The Way of the Bard

The bard's way is an ancient tradition. In this book we shall honor that venerable and worthy tradition. We shall endeavor to recreate it and keep it alive, but in a way relevant to the bard of the twenty-first century. The bard was a poet and storyteller, a musician and enchanter. His craft worked a magic that unbound the soul. It preserved and vivified culture; it remembered. Thus the bard was a person of Otherworldly power who wielded arts that spoke to the deepest soul.

What can you expect if you take up the bardic path? Much study, much practice, and much hard work. Yet you will reap benefits far outweighing the cost as you find yourself walking next to the Otherworld, learning of your true inner self and finding the courage to be that person, and discovering the framework of the ancient Celtic lore that will enrich your life. If you are patient and steadfast, the bard's way will open up reality to you. It will lift the hard edges of perception and expose the mists of mystery and the form of poetry and music beneath.

—Arthur Rowan

About the Author

Arthur Rowan has followed the druidic-bardic path for many years. He is a member of the British Druid Order, one of the oldest druidic groups surviving into the twenty-first century. An accomplished harper and whistle player, he spends much of his time deep in the Alaskan wilderness creating bardic music and poetry. Rowan also practices counseling psychology with youth in crisis.

To Write to the Author

If you wish to contact the author or would like more information about this book, please write to the author in care of Llewellyn Worldwide and we will forward your request. Both the author and publisher appreciate hearing from you and learning of your enjoyment of this book and how it has helped you. Llewellyn Worldwide cannot guarantee that every letter written to the author can be answered, but all will be forwarded. Please write to:

Arthur Rowan
℅ Llewellyn Worldwide
P.O. Box 64383, Dept. 0-7387-0285-4
St. Paul, MN 55164-0383, U.S.A.
Please enclose a self-addressed stamped envelope for reply,
or $1.00 to cover costs. If outside U.S.A., enclose
international postal reply coupon.

Many of Llewellyn's authors have websites with additional information and resources. For more information, please visit our website at:
http://www.llewellyn.com

A Guide to the Celtic & Druid Mysteries

The
Lore
of the
BARD

Arthur Rowan

2003
Llewellyn Publications
St. Paul, Minnesota 55164-0383, U.S.A.

First Edition
First Printing, 2003

Book design and editing by Joanna Willis
Cover design by Gavin Dayton Duffy
Illustration on page 173 by Gavin Dayton Duffy, Llewellyn art department
Illustrations on pages 9, 51, 199, and 231 © 2002 by Cari Buziak
Thanks to Charles de Lint for permission to quote from his books *Dreams Underfoot* and
    Spiritwalk

Library of Congress Cataloging-in-Publication Data
Rowan, Arthur, 1968–
    The lore of the bard: a guide to the Celtic and Druid mysteries / Arthur Rowan.
        p.   cm.
    Includes bibliographical references and index.
    ISBN 0-7387-0285-4
    1. Magic, Celtic. 2. Druids and Druidism—Miscellanea. 3. Bards and bardism—
Miscellanea. I. Title.

    BF1622.C45 R69 2003
    133.4'3'089916—dc21

                                                                    2002040647

Llewellyn Worldwide does not participate in, endorse, or have any authority or responsibility concerning private business transactions between our authors and the public.
    All mail addressed to the author is forwarded but the publisher cannot, unless specifically instructed by the author, give out an address or phone number.
    Any Internet references contained in this work are current at publication time, but the publisher cannot guarantee that a specific location will continue to be maintained. Please refer to the publisher's website for links to authors' websites and other sources.

Llewellyn Publications
A Division of Llewellyn Worldwide, Ltd.
P.O. Box 64383, Dept. 0-7387-0285-4
St. Paul, MN 55164-0383, U.S.A.
www.llewellyn.com

Printed in the United States of America

Contents

PART III   THE POWER OF LEGEND

PART IV   LORE AND TRADITIONS

Acknowledgments

This book could not have been created without building upon the works and research of many fine persons from various fields who have endeavored to record and rediscover the ancient Celtic traditions. To all of you, my sincerest thanks and highest praise for your work. Many of you have been singled out for credit within this book. Many others wrote meaningful literature that influenced my thinking, yet which did not enter so directly into this text as to warrant a specific reference. Nevertheless, I wish to thank you as well. Your work shaped my thoughts in the long hours I pondered the way of the bard.

Of course, this work would be pointless without the old gods who give it meaning, and the *imbas* that gives it strength. Credit is also due to nature and her spirits, who, during my sojourn in the bosom of the wilderness, became richly known to me, and taught me respect and love for that which is wild and intuitive. It is my hope that this work will show those who seek magic, mystery, and beauty a way back to you.

An especial thanks must also go to my precious little daughters, Arielle and Natalia, who gave me peace and quiet when I sat down to type, and who ran me blissfully ragged when the day's writing was done.

Finally, and most especially, I must offer my deepest heartfelt thanks to my dear wife and best friend, who never ceased to believe in me, and who was ever my inspiration and encouragement, my midnight moon and my dawning sun. Daphne, Lady of the Lake, I love you.

introduction

Who Were the Bards of Celtica?

In the smoky halls of Celtic lords, the bards of old practiced their craft, weaving hearthside tales of heroes, battles, palaces, and princesses into intricate patterns of poetry. Chords resounded from the ringing strings of harps, and the warrior race they served was brought to silence, held captive by the power of the bardic vision. Through the bards, the Celts found in themselves a profound love of beauty, nature, and art. The bard's art was to weave magic from word and music—at once a primal, wild, and yet sophisticated enchantment.

The way of the bard is an ancient quest to understand the soul and bring about its growth. The great psychologist Carl Jung might have called bardry the most artistic attempt to individuate the psyche—to reunite the shattered soul in order to realize the potential of the self. The bards of old did this through poetry, music, and profound tales of myth and legend—languages that speak directly to the archetypes within. For the purpose of their quest and as a result of it, they had at their command many magics: from the earthy sorceries of the nature-tuned Celts to the eldritch power of will and word. Yet the way of the bard is first and foremost a quest for growth. All the bard's arts

1

and sciences are the tools by which he or she effects it in himself and others, moving toward that state of total self-realization and fulfillment known to some Welsh mystics as *Ceugant*.

Sadly, today there is a dearth of understanding of the nature of the bardic way, and so its power is lost. Many people view it as so tightly bound to and interwoven with druidry that it becomes a mere stepping stone for those following the druid's path. Others all too often simply believe that being a bard means being a musician or a poet. These misunderstandings have doubtless arisen because, until now, there was no real text clarifying the bardic way as a mystic path. Bits and pieces had to be gleaned from scattered sources, which could often only be located with great effort. Yet bardry, though allied with druidry, has always been a discipline in itself. It may well have been around long before the druids, and it survived some fifteen hundred years after their demise. Indeed, only in the past century and a half has it been broken and scattered. Yet it has not been lost. Enough remained in written and living memory to reconstruct much of the path, and in this tome I have endeavored to do exactly that, bringing the most relevant information together into one book.

What does it mean to be a bard? This question is probably the most important one you should ask yourself as you begin to explore this book, for a bard cannot be described quickly or easily. Nor can you nonchalantly decide to pursue the craft of bardry. The craft requires many years of great dedication to master. A bard is many things, and there are many different kinds of people, each with his or her own individual desires and needs, who might consider bardry appropriate for him- or herself.

True bardry is a quest for the total realization of being. One way it pursues this goal is through artistic exploration. By means of story and poetry, perceptions of existence can be explored and possibilities augured. The inner mind is encouraged to speak to the ego through the creation of characters and plot and exploring their actions.

Related to this and just as important is the role of myth and folklore. Bardry walks the road of myth; it understands its value and power. Myth is a language that arises from the deep, timeless awareness within the basement of the psyche, and is constructed of the archetypes we all share through the collective unconscious. It is shaped and symbolized according to the needs of a culture. When related with bardic skill, it possesses tremendous healing and teaching power. The bard is very aware of myth as a real and vital force that possesses great potency. The Scottish bard Fiona Davidson once told me, "I have never felt purer or more natural in every part of me, more completely integrated, than when I have been spending great stretches of time filling my thoughts with Myth and walking those thoughts through the sacred land."[1] The bard lives in a healthy, active relationship with this force.

In the quest for growth, the bard has at his or her command another powerful force: the richness of music. Music is a wordless language that speaks directly to the innermost mind, that place far down in the subconscious where there is no knowledge of words. Consciousness on that level consists of pure emotion and experiential awareness. While language can affect this place indirectly, music speaks directly to it. It is why music possesses strong emotive power. This level of the mind is very magically potent, for it is a mental facility of pure passion. It can call forth or generate great power, which can then be shaped and directed through higher mental faculties involving language. Bardic music is aware of this raw power and evokes it, directing it toward meditative or magical purposes.

The bard seeks to be an enchanter. Story, poetry, and music complete the triad of elements of bardic sorcery. Yet there is another version of bardic magic (related to traditional Celtic folk magic) that the bard can also utilize. The bard is free to learn and pursue the teachings of the other great magical traditions of the world as well, as did the fabled druid Mog Ruith and others. The use of enchantment has a threefold purpose for the bard: (1) it is a means of empowerment, (2) it opens the gates to the Otherworld, and (3) it assists the bard in the development of an awareness of mystery.

The bard seeks fulfillment by developing a positive relationship with his or her place in time. By this I mean the bard honors the Old Ways, for the past is part of our roots, the former reality of our archetypes, and an inseparable part of our being. Yet the bard is not locked unhealthily into the past, for he or she is aware of the need to evolve, and of the power of the present moment, which is all we truly have. Remembering and honoring the past while using that knowledge to navigate into the future, the bard lives in the powerful between instant of the present moment.

The bard also seeks to hone the mind to razor sharpness. This is done through the power of meditation using traditional Western techniques. I have found methods borrowed from the East that are compatible with bardry as well. The trained mind should be able to focus as well as walk amidst the Otherworld. Both are vital abilities to the development of enchantments, growth, and the great bardic gift of true-sight, which is the mark of the poet-seer.

As you can see, there is a great deal involved in following the path of bardry. It takes a considerable amount of dedication and years of study and training to master the craft, but many old proverbs teach us that the best rewards are the fruit of patience and persistence. I firmly believe that bardry is one of the most rewarding things a person can invest in—if that person is right for bardry! The pursuit of this elder craft of beauty and enchantment will benefit the bard in many ways throughout a lifetime. If the Celtic spiritual path is your cup of tea, and if the bardic mysteries appeal to you, then this book is for you.

Someone once disputed with me whether the bardic mysteries should be available to non-Celts. This person had no idea I was writing a book on the subject, nor that I was descended directly from the Celts. All that is irrelevant, however, because I firmly believe that one might be born a Celt and yet hardly be one. One might also be born to another people, and yet be a Celt in spirit. I have history on my side here. Celtdom is not just a lineage, but a culture, a mythology, and a way of life. The ancient Celts moved into or invaded areas of the old world and either amalgamated the peoples they found there or those people joined them freely. Either one is likely, for the fact is the Celts of old were warriors and conquerors, and yet many people who came into contact with them fell under their spell and joined their race. The eighteenth-century English who tried colonizing Ireland saw this happen often enough, as even nobles and high-ranking military personnel shed their old identities to become more Irish than the Irish. The Irish, for their part, welcomed these immigrants. They became true members of the people, for being a Celt is of the blood, but it is even more of the heart.

The thing I would warn against is a half-hearted attempt at "Celtness." If one is drawn to the Celtic path, learn what it truly means to be Celtic in thought, in spirit, and in the heart, and be it. Only then can one be truly an heir of the Celtic world. Watered-down wannabe Celtness merely dilutes the Old Ways, which bards cherish and strive to preserve.

As you progress though this book, you will notice the use of both gender pronouns (he/she, him/her, e.g.). We can be fairly certain the pre-Christian Celts had female bards and druids, and perhaps they persisted for a time under the Celtic Christian church. So I feel it is perfectly legitimate, in the historical sense, for men or women to take up bardry. I have endeavored to reflect each gender fairly, but constantly writing "he or she," et cetera, is cumbersome, so I have often simply used one gender pronoun or the other. I am a man, so when I use only one gender reference I tend to write in the masculine. This in no way is intended to omit or demean women, for whom I hold only the highest respect. Men and women are welcomed equally on the path of bardry. I know the goddess Brighid (pronounced [*breed*]; also spelled *Brigid*), the patroness of bards, opens her arms to all who would pursue the path of the poet-enchanter without regard to their sex.

You will also notice the appearance of various Celtic words throughout the text. I strongly advise you, the bardic student, to study the pronunciation of Irish, Welsh, and perhaps even the language of Brittany (Breizh) for your own further research into other resources. You needn't necessarily learn the languages; only the rules regarding how to pronounce them. I firmly believe that knowing how to pronounce certain key words will greatly add to your understanding and enjoyment of, as well as immersion in, the linguistic dimension of the Celtic path. However, in this book, I often provide pronunciations in brackets after the Celtic word to assist new students.

The lore taken for this book is derived from many sources spanning all the surviving Celtic countries. The Celts spoke several distinct languages and dialects. In this book, I have often chosen words directly from the languages of these peoples to express concepts, beings, or place names where I felt it was appropriate. I have done this to immerse you, the student, in the Celtic spirit.

I have also chosen to use these words so that you may recognize and understand their meaning when you encounter variations of them in other tomes of Celtic lore. Over time, the spelling of words in any language changes. In the old days before dictionaries, the literate had no standard spelling of words. They spelled according to what made the most sense to them given the phonetic rules of their language. So, when reading other books, you will see occasional variances in the spelling of similar words. For instance, in Irish, the word *sighe* [*shee*] may mean "faerie," but the Irish word *sidhe* [*shee*] may also mean "faerie." These days the second respelling is much more common and generally accepted.

Across the Celtic languages, say from the Gaelic of the Irish to the Cymric of the Welsh, there are words that are similar but different, which also have the same meanings. For instance, *Lug* [*loug*] is Welsh for a Celtic god. The same god's name in Irish is *Lugh* [*lou*]. The *g* becomes silent, the pronunciation of the word slightly changes, but the meaning is the same. The high day of Lug is *Lugnasad* [*LOUG-na-sodt*] in the Welsh language, but *Lughnasadh* [*LUN-a-saw*] in Irish. The changes are more profound, but the words are basically the same. Indeed, they mean the same thing: the high day of the god Lug. In Celtic studies, you will encounter many such instances of variances of words across languages and across time. For now, it is adequate just to know that if the words look similar, you can be pretty sure they imply the same meaning.

I recognize that readers of varying levels of background in Celtic studies will peruse this book. While those who have studied the Celtic ways longer will not be daunted by the complexity of Celtic languages, for the sake of those new to the Celtic path I have endeavored to keep the spellings as consistent as possible. Be aware, though, that I might throw in a variation on the same word here and there to keep you on your toes, so you will understand what you are encountering when you see spelling variations while studying other books of Celtic lore.

Finally, I recommend that you study this entire book in a linear manner. Begin at the beginning and work your way through to the end. There is so much to learn, and a complete study of the bardic way would take up many more volumes. What I have attempted to accomplish in this book is to provide a thorough overview of bardry, from its Celtic roots in the far reaches of the past, to its wisdom and mysteries that enable personal growth, to the enchantment that empowers it. I have surveyed some areas briefly (such as history), and dealt in some depth with others (such as enchantment, meditation, and the bardic arts). A thorough, linear study of this book will help you to get an overall grasp of the path, while developing skill in the bardic crafts. Once you have completed such a study, you should reread the more challenging sections, and turn your attention to the list of recommended reading. Don't rush it. Absorb the knowledge at a comfortable pace. It took many years to train a bard of the elder times, and it takes just as long today.

This book is the product of years of in-depth research, and in those years I have amassed countless thousands of pages of material on the craft. While writing it, I was faced with a dilemma: do I triple the length of this book by providing copious quotations of the ancient Celtic texts of poetry and myth on which I based my research, or do I make it more clear and concise by simply citing the works and elaborating on them, leaving the reader to look up the references for him- or herself? I chose the latter route. Many of these old texts are rather long. I would not have been able to provide complete copies of most of them. You would have ended up paying a lot more for this book (for it would have been very large) and then, later, having to buy the complete versions of some of those old core texts as your studies advance anyway. It is my hope that as your bardic studies progress, you will seek out and read on your own the full versions of the materials I have cited. Many of them can be obtained through libraries. Others you may wish to purchase for your own library.

Finally, you may want to engage in bardic music by taking up a traditional Celtic musical instrument. Some such instruments would be the Irish flute or whistle, the *bodhran* [BO-ran], and the *crwth* [crooth]. Other folk instruments, such as the lute and the hammered dulcimer, work well too, though they are not quite a part of the old tradition. Of course, the ultimate bardic instrument is the Celtic harp, known in Celtic countries as the *clarsach* [CLAR-sack] or the *telyn* [TEL-in]. I have listed some resources to which you may turn to obtain these instruments.

Since Celtic music has a very distinctive sound, you may also want to find some study materials to learn how to make it. The rules that give Celtic music its flavor is really a fascinating study of its own. Yet the rules are not restrictive. They encourage rather than restrict musical expression, much as an alphabet supplies a specific list of sounds one may use to create the infinite variances of language without restricting at all the stories that language may create. Since music is such an integral part of bardry, you cannot begin your study of Celtic music too soon. As you practice the materials in this book, musical skill will aid you along the way. If you do not feel you are very gifted in music, do not despair. You need to develop some musical skill as it is very helpful in spell-casting and meditation, but you can take up an easy instrument. The Irish whistle and the bodhran are among the easiest. Even the clarsach, which is among the hardest of all instruments, can give very pleasing results with just a little practice. Don't be intimidated. It really isn't that hard to learn to make a pleasing sound.

May Brighid, Ceridwen, and Lugh oversee your studies, and the Otherworld bless you with flowing imbas. Welcome to the path of the bard.

PART I
Celt and Bard

chapter one

The Age of Celtica

*All the Gauls assert that they are
descended from the god Dis . . .*

Julius Caesar, *The Gallic Wars*

One might ask, "When did it all begin?" One would be right to do so because it is an important question, perhaps made all the more so because no one knows the answer. Did it all begin at La Tène, that place in the Swiss mountains where Celtic artisans developed surrealistic expression to a high art form more than two thousand years before twentieth-century artists dreamed it up again? Did it began at Halstatt, that beautiful valley in Austria where the Celts first pulled themselves up from historic obscurity and made themselves known as a great people? Perhaps the beginning lies in the dim mists of myth with the gods as the Gallic Celts of the western European continent asserted. In truth, no one knows.

What we do know is that the Celts arose from an incredibly ancient lineage known broadly as the Indo-Europeans. The Indo-Europeans were truly prehistoric; we can only infer their existence from the detailed analysis of linguistic evolution, parallels among folklore and myth, and cultural sleuthing. Four thousand years ago, the Hittites of ancient Anatolia left us the earliest written records of a language of Indo-European origin, yet at this time the Indo-Europeans were already a venerable people.

The Indo-Europeans were the parents of the Celts, the East Indians, the Persians, and a vast array of other peoples spanning from Siberia down through north Africa and into westernmost Europe. They probably originated somewhere between the Baltic and Black Seas. For some reason they dispersed throughout the world. It is not known why. If their influence on history and culture across such a vast area is any indication, it is probable that they did not abandon their homeland due to invasion or vulnerability. More than likely, success led to overcrowding and lack of adequate resources, which combined to drive them from their homeland. It is probably safe to say that the original Indo-Europeans—considering the advanced state of their philosophy, mythology, and language—date back to between 4300 and 7000 B.C.E. This is, however, my speculation based on the evidence I have examined. They could be far older, or a little younger.

Yet even the ancient Indo-Europeans must have had their origins somewhere back in the shadowy recesses of time. Perhaps that story is written in the earth beneath some burial mound in Eurasia. Perhaps a stone lies somewhere unturned that would tell archaeologists more. Even then, history goes back further. Like a vast sea, it stretches on and on. Perhaps there is no end.

So when did it begin? How far back should we look to find the origins of Celtica?

History may yawn before us like an endless sea, but never like a void. The winding roads it follows are rich with tales. In those tales are the foundations of who we are, etched in the memory of time. History lives in artifacts. It snakes up into the present and pushes toward the future in the form of cultural and linguistic survivals. It tells its tales and teaches its lessons by way of folklore. It imparts its spirit through the medium of myth. Indeed, history is graven into our very souls in the form of archetypes that live deep in our unconscious psyches, making us aware of and alive to sensations and thoughts that move us we know not why.

So while we may trace "whens" back forever out of academic curiosity, we never truly find beginnings, for every beginning was originated in other tales with their own beginnings. Everything that will happen is shaped by beginnings happening even now. Our future is written in our past—and our present shapes both. Jungian psychology teaches us that without a knowledge of one's roots, a person cannot know his present, or even his own self, and his future is adrift upon the sea of chance and whim. The people of ancient Celtica, I believe, would have agreed. So we will trace the history of our Celtic forbears as best we can in order to enlighten our present path, yet knowing we cannot truly ever find the beginning.

If we are to look at the tale of old Celtica from the perspective of the ancient Celts, perhaps the time of the beginning itself is not so important. What is of far more importance is the nature of the beginning, for beginnings arise from the work of forces. Such forces are the birthing place of myth. For the ancient Celt, the myth—the ideal—was at least as important as the history, and perhaps more so. Despite whatever historical facts we may know or not know, it is the force of personal myth—a deep-rooted amalgamation of fact, fiction, fantasy, and belief alive deep in our souls— that motivates us and shapes our perception. Knowing the power of myth, and the art of shaping it, is a great bardic mystery, and a source of strength and growth for the bard and those with whom the bard shares his or her art.

So let us begin to explore as best we can the tale of lost Celtica, respecting myth as well as archaeological fact.

Sometimes it seems they came from nowhere; at other times, everywhere. Records disappear prior to about 800 B.C.E. We are left with only speculation—and legends. We know the Celts began as a group of related tribes somewhere north of the Alps. They stood out for their great stature and musculature, their fair red and blond shocks of hair, and their light-blue and green eyes. They wore leather breeches, for they were horsemen. Their women fought as warriors at the sides of their men. They were all renown for their warrior skill, even their love of battle. The Celts craved the challenge of battle, for challenge is the opportunity to test and prove one's mettle, and grow or die trying. The struggle to grow and accomplish something worthwhile for oneself and one's people is the mark of the hero, which we will study more in depth later.

Despite their warlike nature, the Celts were poets in their souls. Poetry stood as a proud art among them. Their poets held high positions of honor, as did their harpers and singers. They reveled in stories of high adventure, great love, and grand deeds. Their storytellers were integral to their society. Harpers, storytellers, and poets were free to travel amongst their tribes, sharing legends and myths, and reciting the deeds of their leaders and heroes.

The Celts were ever a spiritual people. Some might call them animists, though that term is not really adequate. They believed that spirits were everywhere. They saw this world as conjoined to the Otherworld; at some times and at some places more so than others. It is likely they held to a concept of a supreme deity. Deities beneath that deity were considered incarnations or conceptions of supreme power. Their druids—spiritual, intellectual, and philosophical leaders—were held in esteem at least as high as their kings.

For all their love of battle, the Celts were not savages. The ancient Celts are often depicted as primitives who fought naked and hunted heads. Indeed, some Celtic tribes committed these deeds, though one must understand the reasons why they did these things. Suffice it now to say that the Celts did not hunt heads, but took them from the dead when the opportunity presented itself because they believed that in the head resided the power of the soul. Some fought naked as an act of faith in the protective power of their deities. Yet the Celts' love of art and philosophy marked them as a people of high intellectual aspirations. While they were intensely spiritual, that did not interfere with their practicality nor ingenuity in worldly matters. Their inventiveness brought soap to the Romans, improved the wheel with seamless iron rimming, improved agricultural methods and husbandry, and established the Celts as an economic success—the first true civilization north of the Alps.

By 500 B.C.E., the Celts had settled over much of Europe. They were established in Bohemia, south into Italy, north into Germany, and west into the western isles of what is now Britain and Ireland. Now at the height of their continental culture, the Celts further developed their art forms, giving us countless artifacts of the surrealistic imagery we associate with them today. On the isle of Britain, the druids were becoming established as the leaders of their cultural religion and their schools came to be known as the premier schools of druidry. Continental Celts from all over Gaul—and perhaps as far as Cisalpine Gaul and the Italian settlements—began to send their future spiritual leaders to Britain to learn the highest druidic lore.

By 100 B.C.E., the glory of the continental Celts was waning. Pressed by the Germanic tribes to the north and the growing might of Rome to the south, the Celts were in slow retreat. Then a young, ambitious military leader with high political aspirations named Julius Caesar began a campaign against the divided Celtic tribes north and west of Rome. The Italian Celts fell first, then those of the Cisalpine, and then, one after another with almost unbelievable ease, the mighty tribes of Gaul fell beneath the armed might of Rome. In only a few years, Caesar's numerically inferior legions had succeeded in leveling the great nations of continental Celtica.

Why did the Celts fall so easily before the Romans who were vastly outnumbered and far from home and resupply? Alas, it was the very noble nature of the Celt that also made him easy prey for the disciplined Roman military machine. The Celts believed in the value of the individual, and they were constantly trying to prove their self-worth. They were independent, strong-willed free-thinkers. Thus they fought with noble heroism, but with little organization. The gallant attacks of brave men acting largely as individuals could not stand long against the cold strategy of Roman warfare. So, because of who they were, they fell.

I could look back into history and wish the Celts had gotten it together better; that the tribes of Gaul had united under a single king, become organized, disciplined, and stood strong to preserve their beautiful way. I once did, but I came to realize that had this happened, the Celts would have been destroyed in an even more horrible way. For what is a culture defined by if not the nature of its people? The heroic individualism that made them noble and beautiful would have been ended; the Celts becoming the soulless, efficient conformists they fought against. Perhaps it was better that as a nation they fell gallantly, fighting to maintain their old ways. They left behind a legacy of a noble, free people that still lives with pride in our hearts, while the Roman Empire is gone and nowhere missed.

Some misguided historians have thought to make a hero of Julius Caesar. Crushing the Celtic barbarians of Gaul was tantamount to bringing civilization to primitives, they say. Nothing could be further from the truth. The Celts had a highly refined culture, philosophy, religion, and political system. They had a democratic monarchy of elected kingship. Their poetry was second to none. Their art was as beautiful in its surreality as Hellenistic art was in its accuracy. Their technology, such as metallurgy, was the most advanced in its time. The Celts' only crime was in their difference. Their entire way of life was alien to the Roman/Greek/Mediterranean mind. Caesar and his legions acted in the way of ignorant savages, hating and fearing that which they did not understand. So the historians whose declarations would ennoble Caesar are guilty of justifying cultural genocide. For to give approval to Caesar—the man who boasted of having murdered 100,000 men, women, and children of Gaul—is no less than stamping one's approval on militarized bigotry and national murder. It is no less than approving the deeds of the monster Hitler.

Perhaps Caesar's worst crime in this act of aggression was his campaign of disinformation. I am surprised at how naively his statements regarding the Celts are accepted by many to this very day when his words still wrongly sting some 2,100 years later. Caesar accused the druids of religious homicide (human sacrifice in order to prognosticate by reading entrails), the Celtic warriors of deplorable barbarity (berserker bloodlust), and their society of primitive depravity (for their lack of cities and prevailing barter economic system). Much of this he wrote in his commentaries on his exploits in Gaul titled *Commentarii de bello Gallico* (*The Gallic Wars*).

Many historians have swallowed these and other accusations made against the character of the Gallic Celts by Caesar without ever considering his motivations. This is partly because many of these accusations are based on half-truths—some in the form of misdirection, others made without self-evaluation. It is true that the old Celts took some heads of fallen enemies, but they were not headhunters. I am aware of no myths or folktales of Celtic warriors going out in hunting parties with the intention of taking heads. It is true that the Celts fought ferociously when engaged in battle, and they did not back down from it, but their religion and philosophy taught that every Celt should shun the fear of death. Death was only a passage between long life, a mere stepping stone to the next place on the sacred wheel. Many historians also overlook the fact that Caesar was motivated by ambition and held no scruples in political and military dealings. He thought nothing of assassination, murder, treachery, and intrigue. There was little he would not do to further his career or the empire for which he held high aspirations. It was to his profit to infuriate the Roman populace with tales of druidic human sacrifice. Remarking on their rural and largely moneyless lifestyle helped to justify his war as a humanistic endeavor to bring "civilization" to the simpletons. The Celts have suffered Caesar's slander for more than two thousand years, and I think it is high time to set the record straight. One culture has no right to judge another except in matters regarding the ethical treatment of life. The butcherous empire that slaughtered men, women, and children by the tens of thousands for profit is not to be taken as the moral or ethical superior to the Celts.

The tale moves on. The Celts were downtrodden, but not defeated—never defeated. One can crush a political body, a nation-state, even a school of thought, but never a spirit. The insular Celts—those remaining on the British Isles—were eventually invaded by the Romans. Colonies were established. Wars were fought. The Celts were pushed westward literally to the ends of the earth into the mountainous retreats of Scotland and Wales and to the isle of Ireland. During this time the tragic tale of Bouddica occurred. Boadicea, as she is more commonly known, was the Celtic queen who was denied her inheritance by Roman colonists and led the Britons in a nearly successful rebellion against them. Bouddica was defeated through cunning, her troops slaughtered, and she herself committed suicide rather than suffer the horrors and humiliations to which the Romans would have subjected her. Despite Roman oppression and colonization, the Celtic spirit survived.

Druidic thought continued to progress, and the poetic class refined and added to their techniques of composition. The harp, the symbol of Celtic music, was developed into its triangular form, allowing for the creation of the clarsach or the telyn—the distinctly bardic instrument of Celtic legend. The druids continued to press on to new horizons, seeking growth in every sense. Great legends grew up around the magical prowess of the druids, the skill of the bards, and the might of the warriors. According to at least one source, the Celts even made it to North America, though what happened to those that arrived remains a mystery.[1]

Eventually the Roman Empire fell, as empires always do, but the Celts had little peace. Their last refuge was the British Isles and Ireland. Ireland was assaulted by the Norsemen, and Britain was attacked by the Norse, the Saxons, and various other invaders. The Celts could have perhaps held them off, but they felt no national unity. Their fierce individualism that was their hallmark again became their downfall as the British Celts were pushed into present-day Wales, Scotland, and Cornwall. Those nations held fast for centuries, but eventually they, too, fell. Finally Ireland, having thrown off the Norse invaders, fell prey to the English only some three centuries ago. Ireland has at last regained partial independence, and the British Celtic countries now hold a measure of governmental autonomy, but the age of Celtica is lost.

Or is it?

Before answering that, we must ask, "Who exactly were the Celts?" Not as a nation or a culture, but in their spirits. We have briefly glanced at the Celts' history, migrations, and wars, but all peoples have such tales behind them. What made the Celts different, unique, special? What made them worthy of our remembrance and perpetuation today? Perhaps we can best answer this through the bardic power of story, so that we might know them personally. Let us travel back to the elder times, when druids and bards walked among dark woods, and the earth was closer to the Otherworld.

50 C.E.

A lone man is preparing to set out from home, which is a large, round cottage located at the edge of the great wood a mile outside his village. In the village, people are preparing for a great celebration, and members from all over the countryside and several neighboring villages are gathering together. Tonight there will be great bonfires, singing, dancing, feasting, high druidic magic, and bardic poetry, for tonight is the most sacred night of the year. The harvest is all in; it was a good year. Provisions will be ample through the winter. That is just cause to celebrate, but more importantly, tonight is the night when the veil between the worlds grows to its thinnest.

Reaching for a case of soft doe leather, the man lifts an object from a shelf by the wall. Lovingly, he holds it, talks to it, comforts the object in the case with the gentle tones of his mellow voice. The object in the case has a spirit all its own, he knows, a spirit that reflects his very soul. With the attention of a devoted lover he eases the case over his shoulder and walks out of his house, shooing a scratching hen from the doorway with a gentle nudge of his boot.

He stops to breathe deeply of the autumn air—crisp, cool. There is the scent of fading green life still coming from the great forest. There is the pungency of fallen leaves as well, and a hint of sharp winter borne on the cool air's tang mixed with the distant smoke of village fires. He closes his eyes and savors it, then begins to walk into the woods. Though he would love to pause longer and enjoy the scent of this season of change, the sun is lowering in the west. Soon it will be dark, and this of all days is not a time to be in the woods after sunset. Tonight the sidhe [shee] will roam between the worlds at will. The spirits will have their way. On this night, when the Otherworld is barely separate from the world of men, there will be mighty magics and great powers afoot. For this is the eve of Samhain [SAH-ween], the end of the old year and the beginning of the new, the time between times that is a crossroad where barriers fail to hold.

Unlike those less understanding of the way of magic and mystery, the man has only a little fear. It is really more akin to respect for the powers that will roam this night, for he, too, is a creature of enchantment, and he knows the ways of the beings who will roam this eve. He moves into the wood onto a narrow but well-worn path he knows as well as his own home. For him, this path in this wood is also home. He walks a half mile beneath boughs of lordly trees. A mist is beginning to rise from the earth when he arrives at the nemeton, a clearing several hundred feet in diameter. It is surrounded on all sides by great oaks—the sacred tree—that are so old and massive that beside them a man must feel like a flea to an elephant.

He enters the clearing. At the heart of it is a circle of logs set into the ground like great poles—a woodhenge. Between the mighty logs three men and a woman dressed in flowing white robes work at finishing the preparations for this most sacred of nights. The woman is tending a fire of yew, over which a kettle boils. She makes a potion of rowan berries and other protective herbs endowed with many incantations. It will be sprinkled upon the people at the village to protect them from the Otherworldly visitors that will surely come this night and try to tempt them away from the safety of the village.

The three men are standing around a great stone table at the center of the woodhenge. Two hold their hands up high and recite poetry. He hefts the weight to his other shoulder and closes his eyes and listens to the movements of the lines, the patterns of syllables and accent, the primal art of words. They recite well, though not with his consummate skill. They borrow his art for their craft.

A wizened, venerable old soul is the man farthest from him. He stands before the stone table with his eyes closed as if listening intently, completely enraptured by the poetry. He is listening, but not to the poetry, nor to anything mortal ears might ordinarily detect. His spirit is attuned to the Otherworld. He is seeking revelation—what his people always seek.

The man takes the soft case from his shoulder and sets it gently down by his legs. He closes his eyes and focuses his mind on listening as well, but he is listening for something different from the Otherworld; not the revelation of the things to come that the old druid seeks to learn from the sidhe, the faerie spirits, and their kin, but for the sweet sensation of imbas, of inspiration. He focuses his mind on Brighid and Lugh, the goddess and god of his craft, but nothing is forthcoming. After several minutes he opens his eyes. He had hoped to find imbas now in this sacred place, but it is not here. For days he has sought the imbas for this night, and still it eludes him. Now the great night is close at hand, and he does not know what he will do for his people. He bows to the old man out of respect, even though he knows the old man cannot see him, and turns to leave.

"The pool," he hears as he steps away. He stops, turns. The old man is looking at him, a clever twinkle in his blue eyes, as if he knows a secret to which no one else is privy. "What you seek is at the pool."

The man bows again to the old druid, this time in thanks, then takes to the path. Another quarter mile brings him deeper into the wood beyond the nemeton. Here, a crystal spring pools before flowing away between stones colored green by algae. The wood here is hazel, and the trees in this sheltered place grow huge. Everything is cast in shadow as the sun is nearing the horizon now, but the colors of the fall leaves are still vibrant. The place is so beautiful, and the sound of the babbling stream flowing out from the pool is relaxing.

He sits on a fallen log, again setting the soft leather case down beside him. Quietly gathering his thoughts, he ponders over all the tales he knows, all the poetry he has ever heard. Then, realizing that maybe he is trying too hard, he opens the case and pulls from it a smallish harp. It is made of oak and willow, stained a dark rich red, and lined with thin gold strips. He thinks the harp— his clarsach—may be the most beautiful thing he might ever see. Embracing her tenderly upon his lap, he pulls her soundbox to his left shoulder and lays his fingers to strings of silver. At his touch, enchantment spills forth.

He utters no words. Rather, he plays for the stream; the music of flowing crystalline water, bubbling over rocks, cascading down little falls, purest water that swirls and runs and flows and plays at its whim. The notes fall from his fingers effortlessly; he and the music and pool and the wood are one.

Then he stops. There is a certain tension in the air. It is near dark now, but he is unsure how much time has passed. He only knows that soon he must leave. Already the worlds begin to merge. Samhain is nearly here. Instead of leaving, he listens, trying to understand what it is in the air he feels. He sets his harp down on her case and walks over to the pool. For a moment he is certain he sees movement in the darkening water; a shadow slipping into shadows. He kneels, and stares into the depths. Is there a vision waiting for him here? Clearing his mind, he focuses on nothing, and watches the water.

It is nearly full dark now. He knows he should leave immediately.

Something plops suddenly into the water, creating a small splash. He is startled, but only for an instant. Now something is bobbing in the pool. He reaches forth and withdraws a hazel nut. Smiling, he knows that he has been gifted with imbas. By whom? Brighid? Lugh? Some other? He thanks them all as he gathers his harp into its case and hastily leaves the forest.

By the time he passes the woodhenge, the druids have gone. The flame over which the druidess had steeped her potion is now entirely extinguished. He is alone in the wood. The mist is thickening, creeping through the trees like smoke. Certainly, the sighe are on the move. Hugging his harp close to his breast he hurries onward, making his way from the wood.

He passes his cottage and soon enters the village. Pipers are playing wood and bone whistles, and drummers are beating skin drums called bodhrans. Many fires are lit, and ale and mead flow freely. In the safety of the village amidst the protection of the fires and the camaraderie of the feasting, the fears of Samhain night are all but forgotten.

At peace now, in possession of the imbas he will need to accomplish his task this night, he makes his way to the table of the lord of the village where he is invited to take his seat. He graciously accepts, and mead and a dish of pork and bread is laid out before him. He enjoys the good food, and sips the honey wine, but is careful not to imbibe too much lest the nectar of flowers interfere with the sacred duty he must soon perform.

Musicians strike up song at the table, and a man begins to sing to the melody, a whimsical piece about young love. A woman dances gracefully to the melody.

Then the moment of the druids arrives. The elder druid rises from the table, his three young students in tow. They make their way to the fire. The druids stand quietly, and a deep hush settles over the lord's table. Quickly, all the village gathers to witness the event. The druid begins by telling the ancient tale of the rhythms of the seasons, how on this night the sun-father is treacherously slain, and how his death throes make the days grow shorter. He tells of how the world is coming to an end once again, till the month when the earth-mother's love shall revive him and begin to bring him forth from the house of death.

As the elder druid tells the tale, the druidess and the youngest druid have slipped from their robes. Their naked bodies are painted ceremonially: the young druid's all in gold to resemble the light of the sun, and the young druidess decked in paints of blue, white, and scarlet—colors of motherhood, purity, and power. They act out the tale the druid recites; their movements somewhere between a dance and fine prose. The elder druid's voice thunders with authority as he tells the tale. The young druid/sun grows weaker, falling, and waning. As he does, the druidess stands by aloof and cold, not from desire to harm or hurt her beloved sun, but knowing that this must be, for it is part of a cycle that has always been and will continue till the world's end. The elder druid tells of the solstice, when at last the sun is within death's power. At last the druidess/goddess moves to assist. With a loving embrace, she strengthens her beloved sun. With the skill of a wise mother, she tends his wounds and works the magic that resurrects the dead sun. Growing in strength, the sun returns to life, bit by bit, until winter's end when he will wax strong again.

"This is the way of the sacred wheel;" the druid ends his tale, "the way it has been since before the Dagda and Brighid. The sun gives light and life, then dies to night when the moon rules. The season of life ends; all sleeps to be reborn. Then the winter season of death perishes, and life returns. For death is the beginning from which springs life, and now is the between time of Samhain where time is at a crossroads. In this most powerful of between times, the paths amidst the worlds are as thin and grey as fire smoke, as they were at the beginningmost times of primal chaos."

The old druid lifts an object from where it lay at his feet: the well-worn wheel of a wagon. It is large and heavy, but the old druid's strength is surprising for his great age. He lifts it over his head for all to see. The wheel is the symbol of the ceaseless turning of the cycles of nature, day and night, winter and summer, life and death. At this signal, several of the lord's mightiest warriors arise and cover the fire with earth. It is slowly suffocated beneath the rich, black loam. All the other fires throughout the village are likewise extinguished. The many torches lighting the festivities go out one by one. The fires of every home's hearth are smothered till no smoke rises from the thatch roofs overhead. All is darkness, illuminated only by moon and stars.

Now is the harper's moment. He gathers his clarsach, and walks out to the clearing amidst the druids. He kneels on one leg and leans the soundbox of his harp against his left shoulder. When he is ready, he swipes one hand along the strings, then quickly follows with the other, damping strings as he goes so as not to allow the notes to rumble against one another. A silver glissando cascades upward, and at this signal another of the druids takes the single remaining lit torch and lowers it into a pile of timber and straw that has remained unlit until now. The dry straw swiftly catches fire and the druid breathes upon it lovingly, for fire is the transformer, the life and growth of all things of the earth. It becomes a shimmering flame, the flame grows, and shortly the well-dried kindling roars into a blaze that fills the air with the soothing fragrance of oak.

The druidess is again in her white robes. Her red hair and light skin glow radiantly by the flickering light of the great fire as she dips a great goblet into the cauldron in which she was earlier brewing the potion. She takes this to the table of the lord and dips a wand of rowan into it. With a flick of her wrist, she casts droplets of the potion upon the lord and his lady. Then the villagers come, each to be likewise protected. The potion—made of rowan berries, acorns, fairy grass, and other potent herbs—will provide great protection to all who receive it. They will be safe from the faeries this magical night.

When it is done, the druidess pours the remainder of the potion out upon the earth, for none must remain for the sidhe to steal. At this sign, the villagers are relieved to know the spell of protection is complete. They burst into happy chatter and jovially wish their neighbors and themselves luck for the new year. Then, as if commanded by an instinctive law, they grow silent once again and turn their eyes back toward the new fire.

As if they were never there, the druids are gone, having slipped away when no one was watching. The harper smiles. It is an odd talent the druids have, knowing the right moment to vanish. Now, none of their craft but he remains by the flame.

All is silent. There is only the crackling of the flame, and somewhere distant is the hooting of an owl and the nightsounds of the last of the summer crickets. The people are so quiet he can't even hear them breathe. They are waiting on him, expectant.

He draws his fingers across his clarsach's strings, and thus begins his part in tonight's sacred rhythm with music. His playing is not like that of the pipers, the bodhran beaters, or the other musicians. Only he commands the clarsach, the silver-strung harp. Only he, in all this village, has earned the right to lay hands upon the instrument the Celts around him consider the very paragon of musical instruments. He plays the melody that came to him at the pool, its notes of forest and dancing water cascading among the gathered Celts, the ringing harp strings sweet like honey upon new-baked bread.

He moves into another piece. He recites with it in a rich, golden voice a poem of the season; when the year wanes but men are content for the stores in the larders they have worked hard to fill; when they can rest easy from their hard farming knowing their wives and children will be well fed during the time of the sun's retreat from the world of the living.

All eyes remain on him still when he is finished reciting. There is more, and they know it. He rests quietly for a long, pensive moment, and holds his clarsach to him as if embracing an old friend. He thinks of the hazel nut that fell in the pool before his eyes, and considers the message of the omen: knowledge.

That was what the gods wanted him to remember: a tale of knowledge. What better to carry a man or a maid through the three days of Samhain, when the Otherworld is so dangerously close to this one, than knowledge.

He plays again, fingers dancing deftly over the silver wires. As he plays, he tells an old tale through prose and verse; now singing, now reciting. He tells them of the hazel trees of knowledge, of the pool where their nuts fall into water and are eaten by salmon, and of the deeds of the wise who spend lifetimes searching out these blessed fish so that they may eat them and receive complete knowledge. Filled with the lore of the hazel, these wise ones are safeguarded against the wiles of those sidhe of ill intent, and enabled to mighty, noble deeds.

His tale restores his people, heirs of an ancient heritage. It reminds them of who they are, the knowledge they possess, and their place in the scheme of creation. It puts them in touch with the blood that shapes their nature, and gives solidity to the formless archetypes of mind that call to them instinctively. His tale, related with a skill only he possesses, makes them alive to their truest selves, their individuality, and their identity as a people.

When he is finished, the people sit in pensive silence, still chewing over the strength of the words he has imparted and soaking in the wisdom of their myth. He knows that he has done well, and by the gift of imbas has been what his people needed this Samhain.

He has worked mighty enchantment and art this night; as well he should, for he is the bard.

This tale is a snapshot of the ancient, pre-Christian Celts of Britain. We find in it a thoughtful people who are sensitive to nature and the powers of spiritual realities. We see a people desirous of a harmonious existence with the cosmos and its rhythms. We discover a people of sophisticated, high art forms. This is a picture of the deep past and the Old Ways about which we will discuss much, and which are worth preserving.

In our modern world, some would contend that the past is for the past. It is over and is best left behind. They say that the world has moved on; now it belongs to science and hard materialism. This is the age of rockets, computers, nuclear power, and the Internet. To hang on to the past is counterproductive, the result of an inability to deal with this present reality.

Psychology teaches differently. Freud wrote that all our lives are defined by our past, by instincts we genetically acquire through our evolutionary heritage, and by behavioral traits we learn as young children. According to the Freudian school, our lives are forever bound by cycles relating to the past.

Other schools, such as that of Jungian psychology, have a more positive, and, I feel, more realistic outlook. The past, the Jungian school contends, is a foundation and a shaper of our present and our futures. We are in chaos without it. The past molds the archetypes that drive us. It defines the physically rooted instincts that direct us to love, to reproduce, to eat, and to breathe. Approached with the right frame of mind, the past can guide our progress into the future. It is neither realistic nor healthy to imagine that we can abandon our pasts. If we abandon the past—assuming we even could— we abandon the lessons our forebears learned, and the legacy of wisdom they have left behind. This leaves us off balance and directionless, for the past is a scaffold upon which to base the present and an astrolabe with which to navigate into the future.

That is why we need the bard. The bard is the product of an ancient and almost universal tradition. In societies from Australian aboriginals to Native Americans, from African tribesmen to European state dwellers, we find someone like the bard. He or she was at the least a storyteller and lore keeper, and often a musician and a poet. The bard was one who remembered the traditional knowledge of the people, and related it in a meaningful way. In the doing, the bard reminded his listeners of their origins, and never lets them forget how they came into their present. A people who knows these things and takes them to heart is better prepared to understand who they are and where they are going.

More than any other people, the Celts recognized the importance of the bard's role in society. They shaped and molded bardry into a high tradition and revered bards as wisdom bearers—the very voice and memory of their race. It was a high crime to lay a hand upon a bard in violence. They were allowed to pass freely among their territories, irrespective of wars, feuds, and taxes, so as to share their tales and news. They were well paid and well respected.

So nurtured, the Celtic bards fully developed many crafts. They mastered poetry and developed numerous forms for its expression, forms that depended upon metered syllables and accent more than rhyme. Among all instruments, they took to the harp as their premier device of musical expression. They developed playing skills that dazzled continental composers, even during the era of high orchestral music. They developed methodologies of composition and memory enhancement involving sophisticated rituals of meditation and a closeness with nature. They made poetry and music into a powerful magical art, and honed the magical lore of their people.

Because of the Celtic philosophy, which placed great value upon the self, the bards engaged themselves upon quests of personal fulfillment. These quests may be likened to the modern process of psychological individuation, that method Jung identified and refined for defining and fulfilling the self within the context of society, yet independent of it.

The bards contributed significantly to the old Celtic spirituality. Once associated with druidry, no one knows if bardry was always part of it, or was originally a craft unto itself. We do know that the bards conducted religious service with the druids, and that they survived long after the demise of the druids. As bardry was tolerated under the Romans and the Christians while druidry was not, it is suspected that many druids continued as bards. Thus, the bards became the means to continue the lore of the elder times, and druidry and bardry became inseparably commingled.

The age of Celtica may be changed, but it is not lost. The prominence of the Celtic nations is a thing of the past. The Celts have grown with the times, but the spirit of the Celts remains. The legends and lore still survive. The Celtic people still persist. In fact, they are more far-ranging than ever. The Welsh have settled intensively in Patagonia. The Irish and Scottish have made their homes in the U.S. and Canada. Brittany is, in a sense, a Welsh colony on the European continent. More importantly, peoples the world 'round are discovering the value and beauty of the Celts' culture. Their folklore is being preserved and actively revived. Their music speaks to us in heartfelt tones. Their mythos and druidic lore calls us back to a time of primeval forests and green-scented mists, an age of legends and heroes, a time that speaks powerfully to our inner archetypes.

Just as the revival of Celtica makes us more aware of a deep-seated human need for roots into the past and the need for and the power of myth, so does this awareness cry out for one who is a nexus. The nexus is the bard—the memory of the people, the bearer of myth and folklore, the eldritch poet who makes Otherworld contact real, and whose art helps us all to understand what makes us who we are.

chapter two

Jung Meets Vercingetorix

[Myth] is more than tradition, it imparts meaning to life . . .

A. Cliff Séruntine, "True Dreams Therapy"

All peoples have a psychology; we usually refer to it as a philosophy. For some peoples, this psychology may be little more than a loose collection of fables that gives them a vague idea of their origins and some ethical direction. More often than not, however, the psychology of a people is shaped within a complicated tapestry woven of myth, folklore, fact, and history. The Celts have an enormous store of lore on which to base their psychology. Unfortunately, most of this has been lost between the depredations of culturocidal empire-builders like Caesar and book-burners such as the imperial English and zealous, misguided saints. Yet so ingrained was the living, oral tradition of their lore, the remaining Celts on the western fringe of Europe have managed to maintain their identity, way of life, and even their language.

To understand the bard, we must understand the old Celtic psychology. The bards were the very expression of their people's way of life. In effect, they were the incarnations of the lore of the Celts.

As stated in the first chapter, the Celts, ancient as they are, originated from a much more ancient people known broadly today as Indo-Europeans. For some reason the Indo-Europeans dispersed from their homeland, which was probably located somewhere near the Baltic Sea. The state of their philosophical and mythological systems at the time of dispersal is very important. Whenever the dispersal occurred, both were firmly entrenched such that at this current day, over four thousand years later, the effects of this prehistoric system remain strong and wide-ranging. This has two implications: (1) the prehistoric Indo-Europeans' ideas must have possessed some legitimate value for them to have survived so long, and (2) at the time of the dispersal, these ideas were advanced, time-proven, and of sacred value; thus they were already ancient.

Assuming the Indo-European expansion did begin in the Baltic area, they dispersed east, west, and south. Those who went east were influenced by the ancient, extant cultures of those lands and the Indo-European system eventually evolved into what we know today as Hinduism and, later, Buddhism. Those who went east along a more northerly route eventually found themselves in the harsh and demanding country of Siberia. There proved to be little time for the development of philosophy or myth in that unforgiving land where mere survival was a constant endeavor. Thus, the original Indo-European system was eventually pared down to its shamanistic core; its more advanced traditions and philosophies largely forgotten. Those who went south settled in Iran and neighboring regions and established empires that were at first successful, but were eventually overrun by later empires. The people and their traditions were largely absorbed and lost. Those who went west spread throughout Europe and flourished.

One group of European colonists settled in a region between eastern France, western Germany, and northern Austria. They formed a confederation of tribes and became known as the Celts. The Celts were inventive and possessed among the highest technologies of their time. More than that, they were noted for their inquisitiveness into all things. They had an evolved religion and philosophy, a high degree of artistic skill, and they studied nature and the heavens. They possessed the concept of the immortality of the soul. They even had their own ideas regarding metempsychosis that has had scholars debating for at least two centuries on whether the great Greek philosopher and mathematician Pythagoras taught his concepts to the Celts or if the Celts taught them to him.

Unfortunately, it is a demanding labor to trace the thought of the Celts prior to 500 C.E. This is because the Celts believed the word held eldritch power. As long as it remained unwritten, it could be used with some safety. Write the word down and it became a talisman of unending power, timeless as writing is timeless. Thus, there was a sacred druidic injunction against writing, making pre-Christian documents few and far between.

Nevertheless, it is possible to trace Celtic thought through circumspect means. This involves the application of numerous disciplines. Anthropology gives us the tools to analyze and understand the Celts' culture. Archaeology allows us to take this further through a study of their material artifacts. Archaeological techniques also help us date the eras of Celtic history and grasp their evolving periods of artistic conception, which is very important in understanding the Celts. Studies of folklore and mythology help us grasp the ancient Celtic culture by reassembling and analyzing the tales and religious beliefs that shape and define their worldview. Philology helps us understand the course of their languages, law, and literature, which express cultural values and lifeways.

To understand the psychology of the Celts, we must understand what they believed. To understand that, we must examine some key aspects of druidry along the way.

Druidry

If you ask people today what the old Celts believed in, they will probably tell you druidry. If asked to describe druidry, they may respond that it was the embodiment of mystery and magic, as is seen in Merlin's character in the original Arthurian tales. They may also reply that the druids were the historical prototypes for the fantastic sorcerers found in modern works of fantasy like J. R. R. Tolkien's *The Lord of the Rings* and Terry Brooks's *The Sword of Shannara*. Then there is the neodruidic movement, some of which sincerely tries to understand and recreate druidry, but much of which merely mixes modern, and often hazy, concepts of shamanism, crystals, and other

New Age paraphernalia quite liberally with the timeless thought of the old druidic religion. Yet druidry was really none of the above, though it probably bore some resemblance to them all.

Druidry was first and foremost a philosophical monism, to borrow a concept presented by Celtic scholar Jean Markale.[1] It recognized no distinctions between the spiritual and material, between the sacred and the ordinary, or between good and evil. Each is a necessary depiction of a unity in balance. At the same time, it recognized that each part of the unity is fully individual and independent in its own right. Applied to people, this is to say that druidry fully valued both the individual over society, and the society over the individual. It held the gods over man, man over the gods, and a supreme being over all, yet affected by all.

Philosophers often debate as to whether true monism should be spiritual or physical. The druids probably would have held this argument as meaningless. In their view, the Otherworld and this world were of one essence, and when conditions were right and the mists dividing the worlds became thin, they would commingle. To grasp this concept, we must turn to folklore and myth, the only surviving record of ancient druidic thought available to us today.

In the *Mabinogion* (also known as the *Mabinogi*), a collection of Welsh myths, we find the tale "Pwyll, Prince of Dyfed" (it may be titled differently according to the translation you read). In this tale, as in all the tales of the *Mabinogion*, we witness many acts of magic. Of particular importance to us here is Prince Pwyll's [*pweel*] encounter with the Otherworld. While on a hunt, his hounds pick up the scent of a stag. In a clearing he spies the beast, which has been set upon by a pack of white hounds with red ears. He drives off the pack and feeds his dogs on it.

Red and white are, in Welsh myth, colors representative of the Otherworld. It seems that in the heat of the hunt, Prince Pwyll overlooked that fact and chased the Otherworldly animals away. Shortly thereafter appeared King Arawn of Annwfn [*AN-noo-vin*], a realm of the Otherworld. Arawn cites Pwyll's misdeed and Pwyll agrees to do him whatever services he demands as recompense for his discourtesy, for among the Celts discourtesy was intolerable, especially among men of stature.

Without going further into the story, we can see something of extreme importance in regard to our paradoxical Celtic monism: the Otherworld and this world are intimately commingled. Pwyll is not on a quest of shamanic or any other magical nature to find the Otherworld, he simply stumbles upon it.

In countless other tales from the remaining Celtic peoples, encounters with the Otherworld are common and occur by similar accident. We see this in the Irish legends of the hero Cuchulainn [*KU-ku-lin*] and his dealings with the sidhe folk (commonly mistaken for the faeries of Victorian myth), in the legend of the sunken Breton city of Ker-Ys, in the Manx tale *Island of the Ocean God*,[2] and in the fabulous recountings of the Celtic paradise Tir-n'an-Og. The ubiquitous appearance of this theme is a parallel that testifies to the ancient druidic doctrine of oneness between the spirit world (that is, the Otherworld) and our material world. It is the realm that the deceased attain through metempsychosis. Yet it is only a shade apart from our universe. So close indeed that, on occasion, the unwary traveler stumbles into it.

It is also important to understand that the Celtic Otherworld is no mere ethereal spirit realm, insubstantial as smoke. The druidic monistic philosophy recognizes a oneness of essence between the Otherworld and ours. Thus, the Otherworld is as substantial a place as this one. The laws there concerning the workings of time and physics may differ—for instance, the inhabitants of that world do not age as they do here, and magic is more powerful and commonplace there—but the Otherworld realm is made of earth, wind, and water. It is energized by fire and like energies. All of this makes it parallel to this world. Its substructure undeniably differs, for what is magical and rare here are commonplace there, but it is similar on an essential level. The creatures of the Otherworld are spirit beings, but their nature has definite physical form.

This oneness between the spiritual and the physical reflects a druidic philosophy of balance between spirit and flesh, a unity the druids held as a natural, healthy, and necessary state. It is an old parallel to psychologist Carl Jung's rediscovery of the need for unity and balance between the conscious and unconscious minds. According to Jung, the mind is divided between the conscious and unconscious, and to complicate matters, it is further torn by various facets of personality. There is the persona, that part of ourselves we present to the world. There is the shadow, our darker side, and our instincts, which we often try to hide. There is the anima, the male's feminine side; and there is the animus, the female's masculine side. There are a goodly number of other facets as well. This division of the psyche occurs as a survival response to a hostile world that demands at one instant we be one thing, and at another we be something else. In response to dark forces, we may cope with the shadow part of ourselves. In response to the drive to find a mate, we seek the ideal represented in the anima/animus. However, this division of the soul represents an immature way of coping. As individuals mature, the psyche should naturally reintegrate, which is to say that people should become more aware of and true to themselves. However, this process might be arrested for reasons of stress or lack of opportunity. Jung developed a psychotherapy designed around developing individuality and reintegrating the broken psyche. The goal of this process is to bring together the spiritual and the rational, and the conscious and dreams, the end result being deep personal understanding, distinct and unashamed individuality, and peace with one's total self. Amazingly, the Celt's approach to life was a quest to accomplish these same goals.

Recognizing this quest as the primary goal of the pre-Christian Celtic psychology helps us understand the old Celts' historic reckless courage, their love of war, their value of hospitality, their skill at satire, their ardent and sincere openness, and their passionate love of art, music, and profound thought. For in pursuit of these seemingly contradictory extremes, they sought to be one to the fullest with all the forces in life, whether it be the beauty of a skillfully struck harp or the heat of battle. Understanding their full commitment to every part of their being will help us understand how we may go about fulfilling ourselves.

The Hero's Quest

At the heart and soul of Celtic psychology is the hero's quest. Celtic folktales are replete with the theme of the hero's quest. Cuchulainn was a legendary Irish warrior who was in many ways the equal of the later Arthur. At the beginning of his life, rather than pulling a sword from a stone, he is confronted by a vicious hound, which he imprudently kills. The hound belonged to a great blacksmith. Cuchulainn shortly discovers this and honor binds him to make amends for the loss of the blacksmith's guardian animal, for the Celts revered their masterful metalworkers in the way we would revere Picasso today. His first task is to guard the blacksmith in the manner of the dog, and from this humble beginning he takes his first step onto the long, hard road of the hero. Over the years he fights many hard battles against supernatural and natural foes for the protection of his kingdom, his family, and his honor.

When Arthur assigns the knight Cei [*kay* or *kye*] to recover the daughter of the giant Ysbaddaden [*ISS-bath-a-den*] to be the wife of his nephew, Cei must overcome a barrage of insurmountable obstacles. Defeating the impossible was his hero's quest.

When the goddess Rhiannon is wrongly accused of infanticide in the tales of the *Mabinogi*, she takes up the unbearably humiliating role of acting as a horse for the lord's guests as punishment. She bears her ill-given sentence with dignity and honor till she can be proven innocent. This impossible forfeiture of honor (in the Celtic way of seeing things) is also a hero's quest, for the quester must journey to fulfill the self and preserve the balance of order and chaos even against the most daunting circumstances.

What is the hero's quest? It is the hard road of change. The hero faces opponents of this world and the other in his battle to bring about order, to make the world a better place for himself and his people, and to bring about justice. A hero has only one way to succeed on the quest, and that is to grow. The hero must acquire martial, intellectual, and magical skill; in other words, the hero must fulfill every aspect of being. Ysbaddaden challenges Cei to take the comb of the Otherworldly boar-monster Twrch Trwydd [*TO-ork TROO-ith*], a terrible beast capable of decimating armies and laying waste to whole kingdoms. It seems impossible, for the accursed boar has slain whole realms, but it is only in overcoming the impossible that the hero of the tale can grow. Thus he needs the challenge to effect, or practice, the personal fulfillment of potential. To overcome Twrch Trwydd, Cei must exercise the skills of a tactician and warrior. Rhiannon, a lady of the Otherworld and a goddess, stoically shoulders the shameful, false judgment rendered against her in order to redeem herself with honor, though it is long that she suffers beneath the sentence and with no certain redemption in sight.

In the tale of Taliesin found in the *Mabinogi,* we read how the great bard was forced to use enchantment to deal with the arrogance of Maelgwn [*MAA-el-goon*], the wicked king of Gwynedd [*GWI-neth*] who imprisoned Taliesin's adopted father. He draws upon the magical power of the Otherworld, which, as the metempsychotic child of the goddess Ceridwen and one who has tasted of the cauldron of wisdom, is his birthright. Despite his magical origin and bardic skill, the odds are greatly against him and his valiant defense of his innocent father is a noble hero's quest, for the Celtic gods and demigods are far from omnipotent.

What we find is that the hero's quest is as much a benefit for he or she who undertakes it as it is a burden. In the Celtic tradition, heroes had to meet high standards. They had to be physically, mentally, and spiritually honed. Among the Celts, the study of languages and poetry and skill with music were highly prized. Schooling by druids in philosophy, natural science, medicine, and religion was often required. At the very least, heroes had to understand the nature of the Otherworld in order to deal with the magical opposition they would encounter from it. Warriors were even fined for growing out of shape. The training of a druid or bard could last as much as twenty-one years, yet the hero was to be a master of martial *and* druidic *and* bardic skills. In other words, the hero's quest was the quest of a lifetime, a never-ending pursuit of total potential fulfillment and individual growth. The objective was not to make the hero fit a mold, but to make the hero become the finest individual he or she had the potential to become.

The Celts also held to an idea of a blessing/curse that heroes incurred called the *geas* [goss]. The geas was a magical limitation set upon certain individuals. Powerful kings and warriors often bore many geasa [*GUESS-a*]. Every hero bore at least one. The geas was not like a prohibition to avert bad luck, but rather like a two-sided injunction. To break it bore ill. To obey it boded well. Unlike prohibitions against bad luck such as the universal Western prohibition against breaking a mirror, the geasa did not apply to one and all. They were custom-tailored to an individual. One warrior was forbidden to eat dog meat. A particular king was forbidden to sleep in a shelter where a light was to be found after dark. Though the geas might seem senseless to the modern person, a study of the individual upon which it is placed reveals its hidden reason. The custom-tailored limitation of the geas reflects the bearer's individual need for a fence, and serves as a reminder of his limitations as well as potential. Thus, the geasa bore an important, if difficult-to-understand role in defining the individual.

This is important when we consider the value the Celts held for the individual. The individual was valued over society, and the reverse was true as well. The individual Celt was a freeman. Even the Celtic political system emphasized the value of the individual. The king was elected. The individuals had to be satisfied or the king could be dethroned. If an individual did not like the goals of his tribe, he was free to go his own way. If a war bored him, he could walk away from the battle without fear of retribution.

Yet the society was of great importance. As important as the individual might be, his work was not of worth unless it helped the society in some way. Once again, we find the paradoxical monism. In this sense, Celtic society of two thousand years ago represents the particular individualistic values of modern Americans in this day, best bespoken in the famous expression "One for all, and all for one." Society must benefit if the individual is to be of worth, yet the society that doesn't allow complete individualism is of no worth.

Metempsychosis

The druids seem to have held to a concept of metempsychosis. They believed that upon death, the soul was reborn in another body. According to the ancient book *Pharsalia*, written by the classical historian Lucan, the druids said that death is only a middle point of a long life. This all-important spiritual concept is represented in many Celtic symbols: the wheel, Celtic knotwork patterns, and the fabled druid egg. However, their metempsychosis was not at all like the reincarnation of the Eastern religions. Rather, it involved a rebirth into a new physical body in the Otherworld. From there, according to some scholars, one would continue to be reborn into other worlds. According to others, one would come back to this world in the following rebirth. The body, however, is always that of a human, and apparently of the same gender. Metempsychotic rebirth in the Celtic sense doesn't seem to involve transspecies or transgender evolution. The theme is one of perpetual improvement of the essential self: the spirit, the mind, and the template of a body. Since the Celts, prior to the advent of Christendom, did not seem to hold women as inferior to men, it is only natural, then, that they should assume that transgender metempsychosis was unnecessary for personal growth. There was no need to change physical form in order to accomplish full growth. Rebirth was about new chances to fulfill the potential of who we are, to step upon the wheel of the hero's quest and to become more individual and integrated. It was not about repaying karma or trying out every way of being.

The theme that pulsates in every aspect of the Celtic psychology is that there is always a desperate need for individuality, self-knowledge, and growth.

One never *arrived*. Life was ever about improvement. Modern existential psychology theory teaches us much the same, except it adds a chasm of guilt that always haunts every person. Because in one mere lifetime nobody can fulfill all their growth potential—that is true. One could not do "everything" in a thousand lifetimes. Within the Celtic concept, however, there is no need for guilt, for what cannot be done in this life can be done in a future one. The crime is in wasting a life, and failing to grow as much as possible in the moment one has.

Art

Let us finally touch upon art. Celtic visual art was quite different from the art of the surrounding cultures of the ancient eras, particularly by the commencement of the La Tène period (circa 500–100 B.C.E.). The Celts were creating surrealism long before Picasso and Dali reinvented it. An examination of their coinage àlone reveals their surrealistic penchant.[3] Lines are exaggerated, and form is broken and fantasized. Examples of Celtic jewelry reveal their meticulous attention to detail, and the repeating theme of the spiral, which was so vital to pre-Christian Celtic religious belief. (Photos of many artistic Celtic creations can be found in T. G. E. Powell's book *The Celts*).

Let us also consider the less tangible arts of literature and music. The Celts were an extremely musical and literate people. Their tales are ancient and their color and quality stands out to this very day. A reading of the modern translations of Celtic folklore such as *Na Tain* will quickly reveal this. The stirring sagas of Cuchulainn and Finn MacCumhail [*mac-CU-val*], the haunting faerie legends of the Tuatha de Danaan [*tua day DA-naan*], and the passionate, developed poetry of the Irish bards testify to their soul-moving, storytelling skill.

Sometimes playful and frolicking, other times moody and dark, Celtic music is always distinctive. It retains a particular flavor marked by a unique use of ornamentation and repetition underlain by a lean simplicity of natural theme that speaks of spirals and chaos underlying form.

What was the purpose of these art forms for them? Why were they so highly developed so early and why did they manage to persist into the modern era? Through the arts, the Celts expressed the soul's cry, their longings, and their myths. Through their arts they were able to live the hero's quest, even if the realities of hearth and farm prevented the average Celt from physically taking up the quest. Through their art they were able to touch the primal archetypal images their folklore evoked. Through their art they were able to express the Otherworld, which they tasted in dreams and sensed just beyond the twilight. In a very real sense, art for the Celt was integration; the merging of conscious to unconscious, dreams to waking, the Otherworld to the here and now. It was magic made manifest. The magic it offered was the magic of fulfillment, when the spiritual touches the here and now and makes a person whole.

What does all this have to do with psychologist Carl Jung and the last continental Gallic Celtic monarch Vercingetorix?

Jung was a great psychologist who pioneered studies of the importance of myth, art, and the development of the self. His work led him down the trail of occult lore from worldwide mythology to Western alchemy as he sought to trace parallels of archetypal symbolism and comprehend ancient man's knowledge of the development of the self. Jung believed that ancient man, in tune with nature and the elements, was more aware of the unconscious than moderns. He developed a deep appreciation for the function of myth and its necessity to the individual. He even originated a radical new approach to developing the self through individuation (developing one's individual uniqueness and potential) and integration (uniting the facets of the psyche).

At the time of an ultramaterialistic age, Jung came to recognize the importance of the spiritual—and even the mystical—experience. Going against the grain of the more orthodox schools of psychology at the time, he recognized and admitted that the inner workings of the mind cannot be conveniently broken down, put in a test tube, measured, quantified, and explicated. For this he was scolded by Freud and all but excommunicated by the psychological community before his theories came to be appreciated and in some ways validated. Yet even today he remains a controversial figure among those who would like to pretend that the mind is no more than an organic computer. Jung's work points out, perhaps more poignantly than any other psychological school, that there is a ghost in the machine. The theme of Jung is that the brain is a machine with a soul. The Celtic culture fascinates me because it is built upon a similar fundamental concept: the spiritual and the physical are inseparable. It is not animism, but rather the idea that only in the in-between places where spirit and matter meet can a thing be enchanted or made alive.

Among Jung's many controversial theories is the concept of a collective unconscious. This is the concept that powerful ideas and experiences are stored in some inheritable fashion in the minds of all humans. The concept goes beyond race memory. According to it, somewhere deep in the recesses of our minds, memory traces may remain from our earliest evolutionary stages. Perhaps they trace back to when an early hominid first looked up in awe at the full moon, or perhaps they trace back beyond the era of the great reptiles—no one knows. The collective unconscious is a powerful force within our minds that is not healthy to ignore. It is the source of ancient and time-proven instincts that are not only necessary for our survival, but are fundamental, natural, and necessary parts of our being.

The collective unconscious does not express itself directly as imagery or symbols often. That is, we don't dream of being a prototypical, primitive shrew-like mammal fleeing through the underbrush of a tropical jungle being chased by small, predacious dinosaurs. It usually expresses itself more subtly, most often through feelings and affinities for which we cannot account. Thus we may feel great comfort in a forest—the forest being a haven of high, safe trees where fleeing creatures could have sought refuge. In another example, the sight of a castle might evoke feelings of security, harkening back to the days when castles provided strongholds in times of invasion. In a final example, a person might treasure the feel of earth, finding in dark, cool loam a comforting sweetness akin to maternity. As most people before the industrial age were ruralites involved in farming, this is a natural, deeply ingrained feeling toward the element that provides us our daily nourishment as a mother's breast provides a baby's milk. In all the above examples, archetypes are guiding the collective unconscious into evoking feelings summoned through these symbols.

However, the archetypes contained within the collective memory weave a complicated pattern. Meandering in and out amongst the matrices of the mind and intermingling freely, they become hazy and linked. An experience that triggers an archetype to move toward conscious awareness may become associated with other archetypes that are somehow related. The trigger may then have the effect of dredging up those archetypes also. Thus the sight of a deep forest pool may trigger the simultaneous emotions of fear and desire.

The person experiencing this may feel the urge to swim in the cool, crystal waters, yet be afraid to go beyond ankle depth for fear of what may wait in the malignant shadows of the pool's depths. Thus, we see the desire for pleasure mingling with the age-old fear of the dark.

It is within this complicated dreamwork matrix where legends live and become myths. So deeply rooted and independent is this part of the psyche that it is accurate to say that myths are alive within our very souls. Whether they're physically and historically real or the imaginative creation of folktales is moot: myths are a vibrant part of us. They offer us a different perception of reality from the hard and practical working of the pure conscious mind. They work their way up from the mental basement and soften the hard edges of the material universe, perhaps making it more bearable. They realize magic.

Vercingetorix was the last king to unite the Celts of Gaul under a single banner in order to resist the onslaught of Caesar's legions. He wasn't a great military genius, nor particularly gifted at leading men. He was merely an ordinary man who was a monarch, forced to try to rise above extraordinary times. As such, he represents the Celtic ideal of the hero. Against the massive, organized forces of Caesar he stood for his people. Eschewing the risk, he took up the hero's quest and sought a nearly hopeless goal: unifying the independent-thinking Celts and driving off the Romans. This was made more difficult because of the constant need to deal with pressure from the German hordes to the northeast. The number of warriors he commanded were superior to Caesar's, but they were disorganized and undisciplined. His task was not that of commanding an army so much as trying to keep eighty thousand armed individualists focused on a single goal.

This is a great oversimplification of Vercingetorix, of whom we know little except through the records of Caesar's *The Gallic Wars*. What is of importance to us here is that he took up the hero's quest. He faced nearly impossible odds for the sake of the betterment of his people. The act of taking on the impossible is at the very heart of the hero's quest, and so fundamental to Celtic psychology. The need for this hero's quest springs from the same place where myths live. It is that complicated inner side of us that will not passively be molded by the status quo, but will struggle to realize the ideal as it perceives it. The hero does not examine a problem and say, "It is hopeless," and retreats. The hero looks at the insurmountable and is stalwart in the face of the challenge, for in the process of overcoming the challenge lies the potential for growth. The hero knows the road is more important than the victory—or the failure—at the end.

Vercingetorix is a superb prototype of the noble leader, and he personifies the Celtic psychology. He is not so much extraordinary, as he is one who strives after the extraordinary. We could just have easily taken as our example of a hero the warrior-queen Boadicea, who fought and nearly defeated the Romans in Britain, the semimythical Arthur, or the Koadalan of Breton folklore, who was once a peasant yet who rose to defeat an evil, almost godlike wizard. Indeed, we could have chosen among any number of others, for heroes in this psychology of growth are abundant.

Had Jung delved more deeply into Celtic myth, I think he would have found a people long since on the trail of the psychological truths that he was only just then, some two thousand years later, rediscovering. He would have found a people who recognized the power of myth, and who understood the need for applying it to their lives. Myth is the incarnation of our psychological roots. Without it, perhaps we are merely biological computers. It is the magic of being human that makes us more than machine, and myth embodies that magic fully.

Jung would have been to Vercingetorix as a bard is to a king. With wellchosen words, he would have inspired Vercingetorix to pursue his quest and to fulfill himself, for that is the task of the bard. He or she points to the beginning and the haze of the present is cleared away. When the present becomes understood in context with the past, the wisdom to face the future can then be discerned. In this way, our bard from chapter 1 chose his tale with great care in order to give his people wisdom to carry them through Samhain night into the new year.

Today, we have many specialists conducting the work that was once the domain of the bard. Psychologists examine our past experiences to determine our present condition. Historians review history to learn lessons for the future. Folklorists study the old tales to keep them from being forgotten and to learn why people thought as they did. Poets and artists, and singers and storytellers explore life from vantages new and old. Yet none today fulfills in one person the bard's role. The bard takes the stuff of folklore, myth, and legend, and makes it a vibrant unity. The bard crafts tales into poetry of eldritch power, and makes the prose of folk story into the substance of the soul. The bard ensures that history lives on, not as dry text in a dusty book at the back of a library, but as a living experience thriving in the deep psychic realms where myth lives. The bard's craft is vital and necessary in every sense of the word. If one intends to walk the way of the Celt, it is absolutely essential to know the way of the bard. For as the druid is the spirit of Celtdom, so the bard is the soul. How can a tradition remain alive without its soul?

jung

meets

vercingetorix

chapter three

Individual Strings

*T'is believed that this Harp, which I wake
now for thee,
Was a Siren of old, who sung under the
sea . . .*

Thomas Moore, "The Origin of
the Harp"

Consider the harp. Not the massive pedal harps used in modern orchestras, but the smaller Celtic harps, sometimes called *folk harps*. If you
can, go out and take a look at one in a music shop. If you aspire to be
a bard, you may even want to consider buying one, but more on that later. At
the very least, find a picture of one and take a good look at it.

What do you see? Probably you see a roughly triangular instrument of graceful curves and ample body. Between the curves and body you will see between
nineteen and thirty-six strings. If you are fortunate enough to actually see one
at a music shop, run your fingers along the strings one at a time, and then all at
once. You have just played a three-dimensional metaphor for individuation.

As we discussed earlier, individuation is the process Jung identified as the
merging of the ego with the unconscious—that is, uniting that small part of
ourselves of which we are aware with the vast rest of our "self" of which we are

largely ignorant. Jung viewed the ego as that little bit of ourselves over which we have conscious control. It is the part we think of as aware. It is what we steer when we guide our minds to review memories, to focus our attention, or to sit down and eat. The ego is enormously complicated and sophisticated, but it is tiny compared to the rest of the self—that vast, unconscious area that motivates us to do things we don't understand and to feel emotions we can't explain, such as love, desire, and fear. It is that area wherein all our unrecognized memories and dreams abound. Buried in that vast realm is the archetype of the self. For each of us, the self is uniquely special, and the purest expression of our personal inner being. The self is molded by genetics and environment, but it also has form in and of itself. Its existence validates our individuality. It was there before we were born, and it is the expression of our individual essence.

The old Celts have long treasured and nourished the concept of the self. We know this, for at the heart of Celtic psychology and Celtic culture is a deep and sacred value of the individual. The hero's quest was, in effect, a quest to maximize and fulfill the individuality of the quester. Fulfillment had value because the maximized person enhanced society, but fulfillment also held intrinsic value. It needed no justification. The innate task of every being is to realize his or her full potential, reach all boundaries, and, if possible, exceed them. It is the way of things.

Jung carefully observed and identified this process millennia later and called it individuation. His methods and terminology were different from those of the Celts, but the spirit of the idea remained consistent: each person, working within societal and physical limitations, should maximize all of his or her possibilities. It means guiding the conscious ego to a meeting and melding with one's spiritual, artistic, and practical abilities. It means not being shaped by external cultural forces, but finding the strength and courage to shape one's own being. It means pushing oneself to the limit.

It must be understood, however, that it doesn't mean throwing out the baby with the bath water. It doesn't mean shucking off tradition and culture and family and identity and all the other inherited things that are also part of what makes you you. Individuation, especially in the Celtic sense, recognizes the value of tradition and the environment that shapes you. You can no more loose yourself from those things than you can change your skin. Celtic individuation involves finding your individuality within the place nature has deposited you. Modern existential psychology also holds to this idea and calls it *dasein*, a German word referring to our social, temporal, and physical relation to the environment. Dasein is your root; in other words, your grounding to the world. You cannot exist without your grounding to the world, but you can expand yourself through it, or, if your dasein is oppressive, despite it.

Perhaps the bards settled upon the harp as their instrument of choice not only because of its beautiful tone and its remarkable expressiveness, but also because its very form exemplifies the individuation concept. Each string within a harp is like a single talent within an individual. Pluck it and it makes a pleasant enough note, yet like most talents, it is not unique. Just as others have similar talents, so the string will be a note on the musical scale that is common to every other harp. It is how the string is played that will allow for individuation; that is, uniqueness that doesn't show up in the way we are made but in the way we fulfill our total being. When a harp string is plucked, it sounds much like any other harp string. When it is combined with others and played as music by a master harper, it combines uniquely with the other strings (talents), with the musical nuances of the frame of the harp (physical being), and with the harper (spirit) to produce a singularly beautiful piece of music.

Yet just as one doesn't start out a master harper, neither does one start out individuated. One by one the prospective harper learns the strings, first playing with one hand, then with the other. As he struggles, he plays by the same rules everyone else does, reading music and tapping his toes to keep time. His tunes are lean and simple. Anyone could do them. One day, after countless months of hard struggle, he finds that he can play them all with both hands, and with a little skill. The melody arising from the harp is no longer simple and common, but pleasing and complicated. He is on the way to fulfillment, but his music is still common—it does not yet bear the individual mark of his spirit.

Bit by bit, the harper improves. More of himself comes out in the music. He develops deftness, and learns to throw in ornamentation. He learns to bend the rules when his spirit tells him the music will benefit from it. Then, after a couple of years, he discovers that he knows his harp so intimately that he can play with her special characteristics in mind, apply her particular sustain, make use of the way his particular harp chirps a bit on middle C, react to the swiftness of the levers, and minutely refine her sound. Somehow, one day he is a master. The harp seems to know him as well as he knows the harp. He is no longer plucking strings and practicing techniques. Now he is pouring his soul into the music, the harp is receiving it, and a special magic only they two can create bursts forth.

The harp and the harper are a necessary pair. Neither one is a full being without the other. As much potential as the harp has for beauty, it is like the physical body, incapable of anything without a spirit to charge it. The harper is like the spirit, melding understanding with the physical to energize it. Yet, there is still no magic in only the two of them. Together they must find something more; they must integrate with each other, and in that between state they find the equivalent of the "self," a completeness that empowers the creation of the magic that is inspired music.

The frame of the harp is its limitation. It allows for only so many strings, so many talents. However, if you ever listen to a master of the small harp play, you quickly come to understand that beauty arises not from how many strings there are, but how they are executed. Fulfillment comes through maximizing what one is capable of, not bemoaning not having more. In this we see that physical and spiritual limitations need be no real limit to the growth of the self. The challenge that enables growth is to apply what we have to master the obstacles before us.

The frame also shapes the harp's nature. It makes the instrument a harp and a harp only. It cannot be a flute, or a dulcimer, or a guitar, or any other instrument. It is a harp. That is its heritage. Like culture or dasein, it is the destiny to which the harp has been born. Harp and harper must grow together within that grounding, or they will not grow at all. For no matter how much they might wish it (should they wish it), they cannot be something or someone else. That is the way of things.

The way of the bard is largely about fulfilling individuality. Through studying myth, the bard discovers context that illuminates her place in the world. Another way of looking at this is to say that a living relationship with the old lore makes available to the bard a vast fount of wisdom that enables a clear, true vision of the here and now and the potential of the future. This clear-seeing might be called precognition, the second sight, scrying, divination, or any of many more names. It means that illumination is available to choose the roads of one's lifetime wisely in order to best effect individuation.

In this book, I have given this clear-seeing a special name to distinguish it from the second sight, scrying, and the rest (which are not really the same). I call it *true-sight*. A mark of the bard is the development of true-sight.

The way of the bard is a beautiful and fulfilling path toward individuation that bestows personal and spiritual satisfaction. The path is long, and it is not often a path on which answers can be easily found. Part of growth requires finding the answers for oneself. That is why when Myrddin (pronounced [MEER-thin]; known today as Merlin), druid-bard of Arthur, was asked a question, he responded with a question of his own—to make the seeker seek for himself. That is another important lesson in why the druids did not write their knowledge down. Knowledge had no power until it was alive in the mind. Only in the mind could knowledge *belong* to an individual.

Along the bardic path you will not find signposts saying you must do this or that. There are no people you must imitate, no required songs to play, and no prescribed liturgy. There are rituals and enchantments, and there are mysteries and philosophies unique to bardry, not the least of which is a growing relationship with the Otherworld, the source of imbas. Yet these are mere frameworks to the structure of bardry that ensure it remains unique and recognizable as a distinct tradition. Following bardry means you must find your own way along a path that has many routes.

The bard's way is an ancient tradition. In this book we shall honor that venerable and worthy tradition. We shall endeavor to recreate it and keep it alive, but in a way relevant to the bard of the twenty-first century. The bard was a poet and storyteller, a musician and enchanter. His craft worked a magic that unbound the soul. It preserved and vivified culture; it remembered. Thus the bard was a person of Otherworldly power who wielded arts that spoke to the deepest soul, or as modern bard Fiona Davidson puts it, "the place where true dreams live."[1]

Learning the way of bardry will require great effort. It took, according to some legends, more than two decades to become a fully trained bard. We know for certain that it took at least twelve years. It is no wonder: the bard combines the role of the druid and the poet and the harper and the magus into one person. The bard becomes, in effect, psychologist-spiritualist-artist-shaman . . . a singer to the soul.

What can you expect if you take up the bardic path? Much study, much practice, and much hard work. Yet you will reap benefits far outweighing the cost as you find yourself walking next to the Otherworld, learning of your true inner self and finding the courage to be that person, and discovering the framework of the ancient Celtic lore that will enrich your life. If you are patient and steadfast, the bard's way will open up reality to you. It will lift the hard edges of perception and expose the mists of mystery and the form of poetry and music beneath.

You do not need to be born a Celt to benefit from this Celtic tradition. Historically, more people probably became Celts by adoption or amalgamation than by birth. What you do need is the heart of the Celt: a desire for individuality, love of art, honor for the old ways, and a certainty that around the next corner lies another facet of existence that is at once enchanted and full of mystery, yet not quite alien to the here and now. Perhaps most of all you need a heart that is unwilling to let that which is noble and beautiful pass away and be forgotten, as the bardic tradition nearly was. If this is you, then you may have the makings of a bard.

If you think so, then let us begin the journey. There is much to learn, and this book is but the first step.

PART II

Bardcraft

chapter four

In Search of Imbas

I have obtained the muse from the
cauldron of Ceridwen . . .

The Mabinogion

Of all the things a bard can possess, *imbas* (in Irish; also known as *awen* in Welsh) is of the greatest importance. Imbas is that indefinable force without which the bard is lost, his art powerless, and his poetry and music no more enchanted than the rhymes of ordinary verse. Without imbas, the bard's art does not touch the Otherworld, and the Otherworld will not respond. Without imbas, bardic creations have no magical value, because they don't swell up from enchantment and mystery. Imbas is what makes the bard different. It is what sets him or her apart from the mere poet or minstrel; it is what makes his craft meaningful in the spiritual and magical sense. Imbas is to the bard what blood is to life.

Over the centuries, especially after the forced break-up of druidry among the Celts (which was a culturally and spiritually shattering experience for them), some bards began to, in a sense, secularize their craft. They became the puppets of kings, playing and reciting for money and royal privileges. They ordered the poetic and musical arts of bardry into a highly complex system and charged exorbitant prices for their exacting work at lordly courts. Their work, however, became about boosting the egos of their lords and praising them before their guests. It lost its spiritual zest, and its mystical rhythm. It became uninspired.

Not all the bards were guilty of this, of course. The crime was not that they took payment for their crafts. It takes a great investment of time, skill, and resources in order to become a bard, and the bard is entitled to a living for the service he or she performs, as is a poet or musician or any other highly trained professional. Yet when bards took to the craft as merely a means of attaining worldly benefits, their craft lost something vital.

When Taliesin faced Maelgwn, king of Gwynedd, in order to rescue his adopted father from an unjust imprisonment (see the story of Taliesin in the *Mabinogi*), he had to outperform all the bards of Maelgwn—and that he did. Taliesin was a true bard, still in tune with the heart of mystery, and the bards who had sold their craft as profiteers had lost their connection to the Otherworld. He called forth a tempest that proved the power of his poetic gift, and the lesser bards could not equal it.

According to myth, the provision of imbas is within the domain of Brighid, goddess of harpers and poets. It also is in the domain of Lugh, god of all crafts, not the least of which are the harp and poetry. Imbas flows from the Otherworld. It is found near sacred places, and comes to those who are worthy and ready seekers. Those who receive it and use it wisely grow through it and enrich their people. Those who abuse it risk suffering the ire of the gods, who jealously guard the gift.

One of the reasons Celtic society stands out as unique is for the high regard in which they historically held their poets, harpers, and storytellers—that is, their bards. Old Celtic society was stratified into defined castes, but the castes were not as fixed as, say, in East Indian society. One could move up or down as circumstances and talent allowed. Yet the caste system made for a social order in which everyone knew their place. In our modern Western world, we would no doubt find the idea of a caste-based system to be crude and restrictive, and yet it had its advantages. It lent stability in a time of instability, and gave each member a feeling of belonging.

Of particular interest to us here is that within this system, the bards ranked nearly equal to the nobles and druids. A proper king had his druid, and he had his bard.[1] The bardic craft seems to have always been combined within a single person who was harper, poet, and storyteller, and this person was accorded great honor. It is this older, more complete, and more traditional role that we shall pursue as modern followers of this craft to remain true to what it originally meant to be a bard.

In no other culture did the crafts of poetry and music reach such high status as they did among the Celts. Some scholars have remarked that it is nearly unbelievable that a race of warriors and cattle-raisers, whose lifestyle was either aggressive and martial or pastoral, should have so valued the refined arts. Such scholars little understand the power and purpose of the bard's crafts.

The Celts understood that the word held awesome power. Even today the memory of the power of the word echos down to us, firmly fixed into our minds as an archetype. Edward George Bulwer-Lytton noted that the pen is mightier than the sword. Sayings such as "A good word averts wrath" tell us of the word's power to affect emotion. Lawyers and politicians, and businesses and governments battle with words every hour of every day to win the people's favor. The Bible states that from the beginning of time was the word and that the word created all things. The late twentieth and early twenty-first centuries have been characterized as the information age, and the word is the medium that carries information. Within a word is the seed of power, yet today we manage to overlook this fact and pass over the power of the word with accustomed casualness.

If we turn back the pages of time and explore the records of the folklore of ages gone by, we find that earlier man took the power of the word much more seriously. Hardly a legend can be found in which a sorcerer or witch does not use an incantation. The magic may require other elements besides words (herbs, animal parts, stones, and what-not), but usually, once the magical brew is mixed, only the words of the enchanter can bring its potential to fruition. The incantation is the power source behind the magic spell.

The Celts have always been a very earthy people tied into the ebb and flow of natural forces. Yet the Otherworld was just as natural a part of reality as this world. They did not see it as so much supernatural as different; a place similar but more magically charged that runs by parallel but not quite exactly the same rules. Their relationship to the Otherworld was, thus, just as natural. For them, it was quite real. The veils between the worlds are knitted thin, and at certain times and special places it is almost nonexistent. It was wise and right to live in a respectful relationship to the Otherworld—the source of potent magical beings and forces—and that meant a wise relationship to magic.

Thus, arising from the very instinctive core of the Celtic mind is a twofold realization: the naturalness of enchantment, and the close proximity of our lives to enchantment. That is among the many reasons why the Celts appeal so much to modern man. Their entire way of life revolved around an essential relationship to magic. Magic was part of the nature of the here and now as well as mysteries beyond this world. They lived with this magic, and reveled in it while respecting it. It is this soulful attachment to mystery that calls moderns to the Celts, though we barely understand why. It represents a peaceful return to a better Old Way when reality held more potential than we give it credit for now.

Accepting the Celts' relationship to the Otherworld, the Celt would also recognize the power of the word. After all, what is the word if not an incantory force? By the power of shaped sound, ideas and imagery are conjured up within the mind. A person skilled at shaping this magical force of sound can raise men's hearts from fear to noble courage before impossible odds, keep the past alive, and prepare the people for the future. The word is the magic by which ideas are conveyed, and ideas shape the world. What force more powerful could there be than the word, the seed that makes anything possible?

The power of the word is not in the sound, but in the thoughts behind it, their nature, their solidity, and their beauty—and who better to handle this eldritch art than the bard, master of the craft of words? It was only appropriate that the Celts held their bards in such high esteem. A bard was literally memory and vision, heart and soul and passion expressed by the power of the spoken word and music. A bard was as magical a being as a druid. Indeed, there was a time when druidry and bardry were one—but more on that later. Understanding the Celtic reverence for words, we must move on to the bardic search for them.

The Search for Words

The bard—the true bard—did not merely want to compose poetry to make a good poem. The true bard loved poetry and story as a devoted husband loves a wife. His art was a way of touching the most precious mystery and bringing it to the surface. It was a way of presenting the inner Otherworld to the here and now—it was Celtic individuation. The true bard understood this, and reverenced his craft for it. So he did not merely seek to repeat age-old lore, or compose new prose for the sake of novel entertainment. He sought a spiritual unity with his craft; he sought awen, or imbas.

Imbas and awen are two old Celtic words for "inspiration," the former originating out of Ireland, the latter out of Wales. For the bard, touching awen meant so much more than simply receiving ideas or imagining clever word plays to utilize in his or her composition. Receiving the gift of imbas meant drinking from Ceridwen's cauldron, tasting of the hazels of wisdom, receiving the gift of Brighid and Lugh. It meant touching music and words on a level as mystical as pure love, and becoming one with the passion the bardic arts can evoke. To receive imbas was to unite the soul with art. The bard so inspired would reap the benefit of individuation for his own being, and the sharing of his craft would do likewise for his audience. Remember that in the Celtic view, the individual was of foremost importance, but for his or her work to have value it must also help the group. Imbas gave the bard's craft deep value personally and for others. This craft, which arose from the heart of fire and from the bubbling of the cauldron of lore, offered spiritual healing. It was, thus, the bard's most sacred pursuit. Everything relied on acquiring imbas, the sacred inspiration that made poetry and music into magic.

Imbas is not hard to look for. There are many good ways to search it out. Yet it is as elusive as the faerie, always hiding just beyond the next glen, under the next rock, or in the shadowed pool over the dale. One often touches it to be blessed and illuminated by it. It is that sudden realization that you understand; that you know some deep, hidden, inexpressible thing.

I remember sitting on a boat one day, watching the sunset from a hidden cove, surrounded on all sides by a vast forest of spruce. I stared over the gunwale into the water and saw fluid patterns like liquid diamonds dancing on the lake bottom some six feet below. I was struck by a sudden realization of beauty; not just the beauty of seeing nature at her best, but of patterns within patterns as complex and purposeful as every brush stroke of a master painter. I was stunned by the wonder of it all. Something inexpressible welled up in me, which only poetry could touch upon.

> Liquid azure, molten crystal,
> cobwebs tremble by light's weave.

Amidst shores of rock,
mighty sentinels standing darkly
lest they pierce the cyan sky.
Bleeding color, patterns weaving
within glass of depthless depth.
Patterns weaving, truth bespeaking
ancient lore and harp strings wept
on brink of gathered worlds.

This is a poem I wrote in my heart long before I came to understand the craft of bardic poetry, and before I even knew of the sacred inspiration. However, I did not need to know it in my head to touch it in my heart. Imbas touches us all instinctively at some point in our lives. It is an experience we all long for deep within, even if we don't understand it and cannot recognize it. The difference is the bard knows it, pursues it, cherishes it, nurses it, and sets it to boil within the cauldron of his soul to refine it into pure artistic revelation. This endless, driving quest for imbas is the way of the bard, the path of the poetry crafter and storyteller, and the musician who plays from the inmost being.

Imbas can be like a shy maiden. When it is pursued too hard, it will skip away between the trees to hide until an unanticipated moment. Perhaps, if one does not learn to let go and touch the imbas on its own terms, it will flee, never to return. A great and important part of the bard's craft is learning to woo imbas. The rest of this chapter is devoted to just that.

Twilight

Twilight is an extraordinary event to the Celt. It is a time between times; a meeting place between days. All between times have the potential for mystery, for they are the meeting places of the here and now and the Otherworld. They are magical times when the sidhe are said to be their most powerful, when the Otherworld is closest to this one, and when forces flow freely between realities.

There are many twilight times in the Celtic mythology. Samhain, or Halloween, is the strongest. On this night, the Otherworld is at its closest to ours, and the sidhe and spirits are given power to do as they wish in this realm. The other major sacred time of the year is Beltaine (also commonly known as Beltane). This is the other half of the Celtic year, when the sun has returned to power after his cyclic decent into the house of death. According to some old lore, this is the night when the sidhe have greatest power and the veil between worlds is at its thinnest. Two other important, but lesser times when the veil between worlds is also very thin are Imbolc and Lughnasadh. These times are potent because they are at the midpoint between winter and summer, respectively.

During these sacred times—when the boundaries between worlds are feeble—the power of the Otherworld can touch us most freely. In fact, power can flow so easily that there is a danger in it. According to some legends, the Otherworld will drive the unready, or those who are unwittingly caught up in it, mad. In other legends, those who touch it, especially at these times, are carried away into the Otherworld forever and forget this world altogether. In the Scottish tale of Tam Lin, the hero actually becomes a faerie after being transported to that realm, and he takes up its nature as though it were his own. Only the naturally gifted and those who are prepared, open, and have honed the mind can safely make contact with the Otherworld. Otherwise, it is an overwhelming force on the psyche.

The bard must learn to skillfully take advantage of the twilight times. This involves learning control of the mind while allowing the gift of imbas to flow into him or her. In addition, there are twilight places—geographical locations where the veils are always thin. In some lore, these are meeting places of the denizens of the Otherworld: the sidhe. Always at these places there is magic. The bard must learn to find and know these places. He or she must develop the talent of touching the Otherworld through them while not being overwhelmed by its power.

Understand that the Otherworld is not malevolent; it is not out to get you. The Otherworld is not innately evil, or even good for that matter—at least not in the way we are taught to perceive good and evil nowadays. In the old Celtic view, evil is uncontrolled chaos, and even excessive order. Good is a proper balance between these two opposite states. We will deal more with that later. What is important to know now is that a legendary characteristic of the Otherworld is that it is dangerous, but only because it is overwhelming. It must be approached with caution and respect. One must learn to walk the twilight without being overwhelmed. Depending on how open-minded and receptive to its illumination you are, this can be a diffi-cult thing. Perhaps that is why so many artists are known for having gone mad, or why genius is popularly associated with madness. The ones who made contact with the Otherworld, not quite understanding the power that moved them, lost their own sense of balance and were left with a mind that is more attuned to the Otherworld than this world.

The Otherworld need not be dangerous, not if one is in control of the mind. Individuation is the key; you must know who you are deeply and truly and be comfortable with that. At the same time, you must be fully willing to grow beyond your faults and, likewise, build upon your strengths. Learning control of the mind through meditation and the bardic crafts are tools to that end.

Touching Imbas

Thousands of hours of research have led me to a number of methods of safely touching the sacred inspiration. Some involve ritual; others involve routine. Some are quite simple, and others are more demanding. I suggest you experiment with them all, and find the balance with which you are per-sonally most comfortable. It is probably best to get in the habit of using a number of approaches so as not to become too one-sided.

Meditation

Meditation serves many purposes in the bardic way. It calms the mind and soothes the spirit. It enables one to focus deeply upon bardic and Celtic mys-teries. It enables one to tune the self to nature, music, myth, and so on. What bardic meditation does not do is help the bard to attain a Nirvana-like state in any way. The way of the bard—of Celtic spirituality according to the Old Psy-chology we surveyed in chapter 2—has nothing to do with such concepts as transcendental emptying, losing one's selfness to the oversoul, or the illusion of reality. I do not mean this offensively in any way whatsoever to those who may be reading who practice Eastern religions. It is simply a statement of fact. The Celtic psychology not only does not concern itself with these concepts, it completely rejects them, for they are antithetical to the goals of the Celtic spirituality. Druidic doctrine emphasizes individuality across the spiraling timeless expanse of immortality. The goal of the hero's quest is to maximize your personal growth while benefitting others. The bardic way is about uniting the soul with imbas. The Celtic mythology teaches the existence of many worlds, all of which are entirely real. In them, peace is sought not by losing one's selfness in a Nirvana-like total personal emptying, but by finding one's place, realizing one's potential, and attuning one's endless self to the balance of nature and the model of the gods. We will discuss this topic further as we consider bardic mythology and philosophy. For now, let us examine two techniques of meditation beneficial to bardry.

The first meditation technique is mindfulness meditation, which works by excluding all but one thought. I prefer to think of it as focus meditation. The second is visualization, which we will explore in a bit.

Focus meditation is widely practiced today by people seeking religious revelation and by others seeking relaxation. It involves training the mind to become clear, and then focusing only on what the meditator desires. Sounds simple enough, doesn't it? Well, it is one of the hardest forms of meditation to master. Competent psychologists have tried and failed at it. I believe, however, that anyone can learn focus meditation. The trick is to take it one small step at a time and not be discouraged by random intrusions of thought. Just push them away and keep focusing on the object of your meditation. Practice will improve your ability to focus as time passes.

Historical records show the Irish *filidh* (pronounced [*FEE-lee*]; plural for "poets") practiced focus meditation. The students of bardry of old Ireland used to meet at the bardic schools where they would receive from their masters a topic and some illumination on it. Then, after their meal, they would retire to their day chambers and ponder every facet of the topic in the dark upon their beds. The following day they would be tested by their teachers. According to Irish tradition, the place for such meditation was in a distractionless chamber, wherein one would not be disturbed by anything while he gave himself to his lesson. An illuminating text on this is Osborn Bergin's article "Irish Bardic Poetry," found in *The Bardic Source Book* edited by John Matthews.

I do not feel it is necessary for the student of bardry to confine him- or herself to a dark room all day to meditate upon a subject. As I said, this was only an Irish institution. I find no evidence for it among bards of other Celtic lands such as Wales and Brittany. However, it is highly beneficial for the bard to learn to meditate. The founders of bardry knew this to be so.

Preparation. Before you begin any meditative technique, it is a good idea to precede it with a relaxation technique. The one below I borrowed from high magical tradition and Celticized. It will relax your body, take away stress, and help you focus on the task at hand.

Find a quiet place. This could be your easy chair, a study, a solarium, or any other quiet, restful place. Better than an indoors place is an outdoors place. It exposes you to nature and her spirits, and makes for a naturally peaceful setting. Bardry and druidry were deeply intertwined, so it is only natural that for the purpose of focus meditation with bardic goals you should pursue as natural a setting as possible. If you live in the country, or even in the suburbs, finding such a natural setting should be little problem. A quiet place off a trail by a stream is an exceptionally good spot, especially when it is in amongst great trees, and especially when the trees are oaks, yews, birches, or any of the other sacred trees of the druidic tradition (more on this in chapter 8). Hilltops, clearings, or just a grassy site in a meadow can make a perfect spot too. It depends on your preference. My favorite place is a wooded site near my home overlooking a babbling creek. The trees are spruces, but the site is lovely, peaceful, and highly conducive to meditation.

Having found your spot, assume a comfortable sitting position. Some radicals would insist on something like the lotus position—back straight and all that—but really what you're aiming for is comfort. You may even bring a folding chair, or lie down if you feel you can meditate without falling asleep. If you try to do some position that makes you uncomfortable, your mind will constantly fall back to the pain, and that will ruin your meditative effort.

Clear your mind and imagine a ball of cool silver moonlight or warm golden sunlight floating before you. (I imagine cool moonlight on hot days, and warm sun on cool days.) Imagine that the ball extends a shaft of light down to your feet and fills them with liquid light, refreshing and peaceful. As your feet are filled with the light, allow them to relax. Now imagine the beam moves up to your legs, and allow them to relax. Now it moves up to your thighs and they relax. Let the light work slowly up over your entire body in such a way until you reach the top of your head. Wherever the light touches, it brings you into a state of total relaxation; tension melts away, and perfect relaxation takes its place.

Always perform this preparation. Though the light you envision is imaginary, understand that the imagination is a powerful tool; what the mind believes, it can make real in the body. Believe in the tension-relieving power of the light and let yourself to relax as it touches you. This will allow you to shed the day's worries and bring your mind into focus upon the task at hand. Your actual meditation time will then be greatly enriched.

Focus meditation technique. Close your eyes and clear your mind. This part proves to be the hardest part for most beginners learning this kind of meditative technique. We are so used to high-stress lives enveloped by the constant need to jump from one activity to the next, but you must learn to set the world aside for a time and clear your mind. Bardry is partly about finding peace, and this is an important step in establishing the balance necessary for peace.

Start with small goals. Try to clear your mind for only a minute per exercise each day the first week. Then try adding a minute each week until you are up to five minutes. Don't be discouraged or become angry when random thoughts slip in. They do, even for those of us who have been meditating longer. Just let them come and go. Don't fight them, and don't pursue them. They're ghosts; let them flit away as if they never were.

After the first week, you will have had some practice at clearing the mind. This is an important step in learning focus and control. When the second week arrives, it is time to begin following up your clearance session with focusing the thoughts. Find a topic or object relevant to your goals and center your thoughts solely upon it. See if you can maintain focus for two or three minutes. Add a minute of focus time per week over five or six weeks. The goal is to eventually maintain a clear mind for five minutes, followed by focused meditation for ten.

There are many subjects upon which you might choose to focus. As bardry is a Celtic path, it really is best and most harmonious to find a topic to do with the craft. Some topics I use are: the form of my harp, the sound of a harp string, the crescent moon, the yew tree, an acorn, a hazel nut, a line of poetry, an aspect of a legend, the sound a stream makes as it bubbles over stone, a facet of bardic philosophy, a particular piece of Celtic art, a fair lady, a nemeton, and so on. As you can see, there are a great many topics relevant to the Celtic path upon which you can choose to meditate. When you begin exploring them deeply—as you will in this form of meditation— you will discover that each possesses infinite lessons to impart to one with a receptive spirit. Choose a focus that is particularly relevant to you at the time and explore it in your meditations.

Bodying forth. Bodying forth is a concept of existential psychology. Bardry is not existentialism, but bodying forth is a powerful concept of which you should be aware. It demonstrates the incredible power of this form of meditation.

Bodying forth refers to the projection of one's being into another thing. If a cellist loves her instrument, and if she is devoted to it and has mastered it, in a sense she and the instrument attain a special oneness as they play. The cellist is not merely playing the cello, but in a real sense they are playing each other. The cello guides the musician's fingers to the places they ought to go, and the cellist guides the bow as she caresses the body of her instrument. Musician and instrument become one. It is like lovemaking, the fruit being the procreation of sweet melody.

In focus meditation, bodying forth is a oneness the meditator seeks between himself and the focus. When he attains it, he perceives the focus internally. Their spirits have merged, and there may now be a communion between them. Understand that the communion is not with the actual focus, it is with the idea of the focus. If the meditator sets her spirit upon a harp string, she may commune with and learn from all that the idea of a harp string has to impart. If she sets her mind to focus upon a stanza of poetry, her spirit and the idea of it will merge, and she may absorb all the wisdom and beauty it has to teach her. Bear in mind that exactly how much and what kind of illumination the meditator receives depends upon her focus, dedication, talent, and her own unique perspective. The same focus may teach two different talented meditators entirely different lessons, both of which are valid.

Every time you focus meditate, bodying forth occurs to some degree. You want to maximize this experience, for the more you can put yourself into the focus (and thereby join it to you), the greater will be the experience of your meditation. However, it takes time to develop this skill. Do not rush it and do not become discouraged by setbacks. Eastern meditation masters work for years to learn this skill. It will take patience and persistence on your part as well. For the Celtic hero, the journey is as valuable as the arrival, so feel no need to hurry. Patience is the key, as it is in so many things along this path.

Benefits. Focus meditation is rich in benefits for the bard. It teaches the bard to control the mind and to relax, which has proven health benefits. It also teaches the meditator how to explore a topic fully—to see it from every perspective. Also, mental focus is an absolute must in the working of bardic enchantment.

Focus meditation also aids in the process of individuation. The meditator learns to explore the material of the unconscious mind in full, examine its obvious and less obvious implications, and come to a profound understanding of it. This deep processing of unconscious material is what allows the aware ego to join the subaware unconscious and cause the psyche to heal.

Most importantly, focus meditation sensitizes the bard to imbas. By learning to quiet the mind, one develops the ability to sense the subtle gift, become able to hear the tales it whispers, and ponder the winding lane down which it leads. Focus meditation allows the seeker to safely experience the revelation of the Otherworld, for the ability to prepare and control the mind will keep its radically mind-expanding revelation from overwhelming the psyche.

Visualization

This is another form of meditation that, for numerous reasons, is important to the bard. It is another valuable way to deeply explore a topic. It has stress-relieving power. It helps the bard to realize goals. Yet most importantly to the bard, visualization is a wonderful tool for touching the Otherworld through the shamanic journey.

Every time you read a novel and find yourself living the character's experiences, every time you catch yourself daydreaming, and every time you dream at night, you are engaged in visualization. The meditative art of visualization is the process of taking control of your dreams. To do this is to grasp the reins of the unconscious world within, which allows you to tread territory that was as important to the Celts as the material world.

Visualization technique. Begin by following the preparation that was described above. Go to a special place, one that is peaceful and, preferably, magical. Now take a deep breath, hold it for a moment, then release. Do an initial clearing of the mind to allow all the thoughts flitting about to quiet down. Repeat this deep breathing/mind clearing as many times as you feel is beneficial (usually from one to three times). Now imagine the cool beams of the moon or the warm rays of the sun gently passing over and filling each part of your body from the feet up. Allow yourself to come to a completely relaxed state.

Now release the imaginative imagery of the relaxation technique and clear your mind completely. Your goal here is complete nothingness: no thoughts, no images, everything empty. Don't try to force the thoughts out, for that is like trying to grasp dry sand in your fist. The harder you squeeze, the more thoughts will slip through. Just relax and accept that the occasional thought may slip in. When it happens, just pay it no heed and release it. Be still within; silent and at peace. Soon the thoughts will stop intruding.

When the mind is still, you will begin visualizing. In visualization, you do not seek to lock on to and merge with a single idea as with focus meditation. Rather, you set up a milieu within your mind and live there. You explore all that that mental world has to offer. In the process, you want to do two things: (1) make everything as accurate as possible, and (2) allow nothing to come between you and the milieu. This means that if you are visualizing yourself reclining on a moonlit beach listening to the waves rolling up on the shore and watching stars shining overhead, you don't want to let your unconscious mind to take over and start fantasizing about flying or romantic encounters. Nor do you want to allow other thoughts to intrude, such as worrying about work or school. There is a place for all that, which we will get to later. Right now your goal is to stay focused and make the world you are visualizing as real as possible.

Bear in mind that, hypothetically, you can make this psychic world as real for you as the physical one. For everything of the physical world you also know only in your mind, according to how your brain perceives the information gathered through your senses. You can create a psychic construct of a world without the input from your bodily senses using the information of your imagination instead.

That we know the physical world only as a psychic construct within our minds is a difficult concept. Let's take a moment to explore this more fully. Take the book you are looking at right now and feel it in your hands: the grain of the paper, the smoothness of the cover, the coolness of it. You see the words with your eyes. You hear the rasp of pages when you turn them. Yet your mind is not perceiving all these things as if through windows. Everything you perceive is the product of information your body's senses register and translate into electrochemical signals. These signals are relayed through the nervous system to the brain, which interprets them into a mental construct of the physical world. This mental construct is what your ego perceives. So, it (you) essentially lives in a psychic shadow of the physical world.

If you can construct a detailed mental perception of the physical world you live in through the random, sometimes jumbled information of your crude physical senses, then there is no reason why you cannot develop the skill of constructing an imaginary world just as detailed and real through the application of your imagination. You need only to practice developing the imagination to the point where you can create and hold all the details of your milieu until it is quite real. The only difference between the imaginary world you devise and the physical world is that we all pretty much agree on what is real in the physical one; it is the common ground of each ego. The physical world is a place we can experience and interact to similarly. The imaginary world you construct is yours alone.

With practice, you will become able to experience your imaginary world much as you experience the physical one. In the milieu you conjure up, you may walk around, explore, do whatever you like. Don't let the problems of the external world intrude. This milieu is your special place; an Otherworld of your very own. The rest of the world stays out.

Practicing this kind of intense meditation will relax you and teach you the art of visualization. You will realize the ability to perceive objects and milieus entirely through your mental faculties, which will be necessary to master the next step: the Otherworld journey.

The Otherworld Journey

The Otherworld journey is the next technique the bard should learn to use in the quest for imbas. It is a more advanced technique that combines skills from visualization and focus meditation. It should not be attempted until you have a solid base of skill in the previous techniques. If you work on focus meditation and visualization at least four or five times a week, then you may be ready to try moving into the Otherworld journey in a few months. The important thing is not to rush it. Wait until you are comfortable and competent with the previous two techniques.

The Otherworld journey is comparable to the shamanic journey. When I first began exploring the Celtic way, I came across a lot of references to shamanism, yet its place in true Celtic spirituality was unclear. I could not find any direct references to druids or bards having undertaken shamanic journeys in myths or folklore. When contacts are made with the Otherworld in the legends, that realm is as solid and real and effectual as the substances of this realm. It took a long time before I finally figured out what I believe to be the place of a shamanic craft in Celtic spirituality.

For one, indirect mention of shamanic journeys are made in a number of resources, from travelers' descriptions of folk practices of the nineteenth century to *Cormac's Glossary*, found in the *Yellow Book of Lecan*. According to *Cormac's Glossary*, the *file* (pronounced [*FEE-la*]; an Irish bard) would prepare himself for a journey by eating of a recently slain bull, then sleeping in its hide. This was an act of putting one's self in tune with the spirit of the slain bull, which was now in the Otherworld where the bard needed to be in order to receive the bright knowledge. This practice is recorded as having taken place until the nineteenth century.[2] I say the records are indirect because none of them actually calls the soul travels of the bard or druid a "shamanic journey," but by inference we can be pretty sure that that is exactly what they were.

From a study of the shamanic technique as recorded in *Cormac's Glossary* we can infer several essential elements necessary to undertake the journey. The bard had to put himself in touch with a spirit of the Otherworld, develop patience, find a magical place (which we shall discuss later in this chapter), and possess meditative ability and the ability to know how to undertake the journey. Let's discuss each of these elements and put them all together.

Technique. Find a quiet, peaceful, preferably natural place. Certain times and places are more conducive to shamanic journeying than others, and we'll talk about those next, but they are not absolutely necessary. It is most important to simply have a place that you are comfortable in and that is not distracting.

Next, proceed with the relaxation techniques outlined earlier. You must make the mind calm. Once you are relaxed, it is time to use the focus meditation technique of clearing the mind. Empty your thoughts so that you can be receptive and focused. When your mind is quieted, visualize yourself standing in a deep, old wood on a path that approaches a pool. The wood is the metaphorical land of your dreams; the tangle of your thoughts conscious and unconscious. The pool is the gateway to the Otherworld; the place where myth lives.

See the water within the pool. It is so clear it is like air. Reach out and touch it. You should feel it and see it ripple, but when you withdraw your hand, it should not leave it wet. The water is not of this world; it will not follow your hand back out of the pool.

Say silently the following with only your vision self:

"Manannan, let me pass through the waters to the Otherworld."
[*three times*]

"Lugh, grant your harper [*or other instrumentalist if you play something else*] the talent to come to the realm of myth." [*three times*]

"Brighid, grant your poet passage to the realm of imbas." [*three times*]

Three times three is an old and powerful magical formula.

Now see the waters growing cloudy like clean white mists. Know that the bottom of the pool has vanished. Plunge in; it is not wet, or cold. You drift slowly through, as if sinking into great depths, to emerge into the Otherworld. It is full of great trees and dark, beautiful mysteries—and bright knowledge. It reflects the wood you came from, but is much grander, much purer, and of far greater scale. Here live true dreams.[3] Here be the tanglewood of archetypes; the molds within which your thoughts are given form.

Seek here imbas and the bright knowledge of poetry and art and myth, but walk here with respect. How real this place is as compared to the material realm is a subject for philosophers to debate. It is a place of dream substance, unlike the material plane, but know that it has a powerful realness all its own. Remember that dreams and thoughts shape reality and perception. Here live the dreams of your ancestors, and the myths and legends of folk gone by. Here the mists of the wood guard forbidden secrets and lore awaiting a seeker. It is an otherworld. Perhaps not the same Otherworld of the sighe or the gods, but there is more than one Otherworld. This place is just one.

It is best to have a strong understanding of Celtic lore when you explore this place. It gives forms to the archetype, and can point the wise in safe directions of pursuit. Without such wisdom, you may stumble across mysteries or unsainly (malign) things best left undisturbed. This Otherworld is a beautiful place, but go with caution. It is powerful, and it can be dangerous.

A warning that constantly appears from folklore concerns faerie glamours. The lesson that appears over and over again is that faerie glamours are remarkably appealing, and have a hypnotic, binding power. Beware of the them lest they entrap your soul. In this Otherworld, that means knowing when it is time to release the place. When you return to this world, live in it. A relation to the place where true dreams live is a link to imbas, but remember to live in this world, for it, too, is a beautiful Otherworld. It is unhealthy for a being of this world to abandon it before the time comes to step off your current wheel of life.

Now that I have shared the warnings, let me share the encouragement. Here the bard can find much of imbas. Not all, certainly—imbas also flows among other worlds—but in this place, at the heart of dreams, you have a ready source of bardic inspiration. Sometimes you will meet beings here, sometimes entire courts. Learn from them. You may find a willing guide among them.

When dealing with the inhabitants of this Otherworld, remember that they are not all to be trusted. Like the faerie of old lore, remember that some do not intend you well, and they think differently. Their concerns are not necessarily human concerns. Make sure the being you adopt as a guide is a being who can be trusted.

Finally, you may leave any time you wish by breaking the trance. Simply open your eyes. I strongly recommend, however, that you first find your way back to the pool and leave through it as you came. It is a sort of reality adjustment, or a cool-down for the mind, just as a jogger does cool-down exercises after a run. If you simply break the trance in the midst of the journey, you run the risk of corrupting your perception of the Otherworld, and you may find yourself disoriented or dizzy upon awakening.

Sacred Sites and Times

The meditative/magical practices surveyed above can be applied at any time, but there are times and places at which their potency is decreased or increased. It is most effective to coincide your practice with those times *and* places that will positively benefit your work.

Water's edge. At water's edge is a magical place in the Celtic lore. It is a place where the aquatic and the land worlds meet—a place where the elements touch. Thus, it is one of those sacred between places the Celts so treasured, for at the between places, veils between worlds are thin and new insights flow with ease. Thus, such a site is a natural place of enchantment and source of imbas.

Of particularly sacred value were secluded pools and springs. I suspect this may have been because they could be found and enjoyed in solitude, which is highly conducive to pensive inner-searching. Yet the place where any body of water meets land is a good place to seek inspiration: a lakeside trail, a lonely beach, a river bank. They are all between places where worlds may touch and imbas and enchantment flow.

Nemetons. A nemeton is a sacred clearing in the midst of a wooded grove. Such a place was especially valued by the druids of old. It was like a fortress of nature separated from the rest of the world; a private court of the Green Man. Those of the Celtic spirituality will naturally feel an affinity for such a place and draw power from it.

Think about the traits of a nemeton, and you will understand why it is so special to Celtic spirituality. The grove cuts the clearing off from the outside world and all its distractions and interferences. It makes a natural barrier for an area in which spirits are free to frolic. Here the bard can be among them and nature, separate from the illusions of the manmade world of the here and now. The beauty often found in such clearings is supernal. There are green grasses, wild flowers, honeybees, and songbirds, all embraced by the loving touch of warm sunlight or the cool caress of the moon. From within the nemeton the surrounding grove appears dark. The cool forest shadows promise mystery and primal secrets.

A clearing in a wood—especially in a wood of trees sacred to druidry—is a powerful place, a magnet to nature spirits, and the dwelling place of imbas. It is a place of eldritch power, and a sanctuary for the follower of the Celtic ways.

Mounds. As far back as they may be traced, the legends say mounds and small hills are places of supernatural power. The sidhe lived within some mounds. To circle a mound nine times deasil (clockwise) could open a way to faerie. On mounds, altars were erected in honor of the gods. The sacred fires there were kindled to light the way of the dying Samhain sun on his return from the dead come Beltane.

On a mound, one sees the lay of the land in a grand way. One feels closer to the stars and the moon. It is in our gut instincts to feel the beauty of mounds, whether they be mere hillocks or great low mountains such as Tara, the mystical center of Ireland. Tara was the home of the druids of the yew and the bards of high Gaelic poetry and magic.

The circles. Circles of stone and circles of wood—often called *stonehenges* and *woodhenges* after the great Stonehenge in England—are mystical sites as well. Many occultists and modern druids have theorized that such places mark the crossroads of leys of power. If you are fortunate enough to be near an ancient henge, especially a little-known one where you can find some time alone, avail yourself of the opportunity and visit it for meditation sometime.

Holidays. We will be discussing the holidays in more detail later. For right now, know that there are four sacred holidays to the Celts. At these times the veils between worlds are very thin indeed, and at sacred locations at such times, the veils are all but nonexistent. The holidays are especially powerful times for conducting druidic rites, working bardic magic, and touching the Otherworlds. The times are as follows:

1. **Samhain**—The Celtic new year. Traditionally it lasted three days (the Celtic day began at sundown), and begins on October 31. On this night, the veils between worlds are but a flimsy film, and imbas, enchantment, and the gods are just a step from the reality of our here and now.

2. **Imbolc**—The middle of winter. Begins February 1. It is the festival patronized by Brighid, goddess of poets, and thus of special importance to the bard. It is marked by fire and water.

3. **Beltane**—The other great holiday. Occurs in spring on May 1, and marks the return of the sun. Its ceremony and festivals remain very mysterious, but it was the time of the manifestation of energy, when the world came alive again after the long winter's sleep. Some legends mark Beltane as the most powerful night of the sidhe, and the veils between worlds run thin this night.

4. **Lughnasadh**—The festival of Lugh, god of harpers, warriors, crafts-men, and heroes. It occurs at high summer on August 1 and was celebrated with festivities and poetic competitions. This was a celebration of the season of life, and there were no ritual deaths at this time.

The holidays are times of enchantment. The sacred places are locations of enchantment. Practice the meditative arts at such times and places should both greatly assist and inspire you. To combine them—practicing the arts at sacred places during the magic times—will add greatly to the experience and open doors to the Otherworld and to imbas.

Conclusion

There are two things to remember. First, the sacred inspiration is a gift. It flows from the gods and the Otherworld and the very essence of nature, and the bard trains his or her mind to receive it. Others touch it from time to time and know it as inspiration, but they never quite understand it as a force of divine, mysterious, and magical origin and power. Some are naturally in tune with it; they are the great poets and writers, and the great artists and musicians. The bard, however, understands imbas as a sacred force and an essence at the core of magic. It is right that the bard should ask for it humbly and give thanks for it afterward. Brighid and Lugh are the patron gods of the bard—thank them appropriately. A simple, respectful thank-you is enough. In the tradition of the Old Ways, you may want to leave a morsel of bread and a cup of wine or milk on a clay plate, perhaps at your special place, your garden or pool or nemeton, or just your doorstep. Dedicate it to them in thanks and welcome the good people—the sidhe—to it as well.

Second, never ever take the gift of imbas for granted. If you do, you may one day find that it has fluttered away like a shy butterfly. Imbas is a treasure beyond money, for it is the sacred essence of beauty—the very stuff of art. Do not pursue it too heartily, and do not neglect it either. Walk with it, woo it gingerly, let it come and go as it pleases, and always be open to it. The imbas will flow to you, and you will know one of the most wonderful experiences of the craft of the bard.

chapter five

The Forge of Art

Lean is the poetry of bard's unwritten
pen,
light the touch from which stories spin.
Yet from the forge of Awen's craft,
flesh to bones does the loresmith graft.

Arthur Rowan, miscellaneous writings

What is it about a story, a poem, or the lyrics of a song that moves us? What power lies within the simple spoken word that builds civilizations, carries on knowledge, inspires men and women to greatness, and captures dreams to timeless script?

Words carry ideas, and ideas are an ephemeral, insubstantial, ethereal thing. They do not take up space, use energy, or in any way exist in the here and now. Yet ideas shape the world. They have the power to heal and the power to kill. All that mankind has become since we first were lifted above mere survival-oriented animal thought revolves around our mastery of the idea, our ability to shape and mold it, to use it as a template on which to forge reality, and, finally, to pass it on.

Ideas are like magic; they exist between reality and unreality, in that place in between. Like all things from the places between, ideas are enchanted. They possess eldritch power. Words then, are the vessels that encapsulate magic. Whether the vessels be shaped of spoken sound or musical notes, they contain power. The druids understood this. That is why they carefully regulated how words should be transmitted. The bards understood it even better on a deeper, more intimate level, for words were the very heart of bardcraft.

The bards recognized power in the word in three forms, two of which were prose and poetry. We shall discuss the third—music—in the next chapter. A little later, we shall consider the actual magical application of bardic poetry. For now, we will consider words as the medium of bardcraft, and as art in the truest Celtic sense. This is vital to understand, for if the bard's words are not of the art birthed from the pure melding of spirit and imbas, they have no magic.

Prose and poetry are two sides of the same coin. Both are means to tell a story, relate a myth or legend, or preserve lore. The difference lies in the way the words are crafted together and the nature of the bard's task.

The bard had numerous roles in Celtic society. Along with his druidlike role as a communicator with the Otherworld and sorcerer, he was the memory of his people. Each role filled a vital function. As druid, the bard stood as a community's link to the wisdom of the Otherworld through his divinatory power. As sorcerer, he served as enchanter of abundance and victory. He might even possess a degree of knowledge of herbal lore, or concerning the celebration of the holidays. These things were more the area of specialist druids who were not bards, but a bard, being of the druids, could possess such knowledge as well.

The bard is foremost known for his indispensable role as the lorekeeper, the storyteller, and the living memory of the Celts. It was his or her function to remember the deeds of the warriors, lords, and citizens, the lessons of history, and the myths, legends, and knowledge of Celtica, and to keep them alive in the collective mind of the community from generation to generation. The bard was responsible for much of the teaching, and for providing the insight of deep learning at critical times. It was his responsibility to entertain through the long, dark nights. He would spin yarns of heroism, romance, and brave adventures in the Otherworld beside the hearthfire of the hall of his lord, for his guests and warriors, and for the community at large.

Prose, being a natural form of communication like speech, offered an easy way for the bard to relate much of his lore. It lacks the ultrarefined crafting that Celtic poetry possesses, but imbued with imbas, prose can make a tale come to life in a powerful, vibrant, and most meaningful way.

The bard is most noted, however, for poetry. The bards of all the Celtic lands spent years studying the forms of Celtic poetry and working it over until they could compose in any meter with fluent ease. The methods of composure were various and many. Welsh bardic poetry, for instance, was composed in twenty-four recognized meters and utilized a complicated system of internal rhyme and accent called *cynghanedd* [*KING-ha-neth*]. Though less is known about the nature and forms of old bardic poetry from the filidh of Ireland, we know that they, too, spent years studying the poetic arts. The same can be said with certainty of all the bards of the Celtic lands.

We have discussed why the druids held the word as possessed of sacred, eldritch power. From that we can determine why the bards were held in such high esteem, considering that theirs was the mastery of the sublime art of words. Why, then, the emphasis on poetry? What is it about poetry that makes it more special than prose? You would think, what with the general Celtic appreciation of the natural, that poetry, with its unnatural patterns of expression, would not fit in with their general psychology. Well, at first glance, that might seem to be true, but with a more careful consideration of what art meant to the Old Celt, the importance of poetry becomes apparent.

If you look at Celtic visual art, you rarely find literal interpretations of the artist's subject. You find extended lines, swirling designs, and intricate patterns. Whether the Celts were stamping coins, carving a sculpture from wood, or engraving a shield, a penchant for the surreal showed through in all their art. This was because the Celtic mind sought not merely to relate to nature, but to move beyond it. The Celt lived in such close relationship with nature that his art sought to penetrate beyond it to its most deep, Otherworldly essence. Thus, Celtic art did not seek to abandon the reality of the here and now, but to bring a piece of another reality back to enrich it. It amalgamated the real with the mythic to create an ideal perception of what exists that was simultaneously more and less real.

Remember that in the Celtic psychology the mythic was at least as important as the real. The state of things in the here and now was good, but the mythic was a natural state that was better. For us humans, it is not healthy to abandon the realm of the here and now because we are native to it, but it is okay to import a piece of the Otherworld back from the place to which we aspire. This softens the hard edges of this reality with the nebulous, enlivening mystery of enchantment.

The Old Celt did not merely accept things as they were, but sought to change them in ways that were mythically better; this was the hero's vision. Thus, for the Celt, it was naturally better to include the Otherworld in his art. The Otherworld is about possibilities. It is about sidhe, immortality, heroes, and gods. It takes the mundane of this world and lifts its possibilities to where reality should be. Celtic art is a quest to take the here and now and improve upon it by reducing it to its essence and then extending it in every way. It is about fulfillment; the individuation of the here and now forged into the fabric of reality through artistic expression.

Likewise, so is poetry. Prose merely takes natural speech and carefully composes it so that a fine tale can be related from it. Prose can be blessed by imbas, filled with inspiration, and all by itself tell beautiful stories with passionate meaning. Yet it is in the Celtic nature to always strive for improvement. Why merely choose fine words when the words can be skillfully wrought, and sculpted into patterns as wild and paradoxically symmetrical as knotwork? The bards took to this with a zest and refined their language into a medium of highest art. Through poetry, they related entire heroic sagas, or at least the most important, passionate portions of their tales. Through the triple mystery of poetry (which we shall soon cover), they found the means to express the soul's innermost emotions. When it was all said and done, they discovered that they had mastered the very essence of incantory power.

Celtic Languages and Modern Bardic Poetry

An examination of the ancient records will reveal that the bardic schools of Scotland and Ireland taught a meditative form of composure. It allowed the bards to commune with imbas undisturbed so that nothing came between them and the source of their craft. This is one reason why we have studied meditation. In the old teachings, many of the bards would isolate themselves in dark, windowless huts where they could compose uninterrupted day and night.[1] Not all the poets did this, to be sure. The Welsh composed amidst the glory of nature, and records indicate that at least one Gaelic poet broke with meditative tradition and composed out of doors as well. I am certain that others did so also. Wherever and however they composed, they always practiced with a focused, yet open mind. They were perceptive of the realities of the here and now, aware of the deeper context of events, and alert to the hidden meanings and imagery beneath the veneer of outward appearances—that is, the hidden mysteries of the Otherworld.

Rich, otherworldly wordsmithing takes a master craftsman to forge in any language, but the Celtic bards had languages at their disposal that were born for poetry. The languages of Irish Gaelic, Scots Gaelic, and Welsh (known to the Welsh as Cymric) are rich in expressive capability, and utilize rules of accent and definition that make them naturally fit for bardic usage. Irish in particular is a very ancient language, and is notably appropriate for bardic poetry as each Irish word possesses three alternative meanings. Thus, the general gist of poetry written in Irish is clear, while the exact interpretation of it is up to the individual. Such poetry becomes a tool to foster individuation.

Sadly, the vast majority of this book's readers are not speakers of Irish or any of the other Celtic languages. This needn't stop you from creating bardic poetry. If you really want to compose in the bardic tradition using a Celtic language, by all means, begin a study. There are numerous books and recorded courses on how to take up any of the major surviving Celtic languages. You can choose to study the Low or High Gaelic of Scotland, or the Cornish, Irish, or Manx (from the Isle of Man) varieties of Gaelic. You might wish instead to study the venerable language of the Welsh (Cymric) or Breton (the Celtic tongue of Brittany), which are of a different Celtic language family. Irish and Welsh are two of the best to know for reading the old bardic poetry in its original language of composition, but Breton is the most widely spoken surviving Celtic language. All are beautiful tongues, so the choice is a personal one. Languages take a couple of years of hard work to learn well, and more to master for the composition of poetry, unless you are exceptionally gifted. However, for every person that takes up a Celtic language, that is one step further away from linguistic extinction for the old tongues. Even if you don't master the language to such an extent that you can compose in it, you can still widen your sphere of friends and experience by joining another linguistic group. You will also be able to read bardic poetry and tales in the original language without the fog of translation coming between you and the author.

Please understand, however, that while I am convinced it would greatly benefit you—the bardic student—to take up a Celtic tongue, the language barrier need not impede you from bardcraft right now. As the Irish have adopted English and use it to forge their own distinctively Gaelic literary mark in the contemporary world, so can you use your native tongue to craft poetry (and prose) imbued with imbas and the Celtic spirit. What you make of the craft of words with your chosen language is a matter of skill, poetic vision, and your relationship to imbas. Language is the clay of thought; the gift of its molding lies in the soul of the potter.

Composing the Poetry of the Triple Mystery

Bardic poetry in its highest sense incorporates three resonances: it resonates with earthly reality, reflecting what is here and what we commonly know; it reflects multiple perspectives, providing a deeper view of the schemata that lie beneath the overtly mundane occurrences of the here and now; and it relates to the mythic. Bardic poetry exists in that between state; between the here and now and the Otherworld. It is infused with Celtic lore, it lives among myth and legend, and yet it applies as surely and truly to the here and now as does a daily job, a run to the grocery store, or studying for a big exam. It is a member of more than one world, bears more than one shade, and holds truth in every place.

This is the triple mystery of bardic poetry: it is at once earthy, profoundly meaningful, and spiritual. It is the living expression of the "between" places and times.

Composing bardic poetry takes study, practice, skill, and talent. However, most of all, it takes a soul willing to be poured into the vessel of the bard's craft.

Study

To come to an understanding of the nature of bardic composition, you must read the compositions already extant: the poems of Amergin, Taliesin, Aneurin, and others. Many texts of bardic composition survive and may be had from libraries and bookstores. Not to be neglected are also the works of more contemporary Celtic poets, for many of them have sought to conserve their heritage and express themselves in a contemporary world in a distinctively Celtic way.

As a writer, I am of the firm opinion that the best way to learn a literary craft is to study models of the craft. Read the poetry. Mull it over. Soak up its spirit and flavor. Meditate on it. You will feel that distinctively Celtic perspective being imbibed by your own spirit in time. It is also immensely valuable to study the original Celtic techniques of poetic composure. You might want to look up texts on the techniques of Welsh poetic creation such as the popular *cywydd* [KI-weeth], the *awdl* [AW-dle], and the *cynghanedd*, or documentation on the structure and nature of the Gaelic poetry of Scotland and Ireland.

The methods and meters you will learn about can serve as helpful models to experiment with, but bear in mind they were designed to work within the languages that devised them. They will not work cleanly for other tongues. For instance, you will not be able to fit a system of rhyme and accent made for Cymric over English compositions. The idea is to learn the spirit of the poet's craft, and then mold it to fit your language. You want to make the tradition meaningful to your language group without disrupting its bardic theme; not to so change the tradition as to destroy it. Remember, the bard recognizes the value of the Old Ways, for he or she is the living memory of the folk. To fail to protect and preserve the Old Ways would be contrary to the mission of the bard. Learn from the old ways, innovate to keep them relevant, and conserve them in your innovations.

Practice

Write! The bards of old composed in their heads and never wrote, but unless you have worked years to develop such a powerful memory, write! Your efforts needn't be perfect. Writing is practice in the art of sculpting thought, which is what poetry is. You must practice to learn.

Bear in mind, though, that your objective is not to imitate others' styles. You don't want to write like Thomas Moore or even the great Taliesin. You want to be yourself. If the Celtic path is for you, it doesn't mean you are to be like, think like, or create like a stereotypical perception of a Celtic bard. You are your own poet. Write what lives in your soul. When infused with Celtic lore, the theme and spirit of Celtica will be naturally preserved and expanded upon in your writings.

Skill and Talent

The bard must possess skill and talent. Some people are poets born, but even natural talent must be honed. Study; build the skill to shape and understand your talent. If the bard's path is to be yours, there is a great deal of lore you must know to become part of Celtica and so that your creations may resonate with the true Celtic spirit. Only in study can the myth become a living part of your soul, that enchanted place where true dreams live and where conscious thoughts and archetypes meet.

If you do not feel you are a born talent, do not despair. If the bard's path calls out to you, then you are probably pursuing the right tradition. You do not have to be a Taliesin to be among the ranks of the poets. What you *must be* is one who is willing to pour your soul into the craft. That is the first requirement, and the foremost talent.

From there, know that talent and skill can be cultivated. Study and practice are the water and soil that will make them grow. If the love of poetry is in your heart, odds are good you can learn to create it. Remember, it took as much as twelve years or more for the bards to learn their craft. Be patient and work at it. The bard's road is neither quick nor easy. It takes lots of work and dedication. It is a way for a lifetime.

The Seanachie in the Bardic Tradition

Before moving on to the next section of this chapter in which we shall look at a few examples of poetic composition, freedom in composition, and the magic and spirit of poetry, it is important to consider this: you needn't be a composer to follow in the bardic path. All bards were not composers. Some of them were more of the *seanachie* (Irish; pronounced [*SHAWN-a-key*]), or *cyfarwydd* (Welsh; pronounced [*KIH-var-with*]) leaning. The seanachie and cyfarwydd were the storytellers of Celtic society. Much more common than bards, they fulfilled a bardic function by keeping alive the lore, myth, and history of their communities through retelling poetry and tales they had previously learned. They were considered vital, and were deeply respected for their role. To be a seanachie, one didn't even require much in the way of musical talent; they were not fully trained, multitalented bards. Full bards were hard to come by and were expensive as, after years of costly schooling, they were expected to give themselves fully to their craft and be supported by their patrons. Seanachie fulfilled the bardic role in smaller, poorer communities where a full-time, traditionally trained bard could not be afforded. While they were given gifts as tokens of respect and appreciation for their work, they supported themselves primarily through other occupations. So while full bards were rare, the seanachie were ubiquitous; they kept the folk memory alive when no bard could be had to fulfill the function.

However, you greatly limit yourself by not learning all the bardic arts. If you want to be a true bard in the fullest sense, it is best to put in the work and master all the facets of bardcraft. Yet if it is the myth and legends of the folk that you love, and your desire is to keep the magic of those traditions alive, then the way of the seanachie might be for you.

The Smithy of Poetry

Bardic poetry was not only a craft of art, but a way of remembering knowledge. Thus it was art with a very practical value. Bards were expected to memorize vast amounts of poetry during their training (literally hundreds of tales and legends, some of them epic in length), and to learn more as the need arose. Fortunately for them, the druidic injunction against writing led poets to develop the skill of composing poetry that was lean in wordage, yet rich in meaning.

A reading of the poetry of the bards of old such as Amergin will reveal this rich leanness. If you wish to compose and recite from memory as the old bards did, you would do well to learn the art of saying much with little. Latter bards, especially after the advent of Christian times, began to write poetry. In Ireland, it is very possible there was never an injunction against writing, for legends mention St. Patrick burning the druidic books he found upon coming to Ireland. For our purpose of reconstructing bardry, we may gather from these conflicting tales that the modern bard may do either: you may choose to work only from mind and memory, or you may write out your work. Either way, you would do well to develop the skill of leanness in crafting poetry, for leanness imitates the bardic style, imparts your gist while allowing for individual interpretation of your work, and enriches poetry in the fashion of the triple poetic mystery we discussed previously.

Remember, however, that in the druid tradition, committing knowledge to memory made it alive. Knowledge written down and forgotten was dead. So the bardic student should at least memorize certain stories and poems—those that he or she finds especially meaningful. There is no living myth in the literature that is not living in the mind.

Contemporary bard Fiona Davidson once said that when telling an audience a legend, she feels a trance state come over her, but only "if I'm telling a legend that I've memorized." She goes on to say regarding the memorizing of lore: "[My] sense is that myth accesses the part of the psyche where 'True Dreams' live. The doorway to what the ancient Celts called the Otherworld. Some sort of collective or racial unconscious. My experience with this place, over years of working actively—and sacredly—with myth is that frequent visits to this realm cause inner transformation."[2]

The druids knew there was power in keeping the lore of the Celtic folk alive in the mind. The bards also knew it and made it a tradition. Fiona has felt that truth and confirms it in her writing. The lesson is: memorize the lore of the Celts, make it alive in the soul, and touch the Otherworld.

A side effect of this lean, terse manner of composition, wherein so much symbolism is stored up into so few words, was the development of a hidden language within the obvious language. It has been noted that the bards' wisdom became so erudite and specialized that it grew into an extreme state of esotericism. Put another way, the bards had their own jargon that was so highly developed it was indecipherable to the untrained hearer. This language that only poets could understand was called the *dark tongue*.

The ancient tale *The Dispute of the Two Wise Poets* describes a verbal combat that occurs between two esteemed poets over the position of chief poet. Their dialogue is so rich in symbolism that to really understand it, one must be deeply steeped in ancient Irish lore and myth. Otherwise, their arguments are nought but beautifully wrought, meaningless words.

All trades have their professional jargon, but few have ever been able to claim such depth of meaning hidden within every utterance. I strongly recommend a reading of *The Dispute of the Two Wise Poets* (depending on which translation you come across, it could be titled slightly differently in any number of ways). It is both an example of what the bard must aspire to and must not be. His or her poetry must be rich and allow for any number of interpretations, just like Celtic surrealistic art. His or her poetry must also be clear enough to be understood on each level of the poetic triad (worldly, contextually, and Otherworldly), otherwise it is useless to everybody but bards and Celtic scholars.

The first level of meaning, the worldly (or material) level, ought to be readily apparent. It needn't be blatantly transparent, but the average person ought to be able to understand it with no more than normal effort. The second level, the contextual level (which might also be thought of as the level of perceptive depth), ought to be apparent with some deep pondering or meditation. It should reveal things in context of their relations to each other and the Otherworld. The second level, and possibly the first, ought also to bear legitimate multiple interpretations, and the interpretations should be for the reader of the poetry to decide upon, not the author. This ideal is fundamental to the true Celtic style of artistic creation, which uses surrealism to simultaneously express the here and now and the Otherworld, while allowing for individualized interpretation of the work of art.

The last part, the mythic connotation, is where the dark language of poets ought to hide the mysteries, for not everything should be known to all. There are some forms of knowledge to which only the initiated should have access. From the ignorant and the unknowing, some aspects of the bright knowledge must be concealed. The untrained mind is not ready for the deeper druidic and bardic secrets. They will be scorned, unappreciated, or misused. The bright knowledge can even be harmful to a mind not ready to receive it. The dark tongue is the bard's way of circulating craft knowledge while keeping it safely out of reach of those who are not ready for it.

Some Poetic Methods

We've already discussed ways to commune with imbas. We've considered how to study, practice, and develop poetic skill. Now let us briefly consider an old technique of poetic composition. For our example, we shall draw from the well-documented Welsh. Since Welsh compositional methods were made by Cymric speakers for the Cymric language, they will not really work cleanly with other languages. Thus, they cannot be imported into the craft of modern bardry directly. We are going to consider how to adapt their spirit for English.

The *cywydd* is a common Welsh meter for verse. It rhymes couplets in which each line consists of seven syllables. One line's rhyme is accented, the other is not. It also incorporates a system of complex internal rhyme and alliteration called *cynghanedd*.

Right off the bat, we can see that this method of poetry is not going to be compatible with English-language poetry. For one, English doesn't have a fixed method of accent—it varies among national accents (such as the British and American English accents), and even among local pronunciations (for instance, Bronx English and Maine Down Eastern English). For another, the internal rhyme and alliteration system called *cynghanedd* is not going to parallel English-language usage at all.

The bard values tradition, so he or she will want to preserve what can be preserved, while making the method relevant to English speakers. If we look deeply at what the cywydd is trying to accomplish, we see that it is aiming for a system of symmetry (the pattern of rhymes, syllables, and alliteration) with points of emphasis (the accent). The English-speaking bard could match the syllable count per line. He could create a system of alliteration at the beginning of each line, and devise a system of internal rhyme to be followed. What he might end up with is a meter of seven-syllable lines that rhyme on the sixth syllable of each line, with every odd-numbered line beginning with alliteration.

Obviously, we have made substantial changes. We are no longer really dealing with the cywydd, and some conservative Welsh poets might hate me for "bastardizing" their poetic method. Yet that is what happens when you try to conserve a poetic method by adapting it to a language for which it was never meant. It cannot be helped.

Any of the other original methods of composition could also be so adapted. However, I think the English-speaking bard would profit better from a technique more suited to his or her own language from the beginning.

Other Poetic Patterns

In English, Welsh or Gaelic meters will sound rather unnatural. If you are trying to compose from your spirit—as you should be—and English is your first language, then your compositions are most likely going to be in English. To create compositions of quality, you must adapt.

The idea behind the meters of Celtic poetry—with their complicated patterns of syllables, accent, rhyme, and so on—is to create a pattern as complex and beautiful as the famed Celtic knotwork designs. The pattern is not complex for its own sake, but rather represents the intricate interweaving of natural cycles and processes. Nature functions within a strict set of laws, yet its variety is unlimited. All matter and energy is based on only a few subatomic particles and energy states, yet from them springs into being a vast and diverse universe. All things are related, ever-changing, and never quite the same, and yet all things are part of a pattern bound to repetitious cycles. This pattern and cycle of movement is best represented by the turning of wheels within wheels—an ancient, sacred Celtic symbol. In this symbol we find the root behind the methodology of the construction of bardic poetry, for it is a pattern of words bound by a few strict rules, yet it allows for infinite diversity and individuality. The tales of poetry weave a complex pattern, and express the endless cycles of spirit, nature, and being.

Celtic poetry possesses four key elements: (1) it has a tight balance between personal speech and rules of verse (natural law); (2) it says much with little (elements); (3) it is essential (speaks of the events of the sacred wheel); and (4) it is individual (expression is unique, unfettered by the rules). These four essential elements can be imported to poetry composed in English or any other expressive language, for these elements are spiritual essences of nature and the human heart. Let's look again at the fragment of the poem I wrote in chapter 4.

> Liquid azure, molten crystal
> cobwebs tremble by light's weave.
>
> Amidst shores of rock,
> mighty sentinels standing darkly
> lest they pierce the cyan sky.
>
> Bleeding color, patterns weaving
> within glass of depthless depth.
>
> Patterns weaving, truth bespeaking
> ancient lore and harp strings wept
> on brink of gathered worlds.

Here I have broken it down into its natural verses for easier analysis. You may first notice the poem has no system of rhyme. That is because rhyme is not so important in English poetry. It has its place, but fine poetry is easily composed without it in English.

The next thing you may notice is the repetition of two themes. This poem is about the joining of natural worlds (sky and water), the beautiful interweaving of their colors, and the sacred between state that joining creates. Thus, three verses speak of weaving and three of color. The last talks of the Otherworld mystery; the between place where worlds join and imbas makes the mysteries visible. We have a pattern of 3-3-1. We have the material world described, its context or interpretational values incorporated, and finally, its dark tongue value—its reference to Otherworldly mysteries commingling with this one.

Finally, you may notice a syllabic meter. The first and third stanzas each are composed of fifteen syllables. The second and fourth stanzas each are composed of twenty-one syllables. I was not concerned with the syllabic count of the individual lines.

What we have is a poem with a complicated pattern of syllables, themes, and interpretation qualities. It meets the poetic Celtic ideal, for it is a design of intricacy that reflects the potential, the complexity, and the repetition that is the way of life. Yet it varies constantly, so each cycle of syllables is never quite the same as the last, just as life repeats, yet never exactly reruns.

You are free to design your own meters within bardcraft, and you are free to express yourself as only you can. Just remember that to be bardic, your poetry must fit within the framework of the Celtic psychology. It should arise from your heart, bear the triple mysteries of poetry, and be set within a framework of complex, swirling design.

Enchanter

Poetry arises from a timeless place. It is conceived by a spirit that walks between worlds; by a soul that lives on the verge of the Otherworld and the here and now. A language of myth by nature that demands thought and interpretation, it speaks to something primal deep inside each of us. It shapes archetypes into thought and dream, and brings perception and thought down to the place of the archetypes. It is the language of myth; the tongue of that land where true dreams live. Being made of words, and improving upon them in the hero's tradition, poetry is the stuff of enchantment, a fundamental aspect of the bardic art and also of bardic magic.

We shall examine the magical power of poetry more deeply in chapter 7. For now, know that learning the poet's art is one of the two fundamental steps to true, magical bardry; the other being the skill of crafting bardic music. If you can compose what is in your heart in the Celtic tradition, you are well on your way to becoming a true bard.

chapter six

Harp and Lore

Sing, sweet Harp, oh sing to me
Some song of ancient days

Thomas Moore, "Sing, Sweet Harp"

Music and bardry are so interwoven that anyone who plays an instrument today might loosely be referred to as a bard, especially if they perform folk music. There is a degree of truth to this misconception. For true musicians, music arises from their spirits and is the expression of a soulful search. It is likewise for the bard. However, it is inaccurate to confuse a musician with a bard, for there is a profound difference in their understanding and application of music. For the bard, music is as essential and sacred as poetry, a force in harmony with the very order of creation. Bardic music is a twin of poetry, a secret language of the soul, and an agent of enchantment. It is a vehicle for meditation, a means to touch the mystery that precedes magic and imbas, and an artistic force that speaks directly to the mythic realm of the archetypes, the place where true dreams live.

The bardic way cries out for musical expression. To be a bard actually compels you to develop some musical skill, if you do not already have it. If you feel you are not musical, don't throw up your hands and give up just yet. You don't need to be a Mozart or a Madonna. In fact, neither of those are really appropriate. What you need to do is develop a proficiency for musical expression that is deeply meaningful to yourself in some way. You need to find an instrument that you love, and which you can play comfortably. It needs to be an instrument that you can master to the point where the technical points of play do not come between you and the spirit of what you are trying to express. Even your voice can be your instrument.

As I pointed out in the previous chapter, some bards function as seanachai [SHAWN-a-key], or storytellers who are the rememberers of lore. They have the crucial, even sacred function of keeping alive the myths and legends of their people. Other bards may be only poets. Remember that in the Irish tradition of bardry, the role of the bard was for a long time divided up into three divisions: the fíle who composed poetry, the harper who provided the mood music for the poetry, and the reciter who actually spoke the poetry. When you factor in all these different roles, it becomes clear that there is room in bardry for many types of people. However, to be a full bard, you must take up all the bardic arts, and music is fundamental.

In fact, music is so essential to bardry that without it, the bard loses half his or her mystical ability, as well as the power of communing directly with the emotional place of the mind. For music is a most powerful language that speaks to the deepest recesses of the soul. It does not use sound to represent symbols as does spoken language. Its communication works like the pure archetype before it has been covered over by a symbol so that the ego may grasp it. It affects the mind in a basic, essential way. It is pure emotion, spirit, and concept set to sound, and it churns the spirit in ways that go deeper than the logic of symbolic language ever could. It works its magic directly upon the soul, with no medium in between. That is the mystery of the magic and power of music.

Harps

Of all instruments, the harp is most associated with the bard. In fact, the Celts considered the harp to be the paragon of musical instruments. The Welsh even created laws limiting the playing of harps to bards, for the Welsh held the instrument in high regard and did not want to see it vulgarized as a common street player's instrument.

The Irish spent years training their harpers. A prospective harper was expected to begin his studies by the midteen years and study for at least three years. The hours were long and the work demanding. Yet at the end of the training, a master musician could pour his very soul into his instrument and work the three musical enchantments of harpers (more on that later).

In the course of my life I have studied many instruments, from reed instruments to winds and strings. Before I discovered the Celtic harp some years back, I experimented with the clarinet, the flute, the alto sax, alto and tenor recorders, the Irish whistle, and even the lowly autoharp. Of all the instruments I have studied, none has affected me like the Celtic harp. From the time I first saw such a harp, it spoke to me deep within. I felt as if I just had to learn it. I bought one and discovered that I could play it almost immediately; as if we had an old and secret understanding of one another. I learned that harps are instruments with names and individual spirits. They are beings capable of infinite expression, if only they are paired with the fingers of a true harper. Perhaps this affinity just runs in my Celtic soul. Perhaps a harp and I were friends in another lifetime. Whatever the reason, playing my harp is a spiritual experience for me. I believe any person with a bard's soul would and should feel an affinity for this ancient, semimythical instrument. It dates far into the haze of prehistory and has been associated with eldritch enchantment and Otherworldly beauty for thousands of years.

All modern harps built in the Western tradition consist of four basic parts: the harmonic curve (the gracefully curved cut of wood on to which the strings are mounted over the soundbox), the soundbox (the large part that leans against the player and on which the soundboard is attached), and the pillar (the curved shaft that connects the outer end of the harmonic curve to the soundbody), and the strings. These harps come in many flavors. There are the great pedal harps of orchestras, which possess forty strings or more and stand over six feet tall. These harps are extremely expensive and I don't recommend them. For one, they are bulky and heavy and very difficult to transport. For another, they are not traditional at all. The sound they make, and the techniques used in playing them—with their pedals used for gaining the semitone—is alien to Celtic music. They simply don't fit the tradition, and it's just as well, considering they cost upwards of fifteen thousand dollars!

Then there are the lever harps. These are the harps also known as Celtic harps or folk harps in today's vernacular. These harps are significantly smaller, lighter, and less expensive. Prices range from two hundred to about five thousand dollars, depending on quality, size, number of strings, and levers or blades mounted. These harps are the older forbears of the huge, modern pedal harp. They are the direct descendants of ancient harp designs: roughly triangular and, if the design is based on Celtic ideals, stoutly built. The levers or blades are used to make semitones so the harps can play in any key. They usually have between nineteen and thirty-six strings. Lever harps are portable, expressive, and sturdy instruments capable of rich, chromatic musical expression.

If you are considering taking up the harp as your bardic instrument, you should know that Celtic music, particularly Irish music, usually calls for between twenty-eight and thirty-two strings, a nice range that provides ample room for chord accompaniment to go along with the melody. A harp of this size will usually be a medium-sized, free-standing floor harp, weighing in between twenty and thirty pounds and standing between four and five feet high. You may want a harp with a few more strings to get some deeper, richer base sounds, but be aware that anything that has over thirty-two strings gets to be very unportable really fast. Medium-sized harps such as these cost between $600 and $3,500. However, for the deep, rich, powerful voice of these instruments and the wide range of notes, you may consider the size a small limitation. If you don't plan to travel with your harp, it's no limitation at all.

I have learned that I do like to go places with my harp. I play at Renaissance fairs, medieval reenactment events, tea houses, and at other public gatherings. Even more, I love playing it alone in the woods while spending solitary time with the green earth and the Otherworldly spirits. One simply could not lug around a medium or big harp with ease to do this all the time. Small harps have the additional advantage of being less expensive. Compact enough to travel lightly with, they sit on your lap or rest between your knees. Prices range between $200 and $2,500, depending on quality. As a rule, I have learned that with harps, you should buy the finest quality you can afford. It will reward you for a lifetime with durability, playability, and, most importantly, quality of sound. Small harps are strung with between nineteen and twenty-six strings. Small harps are inherently more limited, as they offer less notes and have a lighter, lower-volume sound. However, my main harp is a compact, traditional Irish design that sits comfortably on my lap. Despite her size, she has twenty-six strings and her masterwork design has bestowed upon her the full voice of larger harps. I find her very adequate. The trick is knowing how to use the strings you have—more is not necessarily superior. What size you get, and how you play it, is largely a matter of taste, choice, and how much time you want to devote to developing skill; it actually takes more time to learn to play the smaller harps well. However, with practice, you can learn ornamentation, crossover skill, and other creative techniques that more than allow you to work around the apparent limitation of less strings. For the portability advantage, you may consider this small limitation worth it. Hey, with prices starting at two hundred dollars, you may decide you want a medium harp *and* a small extra harp.

Wire-strung Harps

The harps I have described above are strung with nylon or gut. These harps fit perfectly in with the harping traditions of Wales and Brittany, and are now very popular in all the Celtic countries. However, there is another breed of harp, that is very traditional for Scottish and Irish music and of far more ancient history. These are the wire-strung clarsachs. These are different beasts; they require different playing techniques and are much more difficult to learn. They are strung with brass, silver, or even gold wire, and have a beautiful chiming, bell-like sound. My four-year-old daughter, upon first hearing such a harp, immediately described its voice as "faerie music." Wire-strung harps are worthy instruments of the bard, and if you are up to the challenge of learning to play one, by all means, take it up. My personal harp, which I mentioned above, is of this traditional wire design. Because these harps are played with the fingernails rather than the finger tips, and because the wire strings vibrate less widely, they have the additional advantage of being built much smaller than nylon and gut harps. Therefore, you can have a portable knee harp with as much as thirty strings.

Playing the Harp

Traditionally it took three years of study to produce a professional harper, but fear not. The harp has the rare ability to produce beautiful, expressive music for the novice as well as the master harper. Once you understand how to tell which strings are which, you can easily learn to play single-note melodies with one hand. Learn to play chords using the letter symbol method often seen in music written for guitar and you can quickly begin making lovely harp music. This simple music sounds so nice, in fact, that you may discover you are satisfied with that level of skill and stop there. Much Celtic music has been written in this form, so you'll have plenty of material with which to work. Such simple music makes great accompaniment for stories. It enriches the tale without distracting you from concentrating on the telling of it. Besides, the magic of bardic music does not reside in the technique, but in the spirit the bard pours into his craft (more on that in the next chapter).

Further studies will teach you the art of true two-handed playing. This combines creative chords with multinote melodies to produce astoundingly complex music of intricate expressiveness. Such music can weave webs of patterns, which transform it into a form of the high magical and psychological Celtic art of poetry.

You should also learn the famous glissando, harper's harmonics, and Celtic-style ornamentations (the various rolls, crans, and so on). It will take a long time practicing to master these high harping skills, but when you have, you will have in your grasp the other half of bardic magic: the three enchanted musics. This is the music that summons the beings of the Otherworld, and is the music of meditation and individuation.

These magics require absolute mastery of your instrument. You must be able to play automatically and effortlessly in order to give your mind over to the enchantment that is in your heart. We will discuss this more later in the chapter.

Other Musical Options for the Bard

In the past, it seems all the bards chose to study the harp. The harp was the very mark and emblem of bardry. Though it is a strong tradition, I have never found a rule that says you must play a harp to be a bard. Bear in mind that the bard follows the Celtic path, and as the rememberer of the path, it is his or her duty to value and maintain the traditions of the Old Ways. However, if your musical leanings direct you toward other forms of musical expression, I believe you should pursue them. In fact, we do know that some bards of old also learned other instruments.

Many other instruments are suitable to bardry. As well as the harp, I play the Irish whistle. You may have an interest in the guitar, hammered dulcimer, flute, the bodhran, or what have you. Many kinds of acoustic instruments lend themselves readily to bardcraft, and there is no rule saying your instrument must be of an old style. However, I feel that playing a traditional instrument is more conducive to the practice of bardry. Traditional folk instruments create a link to elder times and old ways that you can feel and see and sense, and they lend themselves to the making of bardic music with a traditional sound. They have a way of setting the proper mood. Below is a brief discussion of several other instruments commonly used in Celtic music today that I believe would serve the modern bard well.

Whistle

The Irish whistle, also known as the tin whistle or the penny whistle, is a kind of fipple flute. It has a whistle attached to one end, and is usually pretty small (about twelve inches long). It is held away from the body and points down, and it has finger holes rather than keys.

The whistle is an expressive little instrument that comes in many keys and sizes. It can play a good range of music of various emotive qualities, but it is best for expressing the spritely music of joy and play. Hence, it is also associated with faeries.

Flute

Most readers will be familiar with the metal transverse flute often played in bands and orchestras. A more traditional flute is the Irish flute. About the same length as the metal flutes, it has open finger holes rather than keys, and is made of wood, which gives it a softer, sweeter sound. It is a demanding, yet not overly difficult instrument to learn. It is also very expressive, as it allows for greater control of embouchure than its cousin, the Irish whistle, and plays many moods of music well.

Fiddle

The fiddle has for centuries held a place of prominence in the making of Celtic music. Like the whistle, flute, and pipes, numerous references to it can be found in folklore from the Celtic countries. It is particularly famous in Scotland and Ireland. It is capable of infinite expression, and is an excellent choice for those determined enough to master it, for it is a demanding instrument to study.

A similar instrument, which is very familiar to the bardic tradition of Wales, is the crwth [pronounced *crooth*, like *hoof*]. It is a kind of bowed, box-shaped fiddle with additional strings that can be plucked during play. They are very hard to find in North America, and are even rare in Wales these days. You will probably have to turn to Welsh music stores to locate one.

Another bowed instrument related to the fiddle and crwth, but which is quite easy to learn and very adequate to the bardic art for those leaning toward this type of instrument, is the bowed psaltery. This instrument looks like an elongated triangle. It has a number of strings stretched over it, and each string provides a fixed note when bowed. It is a very ancient folk instrument, and is becoming quite popular again. Bowed psalteries have been referred to as bowed harps because of their many strings. They are light, inexpensive, and fairly easy to find. Most folk music stores will sell them.

Guitar

A fairly recent import into Celtic music, the guitar is a descendent of the lute and is highly expressive. It plays nice melodies and chords, and is fairly easy to learn to play. If the guitar is your cup of tea, then go for it. If you are good at this fret instrument, but would like to aim for something more traditional, consider the lute. It is a delicate, light instrument, and it produces sweet melodies of various moods and good chord accompaniment.

Voice

If you have a nice voice, you may feel comfortable simply expressing yourself musically by singing. What could be more natural? It is in keeping with the bardic tradition, too, as many bards were singers. However, I strongly recommend that you also take up some kind of instrument. It will offer you an alternative form of expression that will, I am certain, greatly enhance the joy you and others will take in your musical endeavors by providing variety, flavor, and dimension to your craft.

More Instruments

There are, of course, many more kinds of instruments that can be used in creating bardic music. What you must do is choose an instrument that is expressive and natural. It should be capable of producing music that reflects the range of emotions (especially sadness and joy), as well as relaxing music conducive to sleep or meditation. It may require a great deal of technical skill, or only a little. That all depends on what you are drawn to and how much time you are willing to put into your music craft. Even if your instrument requires much technical skill, once you've mastered it, it will be easy to play and you will be able to focus on bardic purposes while performing with it.

There are, however, instruments, that don't really belong in bardcraft, and this includes some traditional Celtic instruments. The Scottish bagpipes are an example. While this instrument is capable of beautiful music, and there are some interesting tales about its enchantment abilities,[1] it is loud and obtrusive to focused thought, and it requires a great deal of breathing effort to play. This makes it poorly fitted for playing the three musics of magic, and even less so for playing meditative music or evocation music. Don't misunderstand me; I enjoy listening to the pipes a great deal. They just do not lend themselves to the requirements of a *bardic* instrument.

Electric instruments are another example of instruments that do not really fit into bardcraft. Electric instruments put an unnatural barrier between the music maker and the music. Keyboards, for instance, require computerized synthesizers to manufacture artificial sound. Electric guitars demand unnatural amplification. Remember that bardry is in harmony with druidry, and druidry is about the organic, the natural, and the wholesome. It is not that beautiful music cannot be made with such instruments; it can. Some of my favorite musicians, including Celtic musicians, make heavy use of electric instruments. Yet such artificial sounds simply don't have a place in the mystical practice of bardry. They are out of sync with nature and its druidic aims.

Notes on Style

Recall that the bard's way is the Celt's way. The music the bard is aiming for derives from the spirit of Celtica. Depending on his or her purpose at the time, the bard's music could be intended to encourage finding the inner quietness required for meditation or the working of enchantment, or it might be made for the simple, noble purpose of providing good entertainment. Either way, bardic music must always reflect the spirit of Celtica. Celtica is the mystical homeland of the bard and the mold of the bardic tradition. His or her music should be shaped by it, sound of it, and feel of it. Yet this is hardly restrictive. There is plenty of room in Celtic music-making to allow for individual expression.

Celtic music has three primary hallmarks: it is lean, it is repetitive, and it is individual.

If you read traditional Celtic music, you will see that the melodies are fairly simple. They may ramble wildly like a dancing elf, or they may gently flow and ebb like a lazy river, but their melody lines are concise and straightforward. This simple pattern of melodic movement reflects an ideal of bardic poetry. It reflects the basic flow of life and nature as it turns upon the sacred wheel.

Though Celtic music is strongly repetitive, it is not fatiguing to listen to. In fact, it hardly even strikes one as repetitive. If you read the music to such old and traditional pieces as "She Moved Through the Fair" from County Donegal, Ireland, or "The Harp That Once" by the nineteenth-century Irish poet Thomas Moore, you see strongly repetitious patterns in the written notation. Yet when you listen to the music being played by a skillful Celtic musician, the repetitiousness all but vanishes. This is because of the rich ornamentation Celtic musicians pour into their music. They add chords and harmonies, and support the lean melodies with the winding turns of long and short rolls, crans, triplets, harmonics, and single, double, and triple grace notes, and many other forms of ornamentation. Properly played Celtic music resembles bardic poetry, for it is concise in notation, yet rich in expression. It parallels the intricate patterns of Celtic knotwork in that it reflects the mystical truth of the repetitiveness of all natural patterns—each one flowing in winding spirals and occurring again and again on the sacred wheel—yet each different and unique in its own special way.

All Celtic music is individualized. Using the rich set of ornamentation tools like an alphabet, the player can spell out tunes in infinite variations. There are no set rules to follow—the best musicians ornament and individualize their music according to their own interpretations of how the tune should flow. Every musician thus puts his own stamp on his work, whether it is an old ballad that has been replayed for centuries or a product of neo-Celtic composition. In this, Celtic music reflects bardic poetry as well: it encourages individual expression while operating within a set of distinctive rules that preserve the overall form of an elder tradition.

Memory

Memory is of the greatest value to the bard. Remember the long years the bards spent learning an entirely oral tradition in the days of the pure Celtic psychology before the Roman Empire and the influence of Christendom. According to druidic teaching, knowledge is not alive and useful until it has been made a part of the spirit.

Accordingly, the bard should memorize as much of the music he or she plays as possible. You cannot very well expect to focus on the emotive content, or the meditative or magical qualities of music, if you have to simultaneously focus upon reading music you haven't memorized. When applying music-craft to any bardic goal, you must give your whole mind over to your goal. So the music, just like your skill at playing your instrument, must be written upon your soul.

The Three Musics of Enchantment

There are three great musics of enchantment in bardcraft. There is the *suantrai* [SWAN-*tree*], which is the music of sleep; there is the *geantrai* [GON-*tree*], which is the music of joy; and there is the *goiltrai* [GIL-*tree*], which is the music of sadness. These three musics coincide with the three needs of the soul. Great joy provides life with incentive and hope. Great sorrow provides perspective and release. Sleep provides rest and clarity.

These musics allow the bard to fulfill the individual's needs by affecting the mystical cauldrons of the soul. The cauldron is a ubiquitous theme in Celtic myth; lore concerning it occurs in many of their tales and poems. It is an archetypal symbol of a container used for transformation. In the legend of the great chief bard Taliesin's creation,[2] a sacred cauldron holds the broth of lore that the goddess Ceridwen brewed and of which Taliesin accidentally tasted. He was transformed by it, having become utterly fulfilled through understanding.

According to one unusual poem, there were two other cauldrons as well: one of craft and one of passion.[3] It is pregnant with mystical meaning, and must have been used by Irish bardic teachers to train new poets in seeking imbas and in understanding growth. This poem has been translated by Annie Power and titled "The Cauldron of Poesy." Noted Celtic scholar and mystic Caitlin Matthews has rendered a new and wonderful translation of it, which she has retitled "The Three Cauldrons."

According to this poem (and bearing in mind the other references to cauldrons in Celtic lore), three cauldrons—lore, craft, and passion—describe the three facets of the soul. Notice the recurrence of the number three. It appears in Celtic thought as a sacred number because it is reflective of so many mystical truths: three facets to the soul; three cauldrons of the spirit; three states of reality—this world, the Otherworld, and the between places. On and on these triads of truths go. No wonder the harp is a sacred instrument to the bardic tradition, with its triad of sides, triad of enchanted musics, and triads of strings used to make chords.

Each cauldron represents a fundamental element of life. The cauldron of passion holds emotion (represented by the two extremes of joy and sorrow and every state in between), which enriches life and makes us human. The cauldron of craft could be called the cauldron of purpose, for it represents the purpose and application of one's life. Finally, the cauldron of lore represents knowledge and understanding, both mystic and natural, by which we perceive and with which we act.

The fullness of any cauldron is representative of the state of one's psychological and spiritual health and fullness. When we are born, the cauldrons of lore and craft are empty, but the cauldron of passion is uninhibited and full. As we grow, what usually happens is the craft and lore cauldrons fill as we learn and apply the knowledge we gain throughout life, but we become inured, cynical, and more inhibited. Our soul shatters (as we discussed earlier in chapter 2, and hence the conception of the individual parts of the personality such as anima, ego, shadow, etc.), and the cauldron of passion empties. When this happens, life loses its brightness, its color, and its meaning. The primary goal of the bard is to balance, align, and refill the three cauldrons. Lore needs to be filled with the good, wholesome elder Celtic lore of life and spirituality; craft with trades, crafts, or professions that are fulfilling and meaningful to one's personal life and path in relation to the Celtic spirituality; and passion needs to be refilled with the power of imbas-inspired song, story, and other art to soften and revive the fragile heart. Through the bardic crafts, the bard gently guides her listeners toward those all-important goals of fulfillment. Such fulfillment is the objective of the hero's quest; the impossible ideal ever to be pursued. Filling every cauldron is archetypally symbolic of fulfillment in the spheres of emotion, purpose, and understanding. Psychologically, it is the reintegration of the soul, the attainment of true individuation, and the discovery of joy and hope in life once again.

Fulfillment is the goal of life, and everything we learn and experience brings us closer toward that goal. Yet it is a goal that is never entirely attained. Even the gods are not entirely fulfilled—just more so than mortals. All beings are born with a purpose, and the purpose is to become a hero—that is, to take up the quest to be the best person one can be. This is the filling of the cauldrons. Such purpose gives us drive and direction, fills us with knowledge, and compels us to experience the full range of the emotions of life. That we never attain perfect fulfillment is a good thing, because it ensures that there is always reason to progress and we never become static.

The three musics of enchantment play an invaluable role in the hero's quest. In fact, without music, it cannot be pursued in fullness. Music is the language that communicates most deeply. It stirs the potion of the cauldron of passion through working directly on the essence of emotion. Constructive bardic music balances and fills the cauldron of passion, and the other cauldrons are dependent upon the state of it. Without passion, lore and craft are quite hollow, and devoid of drive and meaning.

Music is the only language not formed in words. It is the only language that communicates the pure message of emotion without need of symbols, thus it is the only language that can act directly upon the cauldron of passion. Unlike poetry, it is utterly primal. It requires no literacy, and no linguistic skill. It fills the cauldron of passion as nothing else can. That is why the three enchantments of bardic music, though they are derived through the application of developed lore and craft, affect most directly the cauldron of passion. Poetry or prose work by conveying messages through spoken language—the language of symbols. They may therefore affect passion's cauldron indirectly through lore. However, music works the other way around. Being derived from passion and perfected through lore and craft, it works directly upon passion's cauldron. It fills all the cauldrons through the strengthening of passion, which bestows drive and meaning. Music, the product of and mover of passion, is the fundamental, underlying resonance that is birthed of and returns to strengthen the spirit. Indeed, according to many a legend, music's unique strength lies at the foundation of creation itself.

Suantrai

The music of suantrai is deeply relaxing, and hypnotic in flavor. It consists of gently flowing melody, repetitious turns, and sweet chords that often move in cascading arpeggios. It is not demanding to play. If it were, the player would not be able to relax while playing, and the listener would pick up that energy.

If you play the harp or another chord-capable instrument such as the guitar or lute, you will find it very easy to create simple suantrai on the spur of a moment. Simply repeat chords that work together musically in a gently flowing rhythm. Some melody instruments will also lend themselves to this music. The Irish flute is a natural for it, especially when it is used to play music that flows in sweet, slow movement through the low range of the instrument. The harp easily provides sweet, restful melody and chord combinations.

You can also find much written music you can learn that falls into this category. Much of Enya's music, especially her simpler songs such as "Athair Ar Neamh,"[4] fit this category. So does a great deal of native Celtic music, such as "Bonny Portmore" and "She Moved Through the Fair." The skill, you will learn as your music-playing ability develops, is not so much in what you play, but in how you play it. As you develop your music-craft, you should develop a repertoire of the gentle, relaxing pieces suited to suantrai.

Technique. Suantrai is the music of sleep. That is, it has a deeply relaxing, hypnotic quality. Many folktales record bards using the suantrai against enemies in order to escape. Even the Bible records David using suantrai to calm King Saul who was afflicted by evil spirits. Suantrai is the music that calms the soul.

To apply suantrai in your own meditations, prepare your instrument. Find a quiet place where you will not be disturbed and that has a pleasing atmosphere. My favorite places are in natural nemetons and near streams (two classes of sacred sites). Of course, I have the advantage of living in the wilderness, so such sites are abundant. Even if you live in the city, you should be able to find such places with a little effort: lonely parks, arboretums, and the like. Even your own home can work, just so long as you have your own private place.

If you are indoors in your home, I suggest you make it even more suitable to your bardic purposes. Prepare a room as your sanctuary. Fill it with personal things and Celtic things. Make it very much you, yet let it resound with Celtica. You might want to put up pictures, posters, even murals of nat-

ural places, streams, forest glades, and the like. Incense can also be very helpful in creating the setting, especially forest scents. That a proper scent is
important to creating the right feel for your place of meditation is undeni-
able. Some psychologists have found that the sense of smell is much more
powerful psychologically than any of the other four senses. The right incense
can make even an indoor forest setting come alive to your imagination.

When all is ready, play. You will, of course, have to have mastered your
instrument and have memorized your music to the point where both are an
automatic expression of your soul. Assuming that you have, clear your mind
as you play, and allow the music to speak to you in its wordless language. Let
it take you where it may; let it imbue you with its nature.

When you feel you have played enough, you may either meditate upon
the notes of the music, visualize what the music inspires in your heart, or
take up the shamanic journey. The music has worked to clear your mind and
relax your body. It sets you into a resonance with the enchanted. The clarity
it imparts makes you sensitive to the Otherworld. You will find that your
meditations and journeyings will be richer for the application of the suantrai
beforehand.

If others choose to join you, they may likewise benefit from suantrai.
Even if they are not bards or meditators, suantric music is healthful to listen
to: it relieves tension from the body and soul, and fills the cauldron of passion with peace.

Geantrai

The music of joy works similar to suantrai, but it has some other uses. As
before, you should find a private, peaceful place. Best is a natural setting,
but someplace indoors will do if that is your only option. If you are highly
skilled, you may be able to play this music off the cuff, though it is much
harder than suantrai. Otherwise, you should find and memorize some pieces
that speak to you in an especially joyful way. There is an abundance of such
spritely tunes among Celtic music, especially those of the Scots and Irish.

You want to avoid music of passions such as love, battle, rebellion, or any
other cause-motivated music, even if it's for a just cause. What you are after
is music about joy, pure and simple. Some such traditional Celtic tunes that
come to mind are "The Pipers," "The Dogs," and "The Rising of the Lark";
there are thousands more.

Like all the musics of enchantment, geantrai works best when the mind is made clear and receptive. Yet it has the ability of grabbing the mind and making it receptive. The mind naturally wants to be cheered and geantrai attempts to work just that. The more skillful you are as a musician, the better you can employ this magical music for your benefit and that of others.

Geantrai is a great restorative. It invigorates the soul, revives one from sadness, and lends energy. It fills the passion cauldron with the joyous perspective, which assists the cauldron of craft in particular. Joy leads to contentment and purpose.

Geantrai is also the music used to summon the sidhe. In legend, the sidhe find the music of joy irresistible and pass much of their time making it and dancing to it. When musicians win their approval, the sidhe offer the rewards of their protection, knowledge, and luck. However, the sidhe are fickle and unpredictable. Other legends tell of the sidhe carrying off great pipers and fiddlers to play for them in their faerie mounds (also called sidhe mounds or hollow hills). So you may want to be careful.

Technique. If you want to experience the presence of the sidhe, the following is a way to use geantrai.

First, you need to be in a wild place, and preferably some place that folklore indicates may be inhabited by the sidhe. Legends tell us that the sidhe love the same places that are special to the bard and druid: nemetons, hillocks and natural mounds, and water's edge.

It is best to be at such a place on one of the sacred days: Imbolc, Lughnasadh, Beltane, or Samhain. Yet other days and times are also potent. Fridays are said to be a day when the sidhe have especial power. They are often out by day and night, but twilight—the between time of day's end and new day's birth—is the best time to see them. Full moons and new moons are significant to them as well.

Set out an offering. This is not so much a sacrifice or propitiation as a gift. The sidhe value the person who is kind, polite, and generous. They may play pranks on such a one, but will rarely harm him or her.

Traditional foods to set out are bread, cheese, grain, and milk. Wine is another good choice. Set them on simple clay or ceramic dishes. Use no iron and no silver as some legends indicate the sidhe have an aversion to them—especially iron.

Have a poem of enchantment composed and ready for the event. In it, call forth the sidhe, the spirits of nature and the primal enchantment of creation. Invoke protection from the patron deities of bards, and request the help and enlightenment of Cernunnos, the Green Man and the lord of natural things. Your own bardic studies should lead you in the composition of the poem. Bardic magic is not really about repeating well-used formulaic words (which do have a power of their own), but about the more potent magic that arises from the living, imbas-inspired bardic crafts: poetry and music combined with controlled thought. I offer a poem below as a model of what you might do. You are free to experiment with other incantations or modify this one.

> Horned One, Cernunnos,
> lord of natures here and Other,
> summon enchantment from the mists,
> let me walk with mystery.
>
> Brighid, patroness of poets,
> provide protection for your bard,
> your druid–truth seeker,
> that I may share in the mystery.
>
> O sidhe, hidden just beyond the veil between where worlds meet,
> accept this food and joyous music,
> come make real your mystery.

Now build a fire, or at least set out a candle or a lantern. If you use a lantern, be sure it is not made of iron. You can check it with a magnet. Also, use a kerosene one, not a propane or pressurized gas one. The obnoxious hissing of the latter gets in the way of the meditative contact that must be made with nature.

If you are in the right spot at the right time and your music and food is to their liking, the sidhe will come. When they do, you will sense them, if not see them. It feels like the presence of swirling mist prickling with enchantment on the verge of becoming shapes just beyond the shadows. If you are one of the truly fortunate, you may even see them. More will be said on the sidhe in the chapters 10 and 11.[5]

Goiltrai

Finally, we consider the music of sadness. What benefit could there be in sadness? Sadness is the opposite of joy. In whatever flavor it comes—sorrow, loss, anguish, regret—it is the other emotional extreme. It provides balance to joy. Without this balance, even joy would be unhealthy. For instance, in some classic experiments, lab rats have been presented with two levers: one dispenses a euphoria-inducing narcotic, and the other dispenses food. In a setting where there is no limit to the narcotic, the lab rats will drug themselves without eating or resting until they die. A similar experiment on monkeys, wherein they had the option of directly stimulating pleasure centers in the brain, yielded the same result. The monkeys neglected food and rest for a euphoria that, when unchecked, became destructive. Joy (which is euphoria at its extreme) must be balanced, else it is a destructive passion.

Perhaps this concept explains why some legends portray it as dangerous to mingle with the sidhe. In the view of these legends, the sidhe are entities that live in a state of perpetual bliss. They are overwhelmingly beautiful natural beings who seduce humans into a dangerous state of unbalance, which causes them to lose touch with this world. There may be some truth to these legends, though the seduction of the sidhe is most often inadvertent. They are not, in general, malicious. The real danger in communing with the Otherworld is in committing some unwitting offense, encountering sidhe of ill intent, or especially in associating with the Otherworld while the self remains inadequately developed. It is not difficult to lose oneself among the awesome beauty or mystery of the Otherworld if one does not truly know who his or her self is.

The music of goiltrai serves a number of important purposes for bardcraft. It fills and balances the cauldron of passion by giving perspective and release. The invaluable wisdom of perspective that is gained leads to enlightenment within the cauldron of lore. This lore helps to turn the craft cauldron by pointing the bard to ways of service and work that will benefit himself and others.

Like geantrai, the music of joy, goiltrai will grab the mind and fill it with its wordless thoughts and imageless emotions. However, it works best if the mind is cleared and made receptive to it.

Also like geantrai, you want to choose music that speaks of pure sadness. From the strictly musical end of bardcraft, it is not the words of any song you are interested in. You want music that speaks to the soul without the interference of words. Some such old traditional tunes are "The Willow Tree," "The Foggy Dew," "The Harp That Once Through Tara's Halls," and "Farewell to Music."

Technique. As with the music of sleep, the best use of goiltrai is to meditate on it. Go to your private place, relax, and clear your mind by using the techniques described in chapter 4. Having mastered your instrument and memorized your music, play the tune on your heart and give your cleared mind over to it. Soak it up and let it work into your soul. When you have played enough, switch to another such tune if you feel inspired, or set your instrument aside and begin meditating or visualizing. Filled with the imbas of such music, you may find that your meditations lead to some surprising revelations.

You may find a session of goiltraic music leaves you feeling refreshed, if a bit melancholy. Don't be surprised. A bit of balancing sadness is good for the spirit. Also, melancholy is good for the production of art. There is even old Celtic lore that says that the poetic gift cannot manifest in a person without a good dose of sadness. Perhaps with bitter experiences comes wisdom. Perhaps it is because experiencing sadness allows one to appreciate the full depth of life's experiences. In any case, the old Irish filidh used to debate whether joy or sadness was more conducive to inspiration, but it was obvious to them that both were necessary.

A Final Note

Lastly, to be true to the old lore it is important to note that only to harpers do the legends of Celtica attribute the three musics of enchantment. While other instruments are purported as being capable of producing magic (with a gifted musician/mage playing them), those magics are of a different nature; more on the order of charms, invocations, and evocations. It might well be that while other instruments may be able to partially produce the three musics, the full working of suantrai, geantrai, and goiltrai depends on the use of the harp. If you choose to play another instrument in your bardic walk, there is no harm in testing this. There is no lore that says instruments other than harps should not or cannot produce the three enchanted musics. It is only that the lore just records harps making them. So you should be aware that if you opt to play something else, you may be partially handicapping yourself as a bard. If only the harp is capable of the full expression of the three enchanted musics, it would go far toward explaining why the Celts of old held the harp and harper in such high esteem.

Music and Bardic Performance

A couple final notes are necessary. The bard was his community's memory. In the fulfillment of this role, he was the storyteller. Bards understood the power of music to enhance a tale and to make its scenes come alive to the senses. They used the harp to make their tales real for their listeners. With the aid of the harp, one can evoke raindrops on water, the flowing of a stream, the gentle rush of wind through tree boughs, or high mountains beneath the moon. The effects are limited only by the harper's skill.

The bards also understood mood music long before Hollywood started using it in motion picture production. They applied music at strategic times in their tales to heighten the passion and set the listener in the feet of the characters.

These are techniques you should apply to your storycraft. Whatever your instrument, you can breathe new life into your tales by the judicious application of music. For some modern examples of music applied to bardic storytelling, I strongly suggest listening to the CDs *The Storyteller* by Patrick Ball, or *The Language of Birds* by Fiona Davidson.

It is important to understand, too, that bardic storytelling is not merely about providing entertainment in the form of oral fiction. While entertaining, their stories build from the myths, legends, and lore of antiquity. They are pregnant with meaning. They teach while they entertain. They are at the very heart of what it means to follow the Celtic path.

For the bard, fulfilling the roles of memory and storyteller are important tasks in the filling of the craft and lore cauldrons. Like the musics of enchantment, work the telling of tales with all your heart.

chapter seven

Elder Enchantment

In the early twilight Gwydion arose,
and he called unto him his magic and
his power.

The Mabinogion

This chapter is about the high arts of bardic enchantment. The bards and druids also employed the earthier Celtic magic, but high bardic magic is distinguished from lower Celtic magic in a number of ways. The differences include:

1. An understanding that power lies in the sacred, not the profane.

2. A knowledge of the application of mental focus to magical works.

3. A distinctive use of the bardic arts as magical tools.

4. Knowing how to work with the Otherworld, and with nature.

5. Understanding that magic is an incidental characteristic of bardcraft.

Let us consider each of these areas one by one.

Number one: The druids long understood the magic that is worked by an intimate relationship with the forces of nature. It did not actually reside in the material, which was profane, but in the sacred forces themselves. It is important to understand that *profane* in druidry does not mean a thing is unclean or unworthy in any negative sense. It simply means that it is merely material. Matter itself is ordinary and powerless without the forces that empower it. The druids of old understood those forces, and were thus able to manipulate them. The bards, as part of the druidic tradition (and its subsequent heirs as druidry was hounded to extinction by Imperial Rome and, later, the Christian church), inherited this knowledge.

Number two: All traditions incorporating any kind of magical or mystical practice recognize the importance of mental focus. Buddhism sees it as key to the mystical meditative act of attaining *nibbana* (Nirvana). Hermetic and Kabalistic magical systems see it as a key to the working of high magic. The magical traditions of the West recognize its absolute necessity in making magical works effective. Shamanism requires meditative focus and control in order to contact the Otherworlds. Likewise, bardry recognizes this universal occult truth.

Sadly, most people fail to understand the fundamental nature of conscious thought. They view the mind as merely a thinking machine, or a computer isolated from the universe at large and from other minds except through the use of the physical body. They fail entirely to realize how innately mystical a thinking machine is and how incredibly deeply the mind must be linked to the sacred forces we sometimes call magic to even function. Scholars these days are exploring the conscious's relationship to quantum theory, and legitimate scientists are investigating the parapsychological power of the mind. In Europe it is widely recognized that whatever the nature of this parapsychological power, the mind does have some extraordinary capabilities. The high magic arts focus on making use of these abilities. They recognize that meditative focus must be achieved in order to work any kind of magical function.

Number three: All mystical traditions that utilize some form of mental focus have systems and symbolism that the adherents learn to employ. The same is true of bardry. The bard learns the use of music, poetry and prose, and myth as his or her meditative tools.

Number four: The bard learns to have a positive relationship with all aspects of nature, whether that nature is of the here and now or Otherworldly. Bardic magical arts call on the application of the natural forces of the worlds, and these forces are best summoned at those between places where their ebb and flow occurs most freely. The bard must relate to nature so intimately that he or she is sensitive to such places.

Number five: Finally, it is absolutely necessary that the bardic student understand that magical power is not the goal of bardry, but an incidental effect. The goal of bardry is personal growth and fulfillment—the pursuit of the hero's quest. The power of enchantment comes about from the bard's total relationship to the natural and the mystical. The student who takes up bardry merely for the acquisition of magical power will be in for a rude awakening. It will be hard to summon the power, as it requires imbas-inspired music and poetry. This rarely can result in the presence of selfish-ness and power-lust. Of even greater importance is that its misuse will call down the ire of the gods. Dallán Forgaill was a *file* (pronounced [*FEE-la*]; an Irish bard) who misused his power to satisfy his pride and voracious greed. He was first shamed as a warning by a ghost of the Fianna warriors when he tried to use his poetic powers to force another man's wife to become his. Later he was destroyed by the gods who turned his power against him for his refusal to cease abusing it.[1] In a tale from the great book of Welsh legend, the *Mabinogi,* the wizard-god Math terribly punishes his own nephews Gwydion and Gilfaethwy for their dreadful abuse of their magic arts. Their abuse caused the death of a good lord and many fine men, and led to the rape of a maiden in Math's protection.[2]

The bardic magics are incidental powers, to be used firstly for the acqui-sition of wisdom for growth. They may be used for other reasons when needed, but they are not to be used with ill intent. This is tantamount to invoking chaos, and the Celtic gods will not allow such a shift of balance to go unchecked for long.[3]

The Nature of High Bardic Enchantment

Reconstructing Bardic Magic

Sadly, there are no surviving texts on bardic or druidic magic. Texts from that era are very rare (remember the druidic injunction against writing).

However, there are legends that say in Ireland druids had eased up on this interdiction and wrote down many books of enchantment. (This was because druidry in Ireland was isolated from the rest of the world and free to develop in an uninterrupted, almost purely Gaelic-Celtic tradition for centuries.) Yet when St. Patrick came to reform the ancient and sophisticated Celtic civilization of Ireland (which he saw as demonic and primitive because of its Paganism), he ordered the burning of these books. Thus, very few records remain and an understanding of bardic magic must be rebuilt from the surviving folktales of the era. These folktales must be considered in light of surviving Celtic magical practices and compared with the related magical traditions of other parts of the world.

While this method cannot recall the exact nature of bardic magic craft, it can, I believe, go a long way toward showing us how to reconstruct the bards' original mystical way. Legend points out that the druids often went abroad to study the mystical traditions of other lands. The druids added to their native spirituality, and shared of their own while among those peoples. The great Irish druid Cathbhadh [*CAH-vah*] was one who did just that. The legends clearly indicate the peoples the druids studied among, so we know where to look in the world for a Celtic influence, and what other mystic systems might have been incorporated by the druids. Other legends help us to shape our understanding of how the druids interpreted and made use of their learning. We can also trace back through the records of folklore to observe the evolution of the bard's original mystic way and compare it with archaeological and anthropological learning to further refine our understanding of the core Celtic magical beliefs.

Also, by tracing the mystical evolution of other Indo-European peoples (whose beliefs are also documented in bits and pieces), we can gain perspective on old Celtic ideas. This is not to say that the Celtic mysteries are the same as any of these other traditions. In actuality, they are quite distinctly their own. However, they do bear relationships that help to enlighten us on the Celts' Old Ways.

Finally, the Celts are a living people who still survive on the Western fringes of Europe and are dispersed through other parts of the world, such as the Welsh colonists of Patagonia, the Irish settlers of America, and the Scottish settlers of Nova Scotia. Therefore, we have living traditions on which to base final comparisons.

In the end when it is all added up and compared, it means we can put together a good idea of the Old Ways of the Celtic mages. We can't reconstruct it exactly, but we can reclaim many points of their magico-mystical theory. Plus, according to the principles of high druidic/bardic magic, this is sufficient, because the power of enchantment does not lie in the profane—not in mere words or material objects—but in the imbas and spirit of the enchanter.

Theory of Bardic Magic

This section could just as well have been titled "Theory of Druidic Magic," for the two are so tightly related they are, in effect, almost the same. In a nutshell, high bardic magical practice involves focusing the mind and invoking a power. In that sense, it is very similar to the old Hermetic magical tradition, which strongly emphasizes utilizing a mental focus in conjunction with the invoked power of an Otherworldly being. Make no mistake: bardry is not Hermeticism, but there is a relation. Almost certainly ancient druids traveled to the realms where Hermeticists practiced to learn from them, or vice versa.

Considering the Hermetic influence on bardic/druidic magic, it is reasonable to believe that the bard incorporated practices akin to those of the Hermetic *goêteia* [go-AY-see-ah] worker and the magus. Goêteia was the low magic of Hermeticism. It was not low in the sense of immoral, but low in the sense of being simpler, easier to perform, and weaker. It relied on the magical properties inherent within things: words, herbs, stones, and so on. It made little use of the mind of the worker and little of the assistance of Otherworldly beings. It was thus profane. High bardic magic was more similar to the magic of the Hermetic magus in that it made use of some objects, times, and words, but used them not so much for their inherent properties, but as tools upon which to focus a trained mind toward magical work. Of course, the innate magical properties of things, times, and places could also be added to the work of the magus in order to amplify the primary magical work being conducted through the will.

The Hermetic magus also learned to work in intimate conjunction with an Otherworldly power, and actually melded him- or herself to that power. The magus would magically join his ego permanently to a spirit entity, a god, a daimon, or other such being, thus sacrificing his pure individuality in order to greatly add to the power of his individual will. Bards and druids worked in an intimately close relationship with Otherworldly beings as well, but I find no indication in the surviving lore that they went so far as to meld with them. If anything, this would have been repugnant to the Celtic psychology, which so valued individuality.

However, it is important to remember that though bardic magic craft bears some similarity to Hermeticism, it is not of it. Druidry derived from far older traditions and was ancient when Hermeticism was only coming into being. There is reason to believe the druids may have even been the surviving priestly line of the venerable pre-Celts of Western Europe, who were old when the mighty Stonehenge was yet young. I personally doubt this, for druidry seems to have been too vitally bound up in the way of the Celt to have originated from outside Celtica, but druidry was not averse to learning from any beneficial source. Perhaps the druids studied from surviving pre-Celtic mystics. In any case, these are questions for other books. What we are interested in here is the theory behind the bardic magical arts.

All high bardic magic was done in this way: having mastered the art of poetry and music, and having committed the required lore to memory in order to make its enlightenment a living entity of the mind, the bard makes his preparations. He gathers and prepares whatever will be required for the magic he desires to work. For the bard, this often meant a poem of incantation accompanied by music. The purpose of the music and poetry were to focus the mind and to release power at the appropriate moment.

It was also advantageous for the bard to work the magic at the between times and places discussed in chapter 2. The sacred days were the most powerful times, but twilight was a daily powerful time that could be utilized. Nemetons were very powerful places for working magic, and pools or watersides were also highly effective.

Having prepared himself through study, chosen his music, and prepared his incantational poem (either composed for the occasion or taken from extant poetry), the bard set about his personal preparation. The first step was to relax the body and clear the mind; hence, the relaxation technique you studied in chapter 4. After relaxing the body, the mind was emptied of thought. Only when the body is relaxed and the mind is cleared can there be the necessary focus, and freedom from internal distraction.

Once the body and mind were prepared, the next step was to enter a meditative state. The technique chosen depended upon the bard's goal. To cause something to occur, the bard would focus his mind entirely on the goal—so the technique was focus meditation. Here, a living knowledge of myth was most beneficial: the mythological precedent gives symbolic form to the archetypes of the unconscious mind, thus aiding the imagination in visualization. A solid foundation in myth lore gives useful form to archetypes and makes the way of magic alive and potent in the spirit.

When the goal was made real in the mind, the power of the invoked magic was released through the incantory playing of bardic music and the recitation of a poetic spell. The music was appropriate to the nature of the goal. After all, the purpose of the music was to sing in resonance with the forces of enchantment and to assist the bard in mental focusing. The poetry did likewise. Additionally, the poetry: (a) invoked the aid of the appropriate Otherworldly entities, (b) specified the way in which their aid was sought, and (c) specifically named and described the desired effect.

After the enchantment was worked, it was important for the bard to quickly clear his or her mind again so as to release the magic to work without tainting it. If this wasn't done, then any future thoughts could alter the course of the magic. Thus, there was a need for a cooling-off procedure. In Hermeticism, this was accomplished through letting go of all thoughts related to the magical working. In witchcraft, this is accomplished through the ceremony of Cakes and Ale. Similarly, the bard changed the flow of the mind by first clearing it for a couple of minutes through meditation techniques. He would then recite some unrelated lore in the form of poetry or prose, and play some music (this was preferably something complicated and demanding, which fully engaged the mind away from the magical task).

The above order refers only to magic whose goal was to accomplish an effect, such as a spell for a fruitful garden. If the bard's goal was a shamanic journey, divination, or scrying, the poetry and music for the occasion were performed first, which set up a resonance to assist the spirit in entering into the magical-meditative state. Then the procedure for the shamanic journey or divination was begun. At the end of the journey, a cool-down was not necessary. It was better to immediately meditate upon, or simply consider, the knowledge gained through the journey or divinatory act while it was still fresh. This not only permitted one to gain the most enlightenment from the experience while committing it to memory, but it engaged the mind in a different kind of task, which had the same effect as a cool-down.

We see that bardic/druidic magic incorporates the latent power of music and words, the full potency of the mind, and the mystery of the between times and places. It is, in one sense, profane because it recognizes that magical power is inherent within certain things, times, and places, and it utilizes those characteristics. Yet it also recognizes that magic is a force focused by things, times, places, and spirits, that it originates in the forces of nature, and that it is molded and directed by the imbas-inspired human will. Though it relies heavily upon mental strength, it is not really psychic, as the mind works only as a director of natural forces. Though it has traits in common with both the high and low Hermetic magical system, it is not the magic of the Hermetic magician. It never leads to a melding with an Otherworldly entity, but only calls upon the sidhe, divinities, and other spirits, and impels them toward action through the beauty of poetry and music. Finally, underlying the whole process is the special, deep, druidic concern with working in harmony with nature. Bardic/druidic magic, therefore, shares style with some other Western traditions, and even has deep commonalities with some Eastern mystic practices, but it is uniquely itself.

A Theory on How Enchantment May Work

It is well-known that magic may work through the sheer force of belief. That is, a person may be affected by magic because he or she *believes* magic to be efficacious. If that person casts a spell to get a raise, she may work harder and thereby attain that raise. Is this magic? Why not? The end result is the same. A psychic cause works a measurable effect.

What of magic actually affecting objective outcomes, changing states of reality, and possessing a power in and of itself? Can magic do this? I believe it can, and I offer this brief theory as to how it may work. This theory is not presented as fact. You may make of it what you will. I believe it represents a possible explanation for the very real power magic may represent, and it helps you to understand why, as a bard, you must pursue an understanding of magic.

When reality is broken down to its quantum level, we find that all things resolve into waves of probability. A unit of space possesses a probability that within it a thing may occur or exist. A unit of space, for instance, possesses a probability that an atomic particle will occupy it for an instant of time. The chance that something will be in that unit of space is influenced by subtle, even sublime, forces from neighboring units of space. Thus, if you apply force to an object in one area, you increase the probability that the object will appear in an adjacent area. In fact, this probability increases to such a high degree that it becomes a virtual certainty it will appear there (the probability effect flows like a wave into the next area of space, making the object appear there). Force has linked one area of space with another and changed both. The whole universe is linked in this way.

Because everything exists as a manifestation of probability, and probability is not always reliable, we have a way of occasionally observing the truth of this quantum concept. For example, in a cubic meter of space, sometimes particles called *virtual matter* will pop into existence one moment and pop out of existence the next. They have a slight random chance (or probability) of existing in this universe, and even though the chance is indeed very slight, some of them find their way into the here and now. Then, because they have a low probability of continuing to exist (since they are not really connected to this universe), they vanish in an instant.

These virtual particles have been documented and they occur often and everywhere. What makes them really interesting to us is that they appear as if for no reason. Subtle alterations of the waves of probability within the very fabric of space-time brought them here—that is, they appear as if by magic. From inexplicable mystery nothingness springs into existence.

These shifting waves of probability that underlie all things also cause tiny wormholes to constantly open and close in the space of this universe here and now. These wormholes momentarily connect to the space of other realities, far away times, and regions. There are many other quantum effects of such a wondrous nature occurring every moment.

These quantum events teach us several things about the nature of reality. One: all things are interrelated. What affects something in one place may affect something else far away in space, time, and circumstance. Two: there are other Otherworlds, planes, or whatever you want to call them, all existing within the quantum folds of space. Three (perhaps the most important lesson of all): reality is not what it appears. The universe is not a clockwork machine. There is room for the unexplained, as certain phenomena can occur entirely at random, and effects can even precede causes. Quantum probability guarantees that everything will not be predictable. So you can throw out the nineteenth-century concept of a cool, calculating, predictable, Newtonian universe. Mystery is real!

Of late, scholars of many fields have been researching the possible relations between the nature of consciousness and quantum reality. There are indications that being conscious implies more than a mere electrochemical reaction within the neuro-network known as the brain. Consciousness may be rooted directly to the most primal workings of space-time.

Now, an existential psychological concept concerns growing in the world. It teaches that as we fulfill our possibilities for growth, the universe itself grows with us. It implies that the very nature of reality is dependent upon the depth of our perceptive abilities.

It is no great leap from there to realize that the mind, linked to the very fabric of reality as it is, might be capable of influencing reality by exerting the force of will and the power of perception upon the here and now. This validates magic in that it gives it a viable motor (the will of consciousness) and a medium in which to work (the foaming essence of space-time itself). Because very small probabilistic changes can add up over time and distance to effect significant changes (much as a few rolling pebbles can start a rockslide), it means that magic can work like a lever: it amplifies slight and subtle forces, which the magically trained mind may initiate to work profound effects.

Again, this is only a theory of mine (one which I have been researching for years), but it is undeniably feasible.[4] It means that magic is a very real, potent force. Perhaps it is not immediately visible in effect, but it works continuously, subtly, and with profound power. It means there are Otherworlds, other realities beyond the here and now. It also means the universe is full of mystery; it is beautifully unpredictable, and a place of genuine wonder to those who are sensitive to the magic of it.

Growth Through Enchantment

Working with magic teaches control of the mind, and demands the fulfillment of artistic potential through mastery of the bardic arts of poetry, music, and lorecraft. Magic can be employed to seek knowledge and understanding through divination and scrying. The successful working of magic requires an existence in the between places, where magic is at its most potent. It puts one in touch with the deeper nature of reality. Hence, the working of magic is a catalyst for growth.

Therefore, keeping in mind that I have warned of the consequences of misusing magic, also bear in mind that magic is not interdicted. It is, in fact, encouraged, but it must be used rightly. Its purpose is for knowledge and to assist in growth. For instance, it would be unethical for the bard to attempt magic to influence a person to love her. However, there is no reason why magic should not be used to improve oneself, which may have the end result of making oneself more desirable to the person whose love is sought.

Bear in mind that in folklore there were evil bards who misused the formidable magical power of their craft. Their powers were not lifted by the gods. Rather, they were often destroyed or ruined in some way. It is divinely demanded of bards that they work ethically.

The Elder Enchantments

There are several enchantments that fall into the direct domain of the bard. These are: the influence over the elements, the geas, the satire, the poet's curse, the Otherworld journey, shape-changing, and divination. I call these magics the elder enchantments because these are the primal magics; those that are concerned with basic forces and which work through the sheer application of magic power (the power the old gods used to shape creation when time was young). These enchantments require no profane things, and no special ingredients or incantations (though, of course, they will not fail to benefit from the use of harmoniously resonant objects and actions, if for no other reason than the magic worker's will will be enhanced and more focused). They work from the essence of a focused mind, poetry and music being the tools that focus them. Though their power is enhanced and focused by being worked in the between times and places, they are not dependent on such manipulation. These elder enchantments are of primal forces and pure knowledge; the very things that combine to make the here and now, and which will cause personal growth within the bard.

These elder enchantments may be divided up into two main categories: effective magics and lore magics. Effective magics seek to influence a situation to the bard's desire. Lore magics seek knowledge in some way.

Effective Enchantments

We will deal first with effective enchantments. All the effective enchantments are begun in the same way: the body is relaxed and the mind is cleared and focused. Powerful emotion may lend strength to the power of effective magics, so long as a focused mind can be maintained.

Influence over the Elements

When Taliesin faced the wicked king Maelgwn and his bards, he proved his power by summoning a wind to silence the opposition. When the Tuatha de Danaan sent a wind to destroy the invading Milesians, the bard Amergin caused it to cease. Under the curse of the poet, drought could be induced and rivers dried, further demonstrating bardic influence over the weather. Many other legends speak to us of bards and poets exercising authority over the elements. This was a power the bards shared with their druid kindred.

If the bard wishes to try to influence the elements, he must have supernatural assistance. The attention of the Otherworld is gained through imbas-wrought music and mighty poetry. The music must reflect the mood of the change sought with skill and consummate passion. The poetry proclaims the invocation to the Otherworldly powers; the call to the gods and sidhe. It invokes a sympathy between the elements and the bard through descriptively comparing the bard to the manifestations of the element in nature and of the forces that affect it. Finally, it proclaims the bard's desire for the shaping of the element.

During the procedure, the bard's will must be entirely focused upon the task. He must see the Otherworldly beings being called upon, he must become one with the forces being described, and he must visualize with every sense the goal of his incantory poetry.

It is obvious that to accomplish such high and powerful magic, the bard must be a master of the craft of poetry, of the skill of playing his instrument, and of the art of focusing the mind. The incantational poetry and music must be mightily charged with imbas. There is no room during the execution of the enchantment to ponder technique. The bard must be so familiar with his music, poetry, and instrument that they are one with his spirit and flow automatically; much as a good actor must be so familiar with her script that she can pour her heart into her acting without worrying about the text. The knowledge of enchantment-working must be burned into the bard's soul.

I strongly recommend to the bardic student that you study for yourself the Celtic legends, especially those pertaining to the workings of the ancient bards over the elements. Also, the stories of druids doing the same will be most enlightening. The wealth of folk wisdom preserved in such tales will provide a necessary feel for the construction of the poetry of incantation used in this magic.

I offer below a poem as an example of the construction of this type of incantational poetry. This poem is only an example. To possess the primal power of elder magic, the poetry used in your incantational magic should arise from your individual being, and from the very most roots of your soul. Only when it comes from you, created for the working you have intended it, and by the power of your own spirit blended and melded with imbas, will it possess that necessary living link with magic.

> Kernunnos is the lord of the wood and tillage of the soil,
> And Tailtiu looks after the green growing things;
> The Dagda is giver of plenty, his cauldron never leaves
> the brave man or maid wanting.
> They look and see that plentiful is the harvest,
> so great is the Samhain feast.
>
> I am the kernel which grows to perfection,
> I am the green thing that lies in the ground,
> I am the stalk of nine blossoms,
> who yields the fruit of earth, sun, and rain.
> I am the receiver of the sky hearth,
> green grow I beneath the sunbeam,
> I am the riser from the depths,
> with three moors sinking into the earth from which I rose,
> and three shoots rising to grasp the horns of the moon.
>
> From the fruit of the crop does the household eat,
> the garden that grows green and vibrant,
> the garden where Kernunnos takes pleasure,
> whose soil Tailtiu nourishes with her son Lugh's strong beams,
> and the Dagda makes to fill the cauldron.

The first section of this incantational poem invokes the gods of the Celtic pantheon who look after the welfare of natural things, the earth, and grant the blessings of plenty. The second part compares the bard to the growth of plants, which sets up resonances that assist in visualization, and has the additional effect of calling on the Otherworldly powers and shaping forces. The final section proclaims the desire of the bard—a bountiful harvest—and again invokes Otherworldly power in the attainment of the goal. The poem is crafted to make it artistically appealing, for the legends confirm that the gods and the sidhe appreciate and respond to things of beauty.

As I am certain you see by now, this is a poem for the bountiful growth of a garden. It is within the bardic influence over the elements because a garden's growth is the result of the successful melding of earth, wind, and water. It is a natural process empowered by the energy of light—a transforming force synonymous with the element of fire.

Now, the whole thing could be succinctly rewritten in one sentence: "Kernunnos, Tailtiu, Dagda, Lugh, make my garden grow." However, this would be entirely ineffectual. Why? Because such a direct, dry statement would have no more magical power than a legal document. It would not help in visualization, nor invoke any power, nor set up the necessary resonances between bard and element. Such a blatant, direct request would be dry, mundane, and entirely lacking in imbas.

Even more importantly, my studies indicate that, according to the Celtic tradition, a bold, direct request would have been considered quite crass. The Celts were a very generous people. They loved to give gifts and lavish rewards. Their favors were seldom handed over for mere solicitation, for this was the equivalent of begging—a rather lowly and shameful way to go about obtaining something. The Celts freely gave generous gifts as blessings for the pleasure and honor of giving.

The Celts also gave gifts as rewards for deeds well done. Noble warriors received generous portions of the spoils of battle, harpers received gold, land, and even new, expensive instruments for their music, and poets received princely sums for poetry well written. Poets could name the rewards they desired through their poetry, using subtlety and craftiness to make their specific requests polite and clear. That is exactly what you, too, must do in your incantations, for your enchantments are nothing less than poetic requests of the Otherworld. You must name your reward with the deft skill of a true poet and trust the gods and sidhe to provide your request (they are honor-bound to do so) as the reward for well-fashioned poetry.

As you may have guessed, the power to affect the elements means the bard can use her magical craft to work many things. Your creativity and talent, and your relationship to imbas are the vital ingredients of this bardic power. Of course, it being bardic enchantment, which is synonymous with druidic magic, it must work in harmony with nature, else it will be ineffectual, or worse, counterproductive and unpredictable. This form of enchantment may, according to the lore, be used for blessings of abundance, influence over the winds, influence over fire (any energy that empowers or transforms, including light), defense, and other good purposes. The only requirement is that the spell work through the manipulation of natural elements.

The Satire and the Poet's Curse

The satire and the curse were mightily feared by the Celts. Kings would turn over half their kingdom to avert the ire of an offended poet. Even to this very day, traditional Celts in Ireland and Scotland have a strong taboo against offending poets.

The satire was not so much a magical act as a shaming. Poets were held in the highest regard by the Celts. At the top of the status hierarchy were nobles, druids, and poets, and they all ranked relatively equally. Therefore, if a poet disapproved of a noble for some good reason, he was entitled to shame him with the satire. It was a terrible blemish for the honor-bound Celts; as bad or worse than the king's own disapproval. Causes for shaming included stinginess, poor hospitality, vindictiveness, cowardice, and cruelty. A noble so shamed would have such a tarnish on his honor that he would never live it down. Other nobles might refuse to ally with him, his own warriors would lose their respect and loyalty toward him, and the people beneath him would have just cause to scorn him. For the Celts, who valued honor over life, this was the ultimate blemish. Thus, most were careful to avoid the poet's curse by living up to the best of Celtic values.

The poet's curse was a much more dangerous thing. It could cause great illness, misfortune, and even death. Its only justified use was against those who were wanton abusers of power, were cruel without compassion, and who did not fear the shame of satire as a good Celt ought.

The principles for the working of the poet's curse are the same as those for influencing the elements. It requires a total, uninterrupted focus, and music and poetry suitable to the occasion. The poetry must invoke the aid of the Otherworld, bring about a resonance between the bard and the curse by proclaiming the ethical violations the offender has committed, and call down the curse by stating how it is to work.

The poet's curse is a fearsome power. I must remind you: if it is invoked, there must be just cause, otherwise, rest assured, the gods will turn it against the invoker, as the legends make clear. Only those guilty of the most heinous acts justify its use.

The Geas

The geas is the last effective enchantment we shall consider. A geas is a restriction or compulsion laid upon a person by a druid or a bard. To break a geas is to forfeit one's share of luck and possibly one's life.

The geas is very individual. A person may have one or many. They are not given as a form of curse (as is commonly thought). Rather, a geas is a way of pointing out individuality, emphasizing it, and protecting the individual or helping him to grow. The bard, using the gift of true-sight (which we shall consider below), sees the unique nature of a person and renders a geas to declare something as unhealthy for that particular individual to either do or neglect doing. For example, a druid might lay a geas on a child that he is not to drink mead or wine. Perhaps the druid has foreseen that, as an adult, the child will be prone to alcoholism and have trouble controlling his temper while imbibing alcoholic beverages. Conversely, a geas might be laid on a person that he is never to disdain eating in a house where he is invited. Perhaps the druid has seen through true-sight that the person will be prone to shyness and isolation. This geas is given in order to require the person to break the hold of shyness.

For the Celt, the future is not fixed, but offers myriad options leading to less or more probable outcomes. If the child of the former example obeys his geas, it is probable that a negative outcome in the future will be avoided. Likewise, if the person of the latter example disobeys his geas, he may develop a social phobia so paralyzing that he can hardly bear the presence of his fellow human beings, and condemn himself to a life of loneliness. Geasa are not curses, but recognitions of individual needs given to protect and help an individual succeed at life.

The working of the geas, then, while appearing outwardly restrictive and negative, conceals an individual's need beneath a riddle. Riddled or not, so long as the person adheres to the requirements of the geas, his or her life will be the better for it. For the geas to be properly declared, the bard must be skilled in the lore enchantments and a true user of them.

Lore Enchantments

Lore magics are the most important magics in the bardic tradition. Lore magics enlighten the bard about the past, present, and future. Yet they are not only about understanding different reference points in time, they are about true-sight. *True-sight* is a term I derived to refer to the bard's ability to see into the true nature of a thing. It is not to be confused with the oft-heard "second sight." The lore magics are about seeing through the between places, and understanding the inner causes of outward events. The lore magics are about perceiving a reality that transcends the profane world of mere objects and extends into the mythic world of forces, entities, powers, and mystery.

So it is the lore enchantments that perform a key function in filling all three cauldrons of the soul. They add firstly to the cauldron of lore, and this alters the makeup of the cauldron of emotion, for lore adds shades and textures to what we feel. Emotion and lore weave tightly together with imbas to serve in poetic inspiration, which invigorates and empowers bardic artistic expression. The cauldrons of emotion and lore also weave tightly together to affect the potion brewing in the cauldron of craft, which shapes the way a person chooses to use his or her life. Thus we see the lore enchantments have a powerful role to play in the fulfillment of individual potential, which is the goal of the hero's quest within Celtic society.

There are a number of lore enchantments within the Celtic traditions. In the old tales we find the Celts, as a whole, achieve insight through clairvoyance (also called second sight), omens, portents, and through shamanic methods. The bard may utilize these methods or the druidic divinatory skills he or she shares, such as the use of the ogham, auguries, and scrying. Finally, the bard had at his or her unique disposal the insightful power of imbas-charged poetry, which is in itself a mystical force. In the rest of this chapter we shall consider these lore magics, and in the next chapter we will give special attention to the ogham mysteries. Understanding the ogham mysteries is vital to comprehending the bardic mysteries, the doing of augury and divination, and the working of the lesser, but powerful, arcane enchantments of the Celtic tradition.

Celtic Lorecraft

First we will look at a few of the Celtic lorecrafts. These divinatory techniques are not unique to bards or druids; they are generally available to all the Celtic people.

Second sight. The second sight, more generally referred to as clairvoyance, is a gift with which some are born. It is a natural shamanic ability to perceive elements of the Otherworld. People who possess the second sight may see ghostly images, perceive visions of the past, present, or future, or may even catch glimpses of the sidhe. If they are truly fortunate, they will possess all three skills and be able to control them at will, though such a powerful gifting is extremely rare.

Probably many people are gifted with the second sight. It is a widely known phenomenon among psychologists and parapsychologists, though it goes by many names. Jung referred to it as synchronicity; those events that occur with uncanny timing in odd relationship to something we have just thought, felt, or perceived. For instance, you are thinking of an old friend from high school you haven't heard from in years and she just happens to call at that moment. In this instance, your mind somehow became linked with your old friend's, or somehow became sensitive to an impending future event. Unfortunately, in these materialistic times, when so few are privileged to experience a depth of reality that penetrates the profane, most people who have the second sight do not understand it and so can achieve no benefit from it. Even worse is that they fear they are mildly demented and keep it entirely secret. (In the Highlands of Scotland, the second sight is often considered more a curse than a blessing.) However, an open mind can be very helpful in coping with the gift, and a general understanding of Celtic mystical tradition can prepare the sighted to actually benefit from it.

Unfortunately, one is either born with the second sight or not. It is not something that can be learned. That is the way it is with many magical and shamanistic gifts; one is either born with the talent or not. However, Irish poetic lore teaches that such gifting occurs to as many as 50 percent of people. It is just that most are so wrapped up in mere profane materialistic reality that they never make anything of their gifts—that is, they never fill their cauldrons. Yet for the bard there is a kind of second sight that can be learned: the true-sight, which we shall discuss a little later.

Omens and portents. Through the use of omens and portents the Celts sought to discern the future, near or distant. Some such portents make logical sense: red skies in the morning indicate inclement weather, rings around the moon indicate precipitation, that sort of thing. Other omens and portents were of a more mysterious or questionable nature. I say questionable because such omens were interpreted according to the folk traditions, which were not so carefully laid out as the druidic methods of interpretation. Below is a brief list of some folk omens:

- A cricket in the house is a sure sign of good luck.

- Meeting a cat or dog or red-haired woman early in the morning portends bad luck for the day.

- Fridays belong to the faerie; it is a day in which the sidhe hold great power.

- To dream of a woman's kiss portends deceit; to dream of a man's kiss portends friendship.

- To break a geas is to seal one's fate.

- A cuckoo calling on the right means good luck all day.

- Ravens are unlucky birds, being creatures of the war goddess the Mórrígán.

- Itching, hot ears indicate someone is gossiping about you.

- A rooster crowing at the door portends visitors coming.

- A crowing hen is very unlucky.

- Killing a red-breasted robin brings a lifetime of bad luck.

- Horses in dreams are very lucky.

- Meeting a magpie or cat brings bad luck to a journey.

- One magpie prattling at the door is a sign of bad luck, even death, but two augur prosperity.

- Priests in dreams portend bad luck; the devil in dreams portends good luck.

- Disturbing swallows brings ill-favor from nature. Leaving them be brings good favor.

- Never say in the Manx language "cockroach," "cat," or "mouse" while at sea.

- It is not always lucky to find hidden treasure.

The Celts, the Irish, and the Scottish in particular held to thousands of such omens. A complete study of them would take many volumes. However, while some seem to contain druidic wisdom, others are obviously the workings of mere superstition. Often times, the omens even bear contradictory meanings from one place to another. For a more thorough study of Celtic omens, please see the list of additional reading at the end of the book.

Shamanic methods. The Celts never entirely forgot the old druidic shamanic methods. They kept them alive in the form of auguries, divinatory talismans, and, most remarkably, through the *tarbh feis* [*tarv fesh*].

The tarbh feis, originally a druidic practice, devolved to the common folk after the demise of the druid class. The poets did not use it because they had their own unique and effective lore magics. So it was the ordinary people who kept it alive. Alas, they did not possess the deep knowledge of the druidic mysteries, so they laid more importance on the profane form of the ritual than the sacred processes involved.

The tarbh feis was performed as follows: the diviner probably began by fasting for a day or so (at least a meal). Then he would chew a piece of meat from a freshly slaughtered animal (a pig, dog, or ox in the lore). He would then lie down on or wrap himself up in the hide of the animal, preferably at water's edge. Best was rapidly moving water, such as a falls. This served two purposes: (1) it set up a resonance between the shaman and the spirit of the slaughtered animal, and (2) contact becomes easier at water's edge, a place where worlds meet that is full of the abundant energy of motion. Water is also symbolic of the Otherworld, and moving water is a conduit of psychic power in many traditions. The shaman covered his eyes, probably to achieve darkness in which his vision will not be disturbed. Finally, the shaman went into a trance (described as a sleep) to seek out the lore of his quest.

While possessing some value, the problem with such folk traditions is that they are often misunderstood and profaned, not of any ill intention by those who kept them, but because the practitioners have lost the mystical knowledge required of true understanding. The common folk valued and sought to preserve their old spirituality, but without the druid's understanding, the emphasis fell on profane form rather than on the mystical processes that lie beneath the practices. Thus, folk survivals of omens and shamanic practices such as the tarbh feis often tend to be mere shadowy reflections of a far grander way. In the next two sections, we will examine the more refined lorecrafts of druids, then bards. The bardic student will profit from a thorough study of both.

Druidic Augury

We know that the druids augured and divined by a number of methods. They observed the weather, the shapes of clouds, and the flight of birds. The astronomical alignments of the stonehenges and burial places lead us to believe that they also observed the heavens for portents as well. According to some, they even augured by sacrificing humans and observing their death throes and entrails. The veracity of some of these statements is dubious as they were made by ambitious, conquering Romans and pro-Romans who had political motives for propagandizing against the Celts. In any case, the druids were a highly trained, philosophically and scientifically learned class. Their studies required twelve years or more, and through their intense learning, they refined the crafts of augury into a science. Trogue Pompey said that the Gallic Celts surpassed all other nations in their divinatory practices. Unfortunately, we have lost most of the knowledge of their tradition. We do not know how they augured by birds or clouds or by astronomical observance. However, the lore does teach us enough about several druidic lorecrafts that we can reconstruct them. One is the through the ogham, an ancient Celtic script and set of mystery symbols. The ogham really belongs to bards as much as druids, and it is so profound as to warrant its own chapter, so we will consider it in depth in the next chapter. The druidic mysteries appropriate for consideration here are scrying and true-sight.

True-sight. To understand this lorecraft it is important to thoroughly understand an aspect of the Celtic psychology that we briefly considered in chapters 2 and 3: dreams are as significant as the material world. To the Celtic hero, the path to personal growth involves striving to make reality meet the mythic (dreamlike) ideal. The bard does this through imbas-charged artistic creation, which is the act of birthing the beauty of dreams into the realm of reality. So entwined was the idea of mingling the mythic with the material that we can be fairly certain that it was a core druidic doctrine: the worlds were different manifestations of an invisible truth. These worlds commingled, and the imperfections of one were balanced by the perfections of the other. What occurred in the place of true dreams could alter the material here and now, and vice versa. Therefore, dreams had real power. They are alternative perceptions of the same reality; different symbolisms thrown over the same archetypal substratum. The material universe of the here and now is but one veneer of symbolism over the primal forces of creation; a common milieu we humans share for interaction with one another and the universe. Dreams are another kind of awareness—a very personal, individual perception of the same underlying forces.

Now, let us establish that I am not writing of the nonsensical dreams that mince through sleep, but the true dreams that we only know in special moments when the mind touches upon the primal truths. That is the stuff of the mythic realm where archetypes flow fluidly; that place in our psyche where universal truths lie barely symbolized, extant in an essential manner that runs truer than profane form and the symbolism of language.

Such a concept implies that reality is fractured into Otherworlds and possibilities. Further, it implies that while each one is individual and unique, there is an underlying commonality; a substructure of essential forces. Thus, the worlds interrelate. While common perception defines how we interact with the material here and now, dreams, being very personal, can perceive those underlying forces as they relate specifically to the dreamer. Sometimes dream symbolism relates closely enough to another world or possibility that a link is formed. When this happens, perception of another layer of reality is made possible. True-sight is the ability to perceive this depth at will.

Because the mythic and the mystic underlie everything, and all things are directed by cosmic purpose with the goal of total fulfillment and perfection, all things have purpose. All things bear significance and can be used for a truer understanding of the past, present, and future. This is the how and why of druidic/bardic true-sight. It is not an extension of the senses (the opening of the third eye) like the second sight (which is a psychic sense in addition to the body's other five senses), but it is a learned perceptual deepening. It is the key to interpreting the deep significance of all events and developing a living relationship with mystery and the mythic.

It took the druids and bards many years to develop the skill of true-sight. I cannot teach it to you here in a few easy lessons. It is very important for you to understand that the quick way is anything but the true bard's way. The knowledge the bard learns is occultic (secret), mysterious (hidden from the masses), universal (applies broadly), singular (has a single underlying truth that goes deeper than form or symbol), and individual (is perceived differently by each person). Most importantly, the true bard must possess this understanding as living knowledge. That is, it must be committed to memory and perceived with the full, individuated, integrated conscious and unconscious mind. It is irrelevant and useless if it only exists as knowledge within a cold, analytical mind. The truths that make the true-sight come alive in the bard must become part of the whole being of the bard.

I can only point out to you the path to true-sight. You must find your own way upon it.

True-sight is an individuated awareness. It comes from a living relationship with the here and now and the Otherworld, the mythic and the historic, the conscious and the unconscious. Thus, the first step toward true-sight is education. The learning of all things is beneficial and fills the soul's cauldron of lore. Generally, the school system and liberal arts schools fill the need for education in the things of the here and now. Bardry is a Celtic path, so, in particular, the bard should seek the knowledge of the mythic— the legends and lore of Celtica. The old bards had to memorize hundreds of these legends. The idea was to ensure that the bards had a living knowledge of them, so that their truths might become part of the bard's very existence and thereby be imparted to the people for whom they performed their arts.

Of course, the study of the folklore of other peoples can be helpful, too, as it provides material for comparison and contrast. Just don't get too caught up in that. There is a huge amount just within the domain of Celtdom to learn. Anyway, all myths and folklore are just overlying symbols on top of common underlying truths. So a survey of other lore systems is sufficient to provide perspective.

The next step is a profound study of art. Celtic art in particular was an expression of the surreal; an attempt to meld together the realities of this world with those of the Otherworld. Celtic art in all its forms was a reflection of this individualizing, integrating effort, and a study of it will enrich the bard. A bard must be the master of the crafts of beauty (poetry, music, and story), which join the mythic ideal to the less-than-perfect here and now. This understanding will enhance the bard's own artistically creative endeavors and deepen his relationship to imbas.

Because there is no longer a living druidic tradition to teach us about the inner person, bardic students should also study analytical psychology. This was the psychology of Carl Jung, who pioneered work in the concepts of individuation (fulfilling potential), integration (uniting the conscious to the unconscious), archetypes, and dream interpretation. You may find this instruction odd since psychology is outside Celtdom. However, remember that all peoples have a psychology; a way of perceiving the world and understanding it. Analytical psychology has much in common with the Celtic way of perceiving things as it seeks to understand the soul and unite the ego with it; it seeks to realize the potential of the individual and make him aware of the deep mysteries of being. The depth of self-understanding that can be attained from studying analytical psychology will open your eyes to the inner mysteries of our own nature.

Also, Jungian psychology provides rich tools for the analysis of symbols. It teaches principles for the interpretation of everything from the mandala to natural events to sex symbols to ordinary dreams, and then goes on to advise (rightly) that symbols have different meanings for different people. So symbols must be interpreted on a person-by-person basis, in context with the person's environment and the events that surround him or her. Thus, one person's relation to a symbol will be different than another's. True-sight demands this deep understanding of your own self and others' selves, as well as a profound knowledge of the purpose, function, and interpretation of the symbols that appear in dreams, myth, and in day-to-day life.

As was mentioned above, the bard must also become a master of his art: poetry, storycraft, and music. Each craft provides a fundamental, individualizing, artistic outlet that integrates reality with the mythic. Poetry speaks through a highly refined use of symbols and requires intense individual inter-pretation. Bardic stories put us in touch with myth and ancient lore. Music speaks without language directly to the archetypal forces alive in the place of true dreams.

Finally, the bard must make the craft come alive. That is, everyday he or she should put the tools of bardcraft to use through meditation, enchant-ment, or artistic expression.

So, the curriculum required to develop the skill of true-sight consists of the following:

1. General or liberal studies of a material nature

2. Studies of Celtic myths and lore, augmented by surveys of the lores of other cultures.

3. Soul studies, best made these days through a study of analytical psychology

4. Artistic expression as the means to individuation and integration

5. Application or practice

A number of volumes of recommended reading can be found at the back of this book, which will point the reader well along the way.

I know it represents years of study, but this is the long road of the true bard. True-sight, the mark of the developed bard, is not something one can obtain overnight. It comes into being through the cultivation of an educated, inte-grated, fulfilled mind made wise in the ways of this world and the Other. A critic might argue that what I have just laid out makes the bard some kind of mystic artsy psychologist-scholar. Well, that would be almost exactly correct. The bard is one who looks into the depths of the worlds with intuition and educated insight, and perceives with a mind made alive through the skills of enchantment, art, and living wisdom. Though the path is demanding, the price of hard study shall prove worth it in the end when you find that you can hear the secrets known only to trees whispering in the breeze, and discern the hidden meaning of the brush strokes of blue sky on crystalline waters.

It is worth noting that many artists have a natural talent for true-seeing. They have a way of looking at things and seeing more than what is there;

they have a way of perceiving depth and character and, sometimes, purpose, all of which are rendered in their creative expressions as artistic interpretation. Those who can do this are the artists of talent; the ones whose work grabs us with a message, though we may not be able to understand it. The bards of old have always known that art and perception are linked, so the bard pursues the artist's path in earnest.

What true-sight does. True-sight is perhaps the most valuable druidic/bardic lore skill. It would have to be to justify all the work.

True-sight allows perception with depth. It enables the seer to look into the purpose and relationships among things and events in a way that is not outwardly apparent to one who is limited by a shallower, purely materialistic perception. True-sight is not a psychic sense in the way that ESP is. That is to say, it doesn't use a sixth sense. It broadens and enhances the senses we already have, and fulfills their potential to make us aware. True-sight changes the whole mode of awareness in a way that aligns the mind to the Celtic psychology and opens up an understanding of the relationships between all things of the here and now and the Otherworld. This total change of awareness enables a richer understanding of the movement and purpose of things and events than most people ever dream of. It makes possible a constant sense of the magic in existence, and enlightens the person to the truth that just beyond the next shadow is a fantastic world of true-dreams that fills the here and now with the potential for enchantment.

True-sight works by enabling the integration of the feeling and knowing parts of the mind (the artsy-emotional and the logical-intellectual). They are integrated to such a degree that the mind can discern the relationships between things and events. This integration occurs as you nourish the logical-intellectual part of your being with knowledge and make it come alive through the practice of the bardic arts and magic crafts. The mind so nurtured will expand in its potential and learn a broader awareness. It will come to understand that any occurrence and any thing can and does influence other things. Since all things are interconnected, everything relates to everything else in some very real, even if distant, way. True-sight is the ability to perceive these relationships and sense where they are going. As it develops, it can be overwhelming. Those who are true-sighted are swamped with so much information that no sense can be made of anything. However, with practice and growing wisdom, the true-sighted will learn to focus only on what is significant and cull out the rest, just as the brain at any given moment ignores the vast majority of the body's sensory input and focuses only on what is relevant.

True-sight is not a true divinatory method in that it doesn't peer through time to view events that have yet to occur. Instead, true-sight makes the bard fully aware, and informs him or her of the possibilities and probabilities pregnant in a person, place, or thing.

There is, however, a druidic method that does look into time and space. I am speaking of scrying. While true-sight is not necessary to scry, understanding it greatly assists in the use of scrying. Therefore, while it is much easier to learn to scry, and you will be practicing it long before you have developed true-sight, I have presented true-sight here first in order to help you better understand and interpret scrying.

Scrying. Scrying is the art of perceiving visual messages from across time and space by focusing the attention meditatively on an undistracting object and allowing the mind to receive. From the lore wherein druids and bards and ordinary folk receive messages from faeries through looking glasses, enchanted pools, and so on, we can be fairly certain the druids were aware of and practiced scrying. So I offer it here as a part of the bardic path.

Scrying really is not that hard to engage in. All it requires is focus meditative skill, something to focus your mind on, and quiet. In many traditions, such as Wicca and Gypsy magic, a looking glass or a crystal ball is used. In the tradition of bardry, clear, deep, still pools in secluded woods are most appropriate. Otherwise, a fountain in a quiet garden is a good alternative. However, these things are not always available. In such cases, a crystal ball or looking glass is acceptable.

Crystal balls can be purchased from many occult paraphernalia shops, but they can be expensive. Looking glasses are easy to make and inexpensive. Take a piece of glass, squared or rounded and about the size of a grapefruit, and paint one side night black. Glue the glass to a board about one foot square that has also been painted black, and glue another piece of wood perpendicular to the back of the board so it can be stood up.

Now, make yourself comfortable. Do the relaxation techniques for meditation, then clear your mind as in focus meditation. Do not yet look at your scrying tool. After holding your mind clear for a couple minutes, focus your thoughts upon something you would like to know. Hold the focus meditation for a couple minutes more. Then relax and empty your mind and stare into your scrying tool. Do not strain your eyes; allow yourself to blink naturally. Keep your mind blank and let the imagery come of its own. Don't try to force it. After a few minutes you should see sparkles or mist in the scrying tool. The sight should eventually resolve into an interpretable image.

Scrying takes practice. It may take a number of tries before it begins to work for you. Also, do not push yourself too hard; it's counterproductive. Limit your attempts at scrying to fifteen minutes, tops.

One last very important tip: it is a good idea to petition the gods for revelation when practicing scrying. In particular, you may want to petition gods of wisdom, such as Lugh, the master of all crafts. Use your bardic skill with poetry to design a poetic incantation; set it to music if you wish. Music and poetry are the honey and wine of the gods; they will respond to it.

The Bardic Methods of Lorecraft

We know that the bards had at least three of their own unique methods of lorecraft. *Cormac's Glossary* tells us of the *imbas forosna* (pronounced much as it is spelled; manifestation of enlightenment), the *teinm láida* (pronounced *ten LAW-da*; illumination song), and the *dichetal do chennaib* (pronounced *DI-ke-tal doe KEN-nab*; extempore incantation). These lorecrafts are described as the domain of the poet, making them uniquely the bard's.

Imbas forosna (manifestation of enlightenment). This lorecraft was, in form, very similar to the tarbh feis. It involves chewing a piece of flesh, placing it on a flagstone, and making an incantation over it, wherein it is offered to the gods or sidhe. The diviner then invokes the spirits of divination, chants over his palms, and invokes the spirits again. This time he asks to enter into a deep shamanic trance. Then he covers his eyes and enters the trance while others watch over him to ensure he remains undisturbed during the course of the trance. During the trance, knowledge is revealed.

The simple folk understood the imbas forosna in the same way as the tarbh feis: it was the profane actions of the ritual that brought on the revelatory power. However, a deeper understanding of shamanic truth enables us to probe deeper into what is occurring here:

1. In chewing the flesh of a dead animal, the bard is associating himself with a spirit that is in the Otherworld.

2. He makes an offering of flesh (the chewed meat) and poetry (the incantation) upon a stone (a natural vessel).

3. He invokes Otherworldly assistance.

4. He devotes his hands to their work with an additional incantation over them, then evokes darkness (by putting his hands over his eyes and cheeks).

5. He enters the trance of the shamanic journey.

Cormac's Glossary says the poet went to sleep. Yet most shamanic work is actually accomplished in a trance that may resemble sleep. Ignorant of shamanic techniques, the glossary's author probably mistook the trance-state.

You can use the five steps outlined above as a guide to performing the imbas forosna. However, I don't believe it is necessary to chew meat to associate with a spirit. There are other powerful natural spirits in Celtdom. You may choose to do something like chew a twig of oak to associate yourself with the spirit of *duir* [DOO-eer], the oak tree, which is a very powerful spirit of wisdom (we'll cover this more in the next chapter on the ogham). At the same time you could offer acorns, bread, and milk to the Otherworld. Twigs or nuts of the hazel (*coll*; pronounced [*coal*]) tree should also be very potent as this tree is considered the mystical source of wisdom. You may choose to do similarly with any other mystically significant plant (provided it isn't poisonous, of course!). Salmon meat would also seem to make a logical choice, as it is by eating the salmon of wisdom that bards and heroes of myth obtained their great wisdom. Traditionally the meat is raw, and to obtain raw salmon for this ritual, you need only order sushi!

Teinm láida (illumination of song). This was the application of poetic and musical mastery to riddling out a mystery. The process was essentially this: the bard had a subject that required an answer (a riddle). He sought imbas, and, using his bardic knowledge and poetic skill, began to riddle out the question by composing poetry around it, and singing the poetry as he went. The power of artistic perspective, enhanced by imbas, gave new perspective to the subject. Setting the poetry to song, with its powerful emotive powers, added even more perspective. Therefore, by use of the teinm láida, the bard was able to gain a deep and revelatory insight of a subject.

The *Senchus Mor* gives us even more information on the requirements of successfully performing the teinm láida, stating that it required great knowledge in its application. It required a knowledge of the genealogies of the Irish, and a thorough understanding of the techniques of poetry and of storytelling. This tells us that the user of the teinm láida must be very knowledgeable in the standard educational sense and Celtic way of thinking, as well as in the bardic, druidic, and Celtic mysteries. Then to actually apply the teinm láida successfully, she must command the full range of poetic and story skills required of the bard. Such mastery allows the poet performing the teinm láida to compose her subject with the full mind, instead of having to give thought to the technical demands of composition.

One might notice a very important characteristic about the teinm láida: it is not so much a divinatory method as a perception-enhancing method, much like brainstorming. Indeed, it is a rudimentary method of imitating true-sight, wherein the bard consciously grasps toward a deeper perception of a riddle. The difference between it and actual true-sight is, when fully developed, true-sight is always present and works almost unconsciously.

There is no additional technique to study. If you have learned to focus meditate, how to compose poetry, and how to play music, you can perform the teinm láida.

Dichetal do chennaib (extemporary incantation). This is another shamanic method of gaining knowledge, and is akin to psychometric reading. According to the lore, we know it involves the touching of an object with the poet's wand. From what we know of Western and universal shamanic methods, we can infer that it also involves focus meditation to make the mind clear and receptive.

The bard will first need to be in possession of a poet's wand. This is simply a small staff. There are no exact physical dimensions given for a poet's wand, but what is most important is the wood from which it is made. It should be a wood of wisdom, art, or hidden mysteries (as is significant in the ogham). Hazel, being the wood of the tree of knowledge, is probably the best choice. The wand ought to be a couple of inches in diameter and rounded, so that oghams can be carved into it later should you choose. It should be between twelve and twenty-four inches in length. You may leave it simple, or you may inscribe knotwork patterns and other art significant to the Celtic spirit onto it.

It is possible the wand may be forgone entirely, but the ogham mysteries do teach us that certain woods have a resonance with knowledge. Thus, it may be that hazel wood will actually enhance the procedure through an innate power. If nothing else, by making use of its mythical significance, it will assist in focusing the mind to the riddle at hand and in honoring our ancient tradition.

The bard should begin by relaxing, then clearing the mind. The mind should be absolutely clear so as to be the most receptive. The question must be spoken and then meditated upon for a couple of minutes, all the while holding the wand to the object. The answer should make itself known within the mind of the bard, much as an answering image resolves in scrying.

Not everything will respond to the dichetal do chennaib. Some things simply will not possess enough psychometric force to enable a reading. Like all the bardic high enchantments, it requires great skill over the mind, over enchantment, and a living relationship with myth, poetry, music, and imbas.

Conclusion

The high bardic magics require great mastery over the other bardic crafts to be performed properly. One must learn a precise control of the mind, and how to walk with myth and imbas. One must develop a relationship with the Otherworld and an artist's depth of vision. One must also possess extraordinary insight into the soul and great understanding of the archetypes that lie beneath the symbols of perception. Indeed, the bardic path both encourages and demands growth by necessitating the fulfilment of one's potential in all these areas. If the demands seem daunting, you should not allow yourself to become discouraged. Good things always require hard work. The hero's quest teaches us that the path is in fact more to be cherished than the goal, for it is on the path that the challenges that bring growth are to be found.

Finally, we have covered a lot of material in this chapter, and if anything, you will have learned that there is a great deal more yet to learn. A scientist once said that for everything he learned, ten new questions were raised. It does, in truth, take years to master the bardic path, for the more you learn, the more you will discover you need to know. However, there is no reason to rush, and no one to impress but yourself. The bardic path is a path for a lifetime, and as long as there is life reaching forward, there is growth. Life turns on timeless wheels, never ending. Always there is more to come to know, and room to grow.

chapter eight

Ogham Ciphers and the Forest Mysteries

The trees called to her still, a bittersweet air that once again sparked her longing to step under their sweeping boughs and partake of their Mystery.

Charles de Lint, *Spiritwalk*

At the foundation of bardic lore are the druidic mysteries of the forest and their representation through the ogham [pronounced *O-um*]. These mysteries and the ogham combine to create a symbolic representation of lore, a divinatory system that can be applied in a number of ways, a way to perceive nature and forces, and an esoteric way of communicating. Each aspect of the mysteries bears profound significance worthy of intense meditation and exploration, especially through the teinm láida. The understanding of these mysteries relates directly back to Celtic archetypal symbolism and will greatly enhance the development of true-sight.

Understanding the Ogham Script

The ogham script is written on a stave, either left to right horizontally, or vertically going from the bottom up. It is often referred to as the beithluis-nuin [*BEH-loo-ish-noo-in*] which stands for the first, second, and last letter of the first group of ogham characters, according to the Irish alphabet. You may also see *ogham* written as *ogam* or *ogum* in other texts.

The written ogham is divided up into four groups: three sets of consonants, and one set of vowels. Each ogham character relates to a spoken sound and bears numerous symbolic meanings, hence the ogham's arcane significance. Also, the groupings themselves have meaning.

It is commonly thought that the ogham began in the insular Celtic lands sometime after the conquest by the Roman Empire and their introduction of writing. This is fallacious, and is possibly the result of Roman or church propaganda. We now know that the ancient Celts were a literate people who usually chose not to write. Further, there is strong evidence that their writing system dates back some four thousand years. The oldest surviving examples come not from Europe, where many artifacts were intentionally obliterated, but from North America. There is growing evidence to believe that the Celts, among other ancient Western peoples from Africa and Europe, had established a small colonial presence in North America over three thousand years before the coming of Christopher Columbus.

There are many old texts discussing the ogham groups and meanings. Yet being very old, often liberally sprinkled with Latin, Greek, and other classical scholarly languages, and written in old styles, they are hard to understand. In Table 1, I have endeavored to condense this material to its essential core and group it for easier study. (Pronunciations are below, under "Interpreting the Ogham.")

There are also five diphthongs (sounds made by letter combinations) that were added later. Their place and significance to the ogham is disputable, so I have omitted them.

The table shows each ogham character, its relative Roman letter sound, its tree association, and some of the more important associations. There are numerous other old documents on the meanings and interpretation of the ogham, and some of the information in those documents appears contradictory. Usually, however, the other tracts merely relate other ways of looking at the same mysteries.

ogham

ciphers

and

the

forest

mysteries

Irish Ogham Character	Roman Character	Tree/Herb	Associations
Group 1			
⊥ beith	B	birch	beginnings, white or silver
⊥⊥ luis	L	rowan	flame, duck, friend of cattle
⊥⊥⊥ fearn	F	alder	shield, hawk, guardian of milk
⊥⊥⊥⊥ saille	S	willow	pallor, death, activity of bees, music, soul
⊥⊥⊥⊥⊥ nuin	N	ash	peace, fight of women
Group 2			
⊤ huath	H	hawthorn	raven, terror, wolf pack
⊤⊤ duir	D	oak	wren, druid tree, carpenter's wood
⊤⊤⊤ tinne	T	holly	fires of coal
⊤⊤⊤⊤ coll	C	hazel	beautiful forest tree, cracking
⊤⊤⊤⊤⊤ queirt	Q	apple	hind's shelter, lunatics, death sense
Group 3			
⫽ muinn	M	vine	back of ox or man, great effort
⫽⫽ gort	G	ivy	swan, sweet grass
⫽⫽⫽ getal	NG	broom	goose, physician's strength
⫽⫽⫽⫽ straif	STR or Z	blackthorn	alchemy, increasing secrets, tester
⫽⫽⫽⫽⫽ ruis	R	elder	red, blushing, shame
Group 4			
+ ailm	A	fir	groans of illness or wonder, sigh of the newborn, piebald
++ ohn	O	gorse	the wheel, horse helper, the goddess, stone
+++ ur	U	heather	cold dwellings, soil, grower of plants
++++ edad	E	aspen	distinguished wood, friend, swan
+++++ idad	I	yew	eagle, sword, venerable wood

TABLE 1—Ogham Compendium

The bards and druids used the ogham for magical and communicative purposes. The ogham provided them with a secret written language with which they could communicate, with or without making use of the dark tongue. Because the ogham was so rich in meaning, it provided a powerful runelike alphabet for inscribing enchantments. The ogham's rich meanings also made it a tool for divination and the pondering of the mysteries of creation.

Psychology of the Ogham

Each ogham character illuminates an important truth. The bard should commit to memory the oghams and their meanings. Their living presence in the mind will help to awaken true-sight, and provide an enriched perspective of reality by clarifying meaning and relations between objects and events. A living knowledge of ogham lore will also vivify the mystical forces of the woodlands to the bard. It will enlighten the learned to the secrets and hidden resonances of the trees, and give the bard a unique awareness of the Otherworld. Ogham lore illuminates for the bardic student the vital truth that the forest is a living place of enchantment full of wisdom and some danger. It is the dwelling place of the secrets of the old druids and the hiding place of the Old Ways. To know the wood on the mystic level is to have a foothold in the Otherworld through a real place of the here and now.

The mystic forest represents the mind. The deeper and darker the wood, the further into the mind it shows. Open woods full of sunlight and charm reflect the workings of the conscious. The misty, shadowy places deep within the wood represent the unconscious, which is full of the mythic beings of dream. The haunted stands represent the archetype-driven forces Jung would have referred to as *complexes* (powers that dwell within the mind and draw their force from symbol and emotion). The forbidden places represent the haunts of nightmares; those aspects of ourselves we bury and perpetually try to rise above. Finally, the glades are the sacred nemetons where druids reached out to the Otherworld and where bards riddle the mysteries of existence through their art. These are the places where humans reach beyond themselves in the ever-quest of potential fulfillment. Thus, the tree mysteries of the ogham present to us a living likeness of the mind; a way of understanding ourselves by means of metaphorical reflection. The ogham wood reflects our being as much as the Otherworld does. Like us, it is a timeless truth over which we have no initial formative control. However, like ourselves, it is also a place that, when understood, can be cultivated into a beautiful, enchanting thing.

147

ogham

ciphers

and

the

forest

mysteries

Interpreting the Ogham
Beith [beh]

The birch is a graceful, fast-growing tree with a sweet, sometimes minty sap good for syrups and drinking. It is a pioneer tree, among the first to appear after burns have rampaged through an area. Its qualities make it a natural representative of origins, as it is the birch that begins a new forest. Its white or silvery bark represents the purity of genesis and undifferentiated potential. Its healthful, refreshing sap represents a friendly, giving, invigorating nature. The birch is the place of beginnings and the zeal that goes along with it.

Luis [loosh]

The rowan is a tree of old magical repute. Its wood and berries were said to repel evil forces and attract good luck. It is strongly associated with a positive faerie influence. To possess a staff, wand, or even a berry or splinter of the rowan was lucky and provided protection. Its wood was burned for magical fires by the druids,[1] and its flaming red berries were also associated with fire. Fire is the great transformer. Like water, it possesses purifying qualities. Perhaps this is why the rowan is considered so lucky—attractive to good (clean) things, and repugnant to that which is not good (unclean).

The duck is a creature that lives between the three worlds of earth, land, and water. This special centering between three worlds makes it an animal of potent magical resonance. The rowan, likewise, is a member of three worlds: the earth from which it springs, the air to which it ascends, and the Otherworld with which, as folklore has it, it is bound. Thus, the duck and rowan together span all the major nexus places between the worlds, making them very potent. They are things that touch all levels of existence and bridge every world.

Aligned with positive magic, the rowan was used to magically ward cattle. The cattle of old Celtica were in constant need of protection from predators and human theft. Thus, the rowan is also a protector. Just as it protects cattle, so it is known to protect all who utilize it in their enchantments.

Fearn [*fern*]

Alder wood is remarkable for its durability. Hence, it was often made into shields. So the alder equates with strength and protection. The alder was also used to make vessels for milk, thus, again, it is a protector of a precious thing. Yet as shields were often used in medieval times to bear precious things (such as royalty or treasure), the alder represents a supportive role as well. For it to be effective, the wielder must have strength and skill. The greater these qualities within the wielder, the better the alder's protective work. Thus, it supports growth by demanding personal improvement.

In the tale of "The Hawk of Achill," we see the hawk is associated in Celtic mythology with wisdom and reflection. He should inspire us to the same, for they are keys to self-understanding. The hawk is also a powerful predator that symbolizes courage, independence, and pride. He shows us that the great can live by the fruits of the earth without abusing it. The hawk was also an ally to human hunters in bringing down pheasants and other game birds. The hunter's skill lay in finding the game birds. The hawk is what actually retrieved the game, feeding the hunters through its work. Thus, like the hawk, the mystery of the alder is that of a nurturer; building on the strength and talent of the person who works with it to enable success.

Saille [*SA-le*]

Oddly, the willow is associated with both death and pallor and the very vibrant activity of bees. The willow attracts bees because of its fragrant catkins and blooms. Bees are symbolic of community and cooperation, and as a vital food resource to them, the willow also becomes an integral part of their community. The willow plays a role in the productive harmony found in the beehive and benefits from their pollen-sharing activities. Thus, a healthful balance is created.

The association with deathly pallor may arise from the whitish undersides and yellow-brown coloration of the twigs of the European white willow, but another explanation is just as feasible. There are two main types of willow: those that prefer wet soils, and those that prefer drier loams. The shrub-like willows of wet earth are often found in bogs and swamps—dangerous places of quicksand and treacherous paths where unfortunate or unwary travelers often disappear. These places, associated with death and the haunts of evil spirits, have rubbed their reputations off on these willows. The shrub-willows of such places do appear stunted and sickly, even ominous, which further adds to their ill repute.

The willows of drier loams grow to be tall, elegant trees, such as the beautiful white willow. According to Irish legend, such willows are unique in that they possess a soul. Further, the soul speaks the language of music. The wood of this tree does have wonderful acoustic traits, for it was often used in the making of Celtic harps. This makes the tree a natural ally to and symbol of the bard.

This tree's bardic nature, and the fact that it is associated with the month of February and the holiday of Imbolc, makes it sacred to Brighid, the triple goddess, who was the patroness of poets (bards).

Nuin [*NOO-in*]

A mystery tree of complex symbolism, the ash is one of the three sacred trees of Irish druidry, along with the yew and the elder. The ash is associated with the world tree of Norse myth, Yggdrasil, whose roots penetrated to the underworld, whose branches perforated this world, and whose upper reaches sought Valhalla. While the Norse were distantly related to the Celts, we cannot be certain whether the Celts had an equivalent of a world tree in their cosmology. However, the fact that we know the ash was highly sacred to the Celts of Ireland tells us that the tree has strong mythical connections. So, concerning our Celtic approach, it can be said that the ash does have a place in the Otherworld and in this world. This makes it a magical tree; a tree of the between places that link the realities.

The ash also has healing properties within Celtic magic. These powers derive not from its herbal potency—that is, not from any pharmaceutic chemicals inherent to the plant—but from its mystical connections. In Celtic magical tradition, when a child is sick, a split is opened in an ash, the child stripped naked, and then passed through three times head first. Each time, the child is turned deasil (sunwise) back around to the side of the tree

149

ogham

ciphers

and

the

forest

mysteries

where he first was put through for the next pass. Then the rip in the tree is sealed up and if the tree heals, so will the child. The tree is said to take the illness of the child if successful. This practice also still exists among certain Scandinavian peoples.[2]

The ash is also associated with a fight of women and peace. These two connotations may seem contradictory, but I have a hypothesis that may explain them. The ash was the preferred wood for making a weaver's beam. Weaving took place during peace, and was by and large considered a woman's task. The woman's fight was the battle to weave scattered fibers into unity (to make them into cloth), a fight that required deft hands and considerable skill. Hence, the fight of women is a peacetime activity of productivity, and requires ash wood cut into a weaver's beam. This gives the tree a feminine resonance, and associates it with healing and productiveness. Bear in mind this is only a hypothesis; it is my best guess. Confirmation among the surviving lore remains elusive.

Finally, the great European ash produces superb timber that is light and strong. In old times, it was a preferred material for spear hafts, axes, and oars. The ash thus represents mobile, practical strength. This is the shaman's strength, for the shaman must be able to cross the worlds and have the strength of character to conduct the voyage and withstand the challenges and dangers of Otherworld travel.

The ash, then, is the healing wood and the shaman's strength; a penetrator of worlds. The ash is also a symbol of apartness made whole (the weaver's beam uniting fibers), which is healing peace. This is a feminine, productive strength.

Huath [*HU-ah*]

The hawthorn has many dark connotations, and how they arose are easily enough understood when one ponders the nature and use of this shrubby tree. The hawthorn often has nasty thorns. The thorns of one species can reach eight centimeters in length. I have stabbed my own hands deeply on hawthorn thorns by accidentally leaning against the tree while on long forest hikes. It grows densely, and is often used to create hedges to keep farm stock from roaming. It has been used for this purpose for some time with great success in the British Isles. Thus, the hawthorn is a wall, or an entrapper. It holds, not of a nurturing nature as does the alder, but by virtue of its wicked thorns and dense tangle of tough growth that capture and restrict.

It is associated with terror and a pack of wolves. European wolves were more dangerous than their American cousins, and more likely to attack humans. A pack of wolves hunts larger prey by enclosing it, wearing it down, and tearing at it little bits at a time with sharp fangs and claws to slowly bleed it out. This is much like how the hawthorn works to hold whatever it encloses, entrap its victims with numerous members of its thorny pack, wear them down as they try to penetrate the dense shrubbery, and tear at them with wicked barbs.

In Irish myth, the raven is strongly associated with the Mórrígán [MO-ree-gawn], the goddess of war. The sight of a raven was considered an ill omen, and its scavenging nature, especially the way it looted the dead on a battlefield for flesh, was considered hideous, even demonic. The Mórrígán was also the goddess of nightmares, and the raven was a personification she often took. To sight a raven was akin to sighting a demon, and it forebode animosity, ill intent, fear, or a cruel and cunning predator. Even when the Mórrígán appears to be on the side of right, it is rather for the sake of her own self-interest. She satisfies her own lusts and bloody desires.

Thus, the hawthorn is not allied to light or man. It symbolizes the dark side of existence; the spiritual, mythical, and physical forces of the shadow. However, it must be borne in mind that this is not exactly bad in the Celtic psychology. Darkness and chaos are the necessary opposites of order and light. The healthy way is a balanced path between these primal forces; a path that allows for the randomness of chaos in life (the mystery), directed by the positive control of order. This has connotations to the Jungian, Egyptian, and Hermetic ideas of the shadow as an integral part of the personality. The thing to fear is not the influence of darkness and chaos, but the reign of darkness and chaos. Thus, the hawthorn is not a thing to be shunned, but a thing to be respected as it represents a primal, vital force that we need. It must be at all times respected and carefully balanced for positive benefit.

Duir [DOO-eer]

The oak is the druids' tree of the continental Celts of Gaul. A tree of great sacredness, it is referenced time and again throughout the annals of history and folklore.

As the druid's tree, the oak is very sacred. It symbolizes divine provision by Cernunnos in the acorns it provides, which were used to make flour. The

151

ogham

ciphers

and

the

forest

mysteries

Celts of Ireland believed that if they honored the Old Ways, and the king honored his geasa, then the oaks would yield plentiful acorns. It also symbolizes divine linkage in its contact with the sacred druidical herb the mistletoe. It is very rare that mistletoe (known to druids as the *allheal*) grows upon the oak. Yet when it does, it is cause for a ritual harvest and celebration, as the mistletoe will be exceptionally potent.

Even more importantly, the oak is symbolic of the wisdom of the sciences and of the gods. As a great, long-lived tree, it may have been seen as an accumulator of wisdom, perhaps with a soul as the willow is thought to have by the Irish. We know that there is an ancient history of oak worship among the Indo-Europeans (the precursor people of the Celts), and that through them, oak worship became widespread and diversified. It is interesting to note that in Baltic Pagan religions (the Baltic peoples have strong links to the Celts, who once settled that part of the world), the oak is widely seen as the world tree. It is remarked in classical annals that the continental druids thought the oak tree was the very representation of their chief god, and was often associated with the classical Zeus. Other records tell us that the druids believed that everything that grew upon the oak was divine, and that they refused to conduct a ritual without at least a branch of it nearby.

There are countless more references to the divine place of the oak. What they tell us in the end is that the oak is equated with a great Celtic god who was at once a provider for man and a god of nature. This god is by certain authors thought to be the insular Celtic Lugh or the Gallic Tarranis, but in my opinion these characteristics fit more closely with Cernunnos, who is also known in Gaelic as Fearuaine [*FAY-ar-oo-ine*], or the Green Man.

As the carpenter's wood of the ogham, the oak is an extremely strong wood desirable for boat-building, furniture-making, wagon-building, and any other demanding, very practical application. The mighty oak, thus, is the strength that makes great ideas possible.

The wren probably symbolizes the spirit of the oak in bird form. In other mythologies of the West, particularly those of Rome, oak gods took bird forms, though usually as the woodpecker. However, in Ireland, the wren is seen as the king of birds. So it is only natural that this bird would become the animal manifestation of the oak's spirit.

On the Isle of Man and in Ireland, there is a traditional hunt of the wren each year. This occurs because the wren was supposedly the agent of a supernatural treachery, which warranted the eternal hatred of the Gaels. I feel that the hunting of the wren more than likely represents the rejection of this high druidic symbol under the influence of Christendom, and further confirms the wren's status as the faunal symbol of the oak spirit.

Cernunnos is the god of the wild, tillage, and provision at the harvest. Since the oak is a wild tree, yet one that provided a significant harvest, it is only fitting that the horned lord be represented in the oak. With nature as the most potent of forces, it is only natural that the mighty oak should become the high druidic symbol; the living representation of the greatest divine power.

Tinne [*TIN-ne*]

The holly is a mysterious tree; little is known of it. It has long been cultivated for its beauty, and its lovely wood provides veneers. Yet the holly is also an evergreen; it bears its glowing fruit throughout the winter. We probably get its relation to fires of coal from the blazing red fruit. The fruits do resemble little fires, glowing as they do on a tree that refuses to have its bright life muted by the drab greys and whites of deep winter. The tree, then, provides a metaphorical lesson: do not let the coldness of the world sap your brightness away. Coldness represents the hardness of material reality. This metaphorical cold attempts to drown out the mythical and the magical—the bright knowledge. Keep the coals of beauty burning as the holly does on its branches throughout the long winter.

The fact that this tree is an evergreen is also noteworthy. It is always prepared with green leaves, so as long as there is sun, however weak, it can continue its life processes. While other trees are leafless and naked, and wrapped in the thick mantle of deep winter sleep, the holly does not permit death to overcome it. It grasps for life and growth at every possible moment; it is always ready to drink in the brightness of the sun.

Coll [*coal*]

The hazel is a powerful magical tree. It represents elder myths and the highest aspirations of the bard's quest. In Irish myth, the great hazel tree of wisdom grew beside a pool and dropped nuts containing all knowledge into it in its season. Salmon swimming in the pool ate the nuts and swam downstream. People seeking the wisdom of the ages would attempt to catch such

153

ogham

ciphers

and

the

forest

mysteries

a salmon and eat it, thereby absorbing the wisdom of the hazel. While a hazel has other significance and herbal uses, it represents, more than anything else for the bard, the never-ending quest for the wisdom that is the key to personal growth, the understanding of the mysteries, poetry, divination, insight, imbas, magic, and true-sight.

Queirt [*kert*]

The apple was a staple among the insular Celts. Furthermore, it was sacred; it had numerous mystical connotations and divinatory powers. The apple represents the physical nourishment provided by trees. A good apple harvest represents wealth and provision. A grove of apple trees is the hind's shelter. It is a place of fine browsing on sweet wind-fallen fruits that is protected from the elements. After the overthrow of Arthur, legend has it that Myrddin (Merlin) went mad and exiled himself to the wilderness where he wept for the lost days of glory and his beloved apple grove, which was confiscated and given to another. Myrddin longs for death, but instead lives to a ripe old age, and sees everything he and Arthur built torn down and the Celtic world crushed beneath invading foreign hordes. Thus, apples came to be associated with the madness that comes from the loss of something beloved and precious and the death-longing or sensitivity to death (death sense) that arises with that. The mystery of the apple, then, is the forest provider of basic needs and the danger of loving too much, a passion to which those of Celtic spirit are prone.

Muinn [*MU-in*]

Contrary to what some authors have written in error, this ogham does not represent the grapevine. Grapes were not significant to the insular Celts as the island climes were too cold to produce good fruit. Grapes were either imported in the form of wine, or the Celts made their wine from honey.

The ogham of the vine refers to any of the various woody vine species of the Britannic isles, and most likely to members of the rose order. The vine is associated clearly with the back of a man or ox, for it is a tough, woody plant that is not easily deterred. It can climb rock, trees, and other obstacles to reach the sun, and it holds its grip tenaciously. It is very powerful, and is able to support great weight. Oxen and men likewise can perform mighty deeds. Like the vine, they establish themselves in a place, till and build great works, and tightly hold to what they have built. The vine, therefore, represents strength, effort, and determination.

Gort [*gort*]

The ivy plant tells a mixed story. Its ogham relation to the swan tells us that it has to do with the element of air, the domain of the spirits, and some of the magical sidhe. The swan is often the form taken by the Tuatha de Danaan and the gods of Celtdom. Their supernatural appearance indicates magical events in the making.

This ogham is also associated with sweet grass. Sweet grass is an important fodder for livestock, but the ivy is mildly poisonous and so is not quite fully comparable in that way. Sweet grass does, however, make for verdant, lovely meadows, just as the ivy enhances the walls and trees it grows upon with its dark, glossy green.

Ivy, like the swan or a grass shoot, is a delicate, graceful thing of beauty. Yet as well as being somewhat toxic, there is another sinister characteristic to the ivy: it is parasitic. A heavy growth of ivy on a tree will literally sap the life from it.

Ivy grows in a helix form. The helix is a common theme of Celtic patterns and it represents the complicated weavings of existence on the wheel of life. From this symbolism we can deduce the complicated mystery of the ivy. In its helix form it represents life striving for betterment; reaching into the air from the shady earth where it begins, it aspires to the sun.

Just as the swan chooses a mate for life, a fundamental part of human life is love, which will inevitably include grief as well as joy. All things must be done in harmony with the sacred druidic principle of balance. Love can smother and kill if it clings too thickly, just like ivy. Thus the ivy is a grey mystery of dark and light that weaves the complicated facets of pleasure with pain. Its very form, which is similar to DNA's double helix, represents the necessary pattern of life in balance.

Getal [*GET-al*]

The broom has connotations of a physician's strength because it possesses such diversified herbal potency. It is used in the treatment of everything from malaria to lice. This links directly to the broom's goose connection. The goose, as a high-flying diurnal water bird, is a solar symbol that exists in an

ogham

ciphers

and

the

forest

mysteries

especially powerful between place—between the three elements of earth, air, and water. Its solar nature, coupled with its lifeway as a powerful penetrator of the three elements, shows its potency as a panacea that infuses light into the three elements.

As the goose mates for life and is an ardent defender of its territory and family, it further symbolizes the broom as healer; for to heal is to defend and strengthen the body and soul. With all its healing symbolism, it is no wonder that the Celts believed goose fat had remedial properties.

The plant itself bears beautiful golden flowers in spring and grows as much as seven feet (two meters) high on a stout stalk. Its sunlight-colored blossoms and sky-reaching stalk also make it a solar symbol. When it was dried, the plant was traditionally used to make brooms (hence the name for the floor-sweeping device, which is now seldom made of actual broom). This is a cleansing property. All things taken together, the broom represents a thoroughly cleansing healing of the hearth and home—that is, the body and soul. Its solar relation reflects the truth that it is light which illuminates and enables such positive transformation. Broom, then, is the strength of light and healing.

Straif [*straf*]

The blackthorn's symbolism is plainly revealed in its alchemical oghamic cognates. As the plant of alchemy, it is the force of transformation, which relates it to fire. Alchemy, in the vulgar sense, is about changing lead into gold; alchemy in its pure and true sense is about transforming spiritual lead into gold and bringing the self toward perfection. This alchemical transformation involves understanding the deeper mysteries, hence an increase in secrets. The goal of alchemy was to create the transformative elixir.

Ruis [*RU-ish*]

The elder tree is well known for its fruit, which produces excellent wines. The tree also has numerous herbal usages. However, of greatest importance concerning its mystical significance as an ogham is its location on the ogham calendar (see below for further information). Because the elder represents the last month of the year, the tree symbolizes endings. The endings could be anything from death to the end of an era in one's life, such as graduation from school or a career change. It is important to remember that in the Celtic framework, beginnings and endings are not definitive points on a line, but rather positions on a wheel. All things occur in cycles, and spiral forever on the endless turns of the sacred wheel. One ending represents another new beginning. That which has come to pass will find a new origin in some other time and place.

Alternatively, the elder represents the red blush of shame because of the scarlet hue of its berries. Thus the elder stands for the deeds a person has performed or may perform that he or she will regret or would rather not have revealed. Such shameful things are little deaths: ends of innocence, ends of goodness, ends of faithfulness, and so on.

Between its connections to endings, shame, and little deaths, the elder is perceived as a dark, shadowy tree. This explains why it was feared as unlucky or even malevolent in a number of Western folklore traditions, despite its fabulous berries. However, while shame is a negative force, it is a basic emotional signal, which, if heeded, can impel one toward rectification and regeneration. In the Celtic psychology, death is the beginning of a long life, for it is the beginning place of birth. So while endings are sad in that they represent permanent changes, they also signify the onset of fresh new opportunities. The wisdom the elder has to impart, then, is a proper attitude toward change and shame. With such wisdom, these forces can be turned to light. A being incapable of shame and who will not accept change is a monster without a conscience and who is driven by fear—a dangerous combination. This is the darkness the elder's symbolism shows us.

Ailm [*alm*]

The tree of this ogham may be the silver fir of the mountains of Europe, or another fir of the high country predominately in western Ireland and northern Scotland and north Wales. The silver fir is a majestic tree that grows in the high country and rises straight and true to as much as 150 feet (30 meters). Its symbolic significance is very clear in its form, growth habits, and ogham references. Because of the heights to which the fir grows, and because of the high altitudes at which it grows, the fir is privy to a panoramic view. In some old ogham tracts, the fir is likened to the sigh of newborns and groans of wonder. These relate to the silver fir's awesome view; just as the baby sighs for wonder at the new world it has entered, and an adult groans in amazement when he comes to realize the grandeur of creation, the world is spectacular as perceived by the fir.

157

ogham

ciphers

and

the

forest

mysteries

It is important to understand that view is not simply about seeing, it is about perspective. An unenlightened person may look out upon the fir's grand view and see only a vast landscape. Yet to the person gifted with imbas, the view reveals itself on a more profound level. It conveys not only its physical beauty, but also something beneath: the sublime mystery that imbues creation, the semimythic quantum essence of possibilities that is at the heart of magic and beauty and which is the base of all things. The poet knows this as the indescribable for which she must forever seek the right words. The musician knows this as the haunting melody of enchantment; that music beneath music that stirs the spirit. The bard knows this as imbas: the ability to sense relations amidst form and substance, and order and chaos, and perceive the mystery therein. Indeed, the view of the fir is akin to true-sight—the enlightened vision.

The fir has also been likened to the groans of illness and piebald coloration. Seeing the complicated mix of colors that make something piebald is the effect of the fir's vision. One so gifted with it understands that most things are not simple, and are not easily broken down into clear hemispheres of black and white. Things are mixed, complex, and often confusing. Wisdom is not daunted by this complexity, and sees it instead as the richness that makes life interesting. However, to the simple-minded person who demands black and white, such a view can be very intimidating, even terrifying. So the sigh of wonder is transformed into a groan of illness. This is the reaction of the narrow-minded to life's intricate tapestry.

Ohn [oen]

The gorse is an appropriate symbol of the sacred wheel. It flowers all year with yellow blooms that bear nectar and pollen, thus reminding us that the wheel is an ever-turning and ever-productive constant. The wheel moves all things—changing them and sending them on to other wheels—but as one steps off, another steps on and the cycle recommences.

The gorse is also symbolic of the goddess and the helper of horses. In Welsh, this goddess was known as Rhiannon, in Irish as Macha, and in Gaulish as Epona. In all cases, she was allied to horses. The horse was very important to the Celts of old. They fought from horse-drawn chariots and managed cattle using horses as steeds. The horse was the backbone of the old Celtic lifestyle before they became more settled and agrarian, and even then it was an important beast of transportation and war. The goddess who looks after horses looks after the Celt as well.

Stone is implacable, strong, and stalwart. In Wales, the ubiquitous gorse grows everywhere in the stony soil, seeming as tough as the rock from which it rises. As stone, the gorse represents strength and the unchangeable. It represents the immutable character of the wheel and the strength that's needed to move on through the cycles of the wheel successfully, including growing with each new cycle in pursuit of the hero's quest of perfection.

So the gorse symbolizes the wheel-like cycles of time; the endless repetitions that are never quite the same so long as one possesses the strength to move on to the next wheel when it is time step off the old one. In addition, beneath it all is Epona, the friend of horses, lending strength indirectly as a guiding power of enchantment.

Ur [*ewr*]

Heather is a plant of infinite uses. Man utilizes it for making brooms, fuel, ale, and shelter. Bees use its pollen and nectar to make a fine honey from it. Birds eat its seeds. It has many uses besides. The ogham cognates of heather are cold dwellings, soil, and a grower of plants. The heather, then, represents the goodness of nature. It is widespread, being the chief plant throughout many regions of western and northern Europe. It is industrious, as it provides for man and beast in many ways. It also stabilizes the soil by composting into the earth and making it possible for other, less hardy plants to grow in areas that otherwise would be too harsh for them. This makes heather also a paternal symbol—a provider and protector.

Edad [*ED-ad*]

The aspen is a tree of complicated symbolism. It is well-known as a talkative tree for the sounds it makes every time it is touched by a breath of wind. Even the slightest breeze will set its leaves to chattering unintelligible secrets. Yet, the tree's ogham significance has more to do with its relation to the swan, the friend, and its place as a distinguished wood.

The swan is the bird-form the Celtic gods often took. The children of Lir [*leer*], the offspring of the Tuatha de Danaan, were also transformed into swans. Like the swan, the aspen represents elegance, for it is a tree of delicate, graceful form. It may also speak of secrets, as the gods in swan form

159

ogham

ciphers

and

the

forest

mysteries

were repositories of hidden wisdom. The aspen seems a tree full of secrets as it mutters uninterpretable things in the language of wind and leaf.

The wood of the aspen is distinguished for its strength and resilience (it was once used as a shield material). Yet the tree as a whole is more distinguishable for its beauty, and even more so for its perpetual "speech." This relates the tree to the Gallic Ogmios, cognate of the Irish Ogma, god of the strength of eloquent speech. His chains made of words bound hearts with worthy inspiration.[3] Such an inspirer is a friend indeed. This is an encourager, a hope-giver, and a guide of worth. Such is also the aspen—poet's friend, distinguished tree of the forest, and whisperer of the linguistic arts.

Idad [ID-ad]

The old man of the trees, the yew is renowned for its longevity. Yew groves planted by the druids two millennia ago still stand in the British Isles. As age is associated with wisdom, so is the yew. Thus, where the oak was the most sacred tree of the Gallic and British druids, the yew was the most sacred tree of the Irish druids, who so valued wisdom.

The yew is also a very poisonous tree, so it is related to the deadly weapon the sword. Death is the beginning of life, and this is reflected in the yew's growth habits. Yews grow from a central root system beneath the ground. As one trunk grows old and rots, a new one rises from the earth to replace it—a life cycle that clearly shows the spiraling turns of rebirth. Even its leaves attach spirally to the twigs. This creates a form that reflects the thematic spirals of Celtic art and indicates the turning mysteries of the sacred wheel. Yet the spiral growth of the leaves is hidden as the leaves bend out into a horizontal plane, one on either side of the twig. The average observer would never notice it. So, the mystery of the spiral is only perceivable by those who have obtained wisdom and know how to perceive a thing in depth; it remains hidden (occultic) from those unprepared to look for it. Therefore the yew—revealer of truths, keeper of secrets, harborer of wisdom, and dangerous as a sword to those who do not approach it wisely—is a metaphor of druidic truth in every aspect of its form and being. It shows how it earned its place as the most sacred tree of the Irish druids.

In addition to the yew, the ogham finds fitting symbolism in the eagle. In Welsh myth, the eagle is one of the oldest creatures in the world. Indeed, an eagle can live to a ripe old age of more than fifty years—an extraordinarily long time for a wild animal. As a great predator surviving at the top of the food web, the eagle has a poisonous nature, like the yew. Yet, most importantly, the eagle is a truly intelligent bird, which reflects the aged wisdom attributed to the yew.

The yew is the wise old forest man; a venerable wood of wisdom. Yet the yew is deadly poisonous, and as eagle and sword, it reminds us that the revelation of the mysteries is dangerous business, one only the worthy adept is fit to pursue. For wisdom is power as well as enlightenment, and without enlightenment, power corrupts and is capable of much harm.

161

ogham

ciphers

and

the

forest

mysteries

The Calendrical Ogham Mysteries

It is obvious by now that the ogham is much more than a mere writing system. It is also a system of mystery wisdom symbolism, and a deep understanding of it is fundamental to the development of true-sight and a profound knowledge of the Celtic lore. In the next chapter we shall study the ogham's power as a divinatory system, but first, the ogham is also a calendrical system. As such it teaches us even more about druidic/bardic thought and their mysteries.

The insular Celtic calender was a lunar calendar. A new day began at sundown. It was based on agrarian concerns, so it was more occupied with the practical implications of the turning of the seasons than with mathematical accuracy. Put simply, this means that the Celts put their calendar second to utility; they didn't declare it was spring until it felt like spring. Their calendar was based on four seasons that cycled around folk life: the seasons of Samhain, Imbolc, Beltane, and Lughnasadh.

Samhain was the season of the waning of the sun's power. Autumn symbolized the sun's death, which occurred at the very end of summer. Over the coming dark months, the sun would symbolically enter the house of death, and the world would go into a dying process along with it. Just as twilight is the death of one day and the beginning of another, so Samhain marks the death of one year and the birth of a new one.

It may seem odd to begin a new year at the onset of the cold and dark of winter, but we must remember the druidic philosophy that from darkness springs creation. Life springs anew from a cycle begun in death. As Samhain marks the dying of the sun, it is only appropriate that it begins the year's new life cycle.

Samhain was a very special time, for at its end came the mysterious thirteenth month: a short, three-day period that was between either year. It was a time that was neither here nor there, and at its apex—sundown on October 31 by our modern calendar's reckoning—the barriers between the Otherworld and our own had all but dissolved. This was a time of incredible magical power, and the beings of the Otherworld as well as the dead could enter and roam our world at will.

Imbolc marked the first sign of the return of spring when the ewes gave birth and began lactating. Again, in the Celtic mind we see a concern not with numerical accuracy when determining the date of the midwinter celebration, but with the most important sign of the coming spring. As an agrarian people, the birth of the new year's stock and the lactation of the ewes was of immense importance. It signified the sun's return to life and the continuance of life on earth. This festival was a very local affair, and not nearly so important as Samhain, for the lords were not so immediately dependent on the land as were the common people.

Beltane, the other major Celtic festival, was an important spring festival. It was a joyous celebration of the return of life to the land. The sun had been reborn or reinvigorated by the goddess. The world leaves the dark months for the light months, and the love of the god and the goddess makes the goddess fertile, which in turn makes the earth fertile. Where Samhain commemorated dying, Beltane celebrated living. This was a time to relish in nature and life, and the festivities were carried on out of doors with walks in the woods, picnics in glens and meadows, and dancing.

Lughnasadh was a celebration of the height of summer. In it we remember the mother goddess, who sacrificed herself for the benefit of her offspring, and Lugh, who is the god of many talents and is associated with the sun. At this time the first products of summer were harvested and the king of the land was at the height of his power. Summer was in its full power and life was lush. However, this time marked the beginning of the descent of summer as well. Harvests needed to be brought in and stored, so there wasn't much time for celebration. Therefore, this wasn't a major festival.

The Mysteries of the Ogham Calendar

The correlation of each month to its position in the year relates the mysteries of the ogham calendar. The words in bold denote the translation of the ogham. If you live in a region of the world where the seasons just do not match this calendar at all, such as Alaska or Australia, you may find it much more conducive to follow the ancient Celtic practice of reckoning the holidays to occur at nature's first sign of the beginning of the season in your region. Thus, if you are in Australia, Lughnasadh and not Imbolc might occur at the end of January.

163

ogham

ciphers

and

the

forest

mysteries

November—Beith

The **birch** is the tree of beginnings, as this is the first month of the year. It is a time to put the old behind and welcome the next annual revolution of the wheel.

December—Luis

At this time, luck was needed by the Celts, for they were well into winter, and spring was a long way off. Livestock and humans were in danger of illness and starvation. The **rowan** was an amulet in a time of need; nature's protection against ill luck.

January—Fearn

In the **alder** we see protective power again, this time in the form of a shield. As the shield provides protection from the onslaught of the enemy, so nature has protected earth's children with shelter, clothing, and substance with which to pass through the winter.

February—Saille

The **willow's** association with death comes to the fore as the year has now been locked into the frozen depths of winter for some time. Yet its bee association also rings through because spring is now in sight. Animals are calving and the farmers are preparing for the busy season.

Imbolc begins at sundown of the last day of January. As the tree of Imbolc, Brighid's festival, the musical willow is symbolic of imbas. Now the first hints of spring are reaching the poet and setting the cauldrons of the soul aboil with delighted poetry. The willow, then, is inspiration and hope in a dark place.

March—Nuin

The **ash** is the shaman penetrator of worlds and light in the darkness. It breaks through winter's night, and brings spring life and healing to the dormant land. The nuin is the awakening tree month.

April—Huath

The sun is rising to life with strength now; vibrant nature is once again at work. Because animals have new young to tend to, they can be dangerous, for they will vigorously defend their hapless offspring. Also, some of the larger, more dangerous animals are gorging after a long winter's fast, and they may not be picky about what they choose for a meal. The treacherous weather of spring—sometimes deceptively perfect and placid, other times stormy and almost wintry—is experienced. Winter could yet return for one last gasp. All this represents unpredictable danger. The lesson is that even though spring is here, we must not take nature for granted. Balance demands a recognition of the dark side. Thus the **hawthorn** represents the untamed, wild side of nature. It is not a thing to be shunned, but respected. This is Cernunnos's primal nature.

May—Duir

As the **oak** month, this is the beginning of the season of Beltane, the opposite of the season of Samhain. Beltane begins at sundown of the last day of April. It marks the commencement of light and warmth, for the sun is coming into his power. The oak, then, marks the mystery of the sun, life, and the beneficence of nature. It is Cernunnos's bright, benevolent side.

June—Tinne

Coming into summer's heat and the height of the growing season, the **holly** is ready with glossy green leaves outspread and receptive to the sun. As it was green and alive with coal-like red berries during the winter, it is all the more a vibrant life symbol now, exalting in the gift of summer.

July—Coll

This is a lush time for bards and druids and other creatures of nature. With summer at its height, it is the season for seeking imbas in sultry night breezes and sensing the between in the movement of water and in the essence of enchanted places. The **hazel** represents the gift of imbas from the summer country, just as this season represents the gifts of nature. These gifts are highly treasured by the bard, for they inspire wisdom and fuel art.

August—Muinn

The **vine,** which is symbolized by the strength of an ox or man's back, is appropriate for this time, for it is now Lughnasadh. Lughnasadh begins at sundown of the last day of July. This is the harvest festival when the first fruits of summer are brought in. It is a time to begin intensive labor as the farmers prepare to bring in the year's planting, which will get them through the black months (as the winter months are known in Brittany). The vine here represents hard work and its rewards.

September—Gort

This is the beginning of the beautiful season of fall. Harvest time is underway now, though many crops will not be brought in for another month. In this time of light, the days are beginning to cool and the foliage shows the first hint of autumn colors. It is the time when dark first begins to mingle with light. The **ivy** is, then, the plant of the month of mixing forces.

Yet the ivy, with its swanlike character, is also a symbol of love, for next month is Samhain, when young lovers will marry. What is love if not a mixing of forces? The forces of male and female are intertwined for great good, fertility, teamwork, and friendship. The ivy, then, is also the ogham plant for the month of preparations, love, and anticipation.

October—Getal

The **broom's** all healing symbolism becomes more apparent here in this final month of the year. At this time, the last of the harvest is reaped and the community is prepared to weather the winter. The home is transformed into a good place full of camaraderie, laughter, and the smells of food being dried, salted, and stored. The broom, which represents the sunlit strength of

165

ogham

ciphers

and

the

forest

mysteries

healing, represents the sun imparting its last strength to the folk of the earth before its descent into death.

Samhain—Ruis

Samhain begins at sundown on October 29 and ends at sundown on November 1. The thirteenth month and the **elder** were feared because of their association with endings. However, as endings are only the beginnings of new turns of the wheel, so this short time is a joining of worlds, when the great wheels of worlds meet for an instant and passage is free. This is a time of tension, when elder magics hold great potential and possibilities become limitless. As such, it is a dangerous time, unless one is prepared. The lesson of the elder is unlucky to the one who lacks druidic understanding, but to the bard who understands the mysteries and has had time to individuate and build personal strength, this is a time to grow. Legends speak of people contacting the Otherworld and becoming poets, sorcerers, and kings. Yet the unprepared may touch it and go mad. One must be learned and open, or one must fear and avoid mystery. The elder is a reminder: do not reach for the deep mysteries unless you are ready.

chapter nine

Arcane Arts

So she resolved according to the arts of the books of the Fferyllt, to boil a cauldron of Inspiration and Science . . .

The Mabinogion

Enchantment runs in the blood of the Celts. To this very day the Celts are noted for their vibrant and earthy magical traditions. Celtic folk magic runs from ritual divinatory techniques to the second sight, from talismans for luck to charms against being faerie-struck. Their magic is based on form, technique, and incantation, and utilizes the properties of substances and invocations to spiritual powers for aid.

We know from old folk tales that the heroes of Celtdom were not averse to utilizing magic. The Irish hero Cuchulainn used an ogham upon a shaft[1] (talisman) to repel his enemies. The Welsh prince Pwyll ascended the enchanted mound of Arberth (a place of magical legend) in order to see a marvel, and witnessed the horse goddess Rhiannon riding by.[2]

The druids, likewise, made use of many magical traditions, be they the traditions of the "high" magic of Europe and the Near East, or the local folk knowledge to their own magical arts. The druid Mog Roith's daughters went to the

Near East to study their magical techniques (most likely Egyptian, Hermetic, and other such traditions). Mog Roith himself used the magic of the faeries to defeat his foes, the forces of King Cormac mac Art of the northern half of Ireland.[3]

Now, it is important to understand that bards were a kind of druid. Some druids carried out priestly services to the Celtic pantheon, while others were dedicated to scholarship, divination, or the perfection of the magical arts. Bards were the music makers and poets of their people, and were in an intimate relationship with imbas and other natural powers and presences. Their magic craft used art and spirit to craft the raw forces of magic and nature and required high training. Thus they had a magico-artistic system that was highly specialized and unique to them. Their high magics (covered in chapter 7) were based on their poetic, musical, and mind-focusing skills, but they were in possession of much more druid lore. Also, like their druid kindred, they were not averse to utilizing the arcane crafts of traditions beyond their native Celtic culture.

If you should choose to take up the bardic path, you should likewise feel free to practice Celtic magic and integrate it with the magic of other traditions. The bards and druids were seekers of wisdom of every kind. An ancient declaration of the Celtic kings was, "The truth against the world."[4] The search for knowledge is of the highest importance to the bard. Bardry and druidry were like vast cauldrons, combining the ancient wisdom of the mystically minded Celts with the knowledge of other peoples the world over. What mattered most was the development of the deep wisdom that is the result of a full perception of knowledge on the material, mythic, and psychic levels. This is what all magic practices are about, be they shamanic, high, or earthy.

What Are the Arcane Arts?

By arcane art, I am referring to Celtic magic that is not rooted in the specific bardic techniques discussed in chapter 7. That chapter discussed the high magic of old, the enchantment that is summoned from the creative power of poetry, the artistic shaping of sound, and the razor-sharp control of thought. This chapter, however, deals with easier-to-harness reflections of that old magic. This is the magic that is related to the properties of substances and words. It is the magic that springs from enchanted woods and faerie rings, ogham talismans and empowered wands. This magic is more about form than forces. Thus it is, in a sense, profane rather than mythic.

Nevertheless, this magic must not be mistaken for useless or evil. Profane in the Celtic way of thought does not imply either. Evil, in the old Celtic mind, is unrestricted chaos. Profane simply means it springs from form. The advantages to this kind of magic are that it is simple to perform and experiment with, it holds little danger unless it is intentionally used for ill reasons, and it can be built upon, which means that skill with it can lead to other, greater arcane skills, or lead the practitioner to greater ability in using elder enchantment.

Finally, there are many other arcane traditions. Some are based on fairly simple folk magics, and others are very demanding and complex. I do not mean to denigrate any of them by classifying the nonbardic/druidic magics as arcane arts. I am referring specifically to the Celtic folk magic system, and I am doing it this way simply in order to distinguish it from high Celtic magic, the elder enchantments you learned of in chapter 7.

There are many resources old and new on the arcane arts. It is not possible in this book to cover them all—that would take many volumes. The Celts are a people with a long history of dealings with magic and we will only be able to survey a small portion of their magical techniques here. You should feel free to augment what you learn here with further studies of other resources. Note that careful analysis of old folk tales can give invaluable insights into the practice of the arcane arts, and add to one's repertoire of arcane magics.

Some General Notes

The arcane arts are not so dependent on a focused mind as are the elder enchantments. They rely, to a large part, on the properties of the substances used and the form of incantations. However, a focused mind greatly increases the potency of all magics. So it is important to keep in practice. Work at meditation so that you may control your thoughts, keep them focused, and let them go upon the completion of a magic working.

The properties of substances are their resonances and their reflections of sublime truths. For instance, the rowan—sometimes referred to as the mountain ash or the service tree—is a tree of the ogham alphabet that has strong magical properties. It is used in defensive magic such as protection. A deep study of this tree's appearances in Celtic folklore and in other Western traditions reveals that it works like a magical amplifier, so long as the magic is positive. It will work to negate negative magics.

You may base your arcane pursuits on traditional magical workings that appear in old accounts of folklore, or, understanding the properties of substances within the Celtic tradition, you may formulate your own magics. This is the basis for magical experimentation.

It is also fairly safe to experiment with arcane magics, so long as you don't attempt to work negative or harmful magics. Bear in mind that anything you do will bear consequences in this world and the Otherworld. Good will be answered with good, and evil with evil. Legends speak of the gods themselves turning evil-intended magic back upon even high poets.[5]

Also, bear in mind that anything you can do with arcane magics, you can likewise accomplish with elder enchantments. The elder enchantments require less resources because all you really need is your poetry, your mind, and your music. The items involved are merely to enhance focusing the mind. Yet the arcane magics are easier because to utilize their properties you needn't have mastered control of the mind. A combination of the best of the elder and arcane techniques may be the most powerful form of magic.

The incantations of arcane magics may sometimes seem similar to the poetic incantations of elder enchantments, but the theme behind them is different. The elder incantations are tools by which the bard focuses the mind, and the poetic form is part of that process. The elder incantations assist the mind by requiring tremendous accuracy and control and by creating beauty, which is a sublime component of the bardic magics.

The arcane incantation, on the other hand, provides a template for the lesser trained. It helps to focus the mind of the nonpoet for an instant on the magical work at hand. Later misunderstandings by the common folk devolved this poetic intent into spoken talismans. The people came to see the incantations as having power in and of themselves, as if the word order or choice or intonation gave them power. This crucial error disempowered the Celtic folk magics that were dependent upon spoken spells because it is possible to learn simple incantations and recite them back without hardly giving a thought to what is being said. This gives no charge to a magic working, for the power arises from the mind working as a shaper of sublime forces. Remember, arcane magics do not derive power from word choice or order. The words are templates for thought. Focus on your goal as you say them, and visualize clearly the imagery appropriate to the incantation.

A magical work heavily utilizing materials with strong magical resonances would have some innate power on the basis of the properties of the substances. However, without some incantation to focus the mind or call upon divine assistance, the powers are unfocused. Anything or nothing could happen.

Finally, when worked properly, using the properties of substances to augment the mind can be quite powerful. In fact, these magics can be worked in perpetuity. For instance, a talisman can be wrought to keep working for years, even centuries. Such things may be of low immediate power, but they have great cumulative effect over time. Do not shun the arcane arts. Learn when to use them, and when to use the elder enchantments. As a rule, if you need to harness a great deal of power now, turn to the elder enchantments. If you want to ensure good luck, effect a long-term change, or work some minor magic, especially over a long period, the arcane arts are a good choice.

Ogham Magics
Druidic Fires

The legendary druidic fire is based on the old technique of creating fires with magical force by burning woods and other plants of certain properties. The form of the wood as it is laid out for the fire, the time at which the fire is lit, and even the direction of the wind are all significant factors as well. Incantations shape and direct the force, and bardic music will further enhance the incantation, though it is not absolutely necessary.

The properties of the ogham trees and plants will serve to help choose of which fuels to use for the fire. For instance, if one's intent is to ask for protection, the rowan would make a good choice, as it is strongly associated in Celtic and related lores to protection. If the intent is to contact the Otherworld, the alder and the hawthorn would make appropriate woods. The alder is the ogham symbol of the Otherworld, and the hawthorn is the home of the faerie. You should refer to the ogham mysteries of chapter 8 for

Ogham Symbol	Meaning
Birch	Knowledge, birth, death, beginnings
Pine	Things rare or precious
Hawthorn	Legendary home of faeries, power of satire
Aspen	Mistletoe properties (healing)
Oak	Leadership, the divine, strength
Gorse	The sun
Hazel	Wisdom, magic power
Wild rose	Strong magical barrier
Holly	Endurance
Rowan	Spell-casting, magical amplification, strong protection, luck, the wind
Alder	The Otherworld
Ivy	Tenacity, longevity (health)
Willow	Bard's tree, solar magic, imbas, the soul, music, the harp
Honeysuckle	Faithfulness, fidelity

TABLE 2—*Ogham Compendium II*

a more in-depth understanding of the properties of the ogham woods. Table 2 gives a concise, yet slightly different review of ogham plant powers. Add this lore to the ogham lore you gained from the previous chapter, and use it all to construct the ogham-related aspects of your spellcraft. (This table is based on a slightly different yet venerable interpretation of the ogham symbols and their corresponding meanings. It will provide you with some new insights and perspectives on the use and meaning of this magical writing system.)

These woods can be applied to the druid fire individually, or they can be mixed. For instance, a druidic fire of holly, ivy, and rowan would make for a fine spell for enduring health. A fire of alder and willow would make for an invocation for artistic inspiration. A fire of gorse and honeysuckle would be perfect for a dedicatory solar ritual, such as at Beltane. I see no reason why other herbs of power could not also be added to such a fire. Choose plants with the resonances you require and add them to the druidic fire in proportion to the amount you wish that plant's resonances to affect your enchantment.

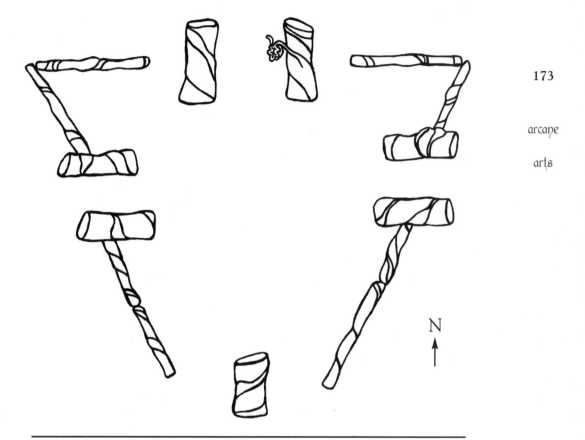

N
↑

FIGURE 1—Druid Fire Layout

The fire must not only be comprised of the correct woods and plants, but it must be built according to the form of a druidic fire. It must have three sides and points (triangular) and seven openings: three in the north, one to the east, one to the west, and two to the south. It should appear as illustrated in Figure 1. This is made by laying out cut logs as shown, with the broad side of the triangle pointed northward. Smaller logs or sticks should be laid perpendicular to the main logs to mark the openings to the cardinal directions. The openings represent opening to the power symbolized by the cardinal directions: north for death, cold, and darkness; south for light, life, and energy; east for the sun, beginnings, and birth; and west for the Otherworld, the spiritual, endings, and the afterlife. The rest of the materials are simply to be heaped within the framework of the druidic fire.[6]

Once the fire is lit and is going well, an incantation should be pronounced over it in order to direct the power of the fire. The bard may write the incantation or use one taken from another source. The incantation should contain the essential elements of a spell: an invocation, a statement of the magic worker's desire, and a thank-you to the spiritual forces who will help actuate your spell. Arcane incantations should be kept fairly simple, though they are best in poetic form. As with all magic working, the mind should first be cleared, then focused. While arcane magics are not so mind-dependent as the higher enchantments, the better the application of the mind, the more potent the magical working will be. Remember, there is no power in the words themselves. The purpose of the incantation is to focus the mind in order to direct the transformative energy of the fire and to summon spiritual assistance. Do not recite off an incantation by rote without giving it any mental effort. That will almost negate the spell.

Bear in mind that a love of beauty is ingrained into the souls of the Celts and their spiritual benefactors. The more beautiful the incantation you create, the more likely Otherworldly powers are to be attracted to it and heed it. In this sense, the incantation does have one powerful property: invocation. A bard should craft it well. Along with this, keep in mind that the more beautiful and well-done the rest of the elements of your spell, the greater the likelihood it will be heard and attended to.

Bardic music also adds to the beauty of the spell. This will further increase its attractiveness and the likelihood that it will be heard and acted upon by Otherworldly forces. As we have discussed, the good bard learns to meditate by the power of the music. Bardic music focuses the mind and empowers it through the primal essence of sound. It should be added, if at all possible, to the druidic fire spell.

Naturally, the druidic fire should be performed out of doors. Bardry, like druidry, is a natural path. While a smaller semblance of the druidic fire could be created indoors and might have some effect, it will not have the purity and power of one worked out of doors, especially in a grove, garden, or an old forest, for such are the places where the spirits of nature dwell.

Like all Celtic magic, the time the spell is worked affects its power. Table 3 is a brief list of the importance and power of daily times and their corresponding holidays, seasons, and directions.

Time	Correspondences
Dawn	Solar magic, origins, beginnings, initiations, spring, Beltane, east
Day	Energy, warmth, light, growth, fertility, nature, summer, Lugnasad, south
Twilight	Between time, Otherworld, afterlife, fall, Samhain, west
Night	Lunar magic, mystery, enchantment, death, endings, winter, Imbolc, north

TABLE 3—Daily Times Correspondences

All Celtic magic is best worked during its corresponding times and in sacred places, and the druid fire is no exception. In addition, a wind blowing out of the direction of correspondence is especially beneficial to the druid fire. Of course, you must exercise caution with the fire. Do not create one on a blustery day when the fire could get out of control, or set a flame near brush. Be sure to thoroughly douse the flame when the ritual is completed.

Ogham Trees

The ogham tree might also be called a living spell. It is a kind of runic magic worked by many cultures. For instance, some North American natives carry out a similar procedure by carving totem faces into the sides of living trees. The face has no long-term harmful effect on the tree, and indeed the magic depends on it, for it is the life of the tree that breathes magic power into the totem face. Ogham tree magic involves carving an ogham into a living tree trunk. The tree's life pours power into the ogham, which works perpetually and grows with the tree.

To work ogham tree magic, you should create an ogham stating your desire in the form of a very concise incantation. Begin by writing out your incantation in your native language, and pare it down to the most concise form possible. You might start with an elaborate poem and pare it down to something like this: "Cernunnos, Lord of Nature, grant protection to the creatures of this, my sacred garden." That's pretty concise. You might further reduce it to "Cernunnos, guard the creatures of this garden." How short it becomes is up to you, just keep it clear. Remember, you don't want to deface the tree, nor harm it. Short ogham inscriptions will be less likely to do either, and are acceptable for the purpose of the ogham tree.

Next, using the Roman-to-ogham letter chart in chapter 8, transcribe the incantation into ogham on a piece of paper. If you can also translate it into a Celtic tongue, so much the better, but your own language will suffice if not.

A special note is in order here: you will soon discover when transcribing English into ogham characters that the ogham does not offer as many sounds as the Roman letters used in the English alphabet do. Therefore, it will be impossible to spell some English words entirely using the ogham beithluis-nuin (pronounced [*BEH-loo-ish-noo-in*]; the ogham alphabet). You can do one of several different things to work around this. One, you can simply skip the sounds that will not transcribe into the ogham beithluisnuin, much as some languages simply omit the writing of vowels. Two, you can use Roman characters to fill in the gaps where ogham characters won't work. Three, you can find a different word that can be completely spelled out using the beith-luisnuin. Which you do is up to you. It depends on how pure and secret you want your transcription to be. Of course, best is translating what you want to write into a Celtic tongue. Dictionaries, a basic language course, and even some computer programs can help you greatly with this.

Now, find a tree that corresponds to the purpose of your magical working. Like all Celtic magic, it will be best if the tree is located in a sacred place: a grove, forest, garden, or something similar. Later, return to it at a magic time that corresponds to the purpose of your spell with a small hammer and chisel to inscribe the ogham into the trunk of the tree. You may inscribe the ogham vertically by writing from the bottom up (this works best for trees), or you may make it horizontal (left to right). As you inscribe the ogham, you should recite it to yourself—to a tune if you wish—meditating upon your magical working as you work. Once the ogham is completed, leave it and clear your mind of it to allow the magic to continue working toward the goal, undiluted and uninterrupted.

The ogham tree is not usually an extremely potent magic in the sense of immediately summoning a great amount of power. Rather, it works subtly and continuously over time, its power building with the strength of the growing tree on which it has been inscribed. Some excellent uses for the ogham tree are to mark your sacred site of study or practice, to welcome Otherworldly beings to the place, to invoke the gods there, or to invoke protection of it from others. It has many other uses, which are limited only by your skill with the arcane arts.

Ogham Divination and the Dallan Wands

We know from the legends that the Celts used the ogham for divination. In one account, a prince of Scotland gave Cuchulainn an ogham in order to determine the whereabouts of missing men. We read of the druid Dallan inscribing oghams on four wands of yew and using this to find Etain after she had been kidnapped from her husband, King Airem, by the faerie Midir. Numerous other accounts abound.

One way of using the ogham for divination—the wisdom way—requires a profound understanding of the ogham mysteries. The bard applies this knowledge to make an educated consideration of the question at hand, much as a psychologist applies his or her knowledge of human nature to interpret the problems presented by a particular patient. For instance, if a person is seeking to understand why he has not received poetic inspiration in some time, it might be wise to consider the mysteries of the birch (tree of beginnings) and the willow (tree of a bard's soul). It may be wise to consider the alder as well, as the alder is a tree of the Otherworld, from which imbas originates. The person making such a consideration may find that he has become bound up in the mundanities of day-to-day life to the point where he has not persisted in his bardic exercises and has failed to keep his mind honed and open to the power of myth. The solution might be to decrease obligations in order to destress and have time to revel in the joy and beauty of nature. This process is not so much divination as it is analysis, and it is highly akin to true-sight—using a developed knowledge of bardic mysteries to interpret events and facts. Yet it is divinatory because it applies the bardic mysteries to see potentialities and solutions you otherwise would not without an illuminating magical power.

Scrying, which was covered in chapter 7, is one of the other great bardic divinatory methods. It allows messages to come directly from the mythic place of the mind (the place where true dreams live) in conjunction with the Otherworld with a minimum of interference. Scrying using a looking glass, crystal ball, clear pool, or any other means can often yield symbolic or unclear results, however. Therefore, we see again that it is important to be familiar with the ogham mysteries in order to interpret the results of scrying accurately.

The druids, who were keenly interested in all manners of discerning knowledge, were constantly on the lookout for omens. They believed that the natural world was deeply sympathetic with the supernatural world. Indeed, in the Celtic view, the worlds intermingled freely. There was an ephemeral boundary between this world and the other that, while it allowed the worlds to maintain their individual natures, was easy enough to cross, so much so that it could be done willfully or even accidentally.

Because of this innate sympathy, and because divination arises from the Otherworld—which doesn't quite flow in time as does ours—nature was full of omens. Some omens were as clear as a foreboding stillness predicting the onset of a mighty storm. Perceiving other omens required a good knowledge of the Celtic mysteries. For instance, three magpies together may foretell ill luck and death. On the other hand, they may just be three magpies hanging out together. How do you tell what is an omen and what is not? For one, omens rarely occur individually. Usually other omens will also occur around the same time to lend context and support to each other, but you must keep a sharp eye out to notice them.

The majority of people today are totally detached from the natural world where most Celtic omens work and they miss its mystic signs entirely. If ill luck bodes in your future, you may have sighted three magpies of late, and you may have had the unusual experience of having a crow fly into your home sometime recently. If good fortune is in your future, you may have the unusual luck of finding a cricket chirruping away in your shoe on several mornings. Real omens tend to be supported by context, so watch for patterns among things in your life that could be omen symbols.

Real omens may also possess the property psychologist Carl Jung referred to as synchronicity. Synchronistic omens may occur at the most unusual or opportune times. You may be wondering if you are going to get a raise at work and look down to find money in your path. You may be thinking a life option available to you is a bad one to take and look out your window to find a crow staring ominously back at you. When omens occur synchronistically and with context, they are the most powerful, most certain to be true, and meaningful omens. Even then, you must possess the wisdom of the Celtic mysteries to correctly interpret them.

To correctly divine with omens, then, requires a few skills: a broad knowledge of the Celtic lore of omen symbols, the wisdom to know when an event is an omen and when it is just an occurrence, and an understanding of the bardic/druidic wisdom—including the ogham mysteries—to make a correct interpretation. Without a thorough mastery of all three of these skills, utilizing omens is little better than guessing at the future.

There is another method of using the ogham for divining. When Dallan sought Etain, he made oghams on four wands of yew. This sounds remarkably similar to dowsing. One gathers the picture from the tale that he created the four wands and then followed their lead to the faerie hill where Etain was being held by Midir. When Cuchulainn was given an ogham to locate missing men, he followed its lead as well. Based on these stories, I have developed a divinatory method that utilizes the ogham as a guiding tool. I cannot say for sure if this is what the ancient druids and bards used; it is what I have been able to reconstruct from my studies.

Ogham wands. The first step involves the construction of four ogham wands. The wands should be made from yew wood, as it is the wood Dallan used in the legendary example. Yew was the most sacred tree of the Irish druids. Alternatively, you may build the wands from oak, which was the most sacred tree of the Britannic and Gallic druids, or from rowan, which was recognized universally throughout the West for its magical powers. However, I highly recommend you stick to the yew of legend.

Each wand should be about twelve inches long, and one to two inches in diameter. To begin with, they should be quite well rounded. You should plane each on five sides evenly so that the wand will be shaped like an elongated pentagon. This is the outline of the pentagram, a shape of high occultic significance that means protection, transformation (relating to the grail mysteries, earlier known as the cauldron mysteries), and is symbolic of Cernunnos.

After the wands have been planed on each side, sand each plane and the ends down to silky smoothness. Then take a wand and, about two inches from the end, inscribe the first ogham of the first five-ogham group: beith. Two inches farther down on the next side going clockwise (deasil) inscribe the next ogham: luis. That places it four inches from the end of the wand. Then, on the next plane, another two inches in, inscribe fearn. The fearn ogham will then be six inches from the end you started on, on the third plane. On the fourth plane, two inches farther down (eight inches from the end), inscribe the ogham for saille. Finally, two inches farther down, inscribe the ogham for nuin on the remaining plane.

On the next wand inscribe the five oghams of the second group in the same manner. Then inscribe the third group on the third wand, and the fourth group on the fourth wand. You have now made your four ogham wands, which, I believe, are similar to what the druid Dallan created. So we will call these Dallan wands. Cleanse and dedicate them as sacred and mystic devices (see chapter 13), and they will be ready for use.

To divine with these wands, you must clear your mind, then carefully choose and clarify your question. You may wish to ask an appropriate deity to answer you through the ogham wands, such as Ceridwen, goddess of wisdom. Take up the four wands and let them fall randomly on a table or the ground. Four oghams will be revealed facing up, one from each group. Using your understanding of the ogham mysteries, interpret the revealed oghams in relation to your question and to each other to gain insight.

Notice that in every ogham-based divination method we have covered, we are more concerned with using the ogham mysteries to increase perception than with just determining the future. While it may be that the old druids and bards used it for simple prognostication, I can find no record of it. Their use of the ogham seems to have been clearly oriented toward deepening their understanding of the whys of things, rather than merely trying to ascertain knowledge of what will be. I believe they would have considered prognostication a lesser, somewhat vulgar ambition. As a divining tool, they used the ogham to provide a supernatural resource to insight what they would not otherwise have had. As the purpose of this book is to honor and preserve the wisdom of the Old Ways, that is how we shall utilize the ogham here as well. It is, in fact, probably the only proper way to use the ogham in divinatory magic.

Now this is not to say that the Celts were uninterested in divining the future. It has been written that of all peoples, the Celts were the most devoted to the arts of divination. However, the tools for that type of discernment seem to have been centered around the use of omens, visions, and prophecies, which are the tools of druidic knowledge, shamanic seeing, and bardic insight, respectively.

So, the ogham is a wisdom tool that can be drawn upon to provide supernatural insight. It is not a tool of simple prognostication. Other techniques are available to serve that lesser function.

Ogham Poles

The ogham pole is similar to the ogham tree, and it has numerous uses. In legend, it was used to warn, to curse, and to threaten with the geas. Cuchulainn at one time used an ogham pole to place a geas on a pursuing force, and it assured him a tactical edge. Another time he used it to proclaim his victory over enemy scouts.

The ogham pole also has more positive uses. Like a talisman, it can call for luck or create a perpetual invocation for the assistance of divine and Otherworldly powers. Remember that among the Celts, the written word was especially powerful. Unlike the spoken word, which is said and done, the written word continues as an unceasing, magically powerful force. Historically, ogham poles were also used to proclaim satires, mark boundaries, and make other kinds of announcements. The advantage of the ogham pole over the ogham tree is that one does not need to scar a mature tree to work it. A small sapling will do. The disadvantage is that its power is set, determined by the skill of its creator. It will not grow with the tree over time.

To create an ogham pole, you will require several things: a sword or machete, a carving knife, a small spade or hand trowel, a suitable sapling (preferably of wood appropriate to the nature of your working), and a natural place where the ogham pole may be set up. A suitable sapling should be no more than two or three inches in diameter—just enough to plane a flat area where an ogham can be carved. Most importantly, the sapling must have four prongs; that is, it must branch in four directions on top, one for each cardinal direction. If the sapling has more branches, you may cut the rest off, but a sapling of four natural prongs is especially potent, as it is a natural symbol and focus of the power of the cardinal directions.

Using what we know of druid herb harvesting procedure, and the example we have from Cuchulainn's legend, we can reconstruct much of the methodology of making an ogham pole. First, the appropriate sapling must be found. (Out of respect for others, this sapling must not come from private or public lands unless you have first obtained permission to harvest it.) You should have the sword or machete with you. Offer thanks to the divine powers of the earth or the wild (such as Tailtiu or Cernunnos) for the gift of the pole, and make an invocation to invest the pole with power. This invocation is best composed by you for the occasion and nature of the magic to be performed. Then you must cut the pole with the sword or machete. It is best if it can be done with a single, mighty swipe of the blade, so make it sharp. If you don't succeed in making the cut the first time, continue until the sapling is cut. The sapling will still be usable, but the less cuts the better.

I believe this has to do with cleanly cutting the sapling from the earth, the source of its earthy power, to leave the power already in it. It also reduces shock to the plant. Be careful not to cut yourself, and make sure no one is anywhere nearby as you swing.

Once the sapling is cut down, take your carving knife and flatten a side of the sapling about halfway up. Flatten only a few inches; just enough to inscribe your ogham. As you are working on the sapling, you should, in the tradition of the shaman, chant your incantation to a tune to which you have set it. Your mind must be cleared of other thoughts and focused on your magical work.

As with the tree ogham instructions, you should have already composed and have ready a concise ogham for the ogham pole. Carefully inscribe this ogham into the pole. Remember that vertical ogham script goes from the bottom up.

When the ogham pole is completed, use your trowel or spade to dig a hole a foot or so deep. Then stand over or near the hole and hold your sapling over your head with both hands. Invoke the Otherworldly powers to grant the request of the ogham you have carved and to recognize your pole as a perpetual reminder. Ask Cernunnos to guard the pole and restore it to life if he so chooses. Maintain focus on your magical work. Now, with both hands, forcefully thrust the pole down into the hole. This act symbolizes a mating between the pole and the earth, and a joining of you with nature as well. Then refill the hole with soil.

Now leave the area and put the magic from your mind. The sapling may grow new roots and continue to grow into a tree. This is an especially potent omen. It may not, however. If it does not, it does not indicate that it has lost its potency. It will continue to act as a magical influence and remind the Otherworldly powers what you have invoked with your ogham.

The most common uses for the ogham pole are druid hedges (magical barriers), warnings, and placers of geasa. As a druid hedge, the ogham pole marks the boundaries of sacred places. It will discourage all others from entry into the region. It serves to protect private property. The druid hedge may be wrought with such an ogham as to discourage only those of ill intent. Ogham poles also make potent protective talismans for use in evocative magic, including the summoning of Otherworldly beings. Like the ogham tree, they have broad usability.

Summary of the Ogham Magics

The ogham magics each have their own appropriate uses. Druid fires are especially potent, active magical forces. They transform their power rapidly through the form of fire, and are directed actively by the bardic arts of poetry and music as the power is being released. The druid fire is best used when great power is needed immediately.

The ogham tree is of tremendous potency, but it is a slow worker. You do not want to scar trees unnecessarily, not even with the tiny markings of an ogham, so you can often use the ogham pole for long-term magic. However, if you need great power over a long period, such as for the protection of a growing child, this is a good method. As the tree grows, so will the strength of the ogham. The ogham tree is a powerful invoker of Otherworldly power and a good marker of sacred places.

The ogham pole does not summon a great deal of magic at once, but it is potent. By the threat of an ogham pole, whole armies have been held back. It acts continually, and it is tied into bardic magic and the strength of the earth, so the ogham pole can have a potent effect over the long-term. It is a magic to use when time is not of the essence, and the changes you wish to work are subtle. It is a powerful protection for a region, as it lays a geas on whoever should cross it. Also, the ogham pole does not scar old trees, so it can be used much more often.

It is important to remember that the ogham is best used as a model of the bardic mysteries. Its true and deep understanding enables true-sight, which leads naturally to perceptive insight. It may also be used as a divinatory method as described above, where it serves also to enhance perception. For prognosticative divination, it is best to turn to a bardic/druidic understanding of omens, scrying, and the shamanic methods such as the shamanic journey.

Staff and Wand

Wands and staffs are a ubiquitous presence in nearly every religion, spiritual tradition, occult order, legend, and myth. We know for certain that the druids and bards possessed them as well, and used them for a variety of purposes. Math, the archetypal druid of Welsh myth, possessed a wand by which he obtained truth concerning Aranrhod's maidenhood. The filidh of

Ireland (Irish bards) carried wands of bronze, silver, or gold, depending on the filid's office and rank. In Cornish myth, an old, wicked druidess uses a wand of hazel to effect shape-changing, as does Math in his branch of the *Mabinogi*. Also, as we have discussed, the druid Dallan used yew wands to divine the location of kidnapped Etain. As the wand is so important to Celtic magic and to the bardic and druidic traditions, it is important that we examine them and their uses.

There appears to be three major types of wands: wands of divination, wands of enchantment, and ritual wands. Wands are variable in size—they may be only a foot or so in length, or as much as six feet or more (a staff). The materials from which they are constructed also vary. They may be made of various metals or woods. They may even be adorned with bells, runes, and other objects or marks.

Ritual Wands

Ritual wands are different from ogham wands and are used in ritual and to indicate status. There were three tiers of Irish bards. The lowest order, the common poets, carried a wand of bronze. The second order, the *anradh* [ONN-rah], carried a wand of silver. The highest order of the filidh, the teacher known as the *ollamh*, carried a wand of gold. These wands were shaped like a small branch, most likely the birch or willow (the bards' trees, though the rowan is another good candidate). These wands also probably were not made of pure metal. They were probably actually made from a branch of the tree and plated in the metal. These delicate wands could be, and often were, hung with tiny, sweet-sounding bells, and it seems the bells were in the form of apples, which was a sacred staple food of the ancient Celts.

These wands were probably awarded to bards as they progressed through their studies, the bronze going to initiates who had completed their beginning studies successfully. They were used primarily as symbols of office and for ritual purposes (to be covered in chapter 13). There are, however, legends of supernatural power attributed to them, especially regarding the silver wands.

The bard was a creature of peace. He did not fight in war, and no weapon was allowed to touch him. The silver wand of the anradh, the second rank of poets, and the gold wand of the ollamh, when shaken with their gently tinkling bells, were powerful invocations to peace. The chief bard Sencha was said to have waved his wand and silenced two armies on the verge of catastrophic bloodshed. Whether this occurred due to a magical property of the wand itself, or because of the tremendous respect the Celts held for their bards, we cannot say for certain. Yet from such magical tales as that of the sleep-bringing wand that was presented to King Cormac, son of Conn, by Manannan mac Lir of the Otherworld, we can glean the idea that its tranquility-bestowing power was in part magical. Its efficacy was probably augmented by the Celts' reverence for the bardic station.

How could a wand possess the power to invoke peace? Remember that the power of bringing deep sleep is one of the three virtues of bardic music, and this power is akin to invoking peace or tranquility. As the bard's music was often used to calm and relax, bards would naturally have come to be associated with peace. It is not surprising, therefore, that the bard, a creature of peace, could summon this gift through another tool of his office. The wand in its branch form symbolizes the bard's artistic crafts. The bells the wands were often adorned with especially symbolize bardic music. The wand, therefore, is a natural symbol of the peace that is part and parcel of bardcraft. This innate peace property is augmented by magical consecration, the embedding of enchantment within the wand (as is done with the ogham pole), and reverence for the bardic office.

Making and consecrating the ritual wand. It should not be too difficult to make or obtain such a ritual wand. If you have no skill at smithing, you can have a smith who works with precious metals make one up for you easily. One of the best places to find skilled silversmiths who can craft such fine work, and who will do it with the care it deserves, is through a Renaissance fair. At these fairs, which happen all over the U.S. and Canada these days, skilled crafters of old arts often assemble to show their wares. Many of them are themselves Pagans and will understand and respect your desire for such a creation. You can also turn to the Society of Creative Anachronism. The SCA is a society of medieval reconstructionists, which has grown to become a phenomenon. They, too, are widespread over North America these days and can even be found in Europe. The local library can usually provide you with SCA contacts in your area.

Having found a silversmith, explain to him or her what you need. Not only do you need a branch of the appropriate wood plated, but to be truly accurate to the tradition, you need a few holes through which to hang the bells of the poet's wand. I have not been able to find a reference saying how many of these bells there should be, so three and nine are good bets, as three and three times three are sacred numbers to the Celts. The bells should be shaped like tiny apples no bigger than the end of your thumb. They should be light, and are probably best made of silver, which is a resonant metal. Perhaps the silversmith knows of a supplier for such things, or he or she can probably make them, though they will doubtless be costly.

Having made your arrangements, all you need is a solid branch of the right kind of wood. I suggest hazel as, more than any other wood, it is symbolic of wisdom. Other good woods for the wand would be oak (also symbolic of wisdom), rowan (for good luck and bright magic), birch (symbolic of the bard), and willow (tree with a soul of music).

You should go into a forest and choose and cut this branch yourself. The day you go should be a day off that you have entirely to yourself. You should precede the trip with invocations to Brighid and Lugh, patroness and patron of bards, and meditations on filling the cauldrons of the soul, the nature of poetry and music, and the bard's work as a fulfiller, a catalyst of individuation and growth, and a worker of peace. To heighten this frame of mind, you may even wish to spend the night before in the forest, perhaps in a sacred place, to attune yourself with nature and the Otherworld and to remove the distracting effects of the artificiality of the urbanized, modern world.

In this myth-tuned state of mind, travel the forest and revel in its natural, wholesome beauty. Know that it is the very incarnation of timeless bardic truths, the ogham mysteries. Find a suitable tree and choose the right branch. The branch should be graceful and slender, but stout enough that it won't be easily broken—about an inch in diameter. It should be straight overall, but with some notches, twists, bends, even forks. In other words, it should look like a branch, not an artificially cut and polished rod that has had its naturalness entirely stripped away. Also, the poet's wand is small; it should be no more than sixteen inches in length.

Having found the correct branch, thank the tree, cut it off with a saw (do not rip it off as this could damage it and harm the bark of the tree), and bring it to your smith. The branch may need to be dried for a while before it can be plated. Have it plated in silver or bronze, depending on your skill. Not only is gold rather expensive, but only an ollamh, a master poet, should have a gold wand. Unless you are a master of poetry and the rest of the bardic arts, you are best going with a less-expensive metal. It is a virtue of bards not be boastful. Use gold only if you are a true master of the craft.

After the wand has been plated, you need to consecrate it. This is a special, one-time function and must be done right to imbue it with the fullest power and significance. Take it to a sacred place at a sacred time. I recommend Beltane, as it is the time of beginnings and a very powerful day for contacting the Otherworld. Whatever day you do the consecration on, it should be performed at dawn, for this is a time of newness, and this time is the beginning of the wand's sacred service.

You should be at the location prior to sunrise. An hour or two before dawn, arise. Take a cleansing bath in a lake or stream, if possible. Once you are fully awake and alert, clear your mind and give it to the forest and to the nature around you. Open yourself to the Old Ways and the old ones, and feel for imbas, the poetic mystery that lies at the heart of every forest and place of mystery. Feel the wet of morning dew; delve into the gleam of living sunlight catching gold in the morning mist. Relish in the songs of birds welcoming the dawn.

When you can see the sun just come over the horizon, hold the wand up to it. Recite a poem of awe for nature, dedication to bardry, and consecration of the wand. Close, and it is done.

You are most free to compose your own poetry, but I offer a model below:

> Golden orb crosses night's threshold,
> shadows retreat beneath rock and bough,
> mystery hides in the shady places,
> enchantment changes,
> moon gives way to sun,
> life springs with golden rays.
>
> Lugh lords the sunbeams brightly harping,
> Brighid bestows the poet's art,
> word and melody flow into daylight,
> mystery lives in shadows or not,
> enchantment is ever transformed
> in the bard by moon and sun.

The wand is the symbol of the poet's craft,
it sings like the chiming of the clarsach,
its voice resonates of the souls of old,
the hazel within the silver speaks of wisdom,
speaks of moon and fey light,
speaks of peace with true life.

The wand is given to the bard's way,
to the Old Way where shadow and light play,
where water sings an old, old song,
and timeless lore remembers riches,
of long-gone eras never gone,
in the here and now and where true dreams live.

The wand belongs to the bard's way,
may her voice be pure as silver,
true as moon,
bright as sun,
the poet's craft and the bard's art,
within the silvered hazel wood.

In the wood,
place of long-forgotten and long-sought lore,
in the wood,
in the wand, [*choose name*],
there be magic and music,
the timeless imbas of poetry.

This poem revels in natural imagery, especially those things dear to the Celt: the forest, the sweet earth, the moon, and the sun. It has been said that druidry is a solar religion and witchcraft is a lunar one. If they are, then bardry walks in the between place—the most Celtic place. Thus it praises sun and moon, Lugh and Brighid, Cernunnos and Ceridwen, equally. (It is important to remember that there aren't any actual sun or moon deities in the Celtic pantheon, but there are representatives of these natural forces, such as the aforementioned deities.)

The poem speaks of magic, which the bard understands is about mystery and sensitivity more than power. So magic is the thing that is always just in the shadows, just beyond sight. It is a bright sparkle in a dark place awaiting discovery, yet shy of it, for to know it changes it forever. Magic is the maybe of mystery; it is the very force of imbas that is the ability to perceive the what-could-be.

Then the poem names the wand. The Celts understood that in names were great power. Know the name of a person and you had control over him. This is because a name in Celtic thought is about much more than a few syllables that designate a person. No, names describe the person and are intimately associated with his being. A proper name is a condensed expression of his essence. So the poem names the wand, and in the doing it describes and claims its purpose, place, nature, and essence, for in the naming it is dedicated to the bard's way. Upon the completion of the poem, the wand is dedicated.

A bard of power could shake the wand and bring peace and sleep. However, the most important uses for the wand are as a powerful ritual symbol to be utilized during the Celtic holidays, the bardic initiation and passage through the bardic grades, and the dedication of instruments and all other material accouterments of the bard. These we will examine in chapters 13 and 14.

The wand is a tool of arcane power, but it is first a ritual instrument. It is a reminder of the bardic work of finding the soul. In this sacred individuation is the deep peace of the shaman, whom the bard is also, for the shaman is the walker between the worlds, the one who touches upon the shaded mysteries. The ritual wand is a visible reminder of that mysterious nature; it is a manifestation of it. Therein lies its greatest power.

Wands of Enchantment

We will now consider the more common form of wands: the wands of enchantment.

These wands, which may range in size from an eight-foot staff to a foot-long wand, are made of woods of potent magic-enhancing properties. The most potent is probably the rowan, also known as the mountain ash or the service tree. The hazel is also often chosen for a wand of enchantment.

These wands are simple to construct. They are little more than a branch cut from a tree, or, in the case of a staff, a shaft cut from a sapling. Once cut, the wand should be trimmed of twigs and the bark peeled off. Once dry, it should be sanded to make it comfortable to carry and splinter-free, and that is it. However, it is the process of harvesting and making the wand, and then finally investing it with power, that makes the wand special.

As with the ritual wand, you should spend the day in the forest. Begin by clearing your mind as you would for a magical work. Focus upon the task of acquiring a wand, and ask the lady of wisdom, Ceridwen, to guide you to the tree. Wander the forest and soak up its beauty and mystery until you find the tree that shall become your wand. Remember: in the forest you are in Cernunnos's realm, so thank him for the tree. Then take some time to get to know the tree: its shape, its size, its spirit. Sit at the base of it and meditate upon the bardic mysteries, especially the ogham mystery of that tree. When you feel ready, cut a branch from the tree for your wand, or cut the sapling if you intend to use a young tree for a staff, and take it to a sacred place.

At twilight, you should burn a druid fire of the same kind of wood and of wood representing the magical task you have in mind for the wand. Then, holding the wand nearby and directing the power of the fire into the wand with incantational poetry, name the wand as you named the ritual wand. Invoke the Otherworldly powers to bestow the wand with power, and name the purpose of the wand poetically, as we did for the ritual wand.

According to legend, there are several appropriate purposes for the wand of enchantment. One is shape-changing. This commonly has been thought to represent changing one's physical form into that of an animal, but this probably has a more shamanic purpose. By assuming animal shapes, the shamanic traveler gains the animal's powers, such as agility, speed, flight, or stealth, which help her to traverse and access the hidden mysteries of the Otherworld during the shamanic journey. The wand in hand is a tool for accomplishing this; it is a focus to help the mind work the necessary meta-morphosing in the Otherworld.

The wand is also used as a talisman for defense and offense. It may be used to invoke a barrier against harmful spiritual beings or magic, and as a charm for luck. As an offensive tool, the pointing of a wand directs a curse or geas on a being, which will rob that being of luck or fate it to an undesirable experience.

Just as Dallan wands are used to obtain truth through divinatory means, some legends say that if a person passes over a wand, then the truth will be revealed whether or not the person wishes it (see the story of Math and Aranrhod in the *Mabinogi*).

The innate magical property of certain woods, such as rowan, makes the wand an amplifier of magical energy, and gives it inherent protective charm-like powers. These innate properties will cause the wand to work at all times like an amulet, whether or not you are actively endeavoring to work magic. Yet the best use of the wand is as an object of focus and enhancement through which the bard exercises the powers of enchantment.

Finally, these less-expensive and easy-to-make wands can substitute for ritual wands. They do not symbolize the bard in any special way like the ritual wands do, but there is nothing wrong with using them for rituals, consecrations, and the like. Like druidry, bardry is a natural, wholesome, earthy path. It is not dependent on complex constructions or manmade wares, except in the crafting of an instrument, which is a fundamental part of the bardic art. Its demands reside in areas that bring about personal growth, not in areas that require wealth or materials.

Composing Spells

The arcane arts of bardry are not very complicated. They are not about intricately complex ritual, nor do they require intense mastery of the mind (though the more you have, the more powerful your spellcraft will be). The Celtic arcane arts are basic, earthy, and natural. They are based foremost upon the natural magical properties of material objects, and, secondarily, the magician directing her will on them. Of course, by adding bardic skills to the process through applying the primal powers of music and poetry, their power can be enhanced even more. Yet whether bardic skills are applied or not, the arcane arts will focus magical power and invoke the Otherworld to one's assistance.

Many material elements are used in Celtic arcane magic-working because they possess certain inherent properties. The properties are basically useless unless knowledge of how to use them is applied. Otherwise, their effects are unpredictable, if they occur at all. There are, though, a few exceptions. For example, the wood of the rowan tree possesses inherent protective power, as does an elfstone or a faerie stone, whether or not the user realizes it. Simply being in possession of such objects wards the possessor.

The purpose of the arcane arts is to allow the magician to work enchantment even when the mind has not been mastered to the point where the person can obtain that pure clarity and focus required of the mighty elder enchantments. However, be aware that at least some minimal level of mental focus is a must. While working the spell, the worker must have an ability to remain undistracted and mentally set on the task at hand. The purpose of the magical elements is to assist where skill over the mind leaves off. Thus, arcane magic is a potent, though lesser magic, being primarily the magic of the less-skilled mage.

In any case, designing and working the arcane magics is based on understanding the potencies of material things and applying spell-casting skills. You, the bard, should compose poetry as your incantational device and set it to music. All poetry should include an invocation to the Otherworld and a naming of the objective of the incantation. Notice I have not instructed you merely to describe your magical objective, but to name it. Remember what we discussed earlier. Names hold mighty power; they are more than just a few syllables that designate a person or thing. A true name springs from the essence of a thing. It is not given, but is a natural extension of the individual being. Bardic poetry is very much in touch with this idea of essential naming. In creating your incantations, you want to *name* what it is you want—that is, define and portray its essence. When such poetry is set to bardic music, it makes for a powerful magical blend.

Always remember that the poetic and musical skills of the bard are as much a mystic art dependent on imbas and a relationship with nature and the Otherworld as they are the products of technical mastery. It takes many years of study, meditation, and pursuit of the Otherworld and imbas to master the bard's skills. Thus, arcane magical elements are added to the apprentice bard's magical craft in order to compensate for lack of skill during the early years of growth into the craft.

Table 4 is a very brief list of some other objects of magical power within the Celtic system. Selecting the ones in sympathy with your intention will enhance your arcane workings.

There are thousands of objects of some magical significance. A complete study of them is a task for other volumes. Fortunately, there are numerous

Object	Power
Salt	A cleanser, repels evil spirits, a protector
Elfstone	A prehistoric arrowhead of Ireland; good luck
Faerie stone	A stone from a streambed with a natural hole through it; for protection from supernatural forces
Spider's web	A styptic, wound stopper, healing
Yarrow	Cures, potions, healings
Four-leaf shamrock	Good luck
Briar	Refreshment, energy
Vervain	Invulnerability, strength against poison
Turf	Repels the faerie-strike when burned and passed over and under an animal or human, supernatural protection
Mint	Intimacy
Hemlock	Love
Clay	From a new grave causes hatred; from forest loam or tilled farm soil brings life and growth
Gold	Sun
Silver	Moon
Sickle	Magical herb harvest
Cauldron	Wisdom, vitality, bounty

TABLE 4—Celtic Objects of Magical Power

books already in print that offer information on their magical properties. The important thing to remember is that bardry is a Celtic path. Your studies should focus on the magical qualities of objects as they are perceived by the Celts.

An Example of an Arcane Magical Working

The following is an incantation I have composed for seeking imbas. It is as much a sensual spell as a magical working. It is earthy, and yet it does not separate the body from the Otherworld or spiritual experience. So it is in harmony with the holistic principles of Celtic thought. As you study it, pay careful attention to the symbolic importance of the items of the incantation and the nature of the poetry. Also note its symmetrical construction, and the naming way it invokes Otherworldly powers, identifies imbas, and requests the gift of inspiration.

Calling down imbas. Items you will need: a small cauldron, hazel or oak wood, nine hazel nuts, pure water, smoked salmon, a white cloth, a cutting board, a cover for the salmon, a ladle (best if perforated to drain the water), a bottle of wine or mead, and a goblet.

Prepare yourself mentally by clearing your mind and making yourself receptive to imbas and focused on your task. Now, go to your sacred place before twilight. Prepare a regular fire of oak or hazel wood (the woods of wisdom), but do not light them. Use a lot of small twigs, dry leaves, and other fuels that will light quickly. (Be sure to build a natural fire. Never use artificial lighters such as barbeque fluid—it does not resonate with the naturalness of the Celtic way.) Set up a spit and hang the cauldron from it so it will be over the fire. Pour in the water and add the hazel nuts. Lay out the cloth and place the salmon on a cutting board upon it. Cover it to keep bugs off if you must.

As the sun reaches the horizon, light the fire. Accompanied by your harp or other instrument, sing a song of wisdom (of your own creation or chosen from Celtic folk music). Put yourself in a meditative state receptive to imbas. Feel Brighid moving about you, her face of wisdom bequeathing the poet's gift. Visualize Ceridwen, mistress of the cauldron of wisdom, stirring the cauldron where the broth of knowledge boils. Allow the music to move within your spirit, touching and opening up your inmost soul to the Otherworld. Allow the inner lights to mingle with the shadows in the place where true dreams live, that place where myth exists in the mind.

When the sun drops entirely behind the horizon, recite the poem of incantation:

> Gwydion sought only to serve his mistress,
> the Lady Ceridwen sought only to bless her son.
> But wisdom goes to whom it will,
> the gift chooses the gifted.
>
> And Brighid smiles upon her poets,
> her triple face illumines the smith of words,
> and wisdom of the deep essences
> is the naming craft of the filid.
>
> I am the poet of the mysteries,
> I seek the cauldron's lore,

the hazel's insight,
the oak fire's transformation.

Pounding essences into verse,
verse for dreams and dreamers,
words that ring true with the essences beneath,
I desire the poet's heart.

Now, remove the nuts from the cauldron. Set them down on the cutting board with the salmon. As darkness falls, eat the nuts and salmon, both symbols of druidic wisdom. Be aware of their significance, of the legends of the hazel nuts of knowledge at the pool, and of the salmon of wisdom who ate them and were then eaten by the druids and bards. Visualize yourself ingesting wisdom as did the bards of legend. Afterward, drink the wine or mead and enjoy the coming of the night. Relish the twilight in the naturalness of your sacred place and the wild beauty of the world. It is the home of the gods and the source of imbas. Feel imbas dancing within the deepening shadows of the growing dark. Feel it merge with the world at the between time. Soak it in.

A Final Note

I encourage you to experiment with composing your own arcane enchantments. Since the bards of legend composed their magic, this is part of the process of rediscovering the path of bardry. Base the poetry of your incantations upon the beauty of tradition. Yet within the bounds of the tradition you are free to develop it as you will. Rightly crafted bardic poetry rings of the Old Ways, yet it is always fresh and alive. These two important essences of Celtic magic—timelessness and newness—amalgamate in yet another paradoxical oneness.

Bardic Garb

The way of bardry is not about things, it is about forces and essences, mystery and enchantment. It is also adaptive. It is a path designed to meet the spiritual needs of the contemporary person by linking him or her to the timeless Old Ways without shunning the fact that we live in a modern world. So bardry does not require any particular garb. All it requires is a heart reaching for imbas, a spirit that loves nature and mystery, and a little artistic skill. I see no reason to require any special clothing for the bard, neither for ritual purposes nor for daily living. The bard's harp (or other instrument) is his or her badge of office. The wand is another. So is the craft of imbas-inspired eldritch poetry, which is a uniquely bardic art.

Even if we were to associate specific costumes with bardry, whose would we choose: those of the Bretons, the Irish, the Welsh, the Gallic or Iberian Celts? Even if we were to settle on a particular tribe of the Celts, what era should we choose to draw the costumes from: the B.C.E. times, the pre-Christian C.E. era, the Middle Ages? Styles change over time, and the Celts of fifth-century C.E. Wales would have little resembled the Celts of fifth-century B.C.E. Iberia. There is no comprehensive "Celtic" style.

However, the Celtic spirit did ring through in all their dress, and being clad in their manner may help set you in the right frame of mind when you practice your craft, especially after having been immersed until that moment in the demands of the modern, urban, techno-centered world. The important thing to understand is that the manner of dress is entirely optional. One's wardrobe does not make one a bard anymore than it makes one a doctor.

I personally suggest that you dress in costume for rituals, and the rest of the time practice in casual garb. For some magical workings (such as those involving a deep resonance with nature) and meditations, you may wish to go skyclad. For rituals, and depending on your personal desires, you may wish to create something as elaborate as a full replication of late medieval Welsh raiment, or something simpler, such as a Scottish-style tunic and kilt. You might find adequate a simple cloak.

Cloaks are certainly one of the most powerfully mood-setting choices of garment. They are also among the easiest to make. Old accounts from the Irish writers indicate that crimson, purple, and green were the colors the old Gaelic Celts preferred for their cloaks. There is good evidence that the druids chose white. As crimson and purple were royal colors, it is probable that bardic cloaks were green—very appropriate for the earthy bards who were so attuned to the natural world from which imbas flowed. Some texts refer to the bards' cloaks being varicolored, striped, and speckled as well. Texts by Iolo Morgannwg indicate bardic raiment should be sky-blue, but as

Iolo forged much of his documentation, most all his contributions must remain suspect.

The Author's Recommendations

I suggest you make a forest-green cloak for ritual and some magical uses. It is probably truest to the old tradition. Cloaks are very simple to make, and, more than any other single garment, seem to convey the spirit of the Old Ways. A hooded cloak virtually wreaks of mystery and enchantment. This garment alone should do nicely for most of your needs.

Add to this minimal costume your magical wand or staff of rowan or hazel (I recommend rowan). Not only do these woods have powerful protective and magic-amplifying properties, but the wand and staff, like the cloak, are potent mood-setters. Wands and staffs are so closely associated with magic that they seem to speak directly to the archetypal regions of the unconscious mind, declaring, "This is an enchanted thing!"

You should consider spell-casting skyclad when working protective enchantments. The old Gallic Celtic warriors fought skyclad as a sign of their faith in the gods to protect them. Likewise, for workings of the most powerful protections (such as creating ogham trees and poles to ward sacred sites) and the calling of luck, it may be most appropriate to also work skyclad. However, that is not by any means mandatory. It is most important to go with what makes you comfortable.

The truest badge of the bard is your instrument and your poetic craft. With these, you communicate the enchantment that arises from the depths of your inmost soul. Clothes, like other magical objects used in the arcane arts, are focusers. They help put your mind in resonance with your work. A master bard who has learned to harness her mind at will uses other material things for their resonances (as enhancers and amplifiers), and for mood setters to help in magical focus. Yet the bard works with art and imbas. In a sense, all the rest is only glamour.

PART III

The Power of Legend

chapter ten

The Language of Myth

*Everything exists, everything is true, and
the earth is only a little dust under our
feet.*

William B. Yeats, *The Celtic Twilight*

Shadowy myths, near-forgotten legends, rumors best whispered—this is
the stuff of folklore. Vile villainy, hellish curses, and fey enchantment
are the key elements of such tales; damsels in need of rescue, old
witchy crones, valiant princes, and poor-but-heroic paupers are the characters.
Folklore is about fairy tales; pretty lies that have no bearing on the real world
or the contemporary person. It is a relic of a bygone age comprised of stories to
charm children's dreams. They are verbal toys told for fun and best forgotten
afterward. Folklore's only value is as an artifact of superstition and an old way
of entertainment.

At least, that is how contemporary people are taught to view folklore.
While it is true that some folklore is no more than imaginative fairy tales primarily remembered and repeated for its entertainment value, all folklore has
psychological value. The very fact that folklore is remembered and repeated
bespeaks its relevance to the human psyche. Such tales teach us about culture,

courage, determination, patience, and countless other lessons of great value. They are satisfying in that they speak to our inmost fantasies, allow us to unconsciously live out our desires and express our fears, and provide examples of others who have surmounted the odds.

For all this, folklore is also so much more. It is a window to the past that reveals the perspective and thought of our ancestors in a way more intimate than any historical account can ever hope to accomplish. Anthropologists are recognizing that recorded history usually tells us little more than the ambitions and doings of monarchs and other nobility, the fights and flights of armies, and the gross trends of entire societies. Yet history is much more than the tale of wealth and nobility, for it is the common people who are the very foundation and force that makes a society work.

Folklore is a relic of the thoughts and dreams of the common people. It circumnavigates history to provide a view of the ordinary members of society. Through its mode of story, it relates the imagery that was significant to them, and tells of their lives, hopes, and aspirations. Through the actions of its characters, it can teach about the daily chores, the requisite skills, and the cultural niches of those people. Thus, folklore is a significant anthropological tool in the historical sense.

Likewise, folklore is a significant anthropological tool in the contemporary sense. Folklore is only remembered and passed on because it is relevant and meaningful, so it provides a dependable perspective on modern culture and minds. It teaches us about everything from modern thinking on sexuality to career orientation. It treads in the realm of myth, reflecting modern concepts of the Otherworld through encounters with the supernatural. It provides insight into our cherished goals, and reveals the forces of sexism, bigotry, and hatred that pervade any society. Folklore provides a way for the societal mind to speak frankly, and by using an ambiguous semimythical medium, it can speak with little fear of reprisal, and without the pangs of guilt. Thus, folklore serves as the conscience of society.

These are mighty truths that were as meaningful to the bards of old as they are for the peoples of the contemporary era. They make folklore more than a storyteller's stock of tall tales, they reveal it as a looking glass, a scrying mirror of insight, and a poet's dark language all at once. The stories of folklore reflect us as whole beings, revealing our darknesses and our bright places. As the product of a culture's unconscious, it is a truthsayer that speaks without fear and without partiality. Yet its truths are concealed behind a careful ambiguity. Without cultural knowledge, its lessons, accusations, and declarations may easily go unrecognized. Its ethical and entertainment value is apparent to all, but its deeper meaning is revealed only to those who have an understanding of the context from which it originates. Often it can take considerable understanding to glean the true mysteries from a tale of folklore.

So folklore is a poet's dark speech, and like mystery, it is truth hidden in shadows. To see it requires the sight that looks into the depths and perceives the shaping of the formless shadows. It requires true-sight. To the true perceiver, folklore is a healing force. It is a kind of psychotherapy—a tool of the Celtic hero's quest for individuation and growth—because it reveals and makes conscious essential truths of our own being that otherwise would have remained unknown. As such, folklore is an essential ingredient in the magic of fulfillment. Is it any wonder then that the bards were tellers of tales, and that folklore was their stock and trade?

Yet folklore is more. Some of it records ancient knowledge in areas as diverse as geography, astronomy, herbal lore, and occult truths. Through analysis of folklore, archaeologists have located lost cities and rare treasures. Through it, alchemists sought the path to the spiritual philosopher's stone wherein the slag of the spirit was cleansed and transformed into gold. Through it, the great psychologists sought out the secret symbols of the archetypes, and traced evidence of the collective unconscious. From this we find that folklore is ancestral memory, a harbinger of literal and spiritual truths, and a revealer of the worlds. Folklore is a real force that can be summoned by the power of mind and storycraft skill in this world and the Other. It is natural then that the bard, master crafter of song and story, would choose folklore as his medium of knowledge.

Why Celtic Lore?

The bardic student must recognize that it is essential to study, understand, and appreciate folklore. The bard is the living memory, the healer, the poet shaman, and the toucher of the Otherworld. Folklore is a great medium of imbas, and knowledge of folklore empowers the bard with the inspiration needed to fulfill those roles. Knowledge of folklore also enhances the gift of true-sight. To benefit fully from folklore, the bard must know it in every sense: for its artistic, anthropological, psychological, mythological, and magical value. Since the bard's way is a Celtic path, he or she must be especially familiar with Celtic lore in order to be grounded in the tradition that gives bardry its fullest context and meaning.

As the living memory, one of the bard's purposes is to preserve the Old Ways—not just as annotations in a book to reside on a dusty shelf at the back of a library, but as a vibrant and meaningful living tradition. The bard, like the druid, reminds the people of man's relationship to nature and the Otherworld, and keeps alive the philosophy of the old Celts who were ever aware of this dynamic oneness. It would be a sad, empty day should the time ever arrive when the ways of the Celt were entirely forgotten and no longer lived. In dismissing this fundamental, simultaneously earthy yet spiritual tradition, we would lose a vital part of our humanity—the part that most separates us from the artificial technological veneer that has come to dominate life in this modern era. We would bid farewell to that part of us that is organic and spiritual by amalgamating it entirely with the mechanistic and physical.

It is also fundamental to study the Celtic folklore because it is one of the oldest and richest records of the Old Ways. Since the Celts were so widespread and enjoyed contact with so many differing peoples, theirs is a rich tapestry of native and incorporated traditions that stretches back thousands of years to the pre-Celtic inhabitants of the Western world. While many of the cultures who shared the ancient world with them have become extinct, the insular Celts and the Celts of West Europe still survive. A study of their surviving lore can lend invaluable insight into the Old Ways of life and thought. Thus, Celtic folklore offers a window into the past.

As a people who lived in oneness with this world and the Other, the Celts were one of the most spiritually aware of peoples. Because their psychology was ever about the struggle of bending reality to fit the mythic ideal, they were not averse to calling upon magic to make real that place of true dreams in the here and now. Thus, Trogue Pompey could truly write that the Gauls outdid all others in augury. The Celtic folklore is replete with supernatural phenomena, and in tale after tale it is seen mingling with and influencing the here and now. The veils between the worlds are thin in the Celtic lore, and their mythology teaches the shaman how to pass between them and use the one to shape the other.

We see that Celtic folklore makes a tremendous psychological and magical resource. It is a treasure trove for those who take the time to understand it. For those who will patiently and intimately get to know it and its lessons on magical practices and spirituality, it provides invaluable and comprehensive insight. In the remainder of this chapter we will study the symbology and lore of the Celtic folk as a vehicle for healing.

The Healing Power of Folklore

Folklore possesses a healing power. It contains lessons that preserve the elder knowledge of healing herbs, natural substances, and wild forces. More importantly for the bard's work, it possesses in itself a salve for the soul. As a reflector of truth, it brings before us our real selves. It presents to us our negative and positive sides. It reflects our shortcomings along with our strengths and talents. It forces us to confront every aspect of our being.

On an outer level, this offers a healing power in the form of relieving stress. Through the story, the listener vicariously lives and resolves the problems of the hero or heroine. By it, he or she rights wrongs, brings justice, avenges the victim, and puts an end to the victimizer.

Yet folklore possesses a deeper soul-healing potential on a more profound psychological level. If one ponders it deeply, it becomes a form of psychotherapy. In the manner of the practice of an analytical psychologist, folklore reflects unbiased truths dark and light, shameful and proud, or simply indifferent, and forces one to face up to the total being within. This honest confrontation with every aspect of one's personal being is the key step to individuation. It is the fundamental process of coming to an understanding of each true part of the self, and integrating the conscious with the unconscious.

This work requires a deep insight into folklore, an insight that can only arise from earnest study, truth-seeking, and meditation. It requires much effort, but the end product is the development of a true being; a person who knows him- or herself, a person who understands his or her needs, and who is not defined by societal and cultural expectations, but by the being within. That being is the self—the primal and most important archetype. We are born with a semihidden nature that is always extant as the very core of our being whether we are living, dead, in the here and now, or the Otherworld.

When we are born, we know the self; we are one with it. However, societal pressures force us to split from it. In the immaturity we all experience at the beginning times of our lives, the self archetype is shattered (this can last from birth until whatever age the person finally finds the inner strength to stop the fracturing). The self archetype splits into specialized areas designed around survival, fitting in, acceptance, and dealing with our dark side. We develop a persona that is the façade we present to the world. Men hide their feminine aspects in the anima and women hide their masculine aspects in the animus. We conceal our dark nature within the shadow. We create a tiny piece of the self to face the world, partly in order to conceal our true whole self from the world because we fear our whole being would be found unacceptable. We also do it partly to conceal the whole self from ourselves because society and culture have left us poorly trained to face our full being-hood in entirety. Instead, we learn to live through only a tiny piece of our fullness: the ego.

Each of these pieces of the fractured soul lives outside the self, orbiting it like planets around a star. These planets are dead without the star. They are essentially massive complexes; pieces of the soul constructed to fulfill certain needs. They provide the ego (the consciously aware part of our being) with a selection of guises to use so that our whole being need never be revealed to the world, and especially so that it need never face the entire self. The self, which is tied into the total being as well as the collective unconscious, is so deep, so massive, and so complex that it is simply overwhelming to the unprepared ego. It is definitely out of place among the shallow personas that the vast majority of people present. These fractured personalities are at best incomplete, and at worst superficial. They exist as the constructs of immaturity. As we mature, we naturally begin to reintegrate them. Most people never do more than a little reintegration. Some avoid it altogether. Integration hurts; it forces us to discard accepted boundaries, to look into the deep, dark places we may rather pretend don't exist, and to delve into our true natures, regardless of anyone's (including our own) expectations.

When people look inside themselves and fear what they see, it is because they have learned to value themselves based on someone else's expectations. Those someone-elses may be important individuals, or culture or society as a whole. Here are some examples: a common Western cultural teaching that we receive from birth is that our sexuality should be concealed. So we live in shame of that fundamental and wonderful part of being alive, and whisper of it only among friends and in the dark. In some cultures we may learn that displaying our emotionality is bad form, so we (especially men) try to hide it beneath a false veneer of strength or indifference. Finally, we all try, at some time or another, to be something we aren't to win someone's affection. This is an attempt to change who we are to fit someone else's preconceived idea of what a desirable person is. In all these cases, we are allowing ourselves to be sculpted and packaged by external forces to fit someone else's conception of right. We are taught to hide from ourselves, our natures, our dreams and desires from the beginning, and tremendous cultural forces go to work right away to make us into another cog in the societal wheel. It is no wonder the self fractures. This unnatural casting creates fear, dishonesty, and anxiety about our inner nature. We learn to reject and loathe what we find on self-examination.

Sadly, most of us are not prepared to deal with what lies just beyond the aware ego either. In our world, it is the romantics who are most naturally in touch with all the sides of their being: the poets and the painters, the musicians who play from the heart, and the writers who shed the offspring of their souls. These kinds of people are considered eccentrics or even mad. They are tolerated in more open cultures, and shunned in others. Among some cultures, they are simply silenced. These people are the shining examples of the soul rejoining; the Otherworld and the here and now enmeshed. Their creative power is the magic that springs from the between place where myth and reality are meeting within them. The fractured self fears the reunification that the most gifted artists present in their creative works. It resists the artist-seers just as the split personalities of the multiple personality disorder victim resist amalgamation. They view the rejoining as countless little deaths rather than what it really is: entry into fuller life. So the dreams of the romantics are seen as odd, flighty, though perhaps strangely beautiful imaginings, then shrugged off as pointless. Their inmost beauty is never touched upon.

Reunification is the whole and healthy state; it is the gathering of the real being from beneath the layers of protective complexes. It is what the sacred wheels of life bring us inevitably toward. Integration is the process of reunification, and individuation (the development and acceptance of one's true individuality) is the fruit.

Pioneer psychologist Carl Jung truly defined the idea of integration, but he did not invent it. It has been the work of the wise throughout time. Nearly every folklore branch speaks of people who have sought perfection. Some pursue it through meditation, others through searching the world's wisdom, and still others through occult lore. The way of the bard incorporates all of the above. It adds to it the shaman's way—journeying between the worlds and through the regions of the mind on a quest to reunite the soul. It also adds to it the artist's way—expressing the inmost soul through poetic, musical, and story creation. In addition, it incorporates the powerful tool of folklore.

Through folklore, the true being can be personified as a villain, hero, magical animal, or enchanted artifact. On the surface, these are only the elements of a tale. To the one who understands why folklore bears such powerful meaning, it becomes a tool of soul searching. Each element is a symbol of the potential being. To ponder and meditate upon folklore, and to learn from it in the deepest sense, is therapeutic; it will point the way toward integration and lead the soul to wholeness and self-acceptance.

folklore as Dark Language

Psychologists have long known that dreams are a necessary part of life. For whatever reason, our minds need them. Perhaps they are expressions of the soul that arise in a private world where the unconscious mind can live its desires and explore its fears safe from any real consequences. Perhaps they are discharges of thought; the shedding of too much cerebration at the end of the day in order to reset and reorient the mind. Whatever the case, it is naturally healthy to dream.

Dreams are rich in symbolism, and when understood and properly applied to the needs of the dreamer, they have incredible therapeutic power. Folklore is very much like this. At a minimum, it is always therapeutic—providing valuable entertainment, relieving stress, and satisfying and encouraging the imagination. Yet just as the symbolism of dreams cannot be fully understood and taken advantage of for psychological healing without the assistance of one trained in understanding it, so Celtic folklore's deep powers of soul healing will not work without an illuminator. To be truly effective, a deep bardic understanding must be cultivated in the mind of the listener. So, like the dark language of the poets, which could only be grasped by those ready with the knowledge to interpret the code, the Celtic myths subtly hide their deepest truths from all but the mind that has been prepared to receive them. Most of the rest of this chapter will deal with the symbolism and meaning of Celtic folklore.

The Forest

The forest represents mystery, enchantment, danger, and promise. It is the place where magics lurk just in the shadows, always on the verge of moving into vision. It is the concealer, the keeper of mysteries. There is nothing negative in this function, for it is protective. It hides the inner truths from all but those who have earned the wisdom to perceive them. Yet the deep mysteries are things that can be fathomed, but never truly revealed. To do so would rob them of a vital, dynamic quality—the promise of the unknown, the wonder of shadows. It would make them no longer mysterious.

The forest betokens danger in that among the mysteries it conceals are some things not friendly toward or aligned with mankind. Yet even more importantly, the mysteries are not meant to be known by the unworthy. This occultic quality is protective as well as innate. Just as the mysteries must be concealed to protect their nature and magical qualities, to reveal them to one and all would make them dangerous and threatening. This is because most humans want things to be clear and to fit into their perspective. Humans instinctively fear those things that challenge their worldview. Perhaps this is why magicians, such as druids and shamans, and other seekers, such as gnostics and occultists, have been shunned and feared by peoples throughout the world. They have dared to pursue the mysteries that challenge human preconceptions. Only the prepared mind is ready to receive the mysteries and can benefit from them. To those who are unprepared and stumble across them, they are fearful, even terrifying, forces that lead to madness or even destruction.

The forest can represent the mind as well: the tangles of complex and confused thought; the glades of clarity; the shadows of uncertainty; the deep, old places of the collective unconscious; the groves where shadow and light, and myth and reality mingle freely. The forest as the Celt perceives it is perhaps the best representation of the mind, and it is deeply ingrained into our beings as an archetypal symbol.

The Druid

The druid is the wise one—the one who knows the mysteries, who is familiar with the Otherworld, and the one who wields mystic power. The druid is a walker between the worlds, and knows both well. He is capable and mysterious, and represents magic incarnate in humanity. He represents what we might attain if we should devote ourselves to his quest.

Conversely, the druid may represent a dark, dreaded force—a person of great power that can neither be understood nor dealt with by conventional means. An evil druid is a terrible thing, and well deserving of fear. Like the forest, the dark druid reminds us that along with the bright side of mystery, dangers lurk in the shadows as well. Only the prepared ought walk the realms of mystery.

The positive druid, the being in white, represents a being to aspire toward. He is a person who is fulfilled and in control of his life and mind, and he is knowledgeable of the meaningful truths—the deeper meanings and natures of things.

The druid may also be represented by the poet, the harper, or the occultic scholar. These are the other sorcerous types of the Celtic tradition. Druids and the like may be male or female.

The Hero/Heroine

The hero is the one who faces great odds for the good of others. The hero's path requires a willingness to grow personally in every possible way. It demands extraordinary work, effort, and dedication. The way of the hero is not so much about the victory at the end of the quest, but the path taken along the way, for therein is the opportunity for growth and lasting, meaningful improvement. If, after the dragon is slain, the hero becomes the old person, mundane, ordinary, unremarkable, not grown, and unindividuated—then his or her fight was of little avail.

The hero's quest is a long and demanding one, and every Celt is called to it. In one way or another, it is the path of each and every one of us. The hero may wield a sword, or he may wield a harp. Whichever it is, the goal is the same: to grow personally, to expand the self and fulfill every potential, and to work good service for others along the way. It is a challenging, life-long path, but the rewards of fulfillment and growth more than make it worth it.

Extraordinary Animals

In Celtic folklore, animals of extraordinary powers abound. Stags know the portals to the Otherworld and back again. Pigs are slain for the feast and found alive the next day. Horses give their masters wise counsel. Ravens portend the future. The list runs as long as the lore of the nature-oriented Celtic folk.

These animals bespeak magic and primal enchantment. They carry with them the lesson that we are never far from the Otherworld, and that its magics should be expected to come from the most seemingly ordinary of places.

Shamanically, they teach us lessons about the creatures the shaman will encounter. The fox is sly; be cautious. The raven is the Mórrígán's minion; be very wary. The bear is strong and solitary; a good friend if you can but earn his friendship. The wolf is a hunter of uncertain nature; unswervingly faithful in friendship, but terrible as an enemy, he is one to learn from and respect. The salmon conveys wisdom. The weasel is mean-spirited and unlucky. The wren is wise as a druid, but a betokener of ill-luck at the wrong time. The list is extensive and broad.

One of the most interesting things about the extraordinary animals we meet in folklore is that when they talk or show uncanny knowledge or magical powers, we think it little extraordinary at all. It is almost expected. This is part of the magic of folklore: it possesses the ability to make the paranormal seem normal, and to fit the Otherworld into our lives. Extraordinary animals are folklore's way of keeping mystery alive in our hearts, and of never letting us forget the magic that gives existence meaning and beauty. Their appearance is a manifestation of the therapeutic power of the folktale.

Faerie

There are many kinds of faerie: from the little winged folk of myth of the past few centuries to the mighty Tuatha de Danaan and Fomori of the most ancient Irish legends. They are beings of magic and speak of elder mysteries and eldritch enchantment. They remind us that the universe is broader than what we can see and full of mysteries we can only strive to understand.

The faerie are magical, but very real, and often earthy beings, as individual as you and I. Though some may look very much like us, they are alien—not human at all. The legends document that they are keenly intelligent, yet possess very different minds with thought processes, values, and motives quite foreign to our own. They cannot be fully understood by any human being. Some are disposed toward mankind, and others are against us, but in all cases the sidhe must be dealt with cautiously. They are powerful, and even the good-natured among them may be easily offended by behavior or statements we consider innocuous. Befriend a faerie and you have a great friend. Earn one's wrath, and you have a powerful enemy. Be cautious and use wisdom when going amongst the good folk.

The Otherworld

The whole concept is very complicated. It is another world, yet it also seems to be many other worlds. The worlds are entirely separate from this reality, yet the separation is not complete. The barrier between the Otherworld and the here and now is most times fairly solid, but never entirely so. At certain times and at certain places it is all but nonexistent. By intent or by accident, one can enter the Otherworld, and beings from there can enter our world as well.

Yet the Otherworld also represents that place in the mind where myth lives. It represents that realm on the verge of the archetypes where the collective unconscious and the individual mind shape old lore into symbols we know as legends and which flow to us in dreams.

The Otherworld, then, denotes places of significantly different natures. On one hand, it is a very real yet mental realm where the mind perceives the things that live in the misty depths of the unconscious, and where the myths and legends of old may wander and work and affect us even when we are engrossed in the hard-edged material reality of the here and now. On the other hand, the Otherworld is an actual external world or worlds; a universe of different natural laws and magical, alien beings.

Yet, are they so different? They both reach us in a profound place of the psyche. Contact with either changes us in significant ways. Whether we speak of the Otherworld within or without, we speak of a place where mystery and supernatural beings dwell. It is a place where wonder is everywhere and things are known to be not what they seem. The Otherworld is full of primal mystery. Its reality keeps alive the wonder of being, the wonder a child sees when snow first falls and washes the world white, the marvel the painter feels when he sets out to capture a beautiful woman with pigments and oils, the awe a poet senses at the sight of sky and forest staining a creek blue-green while smooth, rounded stones give it a voice and song all its own.

The Otherworld speaks of mysteries great and small, and the perpetual amazement we should always know to be part of them. It is no wonder that the bard is ever seeking the Otherworld, and no wonder that from it flows imbas.

The Gods

The Celtic gods represent many things. While the Celts were pantheists and animists, many scholars hold that the druids believed that above them all was one most high being. This being is best reflected and conceived through the forms of the numerous incarnations of the lesser gods and nature itself. These incarnations were highly individual; each possessed his or her own unique nature and existence.

Aside from the old ones—the great god or gods who were responsible for creation—it seems that most of the Celtic gods are not so different from you and me. They have human fallibilities and weaknesses, and their own individual talents and strengths. Their universal lesson is that what they are, we could be like. This is not to say that we, too, could become as powerful as gods, but that we can attain like natures. As we grow—as we individuate and gain an understanding of the mysteries—we approach their fullness. It is a part of the Celtic hero's quest to seek to be like the gods. The goal is not power or prestige or recognition, but growth and fulfillment—always growth and fulfillment. The highest end result is to become our true, full selves, and live at our fully realized potential.

Then, over all the gods is the great god-creator of all things. Toward this being we ever progress, a spiraling pattern from wheel to wheel. This is the quest toward perfection, the reaching of the finite toward the infinite. Along the way is the realization of mystery, the touching of enchantment, and the creation of art. The way is dear and enriching, full of promise and potential. As the druids said, death is only a midpoint between a long life. The goal of life after life is perfection. We may never reach it, but that is not important. The wonder of the hero's quest makes the road itself the goal.

Woman

The old pre-Christian Celtic culture has been remarked as being one of the earliest to accord equal opportunity and respect toward women. Classical accounts speak of Celtic women fighting side by side with their men. Ammianus Marcellinus, a Roman historian, described the female Celtic warriors as being as fierce as the men.[1] Yet a woman needn't be a warrior to be fulfilled or have equal status. To the contrary, there are far more important aspects of femininity than the soldier's trade.

Celtic women were as free to choose their spouses as were the men. Divorce could be initiated by either spouse. Celtic women could rise to rulership. The historical Boadicea, whose battle against Roman oppression is legendary, was a great queen over her people. Yet if a woman chose to be a mother and home-maker, those were also rightly recognized as good and noble trades. Considering the status and respect accorded to Celtic women, it is not unreasonable to think that they were also free to trade, hunt, and otherwise be full and free participants in life.

The insular Celts saw femaleness in the moon. She was the mother-goddess who caused growth, watched over her children, nurtured in gentleness and love, and revived the sun in the midst of his midwinter death. The Gallic Celts saw woman in the sun. There she bestowed life-giving light and warmth upon the world—an act of nurture and love.

Whether her light came by night or by day, the woman as goddess was seen as the mother, the soil, the good nurturer, and a giver of precious light. She was full of mystery, brave and strong, and watched over her children in the darkness. Plus, through it all she was very beautiful and intensely feminine.

The Celts thought of womanhood as a very full essence. She was a being full of potential that was expressed individually in infinite ways. There was no reason a woman could not be strong and brave, a plier of a trade or a mother at the hearth, and all the while profoundly feminine. Such diverse potential is part of the feminine mystery. Indeed, just as one female is the great mother goddess Tailtiu of the soil of Ireland, so the lord of death and nightmares is also a lady in the person of the Mórrígán. Femaleness spanned the spectrum.

The Bard or Poet

On one level, this person is an artist and a magician. More importantly, this is a person questing after imbas—the deep sight that sees the between. In the between are the mysteries, the enchantment, and the magic of being. In the between is full perception—the essence of true-sight—and the bard is a true-seer. His poetic gift, his dark tongue, and his magic all arise from an awareness of the subtle and the sublime things overlooked by others. The bard and his kin—smiths, sculptors, musicians, and other artists—represent perception and the quest for beauty, wonder, and enchantment. They are the representatives of the search for the things that give existence meaning.

The Harp

Many myth cycles speak of creation arising from a note, a song, or music. Others speak of great deeds arising from the power of melody. By melody, the bard Amairgin calmed the sea when the Tuatha de Danaan summoned its fury against the invading Milesians. By music, the Dagda sang the enemies of his people to sleep. By music, heroes summoned the denizens of the Otherworld.

Today, in the shamanic practice, music is recognized as a meditative tool. Some schools teach that there is a certain note or tune that resonates with every individual person. With this tune the person can reach for the Otherworld or sing a lost soul back to health.

In the old Celtic thought, the power of music is best represented by the harp, which to them represented the very paragon of musical instruments. Its form is graceful and as elegant as poetry, yet it is as strong as a warrior hero. Its voice is one of magic bells and fey chirrups. In the hands of a skilled harper, wind can be played soughing through boughs and whispering fey secrets. Rain can be conjured falling in sparkling drops. Passions from the deepest sadness to the highest joy can be evoked, and peace can be conveyed. The harp is, then, a magical being in itself. In the hands of a skilled bard, great wonders can be wrought. Other instruments have similar powers if very skillfully manipulated, but for the Celt there is no other like the harp. Simply to touch the strings evokes shivers.

The harp, then, represents primal magic—the calling forth of passion and the evocation of creation. It is mystery made manifest in sound.

Music

Music was and still remains one of the great treasures of life in the Celtic mind. The lords of old Celtica paid handsomely for it. A harper commanded respect and hefty fees wherever he or she went. Players of pipes, crwths, and other instruments were welcome all over. There was always an inn ready to provide food and lodging for a musician's services. On the road, a farm home was always open to the traveling musical performer. Music was a gift to be cherished. It speaks of beauty in all its forms in a language that transcends words—a language of pitch, tone, and harmonies that communicate directly with the heart.

Even today music is recognized as having the power to heal. Hospitals around the country are beginning to offer programs in harp therapy and psychologists are applying music therapy. The right music can soothe away stress. The Celts recognized music as a primal power of all kinds of potential. It could call down a curse and stay armies, or it could bring joy and make friends. It was a primal magical force to be respected, cherished, and honored.

Nature

The Celts are noteworthy for their respect of nature. While it is doubtful that the druids actually worshiped trees, they did believe that the highest, purest divine powers were directly reflected in them, especially the oak and the yew. They probably believed that some aspects of nature were even linked to the divine. There is reason to think that the druids saw the oak as an actual link with Teutates, the god of thunder, and in the stag they saw Cernunnos, god of nature.

Because of this profound spiritual respect for nature, the Celts maintained a closeness to it. They respected its flora and fauna, lived in harmony with its seasons, and reveled in its beauty. Nature represents a pure force, entirely independent of man, yet one to which man is inextricably bound.

Too often today we become entangled in the endless morass of a technocratic society. Our lives are centered in buildings and corporations, the money we can exchange for our time on this wondrous planet, and the toys we can buy. In the endless race to acquire and build up this artificial industrial world, we forget that the true treasures are abundant around us, free for enjoyment, if we would only remember how to appreciate them.

A life in harmony with nature and content with the free gifts of Cernunnos and Tailtiu is one that is rich in peace and happiness. This person knows and understands the way of the seasons, and cherishes the moment at hand. To spiritually respect and love nature is to know and relish in the very gift of life for life's sake.

Enchanted Places

These are the places where the borders between the worlds run thin, and where magic flows freely. Probably we have all experienced such places. I know them when I visit a hidden stream burbling in a forest of old spruce and cottonwoods. I find them in hidden nemetons in out-of-the-way woods where sunlight dapples needle-covered forest loam. I find them at the edge of lost lakes where white foamy waves caress lonely, rocky shores.

Enchanted places are elsewhere also, to be sure: in the garden by the fountain, in the glen behind the farm, in the starlight of a dark night. With the eyes of the poet, we find that we are rarely ever very far from the Otherworld—enchantment dwells nearby. Life is rich if we do not overlook the riches it naturally offers.

Needless to say, there are far more symbols than can be dealt with in this single volume. An in-depth survey of them would take at least one other book dedicated to the subject, and a thorough study would take many volumes. Fortunately, many resources are available for the interested student of bardry. Compendiums and studies have documented the myth symbols of Celtic lore in great detail. Works of anthropology lend context by explaining the Celtic way of life in the old times. There are also many volumes of tales that cover every branch of Celtic folklore, from the legends of Brittany where the lost city of Ker-Ys lies beneath the waves, to the tales of far-flung Ireland whose druids were coming to America a thousand years before Columbus.[2] A tapestry of rich legend is waiting with yarns of faerie spells and poet charms, terrifying war-goddesses and noble heroes, and every shade in between. A full and rich folklore awaits the bard's exploration when it can let loose its power and heal the fractured self and show the way to fulfillment.

Growing Through Celtic Lore

Simply hearing folklore is helpful and healing. Yet an in-depth understanding of the lore of the Celtic folk is the bard's meat and bread—the very tool of growth and individuation. A program of study should be supported by pondering and meditation, preferably at the places of inspiration. How you go about your studies is up to you, but I recommend that you study at least one tale a week. Read it one day to familiarize yourself with the elements of the tale and their full meaning. In the next day or two, take some time to ponder it over. Go for a walk by a beach, a lake edge, on a forest trail, or some other solitary, natural place. Consider the characters of the tale, what they did, and why they did it. Do not overlook the setting, the milieu, the nature of story's problems, and the losses or victories of the characters. Ponder what the tales mean to you personally, what they can teach you, and how you can benefit from their lessons. When you have found a part of a tale you find deeply meaningful, take some time to meditate and explore that aspect with your full attention.

It is important that you don't overinterpret your readings. The folktales are meant to teach, but their lessons are often subtle as they are woven skillfully into a story rich in entertainment value. It's hard to combine something instructive with something entertaining, so often the lessons may be well hidden and approachable only in a roundabout way. The deep mysteries of folktales may be only visible after you understand the symbolism. Also be sure that your interpretation is based on a well-learned understanding of Celtic lore and symbols, and not on your own opinions or contemporarily based understanding of symbols.

Other times things will stand out as being pregnant with meaning, such as the legends of Cuchulainn or poems such as the "Cad Goddeu." Feel free to delve into those with zeal. You must follow your own intuition.

A key to bardic growth is memory. Committing something to memory has a way of merging it with the soul. Fiona Davidson, a contemporary bard who resides in Scotland, says that when she recites myth from memory at her performances, it has a trancelike effect on her.[3] She finds it more spiritually fulfilling than, say, reciting something off the cuff. When you find a tale that is deeply meaningful to you, it is worthwhile to make it a part of your being through memorization.

Have fun, find the beauty, and enjoy the journey. The joy of the path is integral to the bardic study of the old myths.

A Final Note

A concise catalog of Celtic symbols is given at the back of the book. It is far from complete, but it will give the reader a good beginning in understanding some of the other objects and characters of Celtic myth for which there was not space to deal with here.

Again, I highly recommend the bardic student begin a serious study of Celtic folklore and myth. This is integral to developing the skills and wisdom of bardry. In addition to studying the stories of the Celtic folk, it would be beneficial to become familiar with the science of folkloristics. See the list of recommended reading at the back for some titles that may interest you.

chapter eleven

The Substance of True Dreams

*As soon as sleep had come upon his eyes,
it seemed to him that he was journeying
with his companions across the plain . . .*

The Mabinogion

Within each of us there is a deep, dark place wherein dwell the shadows of the summed experiences of our ancestors. This is the mental realm wherein resides our inmost knowledge. There are conceptions, thoughts, and understanding of which the outermost part of us—the ego—and the upper levels of the unconscious are barely aware. Sometimes we call the constructs of this place "instincts." Other times we may refer to them as "intuition." Writers may call them "gut feelings," or something similar. Our ancestors, who were much closer to the visceral realities of their own being, would have known them as a psychical power of awareness like the second sight, and been much more attuned to them. Most of us today know little more of this place than what we experience in poorly understood dreams. The artificiality we live in—which we know as the modern, technologically centered world—has worked a darkly seductive magic to separate us from this vital aspect of our psyches.

Animals know this place; they live by it. The timeless ghosts of this region arise every fall to summon great flocks of migratory birds to their southern trek. Wordless voices long gone sing to the wolf by night and she sings back with her lonely cry. The hawk guide in the high blue sky is guided down like swift lighting upon the hare, reenacting the timeless deadly dance of predator and prey. At the time of the rut, the stag's hot blood compels him to clash antlers and win the doe. In all these examples, animals are responding to the deep internal force of a mental compulsion. They do not question it or seek to explain it. They only know it is there, it is real, and they wisely follow its lead. It is the knowledge of their generations long past leading them down the path of survival.

In the old times, many humans were very sensitive to this place. The primitive peoples who survive into the twenty-first century still remain aware of it. They live by the timeless rhythm of the seasons, by the intuition of the hunter in the wild place, and by the lore of the gatherer at the camp. It guided, and continues to guide, the shamans of the Native Americans into the spirit world. It speaks to the people of the faerie faith in the green isle of Erin. It enlivens the life of the Siberian nomad with mystery and magic through the long dark months of winter. It also calls to us moderns as well, but we have tried to drown it out. We no longer hear from this primal place and receive its teaching as from a wise guide like we should. We experience it as a nuisance, a primitive relic that no longer has a place in our being. When its specters call to us in the night, we fear madness and drive them away.

This mysterious place is the realm of archetypes, the place of true dreams, the land where shadow and light mingle and timeless wisdom never dies. It is truly an Otherworld, albeit one entirely of the psyche.

No one has ever directly observed an archetype, but their existence is strongly implied. When you perceive something that strikes up an inexplicable chord of sensation in you—a sort of déjà vu—you may well be experiencing the working of an archetype. Other evidence of archetypes has been collected through studies of myth. Jung was the first to recognize that myths from the world over contain powerful, common symbols and themes, the occurrence of which could not be explained away as chance. Other evidence for archetypes comes from the observation that we all seem to be motivated and influenced by similar powerful subconscious compulsions. For instance, men and women may be attracted into romantic relations based on their conceptions of the male or female archetype. Yet, like ghosts, the archetype remains elusive. While plentiful anecdotal evidence testifies that they are there and bear a potent, if subtle, influence, no hard evidence exists. Like ghosts, you cannot capture an archetype, weigh it, dissect it, and label it. Also like ghosts, there is ample evidence to convince one of their reality, but only if one has the strength to be open-minded enough to accept the evidence.

What are archetypes? In the scientific sense, they are the memories of the collective unconscious that exist as basic motifs and are passed down through successive generations through genetics or some other inheritable means. Archetypes may extend not only across the human species, but back into prehuman days. In fact, they may trace back a very long way down the evolutionary ladder. So, archetypes are the memories of our ancestors (and possibly even prehuman ancestors) that still live deep within us. When there is a healthy relationship with the unconscious, the archetypes contribute much to our individual lives by enriching it with sensation, a sense of context, and instinct. When we are in an unhealthy relationship with the unconscious, the archetypes appear as unwanted nuisances. They may be the call of unexplainable urges and inexplicable longings that we can't understand and of which we may even be ashamed. If such an unhealthy relationship is left untreated, it may even cause an archetype to fester into a complex.

A complex is like a whirlwind of mental forces. Its engine is an archetype that has become so strong it takes on a life of its own. It sucks in ideas related to itself and builds them into a construct that can become as powerful as any of the normal constructs of personality. Remember that the personality is fractured from the core of our personal being—the self—into a number of facets as it struggles to survive in the world. This fracturing is a natural, normal phase in our evolution through life, and as we grow and come to understand ourselves, and gain the strength to accept and be ourselves, those fractured facets of the soul reunite. This is the process of individuation. However, a complex is an unnatural fracture. It fights the reintegration of the soul, and if left untreated and allowed to fester, there is the danger that it may even usurp the ego (hence, multiple personalities and any number of other mental disorders). Complexes may center around a parent, one's country, one's lifestyle, a latent fear, or any number of other things. We all have them—most of us at small, manageable levels. Part of the work of the bard is to facilitate the understanding and reintegration of complexes; to bring a part of the fractured soul home. This is a shamanic work of spiritual restoration.

Despite the danger of archetypes running amuck and becoming complexes, they do far more good than harm. That is why we were endowed with them. When we are in a healthy relationship with the unconscious, we can receive much benefit from the archetypal realm. The presence of archetypes means that our ancestors reside within us in a very real way. Their wisdom and experience are available to those who know how to seek it. In older times such people were called shamans, sorcerers, and druids. Today, they might be known as artists and visionaries. Through the ages, they have been known among the Celtic folk as bards.

Flesh and Bones

Though we aren't usually aware of them, archetypes influence us in countless ways. They shape preferences, impart emotional sympathies, and even direct us in the choice of a mate. Their power over the ego (the conscious) is significant, yet their work is usually so subtle and indirect through the channels of the unconscious that we are little aware of their action except as upwelling urges and motivations that arise from we know not where.

Archetypes can express themselves in conscious life so discreetly because of their nature. They are not clearly defined images or concepts within the mind, but are rather substances awaiting form. This may sound very complicated, but it is just the opposite. They are so basic that it is difficult for the sophisticated, conscious ego to grasp them. They are the stuff of deep preconscious, and their nature is too primal for something as sophisticated as spoken language to express. Understand that archetypes do not exist as formulated thought. In the mythic place of the mind—the place of true dreams—they are preconcepts. Perhaps they are best described as inspiration awaiting ideas, or definitions awaiting symbols. For instance, the essential archetype of the goddess may exist as an awareness of a powerful feminine essence of tremendous malleability and potential. Mythology or religion builds upon this archetype, and shapes it in one conception into the Virgin Mary, and in another into the multiple symbolism of Brighid, Tailtiu, and the Mórrígán.

Archetypes interact, and this further complicates understanding them. The archetype of the divine woman interacts with the archetype of deific darkness to produce the Mórrígán, goddess of war and nightmares. The same archetype of darkness interacts with the archetype of the divine male to produce the countless conceptions of a masculine devil. A few examples include Pluto, god of the underworld; Lucifer, fallen angel; and Loki, enemy of the good gods of Valhalla.

So, archetypes are a fairly fluid substance. Each has its own firm nature, yet is plastic enough to fit into countless subtly different molds. They can intermingle to create great variation. Because they exist back in the roots of the mind—in the collective unconscious—they provide a basis for our common human psychologies and instincts. They work their way up to the ego to manifest in daily life. They gift us with knowledge of our ancestors, and keep their spirits alive within us. However, if poorly related to or empowered by terrible experience, they may become the engine-seeds of complexes and wreak devastating effects upon the soul.

The things that whisper directly to the deep unconscious best encompass the archetypes. The primal imagery of myth is one such force, and a powerful one it is. We need myth to put a face on the otherwise faceless archetypes, for, as thinking beings, we need to be able to conceptualize them. Myth accomplishes this very task by providing vessels of symbolism for the semiliquid archetypes to fill. The archetype or archetypes best suited to a vessel-symbol will naturally occupy it. The mythic symbolism may come from classic sources, or by oral tradition. If there is no well of old myth to draw upon, myth will be created to fill the gap, for archetypes seem to demand myth (thus arise modern myths and urban legends). These elements exist in a triad: archetype, myth-symbol, and the tale of the archetype/myth-symbol.

Endowed with a symbol, these powerful inner forces become things that can be conceptualized. The conscious ego is now able to face them and deal with them. Unfortunately, many people deal with them by denying them. They tuck them away into forgotten corners that they label "fairyland," "make-believe," and "fiction," and tell themselves these places have no bearing in the life of a modern, rational person. Some go even further and call the shadowy places of the archetypal realm "madness" and "hell." However, the place of true dreams is none of that. It is a mythical place where magic lives in the heart; a between place where the mind meets the Otherworld within; a place from which can flow inspiration and wonder. It is the work of the bard to be a bridge to this place, and to help people learn from and grow through their inner archetypal realms. As the keeper of myth and lore, the bard accomplishes this by knowing the bones of symbol and the flesh of archetypes. As the storyteller, the bard knits them together with well-wrought tales of legend to give body and being to the inner substances of the human mind. In the doing, the bard becomes shaman, and guides minds that have not learned to grasp things in their essential form toward true perception. Thus, the bard's work with myth is a potent growth function.

To accomplish this sacred work, the bard must be intimate with the tools of meditation, the shamanic journey, and the poet's craft. These skills, when developed, allow the bard to work directly with the archetypes in their essential, plastic form. While others must lay symbols over the archetypes in order to deal with them (which, in effect, keeps them a step away from their essential nature), the bardic skills allow the bard to look deeper, see truer, and communicate directly with these essences of the inner Otherworld. So the bard is able to relate to and reshape his or her own archetypes on a primal level.

This ability to know and understand essence beneath symbol is key to the bard's great potential for growth and magical power. Through it, archetypes at the core of complexes can be disarmed and dismantled, dominating negative archetypes can be reduced in power, and archetypes of perspective can be reworked, mingled, and experimented with to enrich context. It is even possible to work out new cognitive patterns, which can enable higher ways of thinking and perceiving.

Without the skills of bardcraft, myth can only provide a face for the archetypes. This is helpful to the average person because the inner mind is provided a system of symbols that enable better internal comprehension, which facilitates integration and individuation. However, the bard actually has the power to work deep, lasting, positive changes within him- or herself. These are changes that broaden the mind and open it to the Otherworld; changes that unite the fractured self and make the soul whole again;

changes that make the bard alive to every part of his or her psychic being. This is why it is worth traversing the long path of becoming a bard.

The Song of True Dreams

Through storycraft, the bones of symbol and the flesh of archetypes are bound, but this triad is not complete on its own. Another triad of even more primal power must be added to complete true dreams' substance. The triad to which I am referring is that of music: melody, harmony, and rhythm. It works by animating the true dreams, giving the vitality of emotion and spirit to them, and making them meaningful and affective. Some music accomplishes this deep magic with great potency, even though the music maker may not realize it. Many New Age musical creations, much folk music, and the hypnotic drumming of certain shamanic practices propel us into vivid dream. These are the musics that animate myth with their own innate magic.

Music is a language that runs deeper than words. It speaks directly to the soul in tones of passionate joy or sadness, vibrance or rest. With pure music you can convey the feeling essences of the mind, but you cannot convey the refined and clearly articulated ideas of the linguistically based ego. You can tell a soulfelt story with great music that speaks in tones and conjures up incredible imagery. Majestic harmonies speak of great heights and hazy-blue mountain vistas. Slow strains reach into the dark waters of sadness. Rich, flowing, sultry pieces express the passion of romantic love. Subtle contrasts convey mystery. Though it cannot articulate a tale with a sophisticated theme, scenario, or selection of characters, music paints more pictures in a melody than a painter's brush can incarnate in a lifetime. It tells more tales than the most prolific author, and yet it does this without uttering a word. This is because music is more primal than words, and exists deeper than any spoken language. Words, paintings, and even poetry are all the products of symbols. Music uses no symbols. It is substance before meaning. So it is very like the basic archetypes. Therein lies the mystery and the magic of the triad of music.

Its likeness to basic archetypes makes music a powerful magic. Speaking directly to the unconscious, it charges the archetypes with its enchantment. Therefore, music is especially important to the bard. With it, he can manifest the three musical enchantments: joy, sadness, and sleep. With true-sight, the bard can see a person's inmost soul's need, including his or her own. With music, he can speak directly to that need and restore the sacred balance the druids taught was vital to all creation. The bard can evoke the music of gladness to lift the spirit, soulful music to release those in sadness, and the music of rest to calm the stressed. This is using music to counter overwhelming feelings within a person in order to restore balance. It is even used to increase the flow and balance of bodily energies to effect physical healing. In this modern era, the use of the right kind of music to effect this healing magic is recognized in scientific circles—it is called music therapy.

Music may also be used simply to enhance intense emotion, much as one reads a novel or watches a movie to experience the emotions of the characters. With deft fingers, the bard's instrument may summon passion, hope, and peace. The power of bardic music is that it commands the energy to move the soul.

The individual's need is visible to the bard with true-sight, which comes of magical and lore wisdom, poetry, and the heart. The bard is psychotherapist to the soul. The bard's music is the deep language that heals the part of man that is more profound than mere words can express or touch.

Yet never forget, music is but one part of two powerful triads, the other being that of story. Apart, they each work mighty magics and soul-healing wonders. Together, they are a complete force, the sum of which is greater than the parts. Story articulates a message so that a specific purpose can be communicated; music lends primal passion to the tale, adding the fire of emotion to the force of bardic working. There is a time to use them apart, and a time to use them together. Allow true-sight to guide you into knowing which is which.

Touching the Dreaming Place

The bard has three great missions:

1. To grow personally

2. To keep to the paths of the Otherworld and the Old Ways

3. To help others grow and keep to the path of the Old Ways

We know that the bard fulfilled a social role as historian and entertainer. Yet these were the peripheral trades; the things the bard did to be of practical value to his or her society and to earn his or her living. The true purposes of the bard are the three druidic functions listed above.

Personal growth is listed first because without its accomplishment, neither of the other two missions can be achieved. It is the hero's quest, the core of the Celtic psychology, and the bard's first work. Without success in this area, the bard has nothing to offer him- or herself, and so can offer nothing to others.

Keeping to the paths of the Otherworld and the Old Ways involves remembering the enchantment all around us and living in harmony with it. It means walking in the between places and being open and receptive to imbas. It means knowing it is mystery that really matters and that gives life its color and depth. It means knowing the lore of the Otherworld and the Old Ways in a living, vibrant way. Whether the Otherworld becomes alive to you through the sidhe, through visions, or through the deep wood shadows that always promise something more just beyond the next hillock, know it is real, it is out there, and it is real within. It is the eldest elder enchantment; the mysterious *other* reality. If it were lost, then only the surface of things would be perceived. Perception would be diminished until the world was a dry, meaningless husk. So the bard's task is to keep the Otherworld alive by never forgetting the Old Way to reach it. Forgetting it would reduce man in indescribable ways.

Helping others is the end result of the bard's path. Personal growth makes it possible to offer something worthwhile. The Otherworldly connection enchants the bard's work, and gives it spiritual value. The art of the bard is the tool by which to inspire growth.

Throughout the book we have discussed the ways in which you can touch the dreaming places of the inner Otherworld. Imbas is the lifeblood of that connection. The stories of myth and lore give the place form. Poetry manifests it anew by recombining and reshaping the molds to enrich perspective. Music provides the emotive core of the archetypes by speaking directly to them in healing, enriching tones. Meditation is a gate to walking among the true dreams. Working magic is a way of contacting the deep places and bringing them to the surface. The tools are known to you, and now you know why the bard must possess and use them.

Harper and bard Fiona Davidson once stated to me, "[Myth] makes life numinous. It makes every experience pregnant with unknown possibilities. It touches the eternal child within us. And yet it also urges us to grow up, take responsibility. In short, myth can bring us up to how we should be [because] it is an incarnation of the Spirit . . . Myth showed me that I belong to something much bigger than I am."[1] She has poignantly captured the essence of archetypal working through myth in these few lines. Myth is the form of the archetypal substance, and it connects us to the past, the here and now, the future, and mystery in the place of true dreams. Using myth as a guide to the inner Otherworld, the archetypes are empowered to guide and aid us. The true bard opens up this possibility.

Fiona Davidson has produced a CD titled *The Language of Birds*. This, in my opinion, is the best example of bardic work I have ever heard. In her performance, she skillfully overlays myth on to the archetypes, thus shaping our instinctive awareness of the Otherworld. Through music and story-telling, she speaks a haunting truth directly to the soul, one that heals by virtue of its beauty and meaning. Such a work is the very definition of the bard's function.

As a final note, a thorough study of the Celtic lore of symbolism will help you understand the archetypes to which they are speaking. I strongly suggest you get to know the ogham, the list of common symbols provided in chapter 10, and the concise catalog of Celtic symbols in the back, and then add to it from the many resources I have listed in the recommended reading list. It will provide a good, well-rounded foundation from which to begin to garner the meaning of Celtic myth.

PART IV

Lore and Traditions

chapter twelve

Otherworld

*The Otherworld changes people. Without
a strong sense of self, or of purpose, it will
transform you into your deepest desires or
fears.*

Charles de Lint, *Spiritwalk*

So far we have considered some properties of the Otherworld. We have
seen it is an inner psychic landscape where archetypes are shaped by
the form of myth. We have considered it as an external place wherein
dwell the spirits, gods, and sidhe. We have seen it as almost allegorical; the
place from which flow ideas, insight, and vision. We have also examined the
places where the borders between this world and the Other are thin in order to
empower magic at the mixing of these realities.

What does that make of the Otherworld? Is it merely an imaginative conception; a way of looking at the old ways of thinking, which still affect our
lives in the twenty-first century? Is it only a perception; an alternative way of
viewing reality? Is it real, but within us? Does it have a vital, independent,
external existence of its own? The answer is yes to all of the above.

The Otherworld—known in Celtic legend as Tir-n'an-Og (the Land of the
Young), Emain Ablach (Land of Apples), the Distant Isles, Faerie, the Land

under the Sea, the Land of the Summer Stars, and by numerous other appellations—is a complicated alternate reality of manifold natures. It has its own reality, its own beings, its own physical laws, and its own mystical principles. This Otherworld is the home of the sidhe and spirits of lawful and chaotic forces. It is the next stop for humans after death where the spirit is given a new body and a new chance to progress on the sacred wheel. It remains always just out of sight and out of reach of this world. It is also the residence of the gods and heroes, of Ceridwen's cauldron and Brighid's poet face, and the place from whence imbas flows. In many places the veil is thick enough that the Otherworld is all but cut off from us. In others, the veil is all but nonexistent, and only a push in the right direction is needed to stumble into it. Ancient legends speak of such places, such as the giant's couch atop Yr Wyddfa [eer WITH-fa], known in English as Mount Snowdon of Wales. It is said that if one sleeps in such a place, the next morning he will either be found dead, or wake up mad or a poet. These places are very dangerous to those who have not been prepared by the bard's training, because without the druidic, shamanic, and enchanted artistic skills, the mind is unprepared to grip the radical differences between the mundane reality of the here and now and the Otherworld.

It is important to know that just as there is an internal and an external Otherworld, so there are other worlds of the Otherworld. There is perhaps an infinite number of them; one world leading on to the next. As amazingly exotic as this notion might sound, it coincides with both Celtic thought and modern quantum physics. The latter teaches that reality is very likely divided among an infinite number of universes, all of which represent infinite variations of reality. The Celts saw the Otherworld as a place where the spirits of the dead go after death. They don't float about as weak, ethereal wisps of once-human-beings as in classical Greek and Roman myth. They don't persist beyond the corporeal body in a beshadowed, dreary state. In the Otherworld they are reinvested with a new body of flesh and blood and they continue with life. Life is rich and full and abounds with nature, magic, wonder, and opportunities to continue the endless quest of the sacred wheel; that is, opportunities to pursue the hero's quest and grow, fulfill, and serve.

This does not equate the Celtic Otherworld in any way with the paradises of newer religions. The Otherworld is not a perfect, problemless utopia. There are challenges in the Otherworld—upswellings of darkness and chaos that must be subdued beneath the strength of order to maintain the all-important balance without which all creation disintegrates. In the process of subduing chaos, Otherworldly beings can be killed. When they die, they slip from the Otherworld to someplace beyond. Where do they go? Some say back to this world. Yet just as the legends indicate there are so many varieties of the Otherworld with so many names and existing in so many different states, it seems more likely that the spirits move onward from one Otherworld to yet another Otherworld in another state. The wheel turns, moving everything ever onward in the eternal march of fulfillment and individuation.

Quantum theorists have found that material reality is not as solid and predictable as older physics had led us to believe. When we penetrate matter to its very essence—far beneath the level of atoms and the subparticles that comprise them—we find that everything exists as an expression of chance. Everything incarnates into existence from the quantum foam that underlies all things in all places.

That things exist by a kind of fated chance is demonstrated by the existence of the virtual particles we mentioned in chapter 7. Virtual particles have been reliably observed in numerous laboratory experiments. They spring up from the quantum foam and usually disappear into it again, though sometimes they may remain stable (that is, remain in existence). Quantum theory has also theoretically demonstrated the existence of wormholes that open up momentarily to other points in space and time and other universes.[1] Some laboratory experiments have provided evidence of the existence of wormholes.

The science of quantum physics is young and basically theoretical largely because to this point we lack the technical prowess to test its assumptions. Yet, what has been testable to date has been proven correct. What it means is that this universe is full of mystery, things are not what they seem, time and space are malleable, and there is an infinitude of other universes and other worlds across the vast uncharted seas of creation. It seems that quantum theory points to an inner hidden diversity and mystery beneath apparent reality, which opens up to infinite possibilities—the very thing the Celts have known all along.

Knowing that there are many very real Otherworlds, we can easily approach the concept of the inner Otherworld. This world, which I have also variously referred to as the place where true dreams live (because it is the realm of the archetypes) and the collective unconscious, is a purely psychic realm. Yet this does not diminish its reality. The archetypal inhabitants of this realm are very much real beings. They exist apart from you, they existed before you, and they will exist after you. The archetypes may take on forms that the ego can relate to through the individuating power of myth and folklore, but they are separate entities of individual ideas. This means that, if poorly related to, they may also form autonomous complexes that work like personalities in their own right.

It is important to understand that, even when speaking from the hard scientific viewpoint of the Newtonian theory of the universe (that is, the universe is a clockwork mechanism and everything has a logical explanation), psychologists still understand that reality is the product of perception and we live only within that perception. Our senses are not direct windows on to the world. Rather, they pick up and translate information from the universe at large to the mind. The mind interprets that information into a mental construct of the world for the ego, and it is in that mental construct where we (that is, our egos) live. Thus, the conscious part of us is never in direct contact with the universe, but lives entirely in the mind's way of perceiving the universe around it.

In some cases, the mind develops problems with creating a mental construct of the external, objective universe. The person's perception in such cases is so inaccurate that it is dysfunctional, making it impossible for him or her to get by in the external universe in an adequate, self-sufficient manner. We say that that person suffers some form of dissociation from reality. Severe mental illness occurs when this dissociation becomes so extreme the ability to perceive objective reality is almost totally inhibited.

However, whether a person possesses a useful or nonuseful interpretative method, he or she always lives within the construct of his or her mind's interpretation of the universe. Thus, in essence, reality is what we perceive. This is important to our discussion because it means that reality is limited by our perception of it. Objective reality (the here and now) is the external, universal milieu we all share, and subjective reality is the here and now according to each person's individual perception. However, objective reality is not more valuable than subjective reality, for objective reality is only derived from mutually agreed-upon standards of subjective perception. Indeed, no one lives in objective reality—it is only a concept. That makes the individual perception of reality far more important, because for each of us it is the only version of reality we shall ever know.

What's more, it has been demonstrated that perception is so powerful that it can even change objective reality. Once more, the subjective universe is placed over the objective. Therefore, we can correctly make a few statements: (1) one *useable* perspective of reality is no more or less valid or valuable than another, (2) we live entirely within our minds, and therefore (3) the archetypal realm is a plane of the mind as real as the realm of the ego (that which relates to objective reality). So the stuff of the mind is as real as the stuff beyond the objective universe.

The place of true dreams is an integral part of this mind-stuff. It exists in the deep recesses of the mind—regions so primal that form is only transitory and essences are the true state of being. That is why this place is so fundamental to any who follow the bardic, druidic, or shamanic paths; this region deals with the core of being, not the veneer by which the senses comprehend it. As such it is a between place of mystery, and a very real, if entirely psychic world of the Otherworlds.

Why are there Otherworlds? One might as well ask why does a man love a woman? Why does the wind blow free? Why does the sea embrace the shore? Its existence is as much a mystery as that of creation, but it does fulfill some very important functions. The Otherworld exists to harbor enchantment and mystery. From its green shadows and fey beings flows imbas. Awareness of its various realities enriches the mind and bestows true-sight.

The Otherworld also serves to conceal. It keeps unprepared minds from beholding the great mysteries lest they be driven mad or worse. Those who push too hard or who stumble into it are often driven mad by the sudden and overwhelming expansion of the mind. All too often, people fear that the world should change. Even if the change is an improvement, they resist it because of a deep-seated need rooted in fear and prejudice to maintain a familiar, comfortable perspective. The Otherworld holds deep mysteries that can shatter one's cherished perspectives forever. A mind must be capable of not only enduring but embracing truth, mystery, and expansion. This is the danger of the shamanic journey, or the Otherworld visit. All who visit the Otherworld leave changed: the strong and the open-minded for the better; the weak and fearful, and the bigoted and the narrow-minded are found dead or mad.

Among all their other roles, bards are shamans. Eventually the student of bardry will be called upon to visit the Otherworld, either through the spirit journey or in some other way. Be certain that you are ready. Bards are privy to a certain immunity in the Otherworld. This arises partly because of their natural walk with imbas. This empowers them with a deeper perspective that is aware of the enchantment and mystery contained and concealed within the hazy, shifting layers of reality. Their immunity is also granted by the Otherworldly beings who have an ancient respect for the bardic office. This fact is related in numerous legends and reflected in old Irish law concerning the treatment and privileges of poets and bards.

Therefore, the bard as Otherworld quester enjoys a prepared mind and a kind of diplomatic immunity. Still, caution must be exercised. There is darkness as well as light there. Any visitor must act with discretion. Powerful chaotic forces must be carefully avoided.[2] Likewise, the mysteries of the Otherworld are beautiful and seductive. The bard must be patient in learning them, and imbibe only what the mind is ready to receive. Otherwise madness due to overwhelming the psyche awaits.

These warnings are not meant to discourage the bardic relationship with the Otherworld. Indeed, without such a relationship, there is no imbas, and there is no true bardry. Be prudent, go gentle, and go prepared.

In the remainder of this chapter we shall consider some of the beings of the Otherworld—its gods, sidhe, and spirits, as well as its flora, fauna, and topography—in order to prepare you for what you may encounter in this sacred realm.

The Gods of the Otherworld

It would not be entirely correct to say the Celtic gods reside in the Otherworld. Obviously, that we even know of them indicates that they are often in this world exercising considerable influence. However, the legends do indicate that they often reside elsewhere. Legend hints that some gods, who seem to have once been of a nature to spend most of their time in this world (such as Cernunnos), were driven away by man's religious enmity toward them, by his disrespect for the earth, by his greed, and by the mechanized, technological artificiality we know as civilization. Yet, though the gods are away, they are not forgotten, nor have they forgotten us. At times—especially the high days of the Celtic year—they still walk this world, and those of the Old Ways are still their people. It is appropriate that the bard remember and honor them.

Brighid

Other names: Brigid, Brigit, the Triple-Faced Goddess

Attributes: Goddess of three functions. First function: poetry and healing. Second function: martial skills. Third function: smithcraft.

Brighid [pronounced *breed*] means "the high or strong one." She is the daughter of the Dagda and the patroness of poets, smiths, healers, and warriors. Like Ceridwen, she is seen as a keeper of knowledge. As such, she is of special significance for the bard, for each of her aspects relates directly to bardry. The bard as storyteller is the searcher of knowledge and keeper of lore. As poet, the bard participates in the high art of wordsmithing. The bard as enchanter is the ward of his people and the Otherworld. The bard is a healer of the spirit and soul. All three faces of Brighid interrelate to each other. They are tied to the creative act, which is a power center of the eldest magics from the days when worlds were formed and great lore given form in the beings made to inhabit creation.

Brighid inspires all people to seek after wisdom, both of the classical and mystical natures. So from her flows the gifts of the three cauldrons of the soul: craft, lore, and passion. She is the giver of imbas—the power of perception that sees through things to their essence. This is the great power of the bard's gift of true-sight—to see things in richness. Whether knowledge is classical or mystical, the bard does not see it merely as a chain of logical facts. Rather, knowledge is intertwined truths that are rooted in the mystic and pregnant with mystery and potential.

Brighid is revered not only as the patroness of poets, but as their universal mother. Myth holds that she was the mother of Iuchar, Iucharba, and Brien—greats poets all, and the progenitors of all with the poet's gifts. So the blood of Brighid flows within all bards and ties us deeply to the mysteries. The poet's gift, then, is an inheritance of a noble lineage. All who are bards should be proud of this, for they have been granted the ability to see into the sublime as a gift by that which is sublime.

Ceridwen

Other names: Other cognitive goddesses such as Boann, but no direct equivalents; titled Mistress of the Cauldron

Attributes: Goddess of wisdom

Ceridwen is the mistress of the cauldron of wisdom from Cymric (or Welsh) myth. We read of her in the *Mabinogi* tale of "Gwion Bach and the Cauldron of Wisdom." In this tale, Ceridwen is a great sorceress of magic, enchantment, and divination. She and her husband, Tegid Foel, had a son hideous in physical appearance whose name was Morfran, meaning "the great crow." Because of Morfran's ugliness, Ceridwen decides to conjure a great elder magic. She will make a potion that bestows all wisdom upon him. Her hope is that her son will become a great wise man, and that his wisdom will give him value that will cause men to overlook his physical deformity. The potion is to be boiled in a great cauldron for a year and a day. It is made from special herbs harvested on certain days and at certain hours. Its power is augmented by her cleverness and hard work.

This potion is symbolized by the hazel nuts of wisdom and the pool into which they fall. It is also symbolized by the salmon that live in the pool and eat the nuts. These are the Celtic depictions of the ubiquitous theme of the elixir—the liquid of wisdom sought by the alchemists of East and West. It is interesting to note that while in other traditions the elixir is derived through complicated transformations of objects and forces in an alchemical laboratory, wisdom derives from essentially natural origins in the Celtic tradition. This traces the bardic and druidic wisdom tradition from a firm root in the natural world and its sublime power.

Another interesting characteristic of Ceridwen's potion is that if it is not received on the 366th day of the year, it becomes a hideous poison. I believe this represents the terrible potential of knowledge gone stale. That is, great wisdom without a love of mystery is like a toxin. It is what happens to people who become wrapped up in surface views, such as scientists who live only by material facts and philosophers who abandon their humanity for cold logic. It also happens when artists lose their inspiration. It is a world of understanding without imbas, without true-sight, without the enchantment of mystery. The lesson is that wisdom only possesses meaning when it is given depth by the sublime. Otherwise, it is only bland understanding and pointless power. No wonder the poets sought imbas even above knowledge.

In the tale, Gwion Bach (who is later reborn as Taliesin) accidentally receives the wisdom of the potion when three drops of the liquid splash on him. Vengeful, Ceridwen pursues him, a druidic hunt of shape-changing ensues, and she eventually consumes him. (In the Celtic thought, the act of devouring is not destructive, but amalgamative.) Gwion is remade into Tal-iesin, the greatest of all bards, in her womb.

Ceridwen is the divine source of wisdom, and she bestows it liberally. She is also highly protective of it, and reserves the great wisdom for those who are prepared to receive it. The receivers of the deep knowledge must be receptive to imbas, otherwise the wisdom becomes dull, shallow, and a tool of mere knowledge and know-how. The mysteries will dry up with illumination.

Ceridwen's gift will transform one open to imbas. Just as Gwion Bach was transformed from a servant into a bard with druidic powers (from ordinari-ness to mystery and enchantment), so will this deep knowledge have an alchemical effect on the present receiver. It will shape-change. It will alter the mind. It will make a person into a new being, one who is aware of and in tune with the Otherworld and alert to the magical essences that lie beneath the material.

Be warned, though: if it is received after the right time—meaning with-out imbas or when the potential for acceptance and growth is past—it is poison. It reduces the cosmos to a clockwork machinery or drives the receiver mad. Rather than increasing wonder at the sight of the mysteries that make reality all fit together, it robs one of the joy of experiencing the magical. The mysteries become bland parts of a machine. One becomes unable to grasp the wonder of what lies beneath them, the wonder that causes them to even be, much less function as they do. One also loses the ability to peer deeply to the essence beneath from which the mysteries derive their manifestation. Instead, one becomes wrapped up entirely in the illusions of the clockwork surface of things.

So wisdom is a double-edged gift: a boon with imbas; a bane without it. It is no wonder that it is said that ignorance is bliss. Without Brighid's gift of imbas, Ceridwen's gift of knowledge robs one of childlike wonder—a terri-ble fate that leaves the world a dry, uninteresting, cold, and terrifying place.

Cernunnos

Other names: Occasionally spelled Kernunnos, the Horned One, the Lord of
Wild Things, Fearuaine, the Green Man

Attributes: God of nature, animals (strongly associated with the stag), and
tillage of the soil

Cernunnos was a Gallic and British deity who was widely known under a variety of names. His appearance is also well-known from numerous carvings and statues of a nude man's body, slim and well built, with a stag's horns. Cernunnos often appears dispensing bounty in the form of coins and grain.

A powerful god, he is associated with all wild places and all growing things. He is the overseer of animals wild and domestic. The animal most sacred to him appears to be the stag. As lord of growing things, he also has a special significance to tilling and perhaps husbandry. Farmers of elder times called upon him as well as Tailtiu, the goddess of the fertility of the soil, to bless the land with abundance. All those who are close to nature and love her are in natural alignment with the Horned One.

Cernunnos is one of the oldest of the old gods. The oldest physical evidence of the Celts' awareness of him traces back to Val Camonica in the north of Italy and dates to about 400 B.C.E. However, a study of the myth cycles of the neighboring peoples of old Europe traces his history back much further. He was widely known and appears ubiquitously in the myths of other Western cultures as a powerful god of similar attributes, varying names, and somewhat altered appearance, which affirms that he has a history much older than we can trace through the Celts. In fact, it is likely that Cernunnos is entirely pre-Celtic. He may be essentially the same nature god of early Stone Age peoples. It is entirely likely that the druids learned of him, recognized the truth of him, and brought him back to the awareness of the people in their era.

Often attacked by the forces of the early Christian church, Cernunnos was misconstrued as demonic and the lord of sorcerers and witches during the Middle Ages. Thus, we often see medieval illustrations of the witches' sabbath being overseen by a man with a goat's head who represented the devil. Yet Cernunnos, while concerned with primal mystery and the deep, natural enchantments, is concerned not with evil or even so much with sorcery as we tend to think of it today, but with natural forces. The magic of Cernunnos is thus probably intuitive and elemental, as is, I suspect, the knowledge of him. Living in the far reaches of the wilderness as I do much of the time, I often feel a particular affinity toward him and sense his presence nearby. His presence is especially strong in things primal and intensely natural and at times when I am in the sacred between places.

Cernunnos is not really a bardic deity, but we do have a powerful relationship to him. All bards are of the druidic ilk, and thus are priests of nature and the spiritual kindred of all things wild. This means we fulfill, in a sense, a mystical function similar to Cernunnos. As such, we are both his wards and the wardens of the green domain he watches over.

Dagda

Other names: The Good God, the Daghdha [pronounced *da*], possibly the Gallic Teutates, possibly the Welsh Bran

Attributes: Druid, warrior, provider

The Dagda is the father of Brighid, the triple-faced goddess of bards, and is one of the mightiest of the sublime Otherworld beings. He is a member of the Tuatha de Danaan, the mystical race of sidhe folk who first inhabited Ireland before the human sons of the Míle invaded to take the emerald isle. The Dagda's name means "the good god," but it does not mean good in the ethical sense. Rather, it means he is good at whatever he sets his hand to do. He possesses two artifacts: a cauldron that satisfies all those who partake of it, and a great warclub that heals as well as kills.

The Dagda's cauldron symbolizes his power to nourish all those in need, and, like all good Celts, his hospitality is grand. He is happy to provide of his bounty for those who are the friends of his people and his cause. However, his cauldron of provision is not one of wisdom—as is that of Ceridwen—but of material bounty. It was said the Dagda's cauldron could satisfy entire armies. He is well capable of turning the bounty of the land toward his people.

He is a very powerful god, and a lord of the Otherworld, but not in the sense of a supreme being or master. He is more a beneficent director, and leads the sidhe as a good but not overbearing noble.

The Dagda is also the patron of roads and crossroads. He is a superintendent of the routes of travel. Such places are very magical because of the wonder of travel—it leads to new sights, new experiences, new places of nature, and unknown peoples. It is laden with mysteries and potential for growth. Unfortunately, in the modern era we travel entirely separated from the land and its immediate wonders by fast cars, trains, and motorized boats. We become even more separated by air travel. We miss entirely the magic of the road in our rush to get from point A to point B.

The Dagda is also a protector of the wild beasts of the forest, and so is aligned to Cernunnos. Some have suggested that since Cernunnos—the horned lord of nature—does not appear in Irish myth, the Dagda is the Irish conception of him. I feel this is doubtful, for the Dagda fulfills a great many other functions as well.

The Dagda's warclub symbolizes his great strength, for it is a mighty weapon when wielded by him. His powerful, beneficent nature is also revealed by the fact that he may heal with his club as well.

The Dagda is also a lover of the pleasures of excess. This is symbolized by the giant spoon it is said he owns, which is large enough to contain a man and a woman. He is a notorious glutton and enjoys amorous trysts. In this role he symbolizes the pleasures of release; that is, of letting go from time to time and taking pleasure for pleasure's sake.

Finally, the Dagda is a great harper. He is able to play the three bardic musics with such skill as to work mighty enchantments. His music of sleep can leave the hearers unconscious; his music of joy can leave them delirious with ecstacy; and his music of sadness can kill with the pangs of sorrow. He has a harp that will come to him and play only upon his command. As such, the Dagda is aligned to musicians and the bardic craft.

Being a god of nature like Cernunnos, and a god of music, the Dagda is doubly aligned to the bard.

Lugh

Other names: Lleu, Lug, Lugos, Belenos, Nodens, Tyr, Ludd

Attributes: Lord of knowledge, lord of all skills and arts, lord of light or the sun

Lugh may be the mightiest of the Irish Celtic pantheon. He is a very great warrior, and it was his gallant action that saved the day for the Tuatha de Danaan as they battled the Fomori for the green isle. Only he could destroy Balor of the Evil Eye. He stands with the Tuatha de Danaan as a champion of light and justice.

Lugh is also a master of deep knowledge. Supremely skilled in all the crafts, he fulfills the creative role. Likewise skilled in poetry and harping, he fulfills the bardic role. Endowed also with great cunning, as exemplified by his mastery of chess and martial strategy, he completes the requirements of a warrior hero as a true champion of fulfilled potential and individuated being. His only shortcoming is he doesn't seem to be much skilled at enchantment, so he doesn't fulfill the druidic role.

Lugh was widely known throughout Celtica and was associated with the sun. Indeed, one of his titles is Lugh the Radiant. The festival of Lughnasadh, which we will discuss in chapter 14, occurs August 1 and celebrates Lugh's marriage and the triumph of the sun.

Lugh was half of the Tuatha de Danaan, and half of the Fomori. His grandfather was the Fomori leader Balor, whom he killed at the Battle of Mag-Tured. The Fomori represented the primal forces of chaos (the dark side of mystery), which lie beneath the veneer of order that superimposes all the essences of creation. The Tuatha de Danaan represent that order—a beneficent force that allows things to have form and order, to be conceived and useable. Chaos is not evil, nor is order good. They are necessary parts of the mystery of balance. Without the one there cannot be the other. This concept of all things existing in a sacred and necessary balance is a fundamental druidic truth of profound meaning, for it is not merely a mystical concept but a very real need. The mind must be in balance to be healthy and fulfilled. Creation must be in balance or it will become unstable and destructive. Too much chaos and the universe would be only a calamitous convolution of forces and essences. Too much order and it would become entirely stagnant. Because of Lugh's dual origin, he himself is in a between state. He stands between order and chaos, and is empowered by the fullness of both. This is why he is so great. He partakes fully of the two most fundamental necessities.

Lugh is a kind of general overgod. He is celebrated for his near universal mastery of all the arts and smithcrafts, and for his heroic, protective qualities. Yet, sadly, newer Christianized myth has degenerated his memory so that now he is mostly recalled as the leprechaun (a corruption of his name), the little elf who delights in hiding pots of gold and eluding seekers of his wish-giving power.

Manannan

Other names: Alternative spellings of Mannanan and Manánnan, Manawyddan (Welsh)

Attributes: God of the sea, lord of the faerie race, lord of the Otherworld

A great deal of the myth out of Ireland, the Isle of Man, and Scotland deals with Manannan. In the mythology he is principally viewed as a sea god.

A god in this role is rather unique to the insular Celts. The continental Celts had no sea god, perhaps because their homeland was originally landlocked and they had no need to get in contact with the spirits of the great waters. However, spirits of inland waters abounded for the continental Celts, and it seemed as if every spring, lake, and river was associated with its own fey being. So the Celts always had a reverence for and a shamanic sympathy with water. Their myths of the origins of knowledge and the places where the Otherworld was located were very watery. Imbas is found at water's edge. In the cauldron of Ceridwen bubbles a watery potion of wisdom. In the pool of the salmon fall the hazel nuts of wisdom. Yet it is in Manannan that we encounter the first and only true Celtic divinity of the sea.

When the mythology is traced and systematized, we find that it seems that Manannan was not always a sea god. Indeed, his nature as a sea god seems to have come about almost by chance. It seems that in the dawning times, when the world of myth was young, the gods did not live in the Otherworld, but in this one. They battled the Fomori for Ireland and settled there for many a good year. When the sons of the Míle came, they were forced to retreat into the sidhe, Irish for "the hollow hills." There appears to be some symbiotic relationship between the gods and man, for as mankind turned to the new faith of the Mediterranean and forgot the Old Ways, the gods retreated again, fading from this world to the Other. Only Manannan remained, but since he was unable to abide on land any longer, he went to the sea, which was safe from the invasions of man.

Many of the Tuatha de Danaan followed Manannan to the sea. There they dwelt hidden and safe and barely remembered except by the seanachie (the storytellers) and a few isolated peoples of Ireland, the highlands of Scotland, the inhabitants of the lonely Isle of Man. Perhaps it was their memory that kept Manannan in this world at all. Perhaps it was his unwillingness to surrender. In any case, I know of no myth of his final departure. Perhaps he still dwells near Avalon, Alban, and Man, hidden safe beneath the waves.

Manannan is the king of the Tuatha de Danaan who have not retreated. He is known as a lover of women, and visits them in the night. He is also beneficent. He cares for his people—the sidhe—and the mortal people who remember him, especially the dwellers of the Isle of Man. Allied to order and light, it is sad that Manannan has been rejected and cast away.

Math

Other names: Possibly Uath (Irish; pronounced [OO-ah]), possibly Esus (Gaulish)

Attributes: A lord of enchantment, night, and the Otherworld

Math appears most clearly in the collection of Welsh mythology known as the *Mabinogi* where he is portrayed as an upright, just lord and hero of his people. He is the son of Dôn, who is known as Danu in Irish tradition. Danu is the mother of the gods whom myth identifies as the Tuatha de Danaan.

In the branch of the *Mabinogi* in which Math plays a key figure, we discover that he is a master of magic and a lord of the Otherworld. He is a just and upright lord, but is tricked by his nephews Gwydion and Gilfaethwy into a war with a neighboring king, and he slays the king. The brothers began this war as an act of complicated deception designed to allow Gilfaethwy to have a chance to rape the handmaiden of Math, Goewin. When Math discovers their plot, he punishes the brothers by condemning them to several years of shape-shifting and humiliating androgynous reproduction.

Later, the goddess Aranrhod is brought into the tale. She claims to be a maiden, but Math's wand of truth reveals the deception and she gives sudden birth to a child whom she rejects. Having forgiven Gwydion, Math helps Gwydion to raise the child as his own. Together they undo the crippling geasa the resentful Aranrhod had placed upon the child, and then provide for him a wife made from flowers.

Math is a god of enchantment, and as such is a patron of druids, bards, and other enchanters. He serves as a model of manhood in that he is very powerful, yet responsible, kind, forgiving, and honorable; he does not abuse his high office or power. Math is also an exponent of justice and the maintainer of order and harmony.

The Mórrígán

Other names: Mistress of Nightmares, occasionally spelled as the *Morrighan*

Attributes: Goddess of war, of nightmares, and, in a way, of love

The Mórrígán is a dark goddess of complicated nature. Interestingly, she appears to be of the Tuatha de Danaan, the tribe of the goddess Danu who were devoted to order and light. Yet the Mórrígán is without a doubt a goddess of dark affairs.

The daughter of the Irish war-goddess Ernmas, the Mórrígán also had two sisters: Nemain, who confounds armies to slaughter (and which seems to mean she spawns a berserker rage), and Macha, who revels in death. These three represent a triad of Celtic truth grouped around the magical number sacred to Celtdom. It is possible that the triad represents the Mórrígán as a triple goddess, and thus, the antithesis of Brighid.

The triple nature of the Mórrígán is further accentuated by her relation to death, nightmares, and love. Her death aspect is clearly demonstrated through her association with war and violence. Her role as the mistress of nightmares is one of darkness and terror and plainly relates to her war-goddess role. It is felt that a person suffering from nightmares may be suffering the attentions of the dark goddess. In Irish folklore, a raven is the symbol of the Mórrígán, and the unusual presence of a raven is considered a sign of death and ill-fortune. The fear that the Mórrígán inspires, in whatever form she chooses to manifest, certainly brings on dreams that express dark terrors.

Her role as a love-goddess may appear contradictory, but love has both healthy and unhealthy forms. The Mórrígán's love is possessive and controlling. In the myths of the warrior-hero Cuchulainn, he becomes the object of the Mórrígán's affections. When he spurns her amorous offers, she becomes spiteful and determined to kill him, which eventually she manages to accomplish. The Mórrígán's love also appears to be dark and somewhat sadistic, for her desire seems to be founded on the very traits she characterizes: the ability to shed blood, bring death, and kill with a berserker fury.

One branch of Irish folklore tells us that while the rest of the Tuatha de Danaan have retreated to the Otherworld due to man's rejection, the Mórrígán remains to haunt us and inspire the darkness within us. Of all the old gods, she alone has not been rejected. Indeed, because of man's warlike nature and easily evoked bloodlust (which shows itself in national war, local cruelty, murder, and violence for violence's sake), the Mórrígán alone remains almost universally accepted and remembered. Judging from man's love of bloodletting, the Mórrígán seems to enjoy the same dark love from the human race that she occasionally offers.

I believe that, without a doubt, the Mórrígán is still with us. It is a sad statement for our race that we have turned our backs on the gods of peace, beauty, and the bright knowledge, but have kept an open place in our hearts for the queen of fear and bloodlust.

Tailtiu

Other names: Related to Danu

Attributes: Mother goddess, goddess of fertility, the female aspect, the heroine

Little is known of Tailtiu, except that she was the adoptive mother of the god Lugh and was the fertility goddess of the soil of Ireland. It was Lugh who instituted the festival of Lughnasadh to honor her. As a fertility goddess, Tailtiu finds a parallel in Danu, who is the mother of all the Tuatha de Danaan. This makes her, like the Dagda, one of the oldest of the old gods, and a creative founder of the present cosmic order. She and the Dagda represent the opposite yet complimentary forces of masculinity and femininity, which are not complete except in properly conjoined union. Together they are fertile, creative, and life-giving. Each is individual and a completeness within him- or herself, but only together is their creative power fulfilled.

It is important to note that in the Celtic spirituality, masculinity did not connote positivity, activeness, light, or good any more than femininity connoted negativity, passiveness, darkness, or evil. There was no thought of the woman being lesser or darker than the man. The whole Western concept of this kind of oppositeness seems to have originated with Near-Eastern and Mediterranean thought, and is not a universally held concept. Celtic thought held that the woman was complimentarily different from of the man, and each possessed bright and dark attributes that were fulfilled in the other. Having maintained the already very ancient memory of the mother goddess who is integral to creation and the sacred balance, the druids were wise enough to realize that the sexes did not have to be diametrically opposed. There was no need for a woman to be weak, fragile, or faint-of-heart to be her man's appropriate mate. Indeed, this idea weakened the whole race because we came to perceive roughly 52 percent of it—the female half—as a burden to the whole when it became broadly accepted. It was counter to nature, which seeks to create hardy creatures fit for survival. Men and women have more complicated differences of complimentary psychology and physiology, wherein each needs the other to achieve total completion. So maleness was represented by the sun in insular thought because the sun sheds light and warmth upon the world, making it capable of fertility. The light of the sun may be likened to semen. The female received the light and her complimentary nature transformed its good warmth into the spark of life. Neither can accomplish this sublimely creative task without the other. They are bound to each other to form a fertile wholeness in a cyclic relationship; a relationship not built upon positive to negative attraction, but upon a mutually fulfilling nature. This makes the old Western Celtic religion one of the first nonsexist traditions.

We have studied several of the gods fundamental to Celtic spirituality, which is core to the old bardic tradition. Most of the gods examined above derive from Irish and Welsh mythology. They have been selected for this study because they relate either to an aspect of bardry, a fundamental aspect of Celtic spirituality (such as the relationship of the Celt to nature and her rhythms), or because they relate to druidic concepts of especial importance to Celtic psychology (such as the Dagda and Tailtiu who link the old mother/father concepts of divinity).

It is believed among some Celtic scholars that the old druidic religion was probably aware of a supreme, nonanthropomorphic deity above all the others. According to their theory, the lesser gods exist as a means to conceptualize and understand the aspects of the supreme god. This does not mean that the individual gods of the Celtic pantheon were any less real, rather they were the very real expressions of a deeper and truer reality. They were a way for the finite mind of man to conceive of the infinite.

It may be noticed that many of the traits of the gods we have discussed overlap. Cernunnos is the lord of nature, but the Dagda is a lord of wild things too. Brighid is a lady of knowledge, but so is Ceridwen. Tailtiu is representative of the great mother goddess, and so is Danu, who is the mother of the Tuatha de Danaan. Sometimes the differences are similar but complimentary, as is the case of Brighid, who presides over classical knowledge, and Ceridwen, whose knowledge is more profound and enriched by imbas. However, often the areas do overlap. This can occur because the gods of the Celtic pantheon are not so much trait gods as gods of individuals, tribes, and regions. That is, we do not have a specific god of war, of love, of wisdom, and so on, as we do in the classical pantheons of Greece and Rome. Rather, the gods of Celtica have wide-ranging abilities, with talents and preferences specialized to suit the needs of certain regions and peoples.

Finally, some scholars present the gods as ascended heroes. They assert that the hero's quest of total potential fulfillment leads to sublimation. There is good reason to believe this, however, many folktales reject this notion. Koadalan of Breton falls short of the Otherworld because he strives to become like a god after losing his family to the plague. Because of his pride and for attempting to exceed the destiny allotted to man, he was denied even the chance of growth in this life. Also, the wraith of the Finn-ian hero Caoilte [COAL-ta] states that he dwells in the Otherworld with the rest of the heroes of old watching over Ireland, but is unable to return for he is not a god. He had to beg permission of the Mother Goddess to return and set straight an untruth propagated by the wicked chief poet Dal-lan. These particular tales show evidence of the strong influence of Christ-ian doctrine in which the thought of arising to a sublime state is reckoned as a great heresy. Indeed, little if any folklore has survived from the pre-Christian era untainted by church doctrine. However, a deep study of the old druidic spirituality has led me to believe that the Celtic faith held no such reservations. The Celts would have had no trouble believing the hero capable of sublimation. The druids probably reckoned that back in history there was an ancestral divine being—and perhaps an ancestral race of gods—that originated everything. So the old Celtic spirituality would have held that there are gods by nature and gods made.

There is much more we could study in this section on the gods of the Celtic Otherworld. Unfortunately, space does not allow a complete discus-sion of even one of the above-mentioned deities. A whole book could easily be devoted to each. In the case of the Dagda, who represents the primal male father god, and Tailtiu, who represents the primal female mother god-dess, many volumes might not suffice to fully cover them. I recommend the interested reader carry on studies through other resources.

faerie

The Otherworld is alive with spiritual presences. Some myths record dark entities like demons. Others tell us of sidhe that are not much different in stature or body type from human beings, though they are usually very beau-tiful. Other lore speaks of hideous troll-like beings that may be kind or cruel. Still other lore speaks of various fanciful-seeming creatures that may be like tiny, winged people, or the dwarfs of Scandinavian myth, or the elves of Germanic myth. Other myth presents us with sticklike goblins and spirits bound to rocks, trees, and wind.

The picture we derive from the various myths is that the Otherworld is alive with intelligences: springs have their nymphs, forests their sylphs, and bridges their trolls. This Otherworld has been described as animistic, but this is not quite correct if we hold to the truest definition of animism, which is that life resides within a seemingly inanimate object, such as a stone. Rather, the Otherworld is a magical place with a spirit for everything. Any creation from a mighty wind to a minute pebble may be enriched with a living, spiritual being who relates to and reflects the object's essence (its true name).

The oldest of the old myths speak of fey beings such as the Tuatha de Danaan who are essentially like people in stature and appearance. The Otherworld for them is a haven to which they have retreated after defeat and rejection by humanity. It exists as a magical place of living myth where the Tuatha can enjoy life and keep watch over the world for which they still deeply care.

There is an inferred symbiosis between the Otherworld and its creatures, and humanity and our world. It seems that, however fairytale-ish it may sound, the creatures of the Otherworld require belief to exist—at least in our world. From such belief or acceptance they derive substance to manifest in this material reality. This idea is clearly indicated in the legend of the taking of Ireland by the sons of the Míle from the Tuatha de Danaan. As gods, the Tuatha were wiser and stronger than the humans who came to take their land. So how did humanity manage to defeat these sidhe? One theory is that the defeat of these powerful beings was not really won through sword and courage, but that the very fact that man battled them represented a complete rejection of them that disabled them. So weakened, the Milesians were able to defeat them and force them to retreat to the hollow hills.

A common recurrence in myths, legends, and in modern tales of fantasy is the theme that once, long ago, magic was much more powerful and magical beings more commonplace. However, over the years, as man has rejected the Old Ways, the elder magics have been fading until now there is only the faintest whisper left of them to remind us of richer times.

Personally, I don't think it is quite so simple as that. The world today is commonly thought of as a dry, cold cosmos of dead facts and logical realities. However, it is widely overlooked that the very nature of existence speaks in the quantum language of infinite possibility and richness. Perception, as psychologists of the Gestalt school understand, defines what is real to the mind not just in a subjective sense, but in a very real way as well. Therefore, as we have rejected the Otherworld and driven the elder magics from us, so the Otherworld has driven us toward spiritual poverty—not as a retaliative act of punishment, but as the unavoidable consequence of that rejection. Yet the Otherworld is not lost. It is still, as it has always been, nearby, waiting to be rediscovered by those who are open, receptive, those with true-sight and a poet's heart.

Below is a brief catalog of some of the Otherworld beings of Celtic myth. I recommend the interested student to further reading. Many volumes have been written on the nature of the Otherworld and its inhabitants, some of which are listed in the back in the recommended reading.

The Sidhe

The sidhe [pronounced *shee*] are the Otherworldly, spiritlike beings of the old, old myths. The Tuatha de Danaan are among the oldest known of the sidhe folk. Their kindred and traditional enemies are the Fomori. The sidhe are usually aligned to light and order, though the Mórrígán is a notable exception. The Fomori are aligned to chaos and darkness, though they are not really evil. The sidhe are the early gods of Irish Celtic myth, somewhat lesser beings than the great old god and goddess, but sublime powers in their own right.

Faerie

The fey beings are numerous in variety and numbers. Some folklorists believe that the faerie are the devolved diminutive remembrance of the ancient and glorious sidhe. Others feel that they are a different order entirely that represents races of magical beings who are rooted entirely in the Otherworld, and who may visit this world for one reason or another.

In my opinion, the latter idea makes more sense because of the old myths and legends the Irish have preserved through storytellers' and poets' lore. The Tuatha de Danaan are well remembered, even if the memory of them has been altered somewhat in accordance with church doctrine (as in relating the Tuatha to a race of fallen but not damned angels). Plus, legends of faerielike beings abound throughout the world, from New Guinea's wood spirits to Native Americans' manitou, and from the elves of Germania to the dwarves of Scandinavia. This universal recognition bears evidence to a very real Otherworld reality, now rare to encounter for all but shamans.

Some of the sidhe types are listed below.

Giants. Giants often appear as great terrifying humanoid creatures, usually of monstrous appearance and evil nature. They often represent great obstacles, which somehow must be overcome by the hero on a quest.

Elves. The term *elf* is of Germanic origin. They are faerie of slight build and lesser stature than humans. Elves may be of a kind or wicked disposition. They are easily offended, and often for things humans would never imagine. They are also powerful mages, excellent musicians, and fine artisans.

Dwarves. Dwarves originated from Scandinavian mythology. They are stocky, short, and humanoid in appearance. They are adept at mining and smithing.

Nymphs and sylphs. These creatures generally appear as beautiful women. They are tied to a natural thing or place, such as a tree, stone, spring, or lake. Some nymphs desire to harm humans, others are basically beneficent. Most seem to be neutral.

Pixies. Pixies are the little folk commonly associated with the faerie conceptions of the British people. They are generally thought of as small, winged, beautiful beings full of magical capability. Their thinking is quite alien to the way humans think, so they must be approached carefully. As creatures of extremes, they may be unexpectedly pleased by the slightest, oddest kindness and bestow great rewards, or they may be just as easily offended by the same and lay down terrible punishments or geasa.

Goblins. This is a general word for the malevolent or mischievous faerie. They may appear in any number of forms, but are commonly thought of as small, wrinkled, sometimes woody-appearing beings. They may seek to cause serious problems, but are more often maliciously prankish or cunning in their ill-doing.

A complete catalog and study of the faerie would take up many volumes. I recommend the reader go to the resources in the recommended reading for further study.

The Topography of the Otherworld

In witchcraft it is recognized that power can be built up in places where magic is performed regularly. Some legends show that Otherworldly creatures such as the faerie are attracted to magical power and will frequent the places where it abides if these places are wild and lonely, such as a wood or a country garden. As the power built in these places is cumulative, regular ritual practice, artistic crafting, and enchantment worked in such places over time fades the barriers between the here and now and the Otherworld. This fading works like a catalyst of spiritual vitality and casts the area and those who are there into an earlier, healthier, more primal state. It is a state where imbas flows freely and makes us sensitive to nature, wonder, and the proximity of the Otherworld. This is the secret behind the healing power of what is today called nature or wilderness therapy. In beautiful, natural places, the Otherworld is near and imbas is potent. In such places the soul—in fact, the whole being—is enriched and healed.

Therefore, I highly recommend the student of bardry establish a place of study in such a natural place. This place is your nemeton. It should be a regular place for you to conduct the bardic crafts, though you do not need to practice there all or even most of the time. Yet the more you can practice in this special place, the more the magic of the site will build. The growing enchantment that will build there as a result of your regular practice opens the region to the Otherworld and summons its entities. It makes way for imbas, and to the lucky, the second-sighted, or the one who has learned true-sight, a glimpse of a fey being might even occur.

How will the good folk appear? Perhaps as they are, though this is rare. They are usually shrouded in glamours. Perhaps you will see one as a glimmer where an instant before there was only a sunbeam. Perhaps they will appear as a shadow where there should be none. The true-sight of the bard will know.

A side effect of the accumulation of magical power in your place of study is a kind of incidental evocation. Over time, as its enchantment deepens, Otherworldly entities will be drawn to your special place. Some magical traditions teach that you should take great protective measures among such Otherworldly entities. These protections involve the creation of magically charged circles, talismans, and the invocation of holy names.

For the bard, it is different. A bard enjoys a special immunity in the Otherworld. The Celts knew the bard was sacred. No weapon was allowed to touch him or her. The Scots said, "Woe to him who breaks a harp string," indicating their reverence for the bardic tradition. The Otherworldly creatures will most likely honor this tradition too.

However, some may not. In that case, the charms of the arcane magics are there for you. Have something prepared—a rod of rowan should be sufficient. Invoking the protection of the bardic patroness Brighid is a powerful protective spell. Also, the great elder enchantments of harp (or other appropriate instrument), poetry, and imbas-inspired spirit are your greatest assets. In the shamanic aspect of bardry, these are the tools that will ensure your safety and overcome obstacles. Work at the elder magics and the bardic arts. They are intertwined and are among the greatest of all magics—the best protection you could have.

In general, the fey people are at worst neutral. According to the lore, when they are encountered, it is usually in the midst of song and dance beneath Danu's moon, or in a lonely, beautiful place where they frolic amidst the green. Usually, they only want to enjoy the pleasures of the world they gave up so long ago. An encounter with them represents no danger, so long as you do not interfere with them or insult them. If you bring them good music and poetry, you may well even earn friends.

Time

Perhaps the greatest danger of encountering the Otherworld is the way it alters time. Legends and folk accounts from those who stumbled across it tell us of extremely altered perceptions of time. When the warriors of Bran entered the Otherworld, they spent many decades there that seemed to them to pass like days. When Diarmuid entered the realm of the Fomori, the many days he was there seemed to pass like seconds to his comrades waiting for him in this world. In common folk legend, sometimes people are caught up in the moonlight dances of the good people only to find that, at the rising of the sun, years or even centuries have passed. From these stories we can see that time does not work the same way in the Otherworld. It does not even seem to be a constant, as it passes faster or slower depending on who enters where and when. Time in the Otherworld is, in effect, a very subjective experience. If you chance an encounter with the Otherworld, be warned that if you enter it, nothing may be the same when you come back.

Perhaps this is the meaning of the radical time difference. When you encounter the Otherworld, it will change your perspective on everything forever. Even if you return to this world at the time you left, you will find it forever altered because your mind will always be in tune with a new level of awareness. Your perception will be forever deepened, and your heart will be forever in love with the realm of magical shadows and moonlit woods where beauty hangs like stars from ancient trees and summer is always fragrant in the breeze.

The Shamanic Relationship to the Otherworld

A major role of the bard is shamanic. In one way or another, the bard will interact with the Otherworld. Skilled shamans know how to find their way among the spirit realms, but the novice will be in for a shock. The way into the Otherworld, even by way of the shaman's trance, is obstructed by many barriers and fraught with dangers. Just learning how to enter the trance is difficult. The surest bardic method of trance-entry through music is among the hardest of all. Once there, one must learn to navigate the byways of the unconscious, and to carry the ego through the portal of the realm where true dreams live. Once in the Otherworld, barriers will oppose the traveler's progress still more.

These barriers do not exist merely to block the way, nor do they represent hostility from the Otherworld. Rather, they protect the stability of the worlds. The barriers keep the worlds from intermixing too freely, thus bringing chaos. They also exist to prevent the unready from encountering mind-altering revelations for which they are not prepared. The legends clearly warn of the dangers of receiving Otherworldly enlightenment before the mind is able to accept it. Such receivers leave the experience mad, or they never leave at all.

The barriers also serve as a sign of readiness. When the quester acquires the skill to surmount a barrier, he or she will also discover that the mind is ready to partake of the mystery it protects. The barrier itself has served to enlighten and prepare the quester to further the quest into the Otherworld.

chapter thirteen

Practical Bardcraft

*. . . I have a bard who is more skilful than
all the king's bards.*

The Mabinogion

ue to the enmity of religious and political forces who feared the
tremendous influence the bards of old held over the Celtic populace, only bits and pieces of their lore and magical practices remain.
We retain enough written poetry to reassemble the poetic technique of the
westernmost Celtic peoples, but the old musical tradition is a shambles—
especially the harper's tradition. We know that the bards fulfilled a shamanic
role in their contact with the Otherworld and imbas, yet now only fragments
remain to us regarding the actual techniques they used. We can be certain the
bards were revered as great workers of magic, yet because this druidic aspect of
the tradition was largely oral, and what texts the Irish druids did write were
destroyed by the Christian church, we have only distant recounts of their
magical workings.

Such is also the case with the rituals of bardry. We can be very certain the
bards had a number of initiatory, dedicatory, and celebratory rituals, but very
little remains to us of those rituals' language, technique, form, or nature. The

old accounts tell us of their Pagan roots, and of how they were tied into the rhythms of nature, the cycles of the sacred wheel, and the bardic pursuits of the Otherworld. However, we do not know exactly how the bards conducted their rituals.

So, like many other aspects in this book, I have had to reconstruct the way it might have been through piecing together fragments from various sources and postulating the missing parts. In the case of these rituals, this has been especially demanding for several reasons. One, the rituals were especially meaningful, and, as such, the bards would have wanted them committed to memory—where the knowledge and wisdom of the rituals were alive—instead of written down. Second, the rituals would have been among the most obvious Pagan practices of bardry. As such, they would have been among the first targets of censorship by the Christian church. Third, the occult nature of the rituals meant they contained information and revelation intended only for the trained and the worthy to hear, and would have been closely guarded. Secrecy, the oral nature of bardic knowledge, and religious suppression worked triply against these old rituals to bring about their extinction.

So, having almost nothing available in the way of reliable old lore to work with, I have entirely designed and authored the reconstructions of these rituals. I have done so in the spirit of the old bards, bearing in mind what was beautiful to them, what they would have considered sacred and worthy, what would have justified dedication, and the dark truths of mystery and enchantment that remain yet documented. I offer them here to you to utilize in your bardic walk. They are not written in stone; modify them, if you will. Add to them or take away, but always do it in the spirit of the true bard, which is the spirit of the Celt, the druid, nature, and awen (the Welsh word for imbas).

The rituals may be done solitarily or in a group, though they are written with the solitary practitioner specifically in mind. They express deep bardic truths, yet they are basically simple and easy to perform. This is, I feel, in keeping with the bardic tradition. Bardry isn't about pageantry, or the intricate ritual of what is nowadays called high magic. It is about essences and enchantment, poetry, and the nature of things at their core. Bardic ritual should be simple in meaning and tools, yet beautiful in form and language. It should be sacred poetry and elder magic woven together as living art. That is what I have tried to provide below.

The purposes of these rituals are fourfold. One, they are written to keep alive the remembrance of the Old Ways. The traditions and values of our elders are of great worth. They root us to the past, and help us cope with the present by pointing out sublime truths and reminding us of where we come from and who we are.

Two, they are intended to vivify bardry. The working of bardic ritual will make the bardic truths come alive to the practicing bard with living sights, smells, actions, and thoughts. Just as working the bardic magics will open the mind to the Otherworld, so the lighting of the Beltane fire will make alive the old celebrations and bring their truths to the forefront of consciousness. By hearing the crackling of the flame and smelling the burning wood, we will experience the same as the druids of old when our minds are focused upon the Otherworld. Likewise, the dedication of the bardic instrument will raise it from the status of a mere thing. It will enable the bard to see it for what it truly is: a creature with a voice and a magical, imbas-touched spirit capable of expressing the wordless primal beauty of the Otherworld. The purpose of ritual is to make abstract truths come alive.

The third purpose of these rituals is to empower mystery. The rituals, I believe, are attractive to the Otherworld. They speak to its denizens of the primal times past, and help us to resonate with the spirit of those times. They put us in tune with the old forces of enchantment, and attach us to the Otherworld. They declare to the sidhe and the gods that we are aligned to them, and they in turn are aligned to us, for we, the bards, have not forgotten them. We are the living memory—their memory. We are the lore-keepers. The rituals also serve to welcome those mysteries and invite them to be alive in our world again. They say that there are those who will look and listen for the mysteries, and who will cherish the bright knowledge they offer concealed in the shadows of the between places.

Four, ritual has a powerful, subconscious effect akin to meditation. It is both relaxing and invigorating, inspiring and predictable, stable and fluid. It is tremendously adaptable, yet remains of constant character. So it has a powerful therapeutic effect. Ritual is good for us spiritually and psychically.

Finally, a note on clothing: old myth speaks of druids and bards being entitled to wear certain styles of clothing, such as white robes and variously colored cloaks. As these articles of clothing were cultural symbols that are no longer relevant, and they don't seem to have any bearing on magical or mystical bardic practices, I consider the matter of clothing very optional. If it helps you to relate to your mystic practices, then by all means, wear the bardic garb. You may wish to merely augment your normal clothing with the green cloak we discussed in chapter 9. The choice is entirely up to you.

Now, let us examine the rituals.

Initiation and Dedication to Bardcraft

Requirements: If indoors, a brazier and some slivers of birch and willow wood. You may also wish to add some forest-scented incense. If outdoors, enough birch wood to build a small fire and a twig of willow. A silver or gold ring of Celtic knotwork that has already been dedicated is also required (you may do the ring dedication before you yourself have been initiated into bardry). These rings may be obtained through occult shops, historical reproductions stores, or specially made by local silver- and goldsmiths (though that is the costliest option).

Where: Go to your place of study. If you have, or can use a natural, outdoors place, this is best. Otherwise, use the place of study you have established in your home. (Remember, bardry, like druidry, is a natural craft. Outdoors is by far preferable.)

When: At twilight, the between time.

If you can conduct the dedication outdoors, prepare a fire of birch, which is the wood of beginnings. Have a twig of willow ready as well, but keep it aside for now. Remember to practice safe fire habits. Do not build a fire on a windy day or if it is exceptionally dry. If you live in a place where it is very hard to get birch or willow, you may use another wood. For the purposes of the rituals, the wood is symbolic. I believe it adds a strong magical and psychological quality to the ritual to use the appropriate woods.

If you are indoors, you can prepare a fire in a brazier with slivers of the appropriate woods. You can even add forest incense to help attune your mind to nature.

Have everything ready for when the sun touches the horizon. As it does, stand near the unlit fire and face the sinking sun. As you are a bard, come with your instrument to the ritual. If you have a small harp, strum a glissando going slowly up and then down (if another instrument, approximate a glissando or a similar flow of melody or rhythm as best you can) and say the following invocation as you do:

> The Lady of Poetry, Brighid,
> patroness of the fair and sweet art,
> she is invited, may she attend,
> may she answer the summons
> given this moment between night and day.
>
> Let Ceridwen, come and join her,
> bring the broth of manifold wisdom,
> the gift of imbas,
> sweet true-seeing knowledge.
>
> Let the Dagda also attend,
> his harp on his arm,
> the strings ringing sweetly,
> the song of elder magics,
> and new beginnings.

Now, kneel on one knee and light the fire you have prepared. While it catches, sit comfortably and take your instrument and play a melody. It should be something sweet, yet haunting, that yearns of new beginnings. As you play, meditate upon what it means to be a bard, to walk next to the Otherworld, to seek imbas, to live the heart of poetry. When the fire is ready, stand again and face the west once more and recite the following passage:

> Gwion received of Ceridwen's cauldron,
> bright knowledge dwelt deep within,
> In forms he fled the wrathful goddess,
> Till she swallowed him.
> Transformed, she gave him new birth,
> a bard who knew the ways between,
> alive to mystery, to the Otherworld,
> the poet's lore seething within.

I ask the gift of her good cauldron,
Liquid wisdom enchanted of awen;
I ask no less Ceridwen's pursuit,
let her swallow me, a tiny grain,
to be remade from her living womb,
a true bard of the Old Way.

Now take the willow, fabled wood of harps imbued with the bardic soul, and prepare to place it into the fire. Recite this final poem:

I am the weaver of tales,
I am the keeper of the Old Ways,
I am the smith of words,
I am the walker between the worlds,
I am the player of wordless magics,
I am the enchanter of elder myth,
I am given to the way of the bard.
May the cauldrons within me be filled,
may the fire of imbas heat my soul,
may peace warm my spirit.

Place the willow twig into the fire and say:

As this willow represents the soul of the bard,
and as fire is the alchemical transforming force,
let my cauldrons be warmed, my soul transformed,
so let me be fashioned a bard.

Now, take the ring of Celtic knotwork and place it on one of your fingers. As you do, understand that the placement of the ring is the symbol of an alliance formed. It is your declaration that you are aligning yourself with the Celts, their elder path, and the mysteries of druidry, bardry, and the Otherworld. Now declare:

This ring placed upon my finger declares my chosen alliance to
the Old Ways, the elder crafts of bardry and enchantment, and

the pursuit of imbas and the Otherworld. May Ceridwen give me the strength to pursue them with a stout heart, and the wisdom to accept them when I find them.

The ritual is concluded. Sit and play again, pondering this commitment you have made to the bardic way. If outdoors, absorb the beauty of the night: the stars, the trees, the scents upon the air. Remember, nature is where you are closest to the Otherworld. Always strive to develop and increase a mystic relationship with nature, for it is the home of wild shadows, and where the deep and pure mysteries dwell.

The Dedication of an Instrument or Object

Requirements: If indoors, a brazier, coals, and twigs of rowan if they can be found. You may also wish to add some forest-scented incense. If outdoors, prepare a fire, preferably of rowan, hazel, yew, or oak, or all of the above. You will also need the ritual or enchantment wand or staff.

Where: Go to your place of study. If you have, or can use a natural, outdoors place, this is best. Otherwise, use the place of study you have established in your home.

When: At twilight, the between time.

There will, from time to time, be important objects used in bardcraft that you will want to dedicate. Your instrument is a must. You want it to be imbued with the enchantment and imbas of the Otherworld. Your bardic ring is another. As time goes by, you may acquire other items of sacred meaning to you. Some of these items of power will find a place in your crane bag, which is an important aspect of practical bardry that we shall discuss later in this chapter. The bag itself should be dedicated, but not the objects you put in it.

The dedication rituals should not be done until after the bard has been through the initiation ritual (with the exception of the ring, unless there is another who is already a bard who can dedicate the ring for you). Also, if at all possible, you should dedicate the objects before you conduct other rituals or magical workings with them. The dedication ritual is a very simple ritual, and it symbolizes the magical dedication of an object to the bard's path.

Go to your place of study prior to twilight and prepare for the ritual. Set up your fire, but do not light it. As the sun touches the horizon, take up the object to be dedicated and say the following:

> The bard's craft is the poet's way:
>   enriching the mind,
>   joining the soul,
>   making whole.
> It is the between path,
> traveling the byway of the here and now and the Otherworld.
> And this [name object] has been a friend along the way.
> Let its energy imbue me with strength.
> Let its focus fortify my mind.
> Let its essence enrich my craft.
> Let its spirit be before my eyes.

Now, set the object down gently and light the fire. As the flames grow, close your eyes, clear your mind, and try not to merely sense the object, but to experience it. You should be able to imagine its entire presence: its feel, its smell, its sound. Know its essence—its true nature. This is knowing with true-sight—the poet's knowledge, the ability to intimately perceive the deep truth of a thing. When the fire is going well, open your eyes and continue. Point your wand at the object, and say:

> O, Ceridwen, goddess of wisdom and awen, let this [name object]
>   resonate with inspiration and enchantment,
>   and fill me with the wisdom to use it well.
> O, Brighid, patroness of bardic knowledge, give me the knowledge
>   to know its skill with true-sight.
> O, Lugh, many-talented bright one, grant me your talent,
>   so that I might apply it to my craft well.

Touch the object gently with the wand. Then set the wand down beside you and take up the object again. Hold it up as you face the fire and say:

For the craft of bardry,
for the here and now,
and for the Otherworld,
let our essences gather,
let our strengths conjoin,
to keep open the ways between,
to make the divided whole,
to bring peace,
and to keep alive the lore.

You have concluded the dedication.

Other Lore of Bardry

Crane Bags

The crane bag appears in the legends of Fionn. It was made from the skin of a maiden who was transformed into a crane and cursed to live in exile. Manannan eventually acquired the skin of this crane and made it into a bag to hold his great, magical treasures. From this story we can infer that the Irish mystics kept various fetishes, a practice verified by the many charms later Irish were and still are wont to acquire. Like the Native American shamans, they kept their fetishes, charms, and artifacts of power in containers to keep their powers secret and close at hand.

That the magic-using peoples the world over have related practices should be in no way surprising. The same truths were available to the shamans of one land as they were to the druids of another, even if they were perceived in different guises to make them culturally relevant and understandable. We know that the old Celts were coming to North America in druidic times, and they were traveling far into the east also—well up into Siberia. Thus, there was interchange and the chance to influence one another's magical theory. The shamanic peoples of these places all have shared traditions, which probably developed as much through cultural intercourse as through a universal understanding of Otherworldly truths.

In any event, the crane bag is a term I use to refer to Celtic fetish bags. It should be made from an entirely natural source. It needn't be a crane's skin, but it is preferable that the bag be made of the soft leather of some animal significant to the Celtic tradition, such as an ox, deer, or hare. It should have a drawstring closure and be made large enough to hold between a pint and a quart in volume. The fact that the bag is made of leather aligns it to the spirit of that animal, thus enhancing its innate power. Also, if you can make the leather yourself, and then make the bag yourself, the spirit of the bag will be aligned to yours all the more. The crane bag should be dedicated and used only to hold the special artifacts of power you choose to put into it.

What should go into the crane bag? This is a very personal matter. There are numerous items of magical significance in the Celtic tradition. You could not even fit a small sampling of them all in a crane bag. However, sometimes you will come across objects in which you will sense an unusual level of power or that have a special resonance with your spirit. It may be a faerie stone (a rounded stone with a natural whole in the center) you find in a streambed. It might be a small bundle of wind-dried rowan berries you picked from a tree. It might be a four-leaf shamrock. It might even be something as mundane-seeming as an old harp tuning key or a wren feather. You alone can decide what should go into your crane bag.

You shouldn't dedicate the objects that go into the crane bag. You have already sensed a powerful resonance within them—a deep natural strength. You don't want to alter that. Ritual is primarily symbolic, but it does invoke psychic and magical power. The act of ritual over an object meant for the crane bag might well alter its magical properties. When you find something that you are sure belongs in your crane bag, simply add it. The bag is ritually dedicated, and that will focus the object's strength.

A crane bag, like a rowan wand, serves as a charm and a magical amplifier. The innate magical strengths of the objects will help your awareness of the Otherworld and will aid your spell-casting. It is a good idea to keep the crane bag nearby—or better, on your person—especially when working enchantment or conducting a shamanic journey.

Bardic Arts and Performance

Among other things, bards are creative artists. I personally believe that any creative art can add to the quality of the bardic path, whether this be poetry or painting, storytelling or sculpting. However, it must be recognized that the only traditional arts of bardry are storytelling, poetry, singing, and music making, along with the magic arts. Anything else is additional. However, that should not deter you from expressing through other arts the welling creative impulse a relationship with imbas will give you, for artistic expression is a fundamental of the bardic tradition. It is a way of expressing the soul, and of bringing to life the deep undercurrents of inner perceptions.

Artistic expression accomplishes this when it is carried out in the Celtic spirit. That is, it is not about creating straightforward representations of the artist's subject, as demanding as this may be. Celtic art is about relating how the mind perceives and interprets the stuff around and about it. It relates the forces of emotion and spirit as much as the essences of things. Applied in this free, surrealistic manner, bardic art becomes a vital element of soul exploration and individuation that are key parts of personal growth. By expressing what the artist finds without through the way the mind perceives it within, he or she makes a portion of the inner self real and apparent to his or her ego. Once this deep part of the self is known, the ego can begin integrating it.

Whatever form of art you feel is right for you to create in, know that art—true art—is first and foremost a private thing. You needn't feel obligated to share it any more than you would feel obligated to share a diary. That choice is entirely yours. However, in deciding whether or not to share your artistic creations, bear in mind that art created in the Celtic sense is different from a diary. It is not a precise log of your inmost personal being. Its fluidity makes it highly malleable. In other words, it is subject to the perceiver's and the creator's own interpretations. Like any artist, you can rest assured that while your revealed work may hint at your true self, it will not give you entirely away. Your most secret self remains safely secret.

Remember from in our study of Celtic psychology that the hero's work needed first to have inner value. However, it must also have merit for the hero's society as well for it to be of any true value, though this merit may occur as a side effect. Thus, a function of the bard is to serve others, and his or her healing art is the great gift of the bard. Bards do not evangelize or proselytize. They heal with the gift of introspection, by causing people to look deeply into their own souls and grow from what they learn there. Bardic art is, then, a tool you will eventually want to share.

In considering whether or not to perform, take comfort in knowing that there are all kinds of ways to do it. Perhaps you are a born storyteller.

Perhaps your skill lies in oils and canvas. Whatever it is, do yourself and your world a favor: if you feel in the slightest way inclined to let others share your art, then share it in some way. You needn't sit upon a stage to perform. You can recite a poem in a coffeehouse, play a tune beside the hospital bed of a sick person, or donate a painting to a homeless shelter. Sharing your perception through your creative abilities will add value and purpose to your path, and you will find that it will doubly enrich you. As people share their reactions and thoughts on your creation, you will gain new insights into your own self.

A final note to remember: art is not always meant to be pleasing. Sometimes art must disturb, shock, and challenge. The purpose of art is not merely to provide something pretty and amusing. Art awakens the soul. It should haunt as well as enliven. It should explore as much as confirm. So if someone is disturbed by your art, it does not mean you have failed. Indeed, it may mean you have communicated very, very well.

The Kinds and Grades of Bards

Traditionally, there are three grades of bards, and two kinds of lesser bards. These different classes represent gradients of skill and experience and choices of expression. Old Celtic society was very much a caste system. It differed from Hindu society in that the castes were not fixed. A person could rise or fall through them depending on personal skill, talent, and the whims of fortune. In this old society, the bardic grades represented an important system of rank for determining one's honor price, pay scale, and authority.

In contemporary times the bardic grades represent a way for bards to recognize accomplishment, skill, and establish the leadership necessary for the group practice of bardry. The ranks are not about power, or access to revelation, or privilege. There are no popes of bardry who receive unique access to Otherworldly illumination. In bardry, every person must think for him- or herself, else the work of growth cannot proceed, and all expression and magic becomes cheap and meaningless. The ranks are awarded strictly on the basis of time and effort spent on bardry and the development of bardic skill. They serve as recognition of achievement and dedication, and enable the organization of groups.

The great division between the first three grades listed and the final two has to do with fulfillment or intent to fulfill the traditional bardic crafts. To become a full bard, one must pursue with the intent to master all three crafts. If one chooses not to pursue all the crafts, or should fail to master an aspect, one must forever remain a seanachie or minstrel. The bardic crafts are art, knowledge, and enchantment. The traditional arts of the bard are poetry, storytelling, and harping. The traditional knowledge concerns Celtic folklore, myth, and spirituality. Finally, the traditional enchantment lore concerns the arts of Celtic magic we discussed in earlier chapters. While other arts, knowledge, and magic systems may be incorporated into one's practice of bardcraft, it is by this triad of traditional crafts that the bardic grades are determined. (In contemporary bardry, harping has been expanded to include the making of Celtic folk music with any acoustic instrument, including voice. Likewise, poetry and storytelling in Celtic tongues have been expanded to accommodate modern languages.)

When there is so much new knowledge, and so many new ways to make art, why the fixation on tradition in bardry? Bardry is much about honoring the Old Ways. It would be unfaithful to the spirit and tradition of this venerable path to drop this timeless triad of key bardic skills. To do so would effectively abolish what it has always meant to be a bard. It would also destroy the integrity of an age-old system of wisdom that recognized this triad of skills as mutually dependent and supportive of bardcraft.

Let me give you an example of why this is so using poetry. Poetry in the Celtic style must be studied until it is profoundly grasped and the student understands how to create it. It is essential to the practice of bardry, for true poetry is about the development of insight through the divine gift of poets—imbas. Further, poetic composition is absolutely vital in creating the spells to work the elder enchantments. Poetic ability also enhances the skill of communication. It teaches the speaker how to be more intense and vivid in her communicating, which serves to enhance her role as storyteller. Plus, the poet's insight is an essential tool in learning to perceive the essence and true nature of a thing, which is to see with true-sight. While other nontraditionally bardic arts can teach one to see interpretatively, only the poet's art uses the medium of spoken *and* written language at its highest level to convey the idea of a thing (which is, in itself, a kind of deep magic). Finally, with the exception of music, only poetry can be expressed instantaneously when the touch of imbas arrives. Other arts require materials, setup, and preparation. Therefore, through poetry the bard can relate in a lively, communicative manner with imbas, which allows the development of true-sight and the creation of potent magics.

There are equally compelling arguments for the acceptance of the other two traditional bardic crafts as the standard of a full bard. These crafts are like three pillars: each supports the bard in his relationship to imbas, enchantment, and the Otherworld; each enables the bard to fulfill his personal quest for growth; and each enables the bard to serve others. They are the traditional definition of what it is to be a bard. Drop any one of them and bardry is no longer balanced. Indeed, it is no longer bardry at all, but something else. The triad must be preserved.

The Bardic Ranks

Ollamh. This is the highest rank within a bardic group. It is awarded for full mastery of the three crafts of bardry. Traditionally, only one who has mastered all the crafts *and* has been a bard for twelve years or more has earned the right to become an ollamh. This is a high and noble ranking, and we should maintain these requirements in contemporary bardry.

Bard. This is the second grade of bardry. In the Welsh tradition of the past few centuries, expert proficiency in the three traditional bardic arts of poetry, music, and story was all that was required to become a bard. Becoming an expert in these three areas was a significant accomplishment, but it fell far short of the full craft-skill a bard of elder times would have had, thus reducing the bard to merely a very well-trained entertainer. The limiting of bardry to artistic expression was due to limitations imposed upon it by the Christian church. No wonder many people today think of bards only as musicians and storytellers.

For our purposes, and to remain true to elder bardry before it was stripped by politicians and churchmen, we must require full competence in the bardic crafts. Therefore, as with the ollamh, to attain the rank of a true bard, one must also become proficient at the other two bardic crafts as well—that is, magic and lore. It normally took six years of intense training to become a bard. Becoming proficient does not mean one has to master each craft, only that one understands each craft and is fluently capable of using it.

Anruth. The anruth is a novice bard. It includes all bardic practitioners with less than six years of study, and all who have not achieved proficiency in the bardic crafts at any point thereafter. The anruth is a bard in training, but is not limited from any endeavor in any way. The only barrier is his or her extent of experience. To be an anruth, one must aspire to proficiency in all the bardic crafts.

Disciplines of Bardry Not Included in the Bardic Ranks

Seanachie. The seanachie is a kind of limited bard. By the old Irish definition, the seanachie is a storyteller and lorekeeper who lacks professional poetic training. Her purpose was in preserving and passing on the folklore, genealogies, history, and traditions of the local community. As such, the seanachie fulfilled a vital role in history-conscious Celtic society, but lacked the mystical and educated artistic skill of the professional bard.

For the purposes of the contemporary practice of bardry, the seanachie is one who does not wish to fulfill the musical or poetic bardic arts. He is a storyteller, a scholar of folklore, and even an enchanter of the arcane arts. However, he chooses not to pursue the poetic or musical dimensions of the path, nor the elder enchantments.

Minstrels. Traditionally, minstrels were not simply musicians, but were often broadly talented performers. They played instruments, sang, and often recited poetry or told tales. In contemporary bardry, minstrels are those who are interested in the bardic path for its magically empowered artistic crafts. They see art in the Celtic sense—as a powerful, interpretative, psychological force. Their desire is to create art of a Celtic essence with the intent of sharing it. Their art may create beauty, make a statement, or lead to insight, and its nature is to be interpretive rather than literal. Minstrels are, therefore, followers of the Celtic artistic disciplines of bardry only.

Eisteddfod

An *eisteddfod* [pronounced *AI-steth-fodt*] is an assembly of two or more bards. There is no maximum group number, though groups are best kept from getting too large. An eisteddfod functions best when it is large enough to encourage diversified intellectual stimulation, yet small enough to keep the group intimate. I recommend that groups should be no larger than nine in number. That is three times three, which builds upon the sacred triads of Celtic lore.

An eisteddfod should meet on the afternoon of the full moon. All magical and ritual eisteddfod activity should be conducted during the very powerful between time of twilight. Afterward, the group may enjoy themselves with a friendly gathering. It could be similar to the Wiccan Cakes and Ale, which is merely a fun, cooling-down time from the intensity of magical and ritual working. This is a great time for the sharing of art and poetry, good music making, or just soaking up the inspiring beauty of nature in good companionship (if your eisteddfod is fortunate enough to have an outdoors meeting site). It is also a great time to relive the old tradition of storytelling. A tale told skillfully to the accompaniment of a harp or other instrument around a campfire is a timeless, wonderful, and deeply moving experience. It has a deep, universal appeal, and calls up the wonder and mystery of elder times when our ancestors shared their myths in the same potent way.

Every eisteddfod needs an organizer and a leader. This is the position of chief bard, and it is chosen by simple majority vote. The leader should always be chosen from among the bards and ollamhs. If no one in the group has reached either of those high ranks yet, then an anruth may serve as chief bard.

The position of chief bard should be voted upon each Samhain and each Beltane, which is every sixth months at the key turning points of the Celtic year.

chapter fourteen

The Old Ways

Thus, sighing, look thro' the waves of
  time
For the long-faded glories they cover.

Thomas Moore, *Let Erin*
  Remember the Days of Old

T he modern industrial age has undeniably wrought much good. It
has opened venues of communication, created new medical technology, decreased travel time, and, perhaps most of all, pointed out
the great importance of knowledge and education. However, it has worked at
least as much ill as good. Like the legendary Irish Fomor who stood for chaos,
it has brought disharmony to our lives. It has created a state of gross imbalance
that is separating us through a quagmire of urbanity and technology from the
ebb and flow of nature. Most people in the Western world today have little
understanding of the deep significance of the seasons, or the signs of sky
and land. The habits of the wild creatures of woods and plains are as unfamil-
iar to them as those of an alien race from another planet would be. They give
little thought to where the food in the supermarket comes from, and take
no time to thank the beasts and plants that provide the meals upon their
tables. Modern life has given us luxury and convenience, but it has cut us off

from the world to which we were once and should remain intimately linked. This separation robs us of our identity as individuals and as a people by inculcating artificial values and desires, and aiding and abetting the development of stress.

I believe the druids of old understood the human need to remain embedded in the nature of the earth. Their religion was deeply tied to nature, and they understood the profound link it has to a healthy life. Their veneration of nature was a sign of respect for the natural cycles as well as the gods who share the natural realm with humanity. It was also a reminder to the Celts not to forget their ties to the sacred land. The druidic rituals were designed to express that sweet attachment in a holistic, visible, and profoundly significant way.

Bardry is the living expression of this druidic ideal. Bardry is a kind of druidry, but where druidry focused on the sacerdotal linkage to nature, bardry focuses on an artistic and visionary linkage to it. The bard is the artistic expounder of the true perception of the natural world. He propagates in himself and others the essential ability to see the mystery and the magic present everywhere and everywhere overlooked. The bard vivifies a spirituality that accepts the hard reality of the material world, but also accepts equally the heroic ideal and the enchanted Otherworld. The bard understands that the nature of reality is a matter of perception, spirituality, and the quality of one's linkage to the universe at large. Therefore, the bard becomes the poet of the heroic. She overcomes mere mundane reality with all its hard angles and cold callousness, and reaches toward the place where dreams become manifest. Doing this requires a regularly renewed link with the vitality of nature, her rhythms, her plan, and her methods. This is one vital part of the bardic mission; the other being centered around linking the soul with living mystery and magic—that is, the Otherworld. Both missions are vital to the goal of living in the mystery of all nature.

The Celtic high days all represent this druidic/bardic recognition of the importance of a holistic linkage with nature and mystery. They center on ritual commemorating the deeds of gods and goddesses, but they are truly about linking. Just as the Celtic deities represent a way to conceive of mystic forces, the high day rituals allow us to conceptualize the cycles of nature, the working of the seasons, and our intimate, if nearly forgotten, attachment to the natural world.

So while bards are not really a priestly class, being of druid ilk we are obliged to remember and honor the high days with reverence. These sacred days ought to bring to mind our natural connections with an almost sexual intensity. With a deep-rooted awareness of nature as a vital and vibrant process—patient in growth, steady in pattern, intelligent, and enriched with mystery—our own souls are soothed as they are brought into harmony with the natural way of things. Nature can be described as feral, cold, daunting, and sly. It is also nurturant, fertile, receptive, and giving. It can also be portrayed as both predator and prey, giver and taker, friend and foe. It is a teacher who professes commitment to the moment and balance to the one with a poet's heart—that is, an open and receptive spirit.

With this in mind, I offer to you in the following pages rituals for the celebration of the high days. As with the rituals of dedication and initiation in the preceding chapter, the actual wordage is lost beyond recovery. However, enough remains of the old tales and poetry passed down by the bards (particularly the Irish filidh branch of the bards) to recover the spirit of their rites—and it is reliving this vital spirit that is important. Language changes and evolves over time, as does symbolism and technique. The power of magic ritual lies not in those malleable, forgettable things, but in what remains constant: the unchanging cycles of nature, the mystery and the magic, the human spirit, and the relationships the rituals represent. With the truth of these preserved, we can be assured that these rituals are as valid and powerful to the bardic practice today as were the rituals of our elder predecessors.

Additionally, a bard should feel free to rewrite the rituals presented here. There is no dogmatism or orthodoxy in bardry. What is important is the quest for truth, beauty, and fulfillment. As long as you understand and stick with the guiding principles of bardic wisdom, and remain true to the mystic meaning of the holidays, you are practicing bardry. One Beltane, I did something quite different from the usual ritual for this season. I went alone into a wild forest, built a fire at sundown, and played an Irish whistle to the growing powers and presences. Then, just before dark, I recited several impromptu poems to the gods. Finally, I finished with a small offering of grain and wine to the newly spring-warmed earth. It was a very simple, yet beautiful and deeply satisfying experience spiritually, and one as valid as any high ritual. I left that wood knowing I had pleased the gods and nature, and felt their pleasure in the harmony flowing through my soul.

My point is, follow the spirit of bardry. It is not a canon of law, but a pursuit of truth.

Samhain

Samhain, which occurs October 29–31 by our modern calendar, is the turning point of the Celtic year. It begins with the death of the previous year at sundown on October 29. This is when the old sun dies, to be replaced by the new sun of a new year three days later by insular Celtic reckoning. This natural cycle of death before life coincides with the druidic view of death as the midpoint of a long life. For something to live (to be born), it must first have been dead. As the sun dies in the west at the end of the day, a new day is conceived in the deathlike womb of nighttime. Likewise, as the sun dies at this autumn time—when nature is going dormant in preparation to weather the cold, deathlike winter—so begins the Celtic new year, thus fulfilling the timeless cycle of death, rebirth, and new life.

Samhain is one of the two most magically powerful times of the year—the other being Beltane, which arrives at the end of April. Folklore does not establish which holiday is more powerful, but each manifests its power in similar ways. On the night of Samhain, the Otherworld veil is rendered very thin indeed. According to the old lore, at this time more than any other, the spirits of those deceased have license to visit this world, as do the sidhe. Power and inspiration flow mightily across the Otherworld boundaries, and this makes Samhain a night for great magics and divinatory works. The power of Samhain night is attested to by its worldwide recognition and honor. It was celebrated in old Egypt, all throughout ancient Europe, and in Asia. Today its memory is even more widespread, being recognized and remembered in the Old World and the New.

Along with preparing for the night of spirits, on Samhain we give thanks for the bounty of the previous year, ask for protection through the coming winter, and search out the riddles of endings and beginnings. The bard, alone or in the company of an eisteddfod, may wish to celebrate Samhain with the ritual below. It may also be properly celebrated with our brothers and sisters of other mystic traditions, such as druidic or Wiccan fellowships. This is true of the other three holiday rituals as well.

Background Preparations

The ritual occurs at sundown of October 31 by our modern calendar's reckoning, which is the last day of the mysterious three-day Samhain period, the enchanted time between times. It may be celebrated individually or in the company of an eisteddfod. If done individually, the bard should carry out each function him- or herself going deasil (clockwise) around the Samhain fire. The ritual may be conducted in a residence or a building using a cauldron and some candles for the fire and incense to add forest scent, but it is best conducted outdoors, especially at a place of power such as a nemeton (forest glade) or by water's edge.

Requirements

Three members of an eisteddfod: a musician with an instrument (preferably a harp, crwth, or some other traditional instrument to capture the mood), a poet, and a storyteller (to fulfill the three offices of the bard). If indoors, a cauldron, charcoal, and forest incense (you may add other Samhain-related incense as well, such as apples). If outdoors, enough wood to build two bonfires. Indoors or out, you will also need enough water to douse the fire, or shovels to bury it, a carafe of wine, and thirteen candles (one for each month of the Celtic year) with candleholders. Each participant should have his or her own goblet.

Be set up well before sundown. The fire should be prepared, if outdoors. If indoors, the cauldron should be filled with an adequate supply of charcoal and incense. The thirteen candles representing the months should be set around the fire or cauldron. If you have specific candles for each month, November's goes to the west and the others go around deasil.

As the day comes to a close, each bard should find some time alone to ponder the meaning the old year held for him or her, his or her desires for the new year, and the meaning of this sacred time. A few minutes before sundown, everyone should reassemble and gather round the fire. Let one of the bards fill each goblet with a healthy dose of wine. The chief bard, who should fulfill the role of poet, should assume the westerly position (the direction of endings and the Otherworld, for the poet is nearest of all mortals to the Otherworld). The musician should take the eastern position (the position of beginnings and worldly life, for music is a source of enchantment and life). The storyteller should take a central position where he is visible before the fire or cauldron (for the storyteller relates the tales of all times). All other members of the eisteddfod should assemble on the north side of the fire, for now we are moving into the wintertime of death.

When the sun touches the horizon, let the chief bard lift his or her arms. A designated member of the eisteddfod at the north should light the fire if outdoors, or the cauldron and candles if indoors. (The fire should have been built with plenty of good kindling so that it catches easily and quickly rises to a good flame.)

CHIEF BARD: On this sacred night, in this month of the elder tree,
the old year ends, the new year begins,
and now we have entered the between time.

EISTEDDFOD: The between time.

MUSICIAN: [*Playing a haunting tune as the storyteller speaks*]

STORYTELLER: In the olden times—the age past of elder enchantments and great heroes—the learned druids knew the mysteries of the trees, their ogham secrets. They knew the moving of the seasons of the moon, and lived by the whirling dance of the sun. Twelve times the moon rounded our mother in the course of a year, and for three days afterward, there was no year. It was a time between time, when the veil between the worlds was worn very thin, easily rent. It was a time when the good people came across, and our people stumbled into their world. It was a time when our elders who had passed beyond the veil of death were free to visit again. The elder magics flowed freely in this between time.

EISTEDDFOD: The between time.

CHIEF BARD: [*Arms raised, vocal*] Poetry stirred the elder magics.

MUSICIAN: [*Ceases playing*] Music called the primal power.

STORYTELLER: Heroic deeds and great druidry were the order of the age. Yet now there are but echoes.

CHIEF BARD: Yet echoes may still kindle great fires of the spirit, as a tiny spark has lit the flame before us.

MUSICIAN: [*Recommences melody, haunting and powerful*]

STORYTELLER: Belunus, symbol of the sun, is slain. He descends into the house of death. Slow will be his decline, dark the coming days, cold the time of death.

MUSICIAN: [*Ceases play*]

CHIEF BARD: From the cold springs warmth,
from the night springs day,
from death springs life
for the end is a beginning,
and all things turn on a sacred wheel.

STORYTELLER: Indeed, it is so. For the year's sun dies in the northern world, its powers of warmth and light wane, and soon all will be cold and still. Yet the promise of spring is already in the land. The oaks have borne mast, the corn has given grain. Nature prepares for the new spring's birth.

CHIEF BARD: We lament the death of sun,
we welcome the time of death,
it is sleep and rest for all.

At this point, the fire is doused. Once it is pretty much out, a new fire should be built over it and relit. This symbolizes the death of the old year and the beginning of the new.

CHIEF BARD: And in the distance,
life will spring again,
when the wheel comes round again.

STORYTELLER: And so we celebrate the between time. The wheel's turn is completed. Nature sleeps; she will awaken again.

CHIEF BARD: This night the Otherworld is strong,
spirits come and go,
good company is the watchword,
everyone together.
For the realm of spirits is mighty and secret,
its mysteries only for the ready,
spirits of chaos and of good roam there,
and on Samhain they are here as well.

The veil is worn thin,
this is the elder month,
powers and worlds mingle,
in the between time.

EISTEDDFOD: The between time.

STORYTELLER: The Otherworld is for the wise, but not all can bear its wisdom. Caution this night, lest the mysteries prove beyond you, and the
Otherworld drive reason from you.

CHIEF BARD: Yet do not fear the Otherworld,
fear is not for heroes,
nor the way of true bards.
Seek the Otherworld and know it,
find as you become ready,
revel in its mysteries,
grow in imbas's gift.

STORYTELLER: Go with prudence, learn the bard's way well, and fear not the
realm beyond, for it is willful ignorance that makes it dangerous. Learn
wisdom to know where to tread, and the courage not to reject truth,
and then you may journey the Otherworld without fear.

CHIEF BARD: Samhain night, time of mysteries,
month of the elder tree,
we welcome the new year,
and bid farewell to the old,
we welcome the Otherworld,
and seek imbas to know it well,
now, at the between time.

EISTEDDFOD: At the between time.

Now let the Samhain ritual conclude with the drinking of the wine. It
should be followed up with bright bardic music, happy camaraderie, and
drinking and feasting. Traditional foods for the Samhain festival are apples,
pork, and wine. I recommend each member of the eisteddfod contribute a
traditional Celtic dish fit for the season.

Imbolc

Imbolc is a mysterious holiday, of which little information has survived the church-era rewritings of history. What we do know is that it occurred on the last day of January at sundown, exactly three months after Samhain. The word *Imbolc* literally means "in milk" and refers to the livestock giving birth and beginning the spring lactation cycle. Milk was an especially important substance of survival in elder times, as it provided much-needed fats, proteins, calories, and minerals. This holiday was a celebration of the return of the rich gifts of the earth, and the renewing of life with the promise of spring. It signified that even in the midst of frozen winter stillness when the world is dormant, nature is still at work, creating and providing. Imbolc was celebrated with libations of milk and great bonfires.

Imbolc also had important mystical significance. It took place in the dead of winter, exactly three months between Samhain (winter's dawn) and Beltane (winter's dusk). At this time, the sun's power had ebbed to its lowest point. In mystical terms, the sun god Bel had descended into the house of death. Yet even here, in the depths of darkness, light is not entirely extinguished. From this day on, the goddess of the earth, Tailtiu, will give strength to the sun and revive him to his full glory. She awaits him with open arms, bearing the fragrant promise of summer in her love.

Imbolc is a promise. Though locked in winter's deepest day, it signifies that hope is not lost. Many cold days have been withstood and now winter's power can only wane. Soon the warm months will arrive, and the world will spring to life anew. Pleasant green growth and liquid water is the earth-womb the sun's light will fertilize, and the great song of nature will continue its rhythmic air.

As I stated in the section on Samhain, bards may choose to celebrate this ritual alone or in the company of an eisteddfod using the ritual I have provided below. They may also join with our brothers and sisters of other mystic traditions and apply their bardic arts to enhance the holiday celebration.

Background Preparations

The ritual occurs at sundown of the last day of January. If done individually, the bard should carry out each function him- or herself going deasil (clockwise) around the Imbolc fire. It may be celebrated indoors using a cauldron or a brazier and burning candles within the cauldron for a fire. Incense may be used, but its use is questionable because it is difficult to imitate the scent of a frozen winter forest with even the best incense. So, like all the Celtic holidays celebrated by bardry, it is best done outdoors, especially at a place of power such as a nemeton (forest glade) or by water's edge.

For Imbolc, an unused barn in the countryside is an especially good place to conduct the ritual. It is not only atmospherically correct with its connection to livestock and agrarian life, but it provides shelter from the winter weather, which may be quite necessary depending on your location.

Requirements

Three members of an eisteddfod: a musician with an instrument (preferably a harp, crwth, or some other traditionally elder instrument to capture the mood), a poet, and a storyteller (to fulfill the three public offices of the bard). If indoors, a brazier, charcoal, and optional incense (in lieu of incense you may want to consider using small bits of wood to throw on the charcoal for a warm, hearth smell). If outdoors, enough wood for a bonfire. Indoors or out, you will also need thirteen candles (one for each month of the Celtic year), candle holders, a carafe of milk, and each person should have his or her own goblet.

Be set up well before sundown. The fire should be prepared, if outdoors. If indoors, the cauldron should be filled with an adequate supply of charcoal and incense or wood bits. The thirteen candles representing the months should be set around the fire or cauldron. If you have specific candles for each month, February's goes to the north and the others go around deasil.

As the day comes to a close, each bard should find some time alone to meditate upon this most benighted time of year and its symbolic and mystical meaning. A few minutes before sundown, everyone should reassemble and gather round the fire. The chief bard, who should fulfill the role of poet, should assume the westerly position (the direction of endings and the Otherworld, for the poet is nearest of all mortals to the Otherworld). The musician should take the eastern position (the position of beginnings and worldly life, for music is a source of enchantment and life). The storyteller should take a central position where he is visible before the fire or cauldron (for the storyteller relates the tales of all times). All other members of the eisteddfod should assemble on the north side of the fire, for now we are deep within the wintertime of death.

When the sun touches the horizon, let the chief bard lift his or her arms. A designated member of the eisteddfod should light the fire if outdoors, or the brazier and candles if indoors. (The fire should have been built with plenty of good kindling so that it catches easily and quickly rises to a good flame.)

MUSICIAN: [*Strikes up a sad, haunting tune*]

CHIEF BARD: This is the cold twilight, the frozen time,
    the point of the year when the beloved sun is far from us.
    On this night the world sleeps,
    locked in the relentless grip of death.

STORYTELLER: Yet death is but the midpoint of a long existence, so spoke the druids of the elder times. Though we dwell in the black cold, the promise of spring is borne within mothers' wombs. Behold, nature is my witness. The ewes, the cattle, they are in milk. Even now, Tailtiu prepares new life for her people.

MUSICIAN: [*Transits to something a little brighter*]

CHIEF BARD: Now we have come to the heart of the darkness,
    the time between the night.
    The sun has taken abode in the house of death,
    and coldness holds all in its grip.

STORYTELLER: Yet warm is she who seeks after Bel, though he has descended into the cold house of death. With open arms and the promise of welcoming love, she beckons for him to arise and return. She lends him her strength; the bounteous gift of the black earth that is her body. So gifted, he breaks the dungeon bonds of winter, and begins the slow climb back into his power.

MUSICIAN: [*Plays something bright and powerful*]

CHIEF BARD: Some say Bel is dead this day,
    felled by the powers of cold and dark.
    Some say Tailtiu revives him within her womb,
    knitting him anew by their summer love.
    The earth mother's womb gives strength to the light god,

and the light shall fertilize the mother of the earth.
By the love of his lady Bel is reborn,
made whole through the womb of the earth goddess,
he finds strength to climb again,
making for the heights of his summer abode.

STORYTELLER: Consumed in death, Bel wasted in the house of death. Earth died in the cold darkness without him. But full of love, Tailtiu revived him, drawing him forth from that cold winter place into a world she once knew as green.

MUSICIAN: [*An achingly sweet tune*]

CHIEF BARD: Yet dark is the world when first he begins his long climb,
dark and weary with the weight of winter's breath,
though nature has long known the ancient rhythm of seasons,
and trusts in the return of warm summer days.
Nature bears the promise of Tailtiu's succor,
that the sun shall return in brightness,
that Bel shall make the land fertile.
The beasts of the farm now bear their young,
and come into their milk.
Life carries on, and provision for Danu's children is made.

STORYTELLER: Danu remembers her children. Tailtiu calls for Bel. Though dark, the sun will warm the earth mother once more, making her fertile, and we shall return to the summertime.

EISTEDDFOD: Return to the land of summer.

A designee from the eisteddfod goes about the circle, then into the center, filling each goblet with milk from the carafe. Then, led by the chief bard, all raise their goblets to the sun and drink his health in milk. The holiday ritual concludes with a feast and music.

Beltane

The sun has overcome winter, and the days are growing longer, the skies bluer, and the world greener. All the earth springs to life again as Tailtiu is fertilized by Bel. This is symbolized by the seminal sunlight that now penetrates the dark, receptive womb of the earth. It is a time of joy, for the months ahead will be sweet. Beltane is not just a ritual, but a celebration. It is given in remembrance of the summer promise kept. It occurs halfway through the Celtic year at the time opposite to Samhain. Thus it marks the second of the two major divisions of the Celtic annual cycle—winter and summer, dark and light, cold and warmth, death and life. This holiday is perhaps as powerful magically as Samhain: a night when the denizens of faerie and the spirits of the dead may cross the threshold between the worlds.

There are several branches of myth related to Beltane. In one, Bel impregnates the earth goddess and is reborn of her. In another, he is liberated to his full power. It is not so important which is believed or enacted, so long as the mystical drama the myths portray is recognized and remembered in a living, powerful way that keeps us in tune with nature and myth. The theme of the cycle is that the dying or dead sun is revived by the earth mother's great love and rises again by the strength she gives him. In some tales this strength is completed through a bodily renewal (rebirth); in others, by consummating their love. All Danu's children are blessed by this great event, which results in the earth returning to its green state, the resuscitation of nature, the bounty of crops, and the warm, joyful days of the summer months.

Background Preparations

Because of the celebratory nature of this holiday, the bardic ritual is festive. It is taken seriously, but the entire spirit of the event is one of great joy; a sensuous reveling in the bounty of an earth returned to her green and fecund youth.

The festival is celebrated on the last day of April at sundown. As with all the bardic holidays, it may be rewritten to suit the celebrants, so long as it remains true to the Celtic myths and the spirits of the day. It may also be celebrated with our other mystical kindred—druids, Wiccans, and other Pagans—perhaps by applying your bardic arts to enhance the beauty of the event.

Requirements

For the Beltane ritual you should prepare two bonfires (or use cauldrons of charcoal and incense if indoors). It was traditional to build these fires of all the woods of the ogham trees in elder times, and we should remain true to that tradition now. If some of the woods are hard to find where you are located, use the woods you have in abundance and just try to add some small bits of the rarer woods. If you absolutely cannot get any of the ogham woods, you may build the fires without them, though you sacrifice the symbolism and perhaps the power of the magical resonances the ogham woods set up.

You should also have a number of young tree saplings (one for each participant) and enough trowels to go around. If indoors, you will need as many pots as you have saplings, each prepared with loam.

Each bard should have his or her own goblet. You will also need a carafe of wine. Candles for the months of the year may be forgone for this ritual.

For this festival, the chief bard stands in the south, the direction of light and warmth. The storyteller should remain central, as always. The musician should be to the north. The eisteddfod should stand to the east. The symbolism is the chief poet stands in the direction from which springs energy, for the poet represents enchantment. The musician is the guardian of the north, the cardinal direction of the powers of cold and darkness from which the world has just emerged. The musician, then, sustains the eisteddfod against this direction's power with the music of joy. The eisteddfod, in turn, stands to the east, the direction of beginnings and the waxing sun.

As always, each bard should take some time before the day comes to a close to meditate upon the meaning of this time of the year. A few minutes before sundown the group should assemble and prepare. It begins at sundown, as do all the holiday rituals.

Once everyone is in his or her place, let a designee of the eisteddfod go around and fill each goblet with wine from the carafe.

MUSICIAN: [*Playing joyous music, such as a rollicking jig*]

CHIEF BARD: The sun has risen from death's house.
　　　　　Tailtiu's unending love has shown him the way.
　　　　　In their lovemaking the earth grows green and warm.
　　　　　The days stretch to fill the need of the season of the green.

STORYTELLER: It is a time for rejoicing. The sun reigns once more. We have returned to the summertime. For though death's house was a strong prison, love proved stronger still. Tailtiu and Bel are reunited once more. All the earth is blessed by their union. The Green Man dances through wood and meadow, and all things are alive again.

EISTEDDFOD: Let the Green Man dance.

All drink a toast to the Green Man from the wine in their goblets. The musician caps it off by striking a bright, ascending glissando if playing a harp or other chording instrument, or a rising, happy melody run if playing a melody instrument.

CHIEF BARD: This is a time for happiness,
       let all Danu's children revel,
       let all Tailtiu's earth burst forth,
       let the sidhe meet in every glade,
       let the Green Man dance his green dance.

EISTEDDFOD: Let the Green Man dance.

STORYTELLER: The Green Man dances a merry jig, for the earth revels in life renewed and refreshed. The long sleep of winter is ended, and summer power returns to the land. The earth is busy with the business of life: growing green, growing wild, growing beautiful. Ours now is a task of participation, preparing the warm darkness of the fertile earth with the power of our bardic arts. With beauty let us invoke the dance of the Green Man upon the land.

CHIEF BARD: Into the green, green way,
       into the sultry summer time,
       we plant children for the earth
       and the sun to raise with air
       and water
       and earth
       and fire
       and darkness and light,
       to raise them into green growth.

EISTEDDFOD: Let the Green Man dance.

With the musician playing for the progression, the chief bard leads the eisteddfod between the two fires (an ancient act of blessing for health), and then off on a planting ritual, either to pots prepared earlier with soil for this purpose, or, if outdoors, through a meadow or wood. The eisteddfod stops at various predesignated places, one for each member, to plant each sapling. When the last sapling is planted, the eisteddfod returns to the ritual site and resumes its station.

CHIEF BARD: Let the celebration of the green summertime begin.

The ritual finishes with a feast, music, and fun. Traditionally, this includes walks in the forest to revel in springtime's glory, dancing around a Maypole while wrapping it in ribbons, and leaping over the Beltane fires.

Lughnasadh

This holiday, like Imbolc, is one of the two minor holidays of the four revered days of the Celtic year. It occurs at sundown on the last day of July—the middle of summer by druidic reckoning, and halfway between the major festivals of Samhain and Beltane. This festival, according to Irish legend, was established by the god Lugh of the Danaan in honor of his foster mother, Tailtiu, who sacrificed herself for her many children.

Traditionally, this festival did not occupy much time, nor was it very elaborate. With summer halfway done and the work of the harvest approaching, there was little time for feasting and festivities. At the festival, thanks were given for the gift of summer and requests were made for a bountiful harvest to get the people through the dark months of the coming winter.

Mystically, the sun is now at his zenith of power. The earth is warmed and bearing abundance. The green of summer is rich and the enchantment of nature permeates the air. It is a highly magical season, and rich with promise and beauty. Even if it is not a major festival, it is very bardic.

Background Preparations

This festival occurs on the last day of July at sundown. Like all the other festivals, it may be done with an eisteddfod or solitarily. Since it occurs in the heart of summer, it is usually best to try to conduct this ritual out of doors where one can be closest to nature. There is no incense like the natural rich smell of loam, the green scent of a forest, or the colored fragrance of summer blossoms. There is no sight as inspiring as a summer twilight, treetops silhouetted against the magenta west, or the horned moon. Be outdoors if at all possible.

Requirements

If indoors, you will need a cauldron, charcoal, and forest-scented incense (you may add some floral incense too, if you wish). If outdoors, a safe site for the fire is adequate. You will also need fresh bread, mead or cider, and apples for all participants. Every member should have his or her own goblet. Thirteen candles should be set around the fire or cauldron—one for each month. If the candles are coded by month, let November's go in the west, and the rest of the months circle deasil around it.

As with the Beltane festival, the chief bard takes up a position in the south, the storyteller is central, and the musician is in the north. This time, however, the rest of the eisteddfod is west, for we are moving into the end of the summer season now.

Sometime before the ritual begins, every person should find some private time to meditate upon the meaning of this holiday: the sensuous beauty of high summer, the bounty of the new harvest, the rising of the sun to his zenith, and the love and provision of Tailtiu, the mother goddess. A few minutes before the ritual (which begins, as always, at twilight), everyone should assemble. At the signal of the chief bard, a designated bard should light the fire and the ritual begins.

Let three designees disperse the foods for the ritual: one the bread, one the apples, and one the mead or cider.

MUSICIAN: [*Plays something lovely and melodic*]

STORYTELLER: The Green Man has danced his rounds; the summer sun has risen to his zenith. All the fertile earth revels in light and warmth, and even night is laden with the fragrance and melody of the green.

But we stand now at this halfway point with winter's chill dark on the horizon. Yet we do not fear, knowing Bel has descended to the depths and arisen before, and will do so again. And Tailtiu has been good to see to our mortal needs. There is bread and wine and honey. We have no fear and revel in the green.

EISTEDDFOD: We revel in the green.

CHIEF BARD: Crickets fiddle and fireflies dance
merry rounds to nature's tune.
Foxes hunt and twilight owls fly

beneath the horns of the summer moon.
Summer breathes life and green,
a sure and old promise,
bounty flows from Tailtiu's breast,
sun and earth weave harvest.

EISTEDDFOD: Sun and earth weave harvest.

STORYTELLER: The twilight time is at hand this midsummer night. We are at a crossroads; a between time betwixt the seasons of light and cold. Magic—green magic—scents the air. Smell it, taste it, feel it.

MUSICIAN: [*Switches to a haunting, melodious piece*]

CHIEF BARD: Enchantment of life, enchantment of nature
lies upon the familiar earth.
Feel it in the black loam, promising mystery
within every forest shadow.
Hear it in the bubbling gurgle
of the sparkling brook's melody.
Know it by the places
where light and shadow mingle.
The hidden friend,
the poet's power,
the truth that must never quite be known . . .
sacred mystery.
Imbas comes through the summer green,
the strength of our magic and our art.

STORYTELLER: The sun in full strength must now wane and descend. The house of death inexorably draws him down. But he has gifted us with imbas in this green season of wonder, and mystery powers our art and craft. Nature thrives and so do we. We will make song for the sun and his beloved earth mother, and bid them our best. The earth mother will hear and remember our enchantments and win back her bright love. And the Green Man will dance again.

EISTEDDFOD: Let the Green Man dance.

STORYTELLER: We bid farewell to the waning sun, but he is long from departed. Let us celebrate his gifts of harvest and bounty, for he has given us this moment. Let us live our tales in the warm heart of summer.

We have the moment, this green, and pleasant twilight of the heart of summer. Let us toast Lughnasadh.

Each member of the eisteddfod eats a piece of bread, a piece of an apple, and washes it down with mead or cider.

EISTEDDFOD: And let us toast the sun lord.

All drink again.

CHIEF BARD: We have the warm moment, this twilight
of the green summertime.
Let us live in it.
We have the augury,
the sun will wane.
Let us harvest.
We have the promise,
the sun will ascend again.
Let us remember the turning of the wheel.

STORYTELLER: The wheel turns round, as does the year. Summer waxes, summer wanes. Let us live now, in the heart of the green moment. The sun will come again into power. And until then, we have the summer . . . and the harvest.

The festival concludes with a rich feast, which should consist of the fresh produce of summer. Let there be music and gaiety, for we have the green moment.

Other Traditions

There are many other old traditions of Celtdom and bardry that are worthy of our consideration. In the next few pages we will consider two particular traditions of especial interest to us, which will undoubtedly enhance your progress along this path. In addition to these traditions, every student of bardry must research the old lore and learn more for him- or herself. In this way, you will add depth and richness to the bardic path, and build a greater magnitude of understanding of the hidden Old Ways. Do not be afraid to explore the mysteries and experiment. There is little danger in most of the old traditions. When there is, it is usually quite obvious. Let common sense guide you.

Dark Huts

Some very reliable old lore tells us that the Gaelic bards made a practice of meditating in dark huts or dark places.[1] They would enter the darkness for a time of physical stillness, and without any distraction—save a stone upon their bellies—they would compose their finest poetry. Witnesses of the practice, such as Clanricarde, attest that it is very obvious that they do this in order to give their minds wholly over to the creation of poetry. However, Clanricarde's observation does not explain why the bards did it with a stone upon their bellies, as is recorded by Martin Martin in his memoirs of his travels in old Scotland. This practice is significant to us partly because as bards, it is our sacred mission to honor and preserve the memory of the Old Ways, but most importantly because this venerable practice is backed by centuries, if not millennia, of experience and wisdom.

The Marquis of Clanricarde is correct when he postulates that the bards sought separation from earthly distractions in their dark huts. Such a place would be the old equivalent of a modern sensory deprivation tank. By cutting the mind off from external stimuli, it is easier to disengage the psyche from the here and now. With the mind so freed, the psyche can be fully turned upon meditative and shamanic work. In perfect darkness it can walk undisturbed throughout the psychic Otherworld; it can focus undistracted upon the riddles a bard ever seeks to unravel.

Yet we are told in these old accounts that the bards' specific purpose for this practice was to compose. If poetry arises from experience in the here and now of the real world, how could isolation in darkness lead to poetry of value?

To understand this, we must remember that the ancient bards of the pre-Christian Celtic world where this shamanlike practice probably began were oral composers. They were not illiterate, yet they wrote nothing down until far into the church era because of an ancient druidic injunction against writing. (The bards of the Irish tradition are an exception to this statement. Old legend tells us that one of St. Patrick's first acts was to burn all the

Pagan writings of the Irish. So if there is any truth to this, we must assume the Irish were writing their lore even though the rest of the Celts were not. While Celts to the core, the Irish have always been a people apart.)

Even unwritten, the poetry of the bards was complex. It was rich, sometimes epic, and used complicated metrical and rhyming systems. In a situation where writing is forbidden and yet the poetry must still meet the highest standards, the bards of old would have had to devise another effective way to create the art of their craft. It is likely that they took themes from experience and composed them into raw material for poetry in their heads while they were out in the real world, sort of like an unwritten first draft. Having highly trained memories, they mentally stored these first drafts away for when they could return to their huts and meditate upon the poetry. There, in undisturbed darkness and profound meditation, they put the material into a form acceptable to the high Celtic poetic standards.

So why the stone upon the belly? I believe this was no ordinary stone, but most likely some kind of fetish. The Gaels knew many natural objects to be magically empowered or resonant. A piece of rowan wood, a hazel nut, and a spider's web, to name the barest few, were all objects of magic for them. Among the most powerful magical objects were ward stones and faerie stones. Ward stones, also known as faerie stones, were rounded stones with a hole naturally worn through the middle, usually found in dry streambeds. Another kind of faerie stone commonly known as *elf shot* is a prehistoric arrowhead. Black and green stones held healing power when gathered and used properly. Smooth stones could be used for divination. White stones—probably moonstone or some other white quartz—could open the gates to the Otherworld. As the bards sought imbas in their composition, I suspect the stones to which Martin refers were moonstones used to assist opening the way between the worlds and aid the passage of imbas.

The old lore tells us the bards lay upon their backs in their dark huts and placed such a stone upon the belly while they riddled their poetry. According to the ancient Hindu concept of chakras (which may be related to some Celtic mysticism through their common, ancient Indo-European links), a very powerful region is the area at the base of the spine. From there comes potency that, if it the meditator can channel it, can be raised to the high chakras of the head, and illumination results. I think we may have a parallel here. The bards placed the stone near this power region of the body and channeled power through it, or by it, to create an Otherworldly linkage. In this way the bard opened the way to the Otherworld and called upon its power in the form of imbas to charge his poetry with supernatural beauty and power and to enlighten his heart and mind.

This is a practice that may well benefit the contemporary bard. One needs only to find a dark, quiet place to meditate and a fetish stone of smooth white quartz. Then, with a heart given over to the creative work, the bard can *actually evoke imbas*. Practicing this technique will train the bardic student to actively search for and retrieve imbas. It will also hone the mind as you work out your bardic crafts in your meditations.

The Ceilidh

The ceilidh [*KAY-lee*] is an ancient and universal Celtic tradition. In elder times, at the end of a hard work day, it was traditional for the people of a village, and sometimes even lords and nobles, to assemble for the ceilidh. This might take place out of doors, around great bonfires when the weather was pleasant, or it would be held in a home or a barn. On special occasions lords might host it in their great halls.

When the children were settled and every man and woman was comfortably sat with a goblet of ale, mead, or wine, the seanachie would launch into tales of myth and legend. Poetry and music were often welcome additions to the night's ceilidh as well. On the rare occasion that a professional bard might be traveling through, he or she was the guest of honor. The bard would entertain the people with bardic song and story beside the embers of the dying fire till well into the night. The Celts—lovers since the dawn of time of well-wrought tales, poetry, and music—listened raptly until sleep's call beckoned beyond the ability to resist. Contented with the night's yarns, they each went to their own place to dream of encounters with the Otherworld, gallant heroes, and damsels of fey beauty.

The ceilidh tradition seems instinctive to the human spirit and has not only been preserved in cultures related to the Celts, but appears, in some form or another, in every other culture as well. The Native American tribes recognized the immense educative value of story and wove intricate tales of mythology and folk wisdom in order to educate their people in ethics and culture. The Australian aboriginals preserved their mythology with tales of the dreamtime. Kids throughout North America still sit around summer-night campfires to chill each other with ghost stories. All of these forms of the ceilidh evoke vague instinctual memories of powers that confound the otherwise neatly logical material world.

The Celts developed this storytelling session into a regular social event *and* a fine art. Their tales had every kind of story quality: the ability to heal the soul, to teach ethics, to inspire, and to simply entertain. Story, either as poetry or prose, is such a powerful medium because it requires active participation, unlike passive media such as television and radio. Storytelling requires the speaker to work hard at his or her creation and put a piece of the soul into the tale, just as any skilled artist puts a piece of soul into his craft. It requires the listener to attune to the storyteller, to engage the imagination, and to support the story with feedback. When combined with the primal communicative power of music, story's power is amplified manyfold. This is why the old bards, who were masters of the three powerful mediums of communication (prose, poetry, and music), were so treasured by the Celts who understood the deep enchantment of story.

The contemporary bard would do well to revive the ceilidh tradition. It doesn't have to be a regular event. It may only be something to conduct after rituals, or during other eisteddfod assemblies. It may be done with others for fun, perhaps during camp-outs and get-togethers. What is important is that myth and folklore are shared, the Old Way is continued, and the soul of each listener (and the teller) is fed by the bard's craft. Everyone who participates will benefit.

If at all possible, the ceilidh is best held outdoors around a bonfire. When the weather is inclement, an indoors setting will suffice. No one person should hog all the attention, not even if he or she is the only practicing bard present. Ceilidhs are so powerful because they require active participation. The more who contribute, the stronger the overall feeling of community will be, and the more the listener-participants will come away with from the event.

Poetry and prose are acceptable mediums for the ceilidh. Best are tales based on folklore and myth. I have found that tales of the elder legends— which incorporate elements of Otherworldly contact, enchantment, heroes and heroines, and other myth elements—are the most powerful and appropriate for such an event. The tales should not be parables; no one will enjoy this sort of indirect preaching. Rather, they should have strong entertainment value. Believe me, such tales will nevertheless work to engender the growth of the soul as they penetrate to the depths of being with their examples of courage, villainy, and humanity, and plays on luck and magic. I highly recommend Nancy Mellon's *The Art of Storytelling* as a beginning study of the old art and power of storytelling.[2]

If some of the participants are musical, they can greatly enrich the tales with musical accompaniment. Better still is if the storyteller is himself musical, as the bard should be. The tale-teller can then craft the musical accompaniment to add emotional undercurrents that make the tale feel just the way he envisions it.

When providing musical accompaniment, the bard will discover that it is especially useful to be able to play some kind of string or percussion instrument as opposed to wind instruments. This is because if the storyteller is also the musician, he must interrupt telling the tale to add music with wind instruments. No such interruption is necessary for strings and percussion.

I have found that among the most suitable instruments for a ceilidh are the harp, the bodhran, the lute, and the dulcimer. The bodhran's deep rhythmic voice adds power to any tale. The lute and dulcimer are more suitable to many players as they are played similarly to the guitar and add atmosphere to any occasion. The harp, being very capable of emotive chords and melody as well as potent rhythm, is especially appropriate. It is also the archetypal instrument of the bard. It seems to belong in the midst of a ceilidh.

The most important thing is to have fun. Roast some hotdogs and marshmallows. Make some hot chocolate. Drink some good wine or mead or ale. Watch the stars. Enjoy the timeless truth of story. The bard's way is about fulfillment, and the ceilidh is a rich source indeed.

Summary

Note that the two "other traditions" are not magical in themselves. Rather, their practice puts the participant(s) in touch with magic, mystery, and imbas. They also put the participant(s) in touch with nature, the Old Ways, and like-minded community. Both traditions are powerful forces of fulfillment and growth through their ability to touch the psyche.

Referring to the holiday rituals, those readers who are familiar with other magical traditions, such as Wiccan or "high" magic, will note the simplicity of the bardic rituals. There are no circles cast, and no complicated procedures to follow. This is because bardic magic draws its power from very primal sources and from within. The bard wants no protective circle because the powers and presences of the natural world are welcome. Bardic magic originates from and belongs among them; there is no want or need of separation. Also because bards enjoy a special protection among the Otherworld, they have little need of protective circles during their rituals.

While there are no choreographed ritual movements that require great precision as there are in the high magical traditions, precise movement is required of the musical and poetic crafts of bardry. Understand that your music and poetry *are* your primary means of high magic. To utilize them, you must possess well-practiced skill with your instrument, poetic system, and imbas. This is in fact more demanding than the ritual movements of some other magical forms, but its potential is also far greater. The beings of the Otherworld love inspired poetry and music, and they will respond. Poetry is a shaper of emotions, and magical music is a shaper and mover of the psychical and spiritual forces of the worlds.

Remember that the bardic magic and ritual system is still in the process of rediscovery after nearly being lost for almost two centuries. Its rediscovery will depend on accurate research, experimentation, and contact with the Otherworld. Do not be afraid to experiment; just exercise common sense. Do not cast harmful magics, nor work with the spirits of chaos, such as the Fomor. Use protections, such as rowan wands, as you experiment. With research and heart and determination, the magical tradition of bardry can be reconstructed as we who choose the bardic path work to regain all that has been forgotten of the way of enchantment, beauty, and art.

chapter fifteen

Ceridwen's Cauldron

*[O]rganizing Mystery tends to undermine
its essence.*

Charles de Lint, *Paperjack*

Legend holds that in the goddess Ceridwen's great cauldron, a broth made from every herb found in Wales and with many incantations was boiled down into the essence of wisdom. Taliesin Pennbardd (meaning "the great bard") accidentally drank a tiny bit of this sorcerous brew when he was but a boy known as Gwion Bach. He acquired all wisdom, and became the archetypal master of the bardic mysteries. In the following pages we shall examine some of these mysteries and strive to understand what they offer us as modern bards living in contemporary times.

Certain scholars have argued that to be a true bard or druid, and to partake fully in the bardic mysteries, one must be a Celt of the old times. Their argument is that the wisdom of that past age is no longer relevant today; that the world has moved on and left such antiquated thinking behind. Those that proffer this argument say the age of the druids is dead; their relevance can be no more for there is no more place or use for them in the twenty-first century.

Yet we have examined the Celtic psychology and found that many concepts the old Celts knew—the importance of the individual, the ever-present need for growth and fulfillment, the concept of the self, the endless hero's quest—were always present in their thought. Only in the past century are these timeless truths being rediscovered by psychologists as fundamental to a healthy psyche.

We have examined the Celts' art and found in it an enchanted healing virtue that is therapeutic for the body and the soul. We have examined their culture and discovered it possesses a changeless quality and strength our restless modern Western culture, which so glorifies change for change's sake, lacks. The Celts' psychology, art, and culture convey a message of growth, adaptation, resilience, health, peace, stability, and contentment. When did these things become obsolete? The answer is never. They should be just as applicable for human nature today as they were in elder times. While our scientific knowledge and technical prowess have increased, and the appearance of the world has changed, the human being is still the same basic creature that has existed since all the world was a primeval wilderness. Our core psychological and physical beings possess the same timeless needs they have for millions of years.

Perhaps there is a grain of truth to the argument that the wisdom of the old Celts is not for moderns. Without their deep respect for tradition, appreciation for the craft of story and music, and an awareness of the enchantment that lies between the rhythm and cadences of poetry, the bardic mysteries are of little value. Without an awareness of the spiritual value of art, its power to mend the shattered self will be overlooked. Without a spirit made aware of its deep kinship with the natural world, the spirit will not attune to nature, nor find the harmony and healing there that it so craves.

So, in fact, the contention that one must be a Celt of old for the bardic-druidic mysteries to have relevance is, in fact, correct—just not in the way the scholars who proposed it meant. This does not pronounce an end to the order of bards and druids. To bring them back, a rebirth of the old Celtic soul in the modern heart is required. Being a Celt is no mere matter of blood. It is a vital force that runs in the spirit more richly than blood. It is a perspective and a culture that can be learned, a knowledge that can be acquired, and a passion that can be appropriated. The Otherworld is ready for the one with a desire for the green, earthy enchantments who is willing to commit to relearning the Old Ways; it is waiting to pour imbas forth to illuminate the mysteries.

Are you a Celt? If not, you can be.

The Celts' wisdom is the mystical key to nurturing a Celtic spirit. Study it and meditate on it. Make it one with your being through the power of memory. I don't mean you have memorize every word of the lore, but intimately know the spirit of the lore.

Bear in mind that what is presented below is only the beginning. There is oh so much more. In this space I have only been able to provide a foundation. It is up to you to go beyond and fully realize your grasp of the Celt's way so that you can fully appreciate the mysteries of the bardic path.

The forever Quest

A reading of a representative sample of Celtic tales—whether from legend, myth, or modern fiction—reveals an interesting trend: the Celts seemed to thrive on tragedy. Their greatest heroic tales end disastrously. The Irish hero Cuchulainn is finally slain through the Mórrígán's duplicity. Arthur falls to his own son's treachery. The bright Tuatha de Danaan are overrun by the Milesian invaders. The Breton druidic hero Koadalan tragically loses his family to a plague after a heroic struggle to save them, then perishes himself in a terrible abuse of the deep elder enchantments as he struggles to achieve immortality. Yet, despite all the calamity, the Celtic folk grew from these tales, and found the strength to persist as a people who would not perish, even as other cultures all around them came and went. Even the mighty Roman Empire, which had conquered so much of their world and held it for a thousand years, finally left them behind.

From these tales one discerns a mystery of the Celtic way. Their resilience and changelessness does not arise from strength of arms or economic prowess—the things most people equate with power. Indeed, over the past two millennia they have suffered countless military defeats and lost ground. (Having once occupied a vast portion of the Western world, they now are largely confined to the westernmost rim of Europe and a few areas in the New World and elsewhere.) No, their power lies deeper; it is rooted in the old magics, the ancient wisdoms. The Celts are lovers of the quest; they treasure the road more than the place to which it leads. They are a people always becoming, and so are ever charged with the purpose to move on, to evolve, to improve. Their historic disdain is surrender. Knowing that death is but the midpoint of a long life, they do not fear death, and they do not fear defeat. They fear only giving up. For that they are free to give themselves to the hero's quest, free to develop to the fullest their unique gifts and talents, their arts and crafts, their intellects, their magic and music.

The Celts found solace and power in their tragic tales because their outlook made it perfectly valid for them to focus on the goal and not the result. If Koadalan was tragically separated from his family forever for having grasped at godhood, he is a hero for having sought to exceed his bounds. In the old, pre-Christian druidic doctrine, Koadalan would have received another chance to overcome his faults in the Otherworld. If Cuchulainn was defeated by the Mórrígán in Ireland, he would have another chance to overcome his nemesis in the Summer Country (a term for an Otherworld land). The Celts had learned early in their history to value the Otherworld at least as much, if not more, than the here and now. It was not the current circumstances that mattered so much as the pursuit of the ideal. There was no room for stasis, and failure would be met with yet another chance to succeed elsewhere. So the ideal was to steadfastly pursue the hero's quest; to ever be a traveler on the road of growth. No mere defeat of a single lifetime could stop the quester. The great failure was in ceasing to reach for something greater, and in the doing, failing to evolve.

The Celtic way honored no oblivion of Nirvana. They sought no bliss of Eastern passivity. Such a concept would have been anathema to the old Celtic psychology. There was always the struggle to evolve, and there was always evolution. To cease to strive was to devolve—a fate worse than oblivion in the Celtic mind, for it lacked honor and was full of shame. It is not important to the Celtic spirit whether one's efforts are met with worldly success or defeat. The real victory is the change wrought within, the pride of having tried, and the strength of growing through triumph or tragedy. So the Celts grew from their myths, and their losses strengthened them as much as their gains. They became the resilient people, the elder race who would not go the way of the Tuatha de Danaan, the Romans, or the Mohigans. They would persist and they would survive, as they have done for some three thousand years or more. (Indeed, in various names and places, they have persisted for much longer.) Their strength is in the quest, which itself is the goal. Because they never arrived, it was never time to quit. There is always the need to move on and room to grow. The Celtic spirit continues through all lands and all times because continuance is the quest, and the quest is all.

There are two distinct ways to pursue the quest. One may attempt the short road. This is the fast way to enlightenment. It is the foolhardy way, for it is fraught with danger and the quester is liable to lose, for the Otherworld will not admit the unready and the unworthy to its mysteries. Only the very lucky, the divinely protected, and the prodigiously gifted succeed on this quick path, and even then they often meet with terrible failure in the long run having failed their patron protector in wisdom or strength. In modern terms, this short path might be equated to the person who uses dangerous drugs to induce shamanic meditative states rather than patiently learning the techniques of meditation. It could also be equated to the college student who cheats on an exam rather than plodding along with her studies. In the former example, the intrepid shaman stands to lose his mind. In the latter, the student stands to lose her academic career. In a poem attributed to the Pennbardd Taliesin, he declares that he will not reveal the bardic mysteries to the unworthy. This is as much protective as possessive. Few people can handle true enlightenment (true-sight) without adequate preparation, despite whatever they think. Unless they are ready, enlightenment will disappoint them, or perhaps even utterly destroy them. Failure on the short path is nearly always dire. I strongly advise against attempting it.

The other path is the bard's way, which is also the druid's way. It is the way of patiently developing a relationship with the Otherworld, the gods, your arts, and imbas through the techniques you have learned in this book and will study as you discover other reliable sources. It is the way that will launch you on the hero's quest, lead you to growth in knowledge and wisdom, and guide you to knowing yourself through the arduous process of individuation and integration. Remember, it took twelve years to train a bard of old, and though with the profundity of books available today you might be able to gain knowledge a bit faster, it will take many years to absorb and process it. Be patient, and let the gods guide your development so that you proceed in your own best time. The bard is a walker of the long path; it is a time-proven way that cannot be hurried. Yet the reward is a stable relationship with enchantment. Unlike the chooser of the quick path, the true bard need not fear presuming to peer at the mysteries before the soul is ready as happened to some knights of the Arthurian myth who dared hunt out the grail mysteries before they were ready. The bard will know to look where he is ready when he is ready.

The patient, steadfast way of the bard is the true hero's path. It is the unending forever quest; a pursuit that will heal and empower yourself and others, and make you welcome in the Summer Country.

The Power of Naming

It is the nature of the bard's craft to take that which is shallowly understood and peer into it until it is known profoundly—thus naming it. This is the mystery of the artist, and it is this intimate knowing that is the key to the magical power of poetry, song, and music, for it is only when the true nature of a thing is named that the enchanter has real power over it. This is why many magical workings require an article from the person or thing the sorcerer wishes to enchant. Something intimately connected *knows* the nature of that from which it came. More importantly than merely gaining magical power, it is only when a thing is truly and deeply known that the bard can grow from it, for little of lasting value comes from a shallow perception.

Only when something is known deeply can it be given its true name. Until then, we can only think of it in gross terms. For example, we may see a hairy, four-legged beast with a wagging tail, drooling tongue, and unending appetite, and know it only shallowly as a dog. On the other hand, we may bring the creature into our home and get to know it as a friend and companion with a unique personality, eccentric needs, and a penchant for giving furry hugs—thus coming to know the creature profoundly. This learning something deeply is the process of naming. Giving names empowers us to conceive with accuracy in a way that runs deeper than spoken language. We may then say much of it with few, but well-chosen words, which is a principle of the bardic poetry of the old Celtic tradition. A good poet could say a great deal about any person or thing he had named with very few words, thus making for concise, potent verse.

Using his crafts and imbas, the bard expresses a thing in fullness. In this naming act, he makes it a part of his being. The bard effects personal growth through gaining knowledge and wisdom and expanding his sphere of being. He also gains magical influence over the thing that is named, and this is why bardic poetry is so powerful. By its very nature, it shapes and directs magical energy onto the true nature of a thing.

As a bard, when you begin to name things through your crafts, you will discover a new ability to look beyond yourself. You will find yourself growing through this ability and your own self-knowledge expanding. As all things are interrelated, to know something else in fullness is to know a bit more about yourself as well. This is the mystery of naming taking root in your life.

Yet naming is not easy. Few people possess the genuine desire or courage to seek out the true nature of a thing. Really, they would want to know the essence of, say, their mate, no more than they would the bird in the tree beyond the window. This is partly because modern people are taught to be content with shallow, surface appearances: frivolous fashion, the accumulation of possessions, money, and prestige. Yet the real reason the average person fears discerning true names is because it reveals the self. One must search and face one's deep being in order to relate to all there is of another thing. Coming to profoundly know something or someone else forces you to look at parts of yourself you might rather not (especially when it is so much easier to be acceptably superficial), but dare to look! Know yourself and make peace with yourself in order that your growth might not be hindered, and watch your relationships with everyone and everything else deepen and enrich immeasurably. The bard who masters the naming skill and the courage to use it will become a revealer and a scryer; one gifted with true-sight who knows things for the true essence of what they are, and so knows himself as well.

The Cosmology of Bardry

The Celtic cosmology seems simple, but this probably results from the fact that it was systematically wiped from living druidic memory—first by the Roman Empire on the European continent, and, later, by the Roman church in Ireland. The Celts, having chosen to avoid written language because of its perpetual enchantment qualities, lost much of the memory of their knowledge when the continuous line of druidry was interrupted by conquest. If it was not for the bards, who were the only druids acceptable to their conquerors (for their entertainment abilities), their ancient wisdom would have been entirely lost.

That the druids were natural philosophers (an old term for scientists) becomes very clear from an examination of the old literature written about them. This truth is further evidenced by a study of the archaeological relicts they left behind. The Coligny calendar, for example, shows their interest in astronomy, meteorology, zoology, and botany. The druids sought to understand the universe around them and the powers that drove it. Bards, long a fundamental part of druidry, were allied in this quest.

When examined in depth, one discovers that the Celtic view of the universe is really quite intricate, and, like all old cosmologies, its details vary from locale to locale. Amalgamating the wisdom from each region that has survived into the present day, I believe we can put together a close approximation to the ancient Celtic myth of creation. The overall legend is that the world arose from darkness or water. The great supreme being cast the world into being, and set nature into motion. At some point well into the evolutionary progress of nature on earth, humanity arose, and from humankind's humble beginnings, eventually the Tuatha de Danaan arose. The god and goddess then began to oversee the Tuath with love and care. They led them on a wandering pilgrimage that eventually took them into Ireland where they overthrew the Fomor, the tribe of the power of chaos.

Meanwhile, the Indo-Europeans had fractured into various peoples ranging from Siberia to western Europe. Among these were the Celts who settled primarily from the Baltic Sea to Iberia. The Celts, it seems, were the kindred of the older tribe of the Danaan (but as advanced as the Celts were, they were like children compared to the Danaan). Led by visionaries, the Celts eventually entered Britain and Ireland and managed to conquer the older tribe. The Tuatha retreated into the hollow hills to hide from cruel and primitive humanity. Certain gifted bards and druids were allowed to dwell with the Danaan, and they learned the lore of the Danaan, much of which became foundational to druidry. So it was that the isles of Britain became the cornerstone of druidry, the place where the Celts of Gaul sent their druids to study.

In the Celtic cosmology, the cosmos can be conceived of as three concentric wheels. Each wheel has its own properties, principles, and designation. The outermost wheel is sometimes referred to by Cymric (Welsh) mystics as *Annwn* [AN-noon]. This is the outer darkness; the formless primal stuff from which creation was made and all things originate. It is a place of undirected energy, ultimate beginnings, and chaos awaiting order. It is not a hell of punishment, but, being chaotic, it is the abode of demons—or beings devoted to chaos—whose desire is to return the ordered universe to a chaotic state.

The next state is called *Abred,* according to Cymric Celtic mysticism. Other Celts might call it "the here and now" or "the middle kingdom." Even contemporary psychology has a name for it: the *dasein,* which means the place in the universe in which we are grounded. This is the world as we know it; where we now exist. It is sometimes called "the middle kingdom" because it is the place where chaos and order meet and intermingle, and where they are held in balance. It is a place where great powers mix and flow. On either side of the middle kingdom are the Otherworlds. The Otherworlds on one side become more wild and chaotic as they approach Annwn, and those on the other become more ordered as they near brightness and order.

The here and now is both fixed and not fixed. It is as narrow as one's ability and willingness to perceive it, and likewise just as limitless. For the unimaginative, the world is a very dry place. For those with true-sight, second sight, or who are touched by imbas and in love with mystery, the world is rich with beauty, marvels, enchantment, and possibilities. Plus, these perspectives mix continuously, for mere perspective only defines reality for a single individual. As people come into contact and share their views, reality itself is enlarged and changed. This is the mystery of the power of story.

The here and now works by its own rules, and constantly pulls us back and forth from soft-edged mystery to the hard-edged material. Where it tugs us depends on the play of quantum chance and luck. Magic is the skill of influencing the forces of luck and chance at a very basic level. It subtly sets the machinery of the universe to work things out as the enchanter desires. The shifting of the here and now is also the reason why in some places, and at some times, the veil between the worlds is worn thin. Certain times and places have the power to open the way between the worlds and allow magic to flow. Openings may also occur at random for any combination of reasons. The point is, the middle kingdom is a place in flux, and full of magic and possibility to the one who knows how to look for it. The bard develops the ability to perceive this.

The innermost wheel is called *Gwynvid* [pronounced *GWIN-vidt*] in the Cymric tradition of Celtic mysticism. It is what some religions call paradise or heaven, and it is the abode of perfection and divine beings. It is the final world before the realm of the supreme being itself. Every myth tradition of the world seems to indicate that Gwynvid is a place of great beauty, knowledge, and joy. As one approaches Otherworlds closer to Gwynvid, one finds realms of increased perfection. As one grows from being on the hero's quest, one becomes more ready to inhabit this realm.

Do not confuse Gwynvid with the Nirvana of the Eastern religious tradition. The point of the hero's quest is to become more perfect and to grow, not to cast oneself away into the brightness and lose one's personality and identity forever in the divine. As we discussed in chapter 2, to sacrifice the self is anathema in the Celtic mythology. The goal is to pursue individuality and perfection in order to become the best being you can be; to become in the likeness of the divine while still retaining your unique selfness. This growth will make us better individuals and take us on to better things; it is never to end in losing one's own special personality, for the divine is a creator, not a destroyer.

In any case, while becoming so perfect as to be like the divine is the goal, it is not attainable, for we are finite and the divine is infinite. Thus, the hero's quest is the pursuit of an eternity. Existence will forever be made interesting with challenges, relationships, and self-discovery as we grow and move forward among an infinity of Otherworlds. I find this to be an exciting destiny.

No wonder the Celts of old had no fear whatsoever of death, nor a desire for it. As long as they stayed in this world, they could advance themselves through their art, their work, and their druidic skill. When death finally did arrive, they could build on what they learned here in the next world.

Please bear in mind that there are other possible interpretations of the Celtic cosmology. You should allow your own studies to help you develop your understanding. If you find your studies leading you to different conclusions, know that I make no claim to having written infallible truth. I present to you only one bardic student's understanding of the Celtic cosmology after years of intense study. In fact, it is my hope that as others become students of the bardic tradition, they will advance the study of the Celtic cosmology and help to refine and define it. Hopefully, one day it will be fully and properly reconstructed. It may turn out that I have been wrong on many points, but then, being wrong is also a way to growth.

Celtic Divinities

The concept of a supreme being alongside polytheism seems contradictory, yet they are equally valid in the bardic-Celtic way of thinking. Celtic scholar Jean Markale has argued convincingly that the druids possessed a well-developed concept of a supreme being.[1] With this, I tend to agree. However, the Celts were not so vain as to anthropomorphize this deity into a man or woman who could fit their limited human conceptions and be squeezed into the boxes of manmade dogmatic doctrine. Rather, they held that this being was a great creative, intelligent force. Not above compassion and caring for its many creations, but also not being human, the divine is not one to think in an anthropomorphic way. This being is absolute perfection and creativity—the energizing and guiding force at the heart of all the worlds. This being dwells in and, in fact, *is* a place some Cymric mystics called *Ceugant*. Today we might call Ceugant Nirvana, the Light, Paradise, the One God, or the Source, for the term refers to both the divine being and its private domain. *Ceugant* is the thing toward which all creation evolves and seeks to imitate.

That the Celts knew this being to be unanthropomorphizable is demonstrated in history. When the Celtic general Brennus attacked the ancient Greek city of Delphi and took the temple of Apollo, it is said he laughed to see that the Greeks had portrayed the gods as human and molded them in stone. As an educated noble of the Celts, it is almost certain that Brennus received druidic schooling. He would have been aware of their views of the supreme being, and known that to reduce the divine to the likeness of mere man was childish and shortsighted.

However, because the supreme being is so far above humanity as to be all but incomprehensible, the Celts found it convenient to think of it in terms of its manifestations in the natural world—the gods and goddesses. These lesser gods are as real a part of the supreme being as we are. Yet it would seem their natures and functions are defined by the needs of human belief, for they exist to facilitate the limited human capacity to comprehend the divine. They function to reveal attributes of divinity, both empowered and limited by the humans who perceive them. So the Celtic gods are reflections of infinity made finite so that godhood can be grasped by us.

There were many Celtic gods, and they were often localized to the tribes and even villages of various regions throughout old Celtica. These gods reflected the supreme being in ways suitable to the thoughts and needs of the individual people they served. That belief shapes them does not make these finite gods any less real. They are not the mere product of human imagination. Nor are they merely ways to grasp the supreme god with no independent reality. Like us, they are individual and real. They have their own consciousnesses, their own personalities, their own wants, desires, virtues and faults, and all is reflected in the countless tales of them found in Celtic myth. Yet as beings whose root purpose is to reveal the supreme divinity to humanity, their form is malleable. Their appearances shape-change to fit the need of each local people who believes in them. Thus, the gods possess a very real and unique individual personality, yet their forms shift to fit our conceptions and reveal the supreme being as our humanness requires.

Transmigration and the Return of the Soul

It is widely held that the Celts adhered to a belief in reincarnation. This is probably true, though it is not to be taken in the Eastern sense. Celtic transmigration did not involve reincarnation as another animal or even another person. Under normal circumstances, it seemed that a transmigrating human soul would be reconstructed in the Otherworld. His or her body and psyche would remain essentially intact; that is, the person would retain the same gender, personality, and memories he or she possessed in this world. Iolo Morgannwg, the Welsh mystic of the nineteenth century, presented a theory of transmigration in which a soul journeyed over time from the lowest possible lifeform to the highest of being. I presume the latter would be something angelic and just beneath god, or perhaps it was actually united to the supreme being in the end. However, this idea comes more from Gnosticism and Hermeticism than Celtic lore. Iolo wrote as much as he could from a factual basis, but because he was prone to flights of fancy when facts were lacking, all his works are suspect, and we cannot take his theories seriously. Other sources are available to help us understand the mystery of what happens to the soul when it exits this world.

When we look at tales that remain to us of the old Celtic mythology, we see that when people left this world, they emigrated to another. For instance, in the tale of Koadalan, we find that Koadalan's family retained their essential characteristics in the Otherworld after having died from the plague in this one. Likewise, we find a similar situation in the tale "Bro Arc'hant" where the king of the silver land retains his essential form and personality in this world and the Otherworld. Even his Otherworldly body, though it is ageless, remains mortal, for he dies in the tale, and his soul wanders on to yet another world.

An idea emerges from a study of the many Celtic myths and folktales once one eliminates the influences of the church monks who recorded many of these tales and altered a number of events to coincide with their dogma. That idea is that at death, a soul leaves this world to go on to another world more wonderful and magical than the one before, with challenges aplenty to offer opportunities for growth. The soul arrives in the new world much as he or she was before, with his or her skills and learning intact. Once there, the quest for growth—the hero's quest—is taken up again. It is an act of divine kindness that the personality and memories do remain intact, for otherwise it would mean that a person must start over forever at the event of transmigration. The time in the previous world would have been lost and essentially wasted.

Sometimes, it would seem, souls do not cross over to the next world. Instead, they manage to return here. This not only occurs occasionally in the Celtic lore (such as in the heroic legends of Finn and Arthur), but it is also attested to by scholarly studies. The British Society of Psychical Research, an old and respected academic group devoted to the research of paranormal phenomena, has hundreds of well-documented cases of transmigration in its archives. This demonstrates that some spirits do seem to reappear in new bodies in this world after death. Many cases, perhaps hundreds, stand out for their verifiable facts. The claimants' memories of past lives have been checked for accuracy and been found to be so accurate as to surpass the statistical odds of chance-correct recall. The claimants in these cases could not have guessed so precisely the previous life they claim to remember. Further, these cases have been carefully scrutinized for any possibility of fakery, and have been found to be free of fault. For instance, when a young child mysteriously possesses the ability to speak in a rare or extinct language, or can accurately recall the intimate details of a past life that he or she had no way of knowing, there is little possibility of fraud.

Yet usually when people return to this world after a previous life here, their memories are broken or devastated. Nor are they remade in the same essential physical form. They may cross racial or sexual barriers, for instance. Even their psyches might be structured quite differently. In the cosmic scheme of things, not moving on after death seems unnatural, and would cause incredible trauma to the soul that finds itself back in the world where it had previously lived. Perhaps each universe is prepared to hold only one individual for one lifetime. According to the Celtic lore, when souls return to the here and now there is a price. The price does not result from punishment. Rather, it is as if that natural polarity of flow toward improvement is rebutted. Fighting this powerful flow causes tremendous stress to the transmigrating soul, disrupts memories, and radically alters the new incarnation the soul takes.

If this is correct, why do these souls return despite the price? I suspect that the reasons are similar to those for which ghosts remain: unfinished business, an inability to accept death, fear of the beyond, loved ones to whom one is unwilling to say good-bye, and the like. Yet I can only speculate.

The point to remember is that Celtic transmigration is very flexible. It allows for moving on to the Otherworld, receiving a new, corporal body there, and taking up the hero's quest again. If the traveler cannot let go however, then it allows for staying behind, though at a price. If moving on, one seems to retain personality, form, and memory, and can build upon the growth of the previous life to continue his or her hero's quest in the next world. If one remains, there is a disruption of the natural flow, which results in trauma and causes radical alteration of the total person. Progress is broken and the quest must be begun anew.

Bardry, like druidry, is a pursuit of balance and harmony with nature. When one finds these, there is the peace to move on when one's time has come. In this way a life is not wasted, and opportunities for growth resume where they left off in the previous life in a world more wondrous than the last.

Balance and Growth

Balance is a vital part of all things. Nature requires a delicate balance between the elements and energy to create life and maintain it. Any living thing requires a balance between vitamins, minerals, nutrients, water, and energy to stay healthy and reproduce. Life requires a balance between plants, predators, prey, and decomposers to maintain a viable ecosystem, and on it goes. Any system relies upon balance to remain steady and stable. If balance should fail in any area, the system will fall into chaos and end.

Human beings require a balanced life-approach to maintain psychical, spiritual, and mental health. The ancient peoples were well aware of this, for the concept of the human need of balance have survived in modern practices of shamanism, Eastern religions, and Western mysticism. We can trace an awareness of it to the Celts through the lines of myth and folklore clearly and strongly enough that it can be reasonably assumed that balance was a key pursuit of druidry. Yet, oddly enough, modern humans seem to have forgotten the vital need for balance. Many contemporary people seem to feel they are above their basic needs, and will often focus on a small range of activities to the exclusion of their total requirements. Many technology buffs will hack on computers while their bodies and social lives waste from disuse. Business people will ignore family and recreation in pursuit of money and advancement. People who live in the heart of cities will become separated from the natural world and the natural order of things to the point that they no longer understand from where the meat and grain on their tables comes. Thus they fail to give honor to nature and the creatures that provided it.

Losing balance causes a person to become offset and unaware of the full range of reality. It sets one apart from natural rhythms, which is stressful and unhealthy for our bodies and spirits that have been tuned to respond to nature over millions of years. It leads to thinking errors, such as deeming the acquisition of possessions and money as the marker of success. It inevitably leads one to believe he or she is apart from and above the natural world. I think of Freud, who could not accept that our instincts were fundamental, natural, and healthy parts of the human personality. He thought they should be channeled into the "creative" endeavors of civilization. Freud was so wrapped up in the nineteenth-century belief of human superiority over nature that he could not accept that the instinctive side of us did not represent a dark, animal current, but rather our innate healthy connection to the natural world.

Unfortunately, Freud was very influential, and his misguided attempts to steer us away from balance have produced repercussions that are still being felt today, a century later. People fail to accept their total being, and strive to "rise above" their earthiness and become cerebrating, urban, "civilized" persons. They actually struggle to obtain an imbalance that I believe has led to more nervous breakdowns, depression, broken relationships, and harmful misconceptions than any other delusion in history. As I write this, I think of all the girls suffering anorexia nervosa, emaciating their bodies as they battle their healthy instinct to eat in pursuit of the "civilized" conception of the perfect body. I think of the vegetarians who believe it is morally wrong to eat meat. They don't understand that the predator-prey relationship is a natural, healthy relationship within nature, and that its practice by humans—when done with proper respect for nature and the spirit of the slain beast—is a vitalizing spiritual experience. I think of all the people who are working fifty-hour weeks to obtain a big house, techno-toys, a big car, prestige, status, and power, when in this life all that really matters is growth and joy. We are a race that has grown out of sync and off kilter, and now we are teetering on the brink of madness.

Surely this is why so many have divorced themselves from the modern world's ideals in the last fifty years, and turned to spiritualities and philosophies of peace, harmony, and fulfillment. Even if they did not understand what drove them away from the gallop of civilization, they perceived that something had gone awry, that people were not meant to live their lives so speedily and painfully, and that success shouldn't leave one feeling so shammed. As these people were torn from mystery and nature, they were discovering a soul-rending discontentment within. Perceptive people turned to paths that made those things alive again within them.

Bardry, like its cousin druidry, is an ancient path whose mission is to keep the forces of mystery and nature alive within and without. It strives to restore balance by turning the mind back to the spiritual, the artistic, the magical, and the natural. Bardry uses the media of folklore and myth, and tale and song to weave a web of enchantment into the participant's soul. This rejuvenates that which has been strangled by a "civilized" world burdened with priorities not truly in line with the needs of the inner human being.

Yet the path of the bard is not one only of inner spiritual growth, for this, too, would be an imbalance. How can there be effective growth unless there is growth in the total human being? Imbalanced growth is like a cancer that invades and offsets the system and throws it into chaos. True bardry must pursue the comprehensive growth of every vital aspect of being. Too much of a focus on any single aspect of life—be it the outer successes of technology, business, and scientific knowledge, or the inner successes of spirituality and artistry—represents a lifestyle out of balance and is harmful. Only when each life aspect is balanced to the proper degree can they combine to work the fullest positive effect. The great strength of the bard arises from a healthy, full relationship to all the dimensions of being. The bard, as everyone, must hone the entire being to become a complete and balanced person ready to grow as the sacred wheels of life turn.

The body should be cared for and kept fit. The mind should be made razor sharp with a liberal program of study. The spirit should be invigorated with magic and meditation. The whole soul of the being should be explored by the power of art. Balance never allows for stasis, but requires forever cultivating all areas of being.

Balance also requires a balance of passions. The emotions that motivate us and give meaning to life must be channeled so as to make their effects positive and beneficial. For instance, ambition is a fine motivational emotion, and is not negative in itself. Ambition can propel a budding entrepreneur into small-business success and direct a bardic student through the stages of growth. However, it can also push a hungry corporate powermonger into crushing small businesses and grasping for control of entire markets and peoples' lives. When ambition is balanced, its effects will be beneficial; it will provide the entrepreneur with enough impetus to be successful and independent. When it is imbalanced, it will spin out of control and devolve into greed and lust.

Even love can become imbalanced. In its balanced form it is a warmth and affection that leads one to care for and nurture another. When it is imbalanced it devolves into a need for possession and power over another.

The emotions, or passions, must be controlled so as to yield that which is positive. When an emotion no longer has a positive value, it is imbalanced and will inevitably bring harm to the individual experiencing the emotions as well as to others. You gain control over the passions first by meditating or in some way taking a time-out to allow your mind to cool down. Then you must ask yourself the following questions:

- Why do I feel what I feel? (What caused the emotion?)

- What do I want to do with what I feel? (How do I want to react?)

- Who will my reaction help? (Does the emotion promise long-term benefit?)

In the first question, consider if whoever has caused the emotion is aware of what he or she has done. Be empathetic; try to understand the other person's perspective. If you do not believe the other person is aware of having committed actions that caused your emotions, try using communication to work things out.

In the case of the second question, consider the nature of how you want to react to a feeling. Imagine you have a magic looking glass that allows you to see just how the things you will do will occur. Look into that looking glass and imagine how your reaction will pan out. Try to find alternative reactions and imagine how they will pan out as well.

In the final question, determine if any of your imagined reactions will benefit anyone, including yourself. For the reaction to be positive, it must benefit yourself or another, even if all it does is help you to feel better. If it does neither, then it has no therapeutic value and is not a positive reaction, which means it is imbalanced and of no use. Find another way to act upon your emotions.

Even the dark emotions of jealousy, greed, or anger can be balanced by positively channeling them. An example out of Celtic legend is the hero Cuchulainn, who, in times of battle, was overcome by a battle rage. His rage gave him godlike strength to defend and protect his people, which is a positive effect from a dark passion. Anger, for instance, can be channeled against the forces of hunger, poverty, and exploitation. When the dark emotions are allowed to express themselves darkly, as, say, abusive violence, then it is a sign of extreme unbalance. It is negativity begetting negativity. The bard must overcome this negative-begets-negative orientation of psychic force; it is highly destructive to the spirit of the self and others. Balance requires taking the dark forces—the forces of chaos—and channeling them toward the bright forces—the forces of order. Balance does not mean seeking to find the mean between good and evil, pain and pleasure, and order and chaos. It is not the art of mixing black and white to make a perfect gray as some have mistakenly thought. Balance is entirely positive. It is the art of balancing the negative by channeling it into something positive, and balancing the positive by enjoying it while not becoming addicted to it.

Finally, it is important to understand that you cannot fulfill every possible dimension of growth in a lifetime. You cannot become completely and evenly fulfilled in eighty-odd years. There is no shame in this; it is a simple impossibility. There are simply far too many outlets for a single lifetime of growth to actualize them all. That is why our opportunities for growth have been spread among a thousand lifetimes. Each turn upon the wheel allows us to go a step further toward perfection. Take your time as you progress so as to be sure to enjoy in the here and now what you have obtained. The pursuit of balance must be tempered by patience so that one can enjoy the pleasure of growth and avoid the negative forces of stress and the risk of burnout. Grow, but do not be in a rush to grow—there is no peace, no joy, and no fulfillment in that.

Above as Below

There is a link between druidry (and thus bardry) and Pythagoras, the philosopher whose work was foundational to the orders of Gnosticism and Hermeticism. We don't know which way the link flowed—that is, whether it was the druids who taught Pythagoras or Pythagoras who taught the druids—but for our purposes here, it is irrelevant. What is important is a fundamental teaching: as it is above, so it is below. This philosophy seems to be common to both druidry and Gnosticism. What it means is that throughout every other world, the reality of the here and now is a reflection of the divine. The deeper mysteries of the nature of all things contain an element of the sublime. Perceiving these mysteries, which are often woven subtly into the web of reality, is the task of the poet and the artist who scry into them with the inspiration of imbas.

An interesting counterpoint to this philosophy is: as it is below, so it is above. This is to say that the element of chaos also pervades the sublime from the basest world to that closest to the divine. The true-seer should be aware of this as well, for it is the power of the randomness of chaos that keeps life unpredictable, interesting, and full of unforeseen challenges and opportunities for growth. Remember, chaos is not evil. Chaos is the harbinger of mystery. It is not to be spurned, but embraced. One is as necessary to balance as the other. Chaos gives order color and malleability. Order gives chaos form and meaning. They are two opposing forces in need of one another to be functional. Evil, if it is anything, is an imbalance between either force.

Ley Lines

Ley lines are lines of magical power that run through the earth and lie along the land like blood vessels. Indeed, they appear to have a certain life-giving characteristic, as they channel the life force of the earth through the land and into natural, organic creatures. If the bard can develop the skill of finding ley lines, he or she will be able to locate places of great power for the working of enchantment. Ley lines are literally rivers of magical force. Ancient, mystical sites were established at places where ley lines crossed for this very purpose, for they can be tapped into and directed by magical procedures.

Ley lines seem to flow very much like tributaries. In some places they are great rivers, in others mere brooks. Yet even a minor flow of ley power can be a tremendous resource for enchantment. When a place such as a nemeton, a hill, or a stream bank can be found intercepting a ley, abundant energy will be available there to assist magical working. There, magics will work most potently, and the shamanic and meditative arts will be empowered. Magical energy has a way of wearing thin the barriers to the Otherworld as well, and it may from time to time even be possible to physically see or move into and out of the Otherworld where ley lines run, and especially where they intercept.

Intercepting leys locate a magical crossroads, a between place of immense possibility. Such places are powerhouses of magic. Enchantment worked in such places will have exponentially more power than enchantment worked in other places, for the abundant magical energy present can be shaped along with that summoned by the enchanters. Therefore, many practitioners of the Pagan crafts especially seek out these crossroads, if not for their regular rituals, then for their more demanding magical workings.

Leys can be searched out in any number of ways. Some use dowsing, and others of mediumistic talent seem to possess an innate ability to sense them. True-sight is probably one of the best ways of finding and tracing leys, for it endows the ability to sense the mystery within a place. Those places extremely rich in mystery are very likely being fed by leys. The ancients were well aware of ley lines. They often set up markers tracing them, and some even think they may have built roadways along them. Where many leys intercepted, temples were built, such as the famous Stonehenge of Britain.

A warning is in order concerning leys. Legends often speak of travelers getting lost between the worlds at such places, so often do they open the gateways between the worlds. This is not to say you should avoid the places where ley lines intercept, but that they should be approached with respect. There, the primal energy of an older, more magical time is alive and vibrant and the wild magics lie waiting.

Leys are currents of power and it would be wise to think of them very literally as high voltage power lines. Leys can charge magical workings, but magic gone awry at a ley is especially dangerous. Magic is basically a neutral force. It does as it is directed to do by the forces of will and divine power, and is augmented by the resonant components of spellcraft. If concentration should become unfocused or a procedure of spellcasting be done erroneously, the mistakes will be greatly amplified. Where enchantment done poorly away from a ley is likely to simply fizzle out and have little noticeable effect, flawed enchantment done at a ley may spiral into a veritable whirlpool of power before its effects diminish.

The lesson: the mystery of leys is well worth seeking out and exploring. They wear thin the boundaries between the here and now and the Otherworld, and make excellent places for meditation, shamanic journeying, and seeking imbas. However, they are not for casual magic-working, and especially not for use by the novice. Only one adept at enchantment should practice the craft of enchantment at a ley.

Pursuing the Green

The Celts of elder times were profoundly bound to the land. This was in part because in their most ancient beginnings they were a society of deer hunters and lived directly with the natural world. Later, they became livestock raisers and farmers, still tied intimately to the seasons and the whims of nature. Yet so were nearly all the peoples of the ancient world. There was something else about the Celts, something that more deeply wove them into the fabric of the green world. The mystery of this relationship is one that the bard, as a follower of the Celtic path, must understand and emulate.

Among the Celts there was a deeply ingrained reverence for nature. It was rooted deep into their ancient, Pagan druidic religion, and tied so intimately to their cultural psyche that it still reverberates among them in this age of great cities and technological marvels. One need only to sample examples of Celtic poetry to get a feel for their ever-present love and respect of the green. The Cymry (Welsh) delighted in their forests and their untamable mountain land by creating songs and poetry of larks, mighty mountains, and other natural treasures. The Gaels of Alban (Scotland) reveled in their rugged country where verdant meadows rolled out in gentle valleys and the chill north Atlantic wind blew upon the high heathers. This enduring love was founded upon the timeless druidic understanding of nature's sacred worth. The druids saw the green world of flora and fauna as the manifestation of the life force of the divine. They knew the mountains and valleys, and the lochs and streams to be signs of the culmination of titanic forces, and sublime powers of creation and destruction. They were able to sense the soul within the land itself. The green was invigorated with the presence of the sidhe, the gods, the spirits, and the enchantments of countless ages.

Even more, the druids taught the old Celts that nature is the only suitable place of worship. Neither the supreme being nor the gods who reflect it can be properly revered within the confines of manmade buildings. It did not matter how magnificent the temple was. Even the great Stonehenge of England is open to nature. It hides nothing of the natural world from the mind of the worshiper, for sublime powers are far too grand, too potent, and too cosmic to be reflected by manmade craftsmanship. These powers are creators and shapers of nature and are wild themselves—they are nearly incomprehensible by civilized man. True divinity can be boxed into a physical construct no more than it can be boxed into concepts of how we think it should be. The only suitable temple for divine beings is the one they themselves have made; for only amidst nature will a person be suitably inspired to accurately perceive them. So the druids recognized that nature was the only true temple of the deities, and the only place sufficient to reflect them.

At the crossroads of leys, henges of wood and stone were set up. In those places, druids and bards congregated out of doors to honor the mysteries and create beautiful works of music and poetry inspired by the powerful imbas present in such places. In the forests, among the sacred oak and hazel, and the yew and rowan trees, the druids practiced the rites of the deep mysteries. They were the rituals that reflected truths of which the common folk were not yet ready to partake.

With reverence for the land flowing through their veins, bards found themselves in a position to not only honor nature, but to maintain its health. This was done through nourishing the people's awareness of the sacred earth (which is the manifestation of the mother goddess Tailtiu, who may go under other names in the Celtic lore and who is most commonly known in Wicca simply as "the Goddess"). In doing this, the bards ensured that the people remembered to respect and care for the world that gave them life.

It is arguable that it was the bard's task to spiritually revive the earth in her sick places. In those places that were desecrated by man's action or natural disaster, it was the bard who would fill the role of healer and comforter. It was the bard who invigorated the desolated ground with the beauty of imbas-inspired arts, and who called to the spirits of nature to reinvigorate the place.

Likewise, it is arguable that, as shaman and scryer, it was the bard's responsibility to sense the moods of the land. The bard looked into the spirits of the land through true-sight and the divinatory arts, essentially communicating with the mother in order to determine her moods and needs. Thus the bard was in a position to guide the people to prepare for the seasons appropriately, whether is was to make ready for a season of little or a season of plenty.

We also know the bards were singers to the spirits. This is recorded in the classical writings that talk of the bards coming to play their harps with the druids beneath the moon in honor of the spirits. The bards proclaimed a love of the sidhe and of the spirit of the earth itself in a love song that called them to manifest and to invigorate the land with mystery and the beautiful magic of their presence. Without their presence, the world is reduced to cold ground and dry earth where no magic lives and life is barren without wonder.

The mystery of the Celtic binding to nature is reflected in the patterns they recognized and reproduced through their arts. While other mystic traditions, such as those of the Egyptians and the Hellenes, were concerned with finding meaning in geometric shapes (the pyramid, the sphere, the pentagram, and the pentagon), the Celts were seeking meaning in intricate interweaving and various renditions of the wheel. The Celts saw in such patterns the very mysteries of nature. They saw life and death and life again played out in the wheel, which has no beginning nor ending, only endless cycles. Even the turning of the seasons resembled the endless spiraling of the wheel. Thus the wheel became a very sacred symbol for the Celts. The complicated interactions of natural processes and human relationships united into a symmetry displayed best in weaving knotwork. Their weaving, surrealistic art, which sought to show the here and now ever on the verge of becoming something more, showed the endless possibilities of life in growth.

So thoroughly were these forms adopted by the Celts that to this day knotwork and wheels are universally recognized as symbols of Celtica. In them was reflected the fullness of Celtic thought on the course of life and nature. In these symbols, one who is enlightened will recognize a call to pursue the mysteries and live harmoniously with the green.

Every bard has a responsibility to develop the mysterious Celtic relationship with nature. More perhaps than even the lofty druid who is concerned primarily with the divine, it is the bard who must understand nature's intimate connection with the sidhe, the dance of the Green Man among its emerald places, and the love of Tailtiu who keeps this world bounteous. The bard is the healer and the friend of the land who poetically invokes the mysteries and sings health to the wounded green. When this role is engaged, the bard will find that the land is a healer and friend in return that grants peace and harmony, and teaches the lessons of the wheel and its interweaving patterns.

Thus, every follower of the bardic path should wear the symbol of bardry from the time of his or her dedication: the silver or gold ring of Celtic knotwork. In this most perfect symbol are seen the wheel and the weaving of patterns tying endless knots that bind each part of creation to the other. The ring shows our continual devotion to all the mysteries of bardry, and is a constant reminder of the work we undertake upon this path.

Conclusion

There is a great deal more material on the mysteries of the Celts—enough to fill volumes—but it is far beyond the scope of this introductory tome on the practice of bardry. The material is out there and available to the seeker. A list of recommended reading in back will help you to further your exploration of Ceridwen's cauldron.

Author Charles de Lint is right when he says through his intriguing character Jilly Coppercorn that organizing mystery undermines its essence. The objective of a study of mystery is not to develop a dogmatic system of doctrine. I don't believe the Celts or druids were ever concerned about defining the sublime as something that is always one way and not another way. The sublime is infinite and can be whatever it chooses to be at any time. Dogmatism disguises its limitlessness; it disrupts the flow of evolution and stifles possibilities for growth. To be dogmatic is to declare that all truth is now revealed and remains changeless, and this is to fight the natural evolutionary flow of the universe to satisfy our human desire for changelessness. It is an unnatural, counterproductive endeavor, and one that will inevitably lead to frustration, perhaps even destruction. Consider all the wars and hatred that have occurred over the dogmatic doctrinal creations of the world's major religions.

The wisdom of the Celtic mysteries is like a set of guidelines, much like the principles behind Celtic music. They provide a form and pattern whereby mystery might be perceived, which allows for a working conception of it. They give the Celtic perspective a distinctive flavor that attracts those whose spirits naturally harmonize with the primal, intuitive Celtic path. The Celtic mysteries, like Celtic music, must flow from the heart; they are to be practiced more than understood in the academic sense. The goal of the study of mystery is to make one more in tune with it, so that a relation-ship with it will become intuitive and natural.

Also, within the working framework of the Celtic perspective, such a mystical understanding can be taught to other seekers. It cannot be taught in entirety, for each person must experience mystery personally to really know it for him- or herself, but enough can be communicated to set the seeker on the path of discovery.

The great goal of Celtic lore's wisdom is oneness with the mysteries. The goal is to be a living part of the great myth cycle of Celtica, and a traveler on the path of enchantment. It is to be a bard who transforms his understanding into the beauty of art, and so inspires growth in himself and others and brings about the healing of the green world and human spiritual growth.

chapter sixteen

Where Times Mingle

With summons to the bards
For the sweet flowing song,
And wizards' posing lore
And wisdom of Druids.

The Mabinogion

Fiona Davidson once told me, "I remember . . . wishing there were still bards, so that I could learn from them. It soon became clear to me that the bardic practices and lore still did exist in the highlands and islands [of Scotland]. It was just that it was fragmented. All I had to do was use the knowledge I had been gathering and piece it back together again."[1] And that is exactly what she has done. I know of no person who has done a better job at redeeming the artistic qualities of bardry than Fiona has. She has developed a vibrant relationship with myth and the Otherworld, and this shows through in the imbas so rich in her work. Her music and tales leave me astounded by their beauty and depth time and time again, and anyone interested in Celtic music in the true old tradition would benefit immeasurably from listening to her recordings.

Fiona was right: the way of the bard is not lost. It has never been. In the past century and a half it has become fragmented. Many Celts have scattered to the Americas and the new world of the South Pacific, Australia, and New Zealand, taking their oral traditions with them. Others who have remained in their homeland have become scattered in their hearts and divorced themselves from their roots in order to meet the demands of a modern society that has no place for mystery or magic. Yet there are those who remain who have remembered. Some have continued in isolated regions of the western periphery of Europe. Others have been urbanized, and remember only bits and pieces of the old lore passed down to them by their forefathers. Without the glue of the bardic schools, which persisted up until the nineteenth century before at last disintegrating beneath the weight of an ever more technocratic, urbanized society, the skills were set adrift without a cohesive form to give them solidity and cogent meaning. Yet the fragmented Celts have kept the living memory, and the tradition survives. It awaited only the day when someone would come along and reassemble it, and make it alive once more. I am not the first to undertake this task, nor will I be the last. There are now many who have come to understand that the ultramaterialistic techno-industrial world leaves one wanting. It is dry and bare, despite all its glitz and trinkets. There are questers desirous of the mysteries of the earth, the arts, and magic, and so the ways of Celtica are now in the midst of a powerful revitalization.

So why bardry? There are so many ways to the mysteries. Many philosophies and religions and branches of science have sought them. What makes bardry so special that a person should devote to the craft the many years I have plainly indicated it takes to become a true bard? Why is bardry different?

The bard is many things, as we have discussed throughout this book. He or she is a pursuer of fulfillment and the healing of the soul. The bard is a hero, and brings the joy of beauty into the world, which is itself an act of great elder enchantment. The bard is an artist who is in touch with the divinely originating force of imbas. The bard is a priest of nature who has learned to live in harmony with the green mysteries. The bard is an enchanter who opens the door between the worlds and enriches mystery— something which, on this plane, is all too often lacking. The bard is also a quester in the tradition of the old tales, like the questers of the Arthurian myth cycle who pursued the grail—symbol and key to the great truths of the universe.

Yet true bardry originated far, far before the grail myths, which are a product of Christian influence upon Celtic mythology. In fact, recent scholarship has indicated that the Celts date back to as early as 2000 B.C.E. This is evidenced by findings of stones in New England that have their written language—the Iberian ogham—carved on them. Indeed, there is very good reason to believe that between about 1700 B.C.E. to about 200 C.E., the American east from Maryland to Quebec was once a Celtic kingdom known as Iargalon.² This tells us that the Celtic peoples may date back much earlier than scholars have believed until very recent times. So it is more true to say that the bard, being of an institution of the much older pre-Christian Celts, is a pursuer of the cauldron rather than the grail. The bard pursues no less a cauldron than Ceridwen's own cauldron of wisdom, which grants complete knowledge to those who drink of its enchanted potion.

The bard is a seeker of holistic growth. This growth is shared with those within and without bardry not through arguments over dogma and threats of fire and brimstone, but in the giving of beauty and the heroic rendering of humanitarian service. It is lived out in the remembering of the high days and the pursuit of a harmonious relationship with nature. Thus, the bard's way is unique. It is the path that strives to develop the whole physical and spiritual being to the fullest extent through a healing, living relationship with art, magic, mystery, and nature. It remains earthy and rich with the joy of the here and now, like the Celtic warrior of old. It is firmly rooted to the past, like the traditions and lore the druids kept so well. Yet it looks to the future, where there is growth and evolution. The bard is the one who lives in between the times, positively placed between the past and the future and relishing the present. Bardry is the heroic age still alive on the personal and extrapersonal level.

Now you know all you need to of the form of bardry to get started. You are prepared to begin making progress. As you continue to study bardry and the Celtic mysteries, remember that this book was only a starting place. A list of recommended reading is in the back. These materials will take you further. There is so much more to learn and to understand. Still, you must round out knowledge with active participation through the working of enchantment and the creation of art—poetry and music especially, which are the distinctive arts of the bard. You must also develop an intimacy with nature as a material *and* mystical force. Then, between study and active participation, you will find growth happening within. It will arise from knowledge and experience combining together, and make the way alive within you.

Remember, it took twelve years to train a bard; don't rush it. There is plenty of time. In fact, there is forever—life after life—to grow. Go slow so that you may take the time to find the harmony of balance within the soul, and the peace of knowing one's place within nature. These are two great benefits of the bardic path.

You have only just begun the hero's quest, and the adventure of a lifetime. Approach it with courage, strength, and wisdom.

Walk in mystery.

A Concise Catalog of Celtic Symbols

Below is a very brief list of symbols and their meanings in the old Celtic thought. A more thorough study is beyond the scope of this book. However, much information is already in print and awaits only the seeker to search it out.

acorns—*see* mast

animals—in general, all animals are nearer the green mysteries and more aware of the Otherworld; portents; wild energy

apple—divine fruit; immortality

autumn—*see* fall

Avalon—spiritual homeland of today's Celts; land of apples; home

bees—unlucky if a swarm has no owner; symbol of community; provision

beetle—a defender; a protected, respected animal

bagpipes—instrument of mourning or plaintive expression; music of warfare; skilled handling can work other moods and enchantment; occasionally associated with evil

cricket—a very lucky insect; enchanted; wise

crwth—bardic music not of the adept skill; beautiful, but lacking in mastery

Danu—a divine founder of druidry and the revealer of wisdom and the druidic mysteries; founding mother of the Tuatha de Danaan; earth goddess

deasil—the natural, right order; the way of the wheel; clockwise

dragon—guardian of the land; energy

dream—some dreams are the result of the unconscious's interaction with the Otherworld; portentous; self-revealing

druid egg—symbol of druid truths of rebirth; rising above the primordial state; truth

dog—*see* hound

earth—mother or maternal; linked to Danu, great goddess of wisdom and nurture; Tailtiu, Irish goddess of the soil

egg—*see* druid egg

fall—the dying time; season of endings and new beginnings; death is the midpoint of a long existence

fiddle—often associated with festivity, magic

fire—transformative, alchemical force; energy

forest—place of mystery, potential, enchantment; wild power; the Green Man's abode

glade—place of enchantment

ghost—one caught between states; unable or unwilling to progress into the next world

gold—solar symbol; incorruptible; wealth

Green Man—Cernunnos, lord of the forest, the green mysteries, the wild, and of tillage of the soil and the harvest; nature god

hare—unlucky if it crosses your path before sunrise

harp—beauty in sound; the three great enchantments of music (sadness, gladness, sleep); the Dagda and other divine associations

hawk—solar power (Bel); good; great predator (hunter); longevity; strength

hazel nut—great wisdom

heather—a sign of the Pagan peoples, the Old Ways

hind—grace; beauty; gentleness; femininity

horse—power to till; to travel; to make war

hot spring—powerful link to Otherworld; healing virtue

hound—noble defender; faithful; a true friend

iron—repugnant to the faerie folk or evil spirits, so it derives curative power

island—isolation; place to grow, prison; Tir-n'an-Og (the Otherworld in the sea)

juniper—when gathered and processed rightly, it is a charm against evil

knowledge—growth of the intellect; an important facet of self-fulfillment; key to understanding

lake—Otherworldly portal; divine association; imbas

mast—also known as acorns; bounty of the forest; natural food of man and beast; sign of the health of nature

moon—portender of weather; wielder of power over the human body and spirit; the lunar goddess

nettle—physically healing when processed properly

night—time of magic; imbas; mystery is nearer; veils between worlds is thinner

ocean—dwelling of the Fomor and of Manannan; the Otherworld; somewhat of a female symbol

orators—Ogmios of the Gallic Celts is the patron of speakers; power to enchant by way of speech; power over hearts and minds

otter—sacred to Manannan; clever, playful, and wise; friendly toward man; kin to sidhe

pig—meat of the gods; livestock of the Otherworld

pools—dwelling places of sidhe spirits; sources of scrying vision

raven—sign of the Mórrígán; ill omen of death and war

robin—divinely loved bird

salmon—carrier of wisdom; perhaps a totem of knowledge

serpent—wise creature; secretive; cognizant of mysteries

sidhe—a hollow hill that is the home of the sidhe; gateway to the Otherworld; in contemporary usage, it has come to mean the magical races that are sometimes called "faerie".

staff—magical power

stag—wild freedom; strength; courage

stars—portents; markers of time and seasons; power of the heavens

story—way of exploring the Otherworld; teaching ethics and life lessons; relating history as it should be

sun—Bel is the god of the sun; invigoration; fertilization; traditionally a male aspect

swans—Otherworldly beauty and grace; suffering (as when the children of Lir were changed into swans)

Tuatha de Danaan—elder wisdom; link to the goddess Danu

wand—phallic symbol; sexual vitality and fertility; magical potency wheel—endless progression of life, death, and life again

widdershins—unnatural progression; attempt to reverse natural order; very unhealthy; counterclockwise

wren—ill-omen (death, defeat)

zombie—product of offensive magic accomplished by putting a spirit back into a dead body; unnatural state, unlike reincarnation or healing from death as was done at the spring of Dian Cécht, the Irish god of healing; it is to enter a state of reincarnation without potential for growth; an abomination

Sources for Traditional Celtic Instruments and Music

Melody's Traditional Music & Harp Shoppe
9410 FM 1960 W
Houston, TX 77070
1-800-893-HARP
http://www.folkharp.com
melody@folkharp.com

These friendly folks sell all kinds of folk instruments and music books, from whistles to genuine bodhrans. They have an especially nice selection of harps.

Musicmaker's Kits
P.O. Box 2117
Stillwater, MN 55082
1-800-432-5487
http://musikit.com
info@musikit.com

If you are handy, and want to save a buck, this company offers fine kits that will yield good quality instruments. They make everything from autoharps to bowed psalteries.

Sylvia Woods Harp Center
P.O. Box 816
Montrose, CA 91021-0816
1-800-272-4277
http://www.harpcenter.com
harp@netbox.com

Lots and lots and lots of harps and harp stuff.

Mountain Glen Harps
809 W. First Street
Phoenix, OR 97535
541-535-7700
http://www.markwoodstrings.com/mtglen.htm
mtglen@aol.com

If you are looking for a truly traditional instrument in the bardic tradition, such as a replica of the Brian Boru harp, Glen can make it. He builds only custom-designed harps of the highest quality, and incredible as it may sound, they are quite affordable.

Blevins Instruments, Inc.
2591 B ¾ Road
Grand Junction, CO 81503
1-800-398-HARP
http://www.blevinsharps.com
encore34@gj.net

Dwight Blevins makes some very nice, very affordable harps. A real bargain for the quality.

Notes

Introduction

1. Fiona Davidson, interview by author, e-mail, 1998. Her CDs are some of the finest examples of the bardic crafts of storytelling and harping. A study of her work is highly recommended.

Chapter 1

1. Barry Fell, *America B.C.* (New York: Simon & Schuster, Inc., 1989), 3.

Chapter 2

1. Markale elaborates on this concept in his books *The Druids* (Rochester, Vt.: Inner Traditions International, 1999, 213–20) and *The Celts* (Rochester, Vt.: Inner Traditions International, 1978, 297–99). These books cover this concept expansively and with superb scholarship.

2. Peter Ellis, *The Chronicles of the Celts* (New York: Caroll and Graff Publishers, 1999), 130–37.

3. Excellent examples of Celtic coins can be seen in T. G. E. Powell's *The Celts* (London: Thames and Hudson Ltd., 1980, 142).

Chapter 3

1. Fiona Davidson, interview by author, e-mail, 1998.

Chapter 4

1. In Ireland, there was a slight alteration to this traditional order. After the Christianization of the land, the bardic role was divided into a triad: a composer of poetry, a reciter, and a harper. This division probably began during the time of the secularization of the Irish bardic order after the church had forbidden the practice of magic. This was a time when self-serving poets were known to wander from court to court demanding excessive payments for their poetry and threatening to call up the dreaded poet's curse against those courts that would not or could not pay their often unreasonable demands. At least two Irish folktales, *The Proceedings of the Great Bardic Institution* and *The Poet's Curse*, concern just such happenings (see John Matthews's *The Bardic Source Book* and Peter Ellis's *The Chronicles of the Celts*, respectively). So an Irish king's court came to consist of a priest, a poet, and the poet's bardic retinue, including his harper and poet apprentices.

2. Further reading on this can be found in James Bonwick, "Druidical Magic," in *The Druid Source Book*, ed. John Matthews (London: Wellington House, 1997), 253–60. More detailed work can be found in Jean Markales, "The Power of the Word," in *The Druids*, (Rochester, Vt.: Inner Traditions International, 1999), 169–81. Of course, there's also *The Yellow Book of Lecan*, an ancient manuscript recording the practice as it was over six centuries ago.

3. Term coined by Fiona Davidson, a talented modern bard who practices the craft of bardry in the true Gaelic tradition. Interview by author, e-mail, 1998.

Chapter 5

1. Daniel Corkery's article "The Bardic Schools," published in *The Hidden Ireland* (1923) is excellent reading on the training of the Gaelic bards. A reprint can be found in John Matthews, ed., *The Bardic Source Book* (London: Wellington House, 1998), 26–42.

2. Copied with permission from Fiona Davidson's website discussion on myth and the psyche. Her website can be found at http://www.the-bard.co.uk.

Chapter 6

1. See Parragon, "The Wonderful Tune," in *Irish Fairy Tales* (Bristol, U.K.: Parragon, 1998), 196–205. Also, Donn Byrne, "Tale of the Piper," in *Great Irish Ghost Stories of the Supernatural*, ed. Peter Haining (New York: Barnes and Noble Books, 1992), 300–303. The latter is a work of fiction written by an Irish-American based on old legend. Also, the Cornish legend "Nos Calan Gwaf" contains references to pipers (in *The Chronicles of the Celts*, ed. Peter Ellis [New York: Caroll and Graff, 1999], 406–17). A problem with the older folktales is they rarely ever disclose exactly what kind of pipe is being played. They could mean a whistle just as well as a great set of Scottish bagpipes.

2. See Patrick Ford, trans., "The Tale of Gwion Bach," in *The Mabinogi* (Berkeley, Calif.: University of California Press, 1977), 159–63.

3. An excellent, detailed study of the cauldron in Celtic lore may be found in Caitlin and John Matthews, *The Encyclopedia of Celtic Wisdom* (New York: Barnes and Noble Books, 1996), 218–29.

4. Enya, *The Memory of Trees*, Warner Brothers, 46106.

5. If you are truly interested in a superb study of the faerie folk, see W. Y. Evans-Wentz, *The Fairy Faith in Celtic Countries* (1911; reprint, New York: Caroll & Graff Publishers, Inc., 1994). This is an excellent and comprehensive study of sidhe lore.

Chapter 7

1. See Peter Ellis, "The Poet's Curse," in *The Chronicles of the Celts* (New York: Caroll & Graff Publishers, Inc., 1999), 99–108.

2. See Patrick Ford, trans., "Math son of Mathonwy," in *The Mabinogi* (Berkeley, Calif.: University of California Press, 1977), 89–110.

3. Reference the tales of the battle of the Tuatha de Danaan against the Fomori.

4. A thorough study on quantum functioning geared toward the layman may be found in Nick Herbert, *Quantum Reality* (New York: Doubleday, 1985).

Chapter 8

1. Reference the tale of the druid Mog Roith in Caitlin and John Matthews, "The Siege of Druim Damhgaire," in *The Encyclopedia of Celtic Wisdom* (New York: Barnes & Noble Books, 1996), 191–98.

2. Robert Georges and Michael Jones, *Folkloristics: An Introduction* (Indianapolis, Ind.: Indiana University Press, 1995), 50.

3. H. W. and F. G. Fowler, trans., *The Works of Lucian of Samosata*, vol. 3 of *Hercules 1–7* (Oxford, U.K.: Oxford University Press, 1905).

Chapter 9

1. Readings from the *The Book of Leinster*, circa 1160. This compilation is housed at Trinity College Library, Dublin, Ireland.

2. Patrick Ford, trans., *The Mabinogi* (Berkeley, Calif.: University of California Press, 1977), 42.

3. John and Caitlin Matthews, *The Encyclopedia of Celtic Wisdom* (New York: Barnes & Noble Books, 1996), 191–98.

4. Peter Ellis, *The Chronicles of the Celts* (New York: Caroll and Graff Publishers, 1999), 102.

5. Peter Ellis, "The Poet's Curse," in *The Chronicles of the Celts* (New York: Caroll and Graff Publishers, 1999), 99–108.

6. John and Caitlin Matthews, *The Encyclopedia of Celtic Wisdom* (New York: Barnes & Noble Books, 1996), 196–98.

Chapter 10

1. Merle Severy, "The Celts," *National Geographic* 151 (1977): 601.

2. Barry Fell, *America B.C.* (New York: Simon & Schuster, Inc., 1989), 3–6.

3. Fiona Davidson, interview by author, e-mail, 1998.

Chapter 11

1. Fiona Davidson, interview by author, e-mail, 1998.

Chapter 12

1. Kip Thorn, *Black Holes and Time Warps* (New York: W. W. Norton & Co., 1994), 439–45, 485–86.

2. See the Irish tale of "The Jealousy of Émer" about the hero Cuchulainn's battle to save an Otherworld people from a powerful horde of demonic forces.

Chapter 14

1. This is attested to by Martin Martin in his *Description of the Western Islands of Scotland* (published 1703), and Clanricarde's *Memoirs of the Marquis of Clanricarde* (published 1722).

2. Nancy Mellon, *The Art of Storytelling* (Rockport, Mass.: Element Books, Inc., 1992).

Chapter 15

1. Jean Markale, *The Druids* (Rochester, Vt.: Inner Traditions International, 1999), 62–69.

Chapter 16

1. Fiona Davidson, interview by author, e-mail, 1998.

2. Barry Fell, *America B.C.* (New York: Simon & Schuster, Inc., 1989), 6.

Glossary

Abred—The here and now, balanced between chaos and order.

Alban—An ancient Celtic land today occupied by modern Scotland.

Alchemy—The arcane art that seeks change leading to growth through the use of spirituality and enchantment. The goal of alchemy has been vulgarized as being the pursuit of changing lead into gold. More accurately, it would be transforming the base person into a fulfilled spirit.

Amergin—A bard who came to Ireland with the conquering Milesians and took part in their defeat of the Tuatha de Danaan.

Aneurin—A noted early bard, some of whose works seem to still be in existence. I say "seem" because these survivals have been recopied and passed down many times, so it is not likely they remain in their original form.

Animal—On the Celtic path, animals may be mere animals, or powerful harbingers of magic, transformation, and knowledge. Some of the gods and goddesses were even able to assume the forms of animals, such as the Mórrígán who could assume the form of a raven.

Annwn—The outer place of pure chaos. In some religions this place might be mistakenly associated with hell. However, chaos is not evil, only disordered.

Anruth—An Irish word meaning a novice poet—one just beginning his poetic training.

Archetype—The essence of a memory or perception that exists deep in the unconscious. This essence is more than a mere memory; it has a kind of life of its own. It is able to interact with other archetypes in the forest of the unconscious and manifest itself to the ego through waking and sleeping dream and in other ways. Archetypes have no form; they are ideas more primal than form. What they carry is the essential spirit or idea of a conception.

Arthur—A great king of Celtic myth. This myth was originally Pagan and represented the stand of the old Celtic world against the changing times when invaders came into Britain to do away with the Old Ways. It was altered by Christians during the Middle Ages to inspire the peoples of Britain and Brittany to stand against their enemies and value their heritage.

Awen—The Otherworldly force of inspiration and magical empowerment of the bardic arts; a gift of the sublime powers of the Otherworld. It is the Welsh synonym for *imbas*.

Bard—One who gives himself or herself to the imbas-empowered and inspired path of growth, mystery, magic, and nature. Bardry is a kindred path to druidry, but it is different in that it is not primarily sacerdotal. Its focus is upon growth through a mystical closeness with the Otherworld and with nature. The primary tools of growth are myth, music, and poetry. Its tools of growth are means for working magic, as they are charged by the Otherworldly force of imbas.

Bardcraft—The total practices of the bardic path, inclusive of all magical, lore, and growth functions.

Beithluisnuin—The Celtic ogham alphabet. Beith, luis, and nuin are the first three letters and tree symbols of this magical writing system.

Bel—Also known as Belenus, this is another name for a god of the sun, and may be the same as Lugh.

Beltane—Sometimes spelled *Bealtaine*, the second of the two greatest Celtic high days, the other being Samhain. This was a celebration of spring and life and the return of the sun to his rightful place of life-giving strength wherein the world is renewed by his warmth and love for Tailtiu, goddess of the earth. Occurs May 1.

Bodhran—A hand drum of the Gaelic folk music tradition that possesses a rich, deep, full voice.

Bodying forth—A term used in existential psychology that refers to how one's consciousness expands as it becomes engrossed in the universe around it. The nature of this expansion is so complete that what is expanded into becomes, in a most real sense, a part of the body. For instance, a clarinettist enveloped in her music, and playing with consummate skill and devotion could be said to be bodying forth into the instrument.

Brighid—The triple-faced goddess of smithcraft, poetry, and the warrior arts.

Brigid—An alternative and common spelling of Brighid. Derives from the Cymric.

Britain—Encompasses all the western isles off the coast of Gaul, excepting Ireland.

Calendar—The Celtic calendar is a lunar calendar based on the thirteen-month system. At the end of it is a mysterious three-day month (Samhain) that is the between time. It is a time that is neither this nor that, and a powerful temporal between place when the worlds may mingle and magic flows freely.

Cathbhadh—This was a druid of legendary renown according to ancient Irish legend. According to the tales, he studied the magical practices of other peoples and imported them into druidry, thus greatly adding to his magical prowess.

Cauldron—A large spherical pot designed to be heated over open fires. The cauldron represents the potential for the fulfillment of the soul, the container of the elixir of wisdom, and even the original object of the Arthurian quest before later Christians replaced it with the grail.

Ceilidh—An old Celtic tradition; a time for gathering socially, storytelling, reciting poetry, and music making.

Celt—One who is aligned with the philosophy, spirit, and psychology that values myth, mystery, the Otherworld, the Old Ways, and the old gods. One who pursues growth through the hero's quest and values the journey of growth over the destination. One who does not fear failure for the certainty that another chance lies upon another turn of the wheel. Alternatively, a Celt may be born of the race of Celts, or come into the Celtic race through a personal choice to align with the Celtic values and spirit.

Celtica—A metaphorical reference to the combined Celtic world that encompasses all the places and times it has been, is, and will be.

Ceridwen—The sorceress/goddess who created the elixir of wisdom that transformed the mere boy Gwion Bach into the magical Pennbardd Taliesin.

Ceugant—The place wherein dwells full divinity according to some Welsh mystics.

Chaos—Pure chaos is the force of pure chance, wherein anything could happen at any time. In pure chaos, cause need not precede effect, occurrences need not be logically related, and form and substance are completely transitory and have no lasting meaning. Complete maddening randomness is the standard. It is important to understand that chaos is not in itself evil. It is a necessary aspect of the worlds. It is the force that gives the worlds mystery, magic, wonder, and difference.

Clarsach—A Celtic harp. These days the term may refer to many designs of folk harps, as long as they are of the sturdy, triangular, pedalless design. In older days, clarsachs were usually strung with bronze or gold wire and were small enough to be easily portable—an important feature since bards often traveled.

Collective unconscious—The unconscious realm all humans share (indeed, we may share it with other creatures such as animals as well). It is the place wherein dwell the archetypes and the true dreams. It shapes and fashions our actions and personalities through subtle workings only slightly perceived by the unintegrated ego.

Complex—The mind is divided into many facets, and each serves a purpose in aiding the whole being to function. A complex is an ill facet that has broken off from the mind due to trauma. It begins to take control of the mind, drawing strength by aligning other facets and archetypes to itself. Complexes must be checked and should be treated by some form of therapy in order to stop them from damaging or taking over the mind.

Conscious—That part of the mind of which we are most aware; the logical, wakeful part of the mind.

Cosmology—The perception of a people regarding how the universe came into being and the nature of its existence.

Crane bag—A bag of elder myth made of the skin of a maiden who was transformed into a crane. The bag was an enchanted keeper of enchanted things. It appears to have amplified the enchantments of that which it contained.

Crwth—A Welsh bowed instrument similar in some ways to the fiddle, except that it possessed extra strings on which rhythm could be plucked out while tunes were being played. The crwth is now very rare, even in Wales.

Cymru—An ancient Celtic land today occupied by modern Wales.

Dagda—An Irish god. The name means "the good god."

Dallan wands—Wands inscribed with ogham characters used in divination.

Danu—An elder goddess and lady of the Tuatha de Danaan, which means "the tribe of the Danu."

Dark language—During the age of the great Irish poets, their poetic lore became so great that they developed an abstract jargon that those who were not in the know could not follow. Thus they were able to communicate secretly, even while technically speaking Irish among the Irish. This jargon became known as the dark language.

Dasein—A modern term borrowed from existential psychology for the here and now.

Death—Death begins from life, life ends in death, and the wheel turns again to renew the eternal cycle. Death is not an end, but a beginning—a state from which life springs. Through it the spirit goes from world to world, experiencing opportunities for growth with each turn of the wheel.

Dichetal do chennaib—A ritual to obtain magical insight. Akin to psychometry, this method of divination involves touching a magically charged wand to a thing and reading the psychic impressions left upon it.

Druid fire—A fire built with magical purpose. Details of its application were originally recorded in the story of Mog Roith.

Druid's tree—Among the druids of continental Europe, this was the oak. For those of Ireland, this was the yew.

East—A direction associated with the rising sun, newness, warmth, and coming into power. Cognates with spring.

Effective magic—Magic that has as its root purpose the seeking of a change or a transformation. It is magic that requires power over something.

Ego—The aware self.

Elements—Earth, wind, fire, and water. Fire, however, is an energy and a transformative force rather than a true element. As such, it may be equated with other primal and transformative forces, such as chaos and order.

Erin—An ancient Celtic land today occupied by the modern state of Ireland.

Faerie—Also known as the sidhe folk, the good people, the fair folk, and by other names. These are beings of a magical, perhaps spiritual nature. They seem to be able to cross between this world and the other at will. In times past, it appears that they commonly dwelt in this world, though in the modern era they are far more rare here.

Filid—This is an Irish word for "bard."

Fire—An alchemical force of transformative power capable of destroying or purifying.

Focus—A thing that calls the thoughts of the mind to a single purpose. It may also be a thing that directs and channels magical energy.

Folklore—The tales, myths, stories, and knowledge passed down through generations by the common folk of a land. Folklore survives because it has interest, beauty, and value. A study of it discloses the soul of a people because it reveals what mattered most to them, as well as their secret knowledge.

Forest—In addition to its usual meaning as a place of many trees, the forest is a place of mystery, and a between place where sunlight meets shadow and the life force of the earth is strong. It is by nature, then, a place of enchantment and the forest spirits and gods. The forest is also a symbol of the unconscious—a shadowy place wherein lurks beauty, mystery, and even some nightmares. It is where things may not be as they appear, and where logic does not always apply.

Gaul—An ancient land of the continental Celts located in Europe, today occupied by the modern state of France.

Geantrai—This is the enchanted bardic music of joy. As with the other two bardic musics, music such as this can only be effected when it is empowered by imbas.

Geas—A magical restriction placed upon an individual by Otherworldly power. Geasa are highly individualized and serve to mark out the boundaries, individuality, or needs of the one who receives them.

Glamour—An enchantment. Glamours are often disguising or illusory enchantments. For instance, when the faerie folk take on the appearance of animals, they are said to be under a glamour.

Gnosticism—A view that holds matter as evil, knowledge as good, and the shedding of the material universe as the way to god.

God/dess—In the Celtic way of thinking there seems to be several degrees of god/desses. There is the creator, the ultimate and infinite power who made the universe. There are the elder gods who seem to have always had a divine nature. Then there are the ascended gods, such as seem to be Ceridwen and the Rhiannon, who became goddesses through fulfilling the hero's quest.

Goêteia—In the Hermetic tradition, this is the low form of magic. Beings and magical essences of things have to be manipulated through magical means to obtain an effect. This magical theory partially reflects the theory behind bardic magic, however bardry does not hold this form of magic as low.

Goiltrai—The music of sorrow. This enchanted bardic music can only be created when the bard is in harmony with imbas.

Green Man—Known as Cernunnos or Fearuaine (in Gaelic), he is the lord of nature and the tillage of the soil. A wild and very ancient god with whom the nature-oriented bard, as well as any follower of the Celtic tradition, would do well to become acquainted.

Ground—Magically speaking, this is a thing in which to center or ground one's thoughts. Psychologically speaking, a ground for the mind is something that roots the thoughts in the here and now, the dasein, and the shared and workable perception of the universe.

Grove—Wooded groves are an ideal place to practice bardry and its kindred spirituality of druidry, as they are rooted in the beauty and power of nature.

Gwion Bach—The bard Taliesin's boyhood form before he was reborn from Ceridwen's womb as the Pennbardd.

Gwynvid—The place wherein the supreme creator dwells, and to which all humans aspire. It is highly ordered, and full of brightness and knowledge and energy.

Halstatt—One of the oldest known Celtic settlements, today located in modern Austria.

Harp—The Celtic harp is the paragon of musical instruments, according to the old Celtic way of thinking. It is an instrument born of beauty and magic, and capable of evoking the three bardic magic musics of sleep, joy, and sadness.

Henge—Made of wood or stone, henges such as the renowned Stonehenge were many things: markers of ley crossings, astronomical observatories, and places of ritual practice. Today, sensitive visitors to these henges remark on the power one can feel around and about them, their antiquity, and their rich and promising mystery.

Hermeticism—A magico-mystical way strongly rooted in Gnosticism and named after Hermes. Using ritual magic of the kind commonly thought of today as high magic, practitioners of Hermeticism seek to influence the world in the way they desire while aspiring to become like a god through the practice of magic.

Hero's quest—The search for growth. There is no real end to the quest, for the goal is an eternity distant. The goal is the journey itself, and therefrom one derives the joy of the quest—the joy of ever having more to aspire to, challenges to meet, and knowledge to discover.

Huts—According to some old lore, the poets of the old bardic tradition used to meditate in dark huts wherein they could visualize their subject matter and compose their poetry without distraction.

Imbas forosna—A ritual to obtain magical insight very similar to the tarbh feis.

Imbas—The Otherworldly force of inspiration and magical empowerment of the bardic arts. A gift of the sublime powers of the Otherworld. It is the Irish synonym for _awen_.

Imbolc—A lesser Celtic high day celebrating the time the ewes give milk again, which marks the waning of winter and the coming of spring. This holiday celebrates the continuance and revival of life in the grip of cold and death. Occurs February 1.

Incantation—The verbal components of a spell.

Individuation—The process of reuniting the shattered aspects of the personality, including the conscious ego and the unconscious, to form a whole, complete, and distinctly individual person. A maturational process key to the Celtic way of growth.

Indo-European—While there was never an ancient people who actually called themselves Indo-Europeans, ancient artifacts leave a trail of history that tells us that there was once a great people who formed the base of the culture of many peoples. This people expanded throughout the old world, and moved into and settled Africa, Asia, and Europe. The Indo-Europeans were the forefathers of the Celts.

Integration—Bringing together the shattered parts of the mind. Uniting the conscious with the unconscious, and all the aspects of the personality, such as the anima/animus, shadow, and so on.

Irish flute—A wooden transverse flute that has six holes and a sweet, mellow sound. It is fingered like the Irish whistle.

Jung—A psychologist of the analytical school whose views were remarkably optimistic and humanistic compared to those of his predecessor and former mentor, Freud. Jung's psychology recognized the spiritual nature of being, and accepted the probability of paranormal phenomena.

Koadalan—A wizard of Breton myth.

La Tène—A region in France where Celtic artifacts were excavated during the nineteenth century, which indicated advancement in Celtic art and culture.

Ley—A ley is a line or river of power that traverses the surface of the earth. The power of leys can be harnessed for magical workings of many kinds.

Lore magic—Magic that has as its root purpose the seeking of knowledge, which is the seeking of wisdom and growth.

Lug—The Cymric (Welsh) spelling of the name of the god Lugh.

Lugh—The god of light and many talents.

Lughnasadh—A lesser Celtic high day celebrating the height and first fruits of summer, and commemorating Lugh. This high day is often spelled as *Lugnasad*. Occurs August 1.

Lute—An instrument like the guitar but with many more strings. It is a marvelous old instrument for playing chords and melody.

Math—A wizard god of Welsh myth.

Meditation—In the Celtic tradition, the goal of meditation is to teach the mind how to focus upon a magical purpose, and to assist the poet in giving himself entirely to the task of composing imbas-inspired works.

Memory—Memory is a key bardic tool because it is in the living memory that lore is kept alive and meaningful. Knowledge is quite purposeless if it merely sits unread and unappreciated in a musty tome upon dusty shelves. In the memory is where lore lives and mixes with the mind and encourages growth and individuation.

Merlin—Also known as Myrddin, this was the archetypal Otherworldly wizard who guided Arthur and aided his quest to restore the glory and autonomy of the Celtic peoples.

Mog Roith—A great druid of early Irish myth. Also spelled *Mog Ruith*.

Moonstone—A stone I feel may have been used by the poets of old who composed their poetry in dark huts. Such a stone connected them with imbas and the Otherworld.

Mórrígán—The Irish goddess of love, nightmares, and death.

Mound—Many kinds of mounds exist in the Celtic lands, most of which signify that an ancient construct lies buried beneath the accumulated dust of ages. Many of these mounds have come to have paranormal associations, from being haunted by old spirits to being the current dwellings of the sidhe.

Music—A key element of magical and artistic bardcraft that is central to growth, individuation, working with the Otherworld, and working enchantments. Imbas-charged music is a shaper and charmer of Otherworld forces, and a key element in the making of bardic magic

Music therapy—A form of mental therapy that utilizes the power of music, and which speaks directly to the emotional part of the mind. This power to communicate directly with the deep-seated emotions makes music therapy a kind of officially sanctioned modern magic. It has few ties to the ways of logic and is more intuitive; it arises from the artsy, preconscious side of the soul. Such magical music of the modern era serves a very similar function to the healing music of the bards of elder times.

Mystery—The goal of this modern age of reason is to strip mystery—to pour light upon and explain everything. Yet mystery in and of itself is a potent and beautiful force. Some things that might best have been left as mysteries have been illuminated. Other things seem resistant to being demystified. The bard understands that the question of "how" often lends itself to logical understanding and is seldom diminished by having its mystery revealed. However, the question of "why" is much more difficult to riddle out, and may often retain its most meaningful answers when left as mysteries to be known with the heart rather than known with the logical mind.

Naming—Identifying the essence of a person, place, or thing. Such a process gives one true understanding of the named, ergo one has a magical power over the named. Thus, the old Celts guarded their names zealously. However, the word by which one is called is not synonymous with one's true name. This can only be discovered by identifying one's true nature.

Nemeton—A clearing in a forest or grove of trees where druidic practices are conducted.

Nirvana—Also known as nibbana, this is the Hindu concept of a place to which souls aspire through their cycling mortal lives over time. In this place is the light of god that, when a soul is perfected enough to enter it, absorbs the soul's individuality into the great divine being. Some scholars have actually equated this place to the Celtic Gwynvid, however, it must be noted that the two have significant differences. Chiefly, Nirvana is a place where the soul loses its individuality within the greatness of the creative force. In the Celtic spirituality, such a concept is anathema. Gwynvid is the place where the soul attains true individuality and lives in perfect illumination of the bright knowledge of the creator. Differences such as this are so profound that the two cannot be truly equated.

North—A direction associated with cold, death, and winter. A beginning time; a time of transformation when life sleeps in darkness, to arise again from death. Cognates with winter.

Occult—Something occult is simply secret. That which is occult is hidden for a purpose, the purpose being that the majority of people simply are not ready to receive or accept it. It can be a dangerous thing to lay bare occult secrets to the unready mind. Old myth teaches that to do so may kill such a one, or drive him insane.

Ogham—The ancient alphabet of the Celts. According to myth, it was created by the god Ogma, the lord of eloquent speech. The ogham script is a magical script, and is also useful for writing information. Because it is comprised of patterns of straight lines, it is particularly adapted to inscribing on wood and stones.

Ogham pole—A rod inscribed with an ogham and planted in the earth for a magical purpose.

Ogham tree—A tree inscribed with oghams crafted to spin a spell of long-term effect.

Old Ways—The ancient ways of elder days, here specifically referring to the old traditions and practices of the Celtic peoples. The Old Ways give one a sense of place in time and belonging to a people. They survive because of this valuable service, and because of the lore they conserve.

Ollamh—A term denoting a senior druid.

Omen—A sign. In the Celtic context, many things can be omens. They might just as well be random occurrences. The way to differentiate random occurrences from genuine omens is to observe them for patterns that occur in context.

Order—Order cannot be equated to good. Pure order would require zero unpredictability and no randomness. In pure order, cause would always precede effect, and there would be nothing but bland sameness. It would preclude both mystery and magic. Good is obtained by the functional balance between chaos and order; it creates a world ripe with magic and mystery, yet ordered enough to be understandable and livable.

Otherworld—A name for the world beyond the veil that marks the physical boundary of the here and now. There are likely an infinitude of otherworlds, and they may be known as faerie, Tir-n'an-Og, or by other names.

Ovate—A scholarly type of druid.

Pennbardd—A title attributed to the archetypal great bard Taliesin, meaning "great bard" or "chief bard."

Poetry—A concise, even, concentrated form of prose. Poetry possesses patterns that lend it a grace and elegance that make it resemble the twisting, spiraling, surrealistic nature of other forms of Celtic art. This form allows it to resemble the cycles and patterns of nature. Imbas-charged poetry is a shaper and charmer of Otherworld forces, and a key element in the making of bardic magic.

Polytheism—In the Celtic concept, this is the belief in many gods who probably represent the supreme creator in a finite way comprehensible to the limited mind of man. However, that is my interpretation, and it may be flawed. Too little information remains on the old Celtic pantheon to be sure.

Pool—Pools are places that harbor spirits, magical energies, and mystery. They may be used for scrying, or for getting close to the spirits of nature. Being surrounded by land meeting water, they represent a between place—the kind of place where worlds meet, thus making them very magically significant in the bardic tradition.

Portent—*See* omen.

Profane—That which is composed of matter or energy, not of spirit. In the Celtic way of thinking, to be profane does not infer that something is bad or inferior. It merely refers to its nature.

Pythagoras—A Greek mathematician and mystic. He argued for the immortality of the soul. His concepts are believed by some scholars to have been so similar to what the druids believe that it is conceivable that he learned them from them, or vice versa.

Quantum—Dealing with things on a very primal, elementary scale. For instance, quantum mechanics seeks to understand the behavior of matter on the most basic level of elementary particles.

Relaxation—The process of allowing the mind and body to have release from their efforts. When conducted properly, this can be a very rejuvenating, positive experience.

Salmon—This fish, which is a modern favorite and staple of the Irish and British peoples, has old mythological connotations. The flesh of those salmon who ate the hazel nuts that fell from the tree of wisdom was imbued with wisdom. Wise men sought to catch and eat these blessed salmon for themselves in order to attain true enlightenment.

Samhain—The first of the two great Celtic high days, celebrated during the mysterious three-day thirteenth month. This was the time when the Otherworld was nearest to the here and now, and when the veil separating the worlds was thinnest. This is the most powerful magical time of the year. It is a time of great potential, for in the Celtic way of thinking, ends and beginnings occur on wheels or spirals, and signify only a transition and a renewal. Occurs sundown October 29 and lasts until sundown November 1 to make three days by Celtic reckoning.

Second sight—The power to see into the Otherworld. This power is inherited, not earned, so often those who have it are not equipped to cope with it, for the illumination of the Otherworld is a dangerous thing to those who are not prepared in mind and spirit. To them it is a form of madness or malaise. It may thus cause them to be resentful of the Otherworld's mysteries.

Self—This is very difficult to define, but it is the essence of what makes an individual uniquely himself. It is the sum of the personality, the spirit, the memories, and the physical being, yet the self is greater than the sum of these parts. To the definition of self should especially be added the unique being and awareness that is the being in its particular time and space.

Shaman—Shamanism is a magical practice that attempts to identify, work with, and harness natural creatures, spirits, and forces for magical working and conducting the shamanic Otherworldly journey. Bardry has elements akin to shamanism, though it is not actually shamanic.

Shape-changing—The ability to change one's spirit form during the Otherworld journey. Many myths claim this power is also functional in the here and now.

South—A direction associated with warmth, fire, energy, and alchemical transformation. Cognates with summer.

Suantrai—The enchanted bardic music of sleep. Music such as this can only be created when the bard is in harmony with imbas.

Synchronicity—The occurrence of a preternatural coincidence too far-fetched to have happened by random chance. For example, a person catches herself thinking of a longtime friend whom she has not heard from nor thought about in years, and suddenly that very person calls.

Tailtiu—The goddess of the earth, at least in insular Celtic lore.

Taliesin—The Pennbardd, meaning "the greatest of all bards." He was a mighty poet and harper of renown who lived in the northern Welsh kingdom of Gwynnedd. In his youth he had been Gwion Bach until he accidentally partook of the elixir of wisdom being concocted by the goddess/sorceress Ceridwen and was transformed by its wisdom. In revenge, she ate him in the form of a grain of wheat and he was reborn of her womb as the bard Taliesin.

Tarbh feis—A ritual to obtain magical insight. It was conducted by chewing a piece of freshly slaughtered animal meat and wrapping one's self in the skin to align one's spirit with the animal. Then the person entered a shamanic journey into the Otherworld to seek the animal's illumination.

Teinm láida—A ritual to obtain magical insight conducted by applying song and poetic loremastery to the discernment of the meaning of a thing.

Teutates—A god of thunder, perhaps related to the oak.

Three—A number of especial significance in Celtic thought. It represents completeness, a full cycle, and the magical. Many Celtic proverbs and historical events are recorded in groups of three, known as triads.

Tradition—A practice that has been handed down over time. Traditions survive because they have meaning, use, and beauty. The bard seeks to preserve the Celtic traditions.

Transformation—The process of change. Depending on the nature of the transformation, such change may be either good or bad, depending on whether the person being changed grows. If there is negative growth, then change for change's sake is not truly beneficial. If there is growth, individuation, and the development of self, then change is a positive occurrence. Change can be likened metaphorically to alchemical work. Change for change's sake is not beneficial, but rather an unbalancing force.

Triad—British wisdom lore, stated in groups of three.

True dream—In this book, this is a dream rooted in an archetype. This makes it rooted in the truth of a timeless, universal myth common in some form to all humanity.

True-sight—A kind of deep perception possessed by the bard, and developed by her mastery of lore and the bardic arts. True-sight is not really divinatory, nor the second sight, though it may appear as either. Rather, it is the ability to perceive the depth of a thing, to understand its true name, and to foresee possibilities.

Tuatha de Danaan—This ancient tribe lost Ireland when it was wrested from them by the invading Milesians. The Milesians became the Celts, who live on the isle to this day. The Tuatha de Danaan appear to have been a part of the faerie folk, though at the time of the coming of the Milesians, they were firmly settled in this world.

Unconscious—The part of the mind of which the ego—the wakeful, logical thinking part of our being—is not normally aware. The unconscious represents the vast majority of the mind. Within this psychic Otherworld dwell the archetypes often referred to in this book as the true dreams.

Veil—The barrier between this world and the Otherworld. In some places and at some times it is thinner than at others. Certain magics may be able to thin the veil as well.

Vercingetorix—The last king of the Gallic Celts, who is remarkable both because he resisted the Romans in a heroic yet tragic final stand, and because he was able to temporarily unite the divided Celtic tribes of western Europe.

Wand—There are numerous wands in the Celtic myth, some having a place in bardry. The poet's wand is a symbol of office. Dallan wands are tools of divination. Staffs and wands may be charged with magic to make them tools in service of the bardic arts.

Water—A substance of nature. Where water flows, magic seems strong. Still, clear water in pools can be used for scrying.

West—A direction of very mystical significance to the bard. This is the metaphorical (or literal) direction of Tir-n'an-Og, the Land of the Young, which is the home of the sidhe, or the Otherworld. West in general connotes Otherworldly and spiritual things. It also relates to an ending time—the twilight—and the powerful between places and times. It also cognates with fall and the mysterious three-day thirteenth month of the Celtic year culminating in Samhain.

Wheel—A sacred symbol of the Celts that represents the cyclic turning of the seasons and the progression of life. From death life begins, returns, and begins again.

Whistle—A fipple flute ranging in size from the large low whistles as big as flutes to the tiny tin whistles with their high-pitched, merry sounds. Whistles are remarkably expressive instruments and are very easy to learn to play.

Yggdrasil—The world tree of Norse myth.

Recommended Reading & Bibliography

Bardic Thought

Matthews, Caitlin and John. *The Encyclopedia of Celtic Wisdom*. New York: Barnes & Noble Books, 1996.

Matthews, John, ed. *The Bardic Source Book*. London: Wellington House, 1998.

Celtic Philosophy and History

The Celts: Artists and Storytellers. Edison, N.J.: Chartwell Books, 1998.

Fell, Barry. *America B.C.* New York: Simon & Schuster, Inc., 1989.

Markale, Jean. *The Celts*. Rochester, Vt.: Inner Traditions International, 1978.

O'Driscoll, Robert, ed. *The Celtic Consciousness*. New York: The Dolmen Press, 1981.

Powell, T. G. E. *The Celts*. London: Thames and Hudson, 1980.

Druidic Thought and History

Carr-Gomm, Philip. *The Elements of the Druid Tradition*. Rockport, Mass.: Element Books Limited, 1991.

Cunliffe, Barry. *The Ancient Celts*. Oxford, U.K.: Oxford University Press, 1997.

Markale, Jean. *The Druids*. Rochester, Vt.: Inner Traditions International, 1999.

Matthews, John, ed. *The Druid Source Book*. London: Wellington House, 1997.

Nichols, Ross. *The Book of Druidry*. London: Thorsons, 1975.

Piggott, Stuart. *The Druids*. New York: Thames and Hudson, 1975.

Spence, Lewis. *The History and Origins of Druidism*. Van Nuys, Calif.: Newcastle Publishing, 1995.

Enchantment

Buckland, Raymond. *Buckland's Complete Book of Witchcraft*. St. Paul, Minn.: Llewellyn Publications, 1998.

Flowers, Stephen, Ph.D. *Hermetic Magic*. York Beach, Maine: Samuel Weiser, Inc., 1995.

Lady Wilde. *Irish Cures, Mystic Charms, and Superstitions*. New York: Sterling Publishing Company, Inc., 1991.

Matthews, Caitlin and John. *The Encyclopedia of Celtic Wisdom*. New York: Barnes & Noble Books, 1996.

Parker, Derek and Julia. *The Power of Magic*. London: Mitchell Beazley, 1992.

Valiente, Doreen. *Natural Magic*. Custer, Wash.: Phoenix Publishing, Inc., 1975.

Folklore

Ellis, Peter. *The Chronicles of the Celts*. New York: Caroll & Graff Publishers, Inc., 1999.

Evans-Wentz, W. Y. *The Fairy Faith in Celtic Countries*. New York: Citadel Press, 1994.

Georges, Robert, and Michael Jones. *Folkloristics: An Introduction*. Indianapolis, Ind.: Indiana University Press, 1995.

Lady Wilde. *Ancient Legends of Ireland*. New York: Sterling Publishing Company, Inc., 1996.

———. *Irish Cures, Mystic Charms, and Superstitions*. New York: Sterling Publishing Company, Inc., 1991.

Ross, Anne. *The Folklore of the Scottish Highlands*. New York: Barnes & Noble, Inc., 1976.

The Harp

Geller, Janna and Mallory. *Exploring the Folk Harp*. Pacific, Mo.: Mel Bay, 1993.

Larchet Cuthbert, Sheila. *The Irish Harp Book*. New York: Music Sales Corporation, 1993.

Loesberg, John, ed. *The Celtic Harp*. Cork, Ireland: Ossian Publications, 1988.

Sanger, Keith, and Alison Kinnaird. *Tree of Strings*. Midlothian, Scotland: Kinmore Music, 1992.

Woods, Sylvia. *Songs of the Harp*. Montrose, Calif.: Woods Music & Books, Inc., 1993.

———. *Teach Yourself to Play the Folk Harp*. Montrose: Woods Music & Books, Inc., 1978.

Yeats, Gráine. *The Harp of Ireland*. Belfast, Northern Ireland: Belfast Harpers' Bicentenary Ltd., 1992.

Mythology

Ellis, Peter. *The Chronicles of the Celts*. New York: Caroll & Graff Publishers, Inc., 1999.

Ford, Patrick, trans. *The Mabinogi*. Berkeley, Calif.: University of California Press, 1977.

Rutherford, Ward. *Celtic Lore*. London: Thorsons/Aquarian, 1993.

Poetry and Story

Collom, Jack, and Sheryl Noethe. *Poetry Everywhere*. New York: Teachers and Writers Collaborative, 1994.

Downs, Chris, ed. *Celtic Dreams*. London: Blandord, 1998.

Matthews, Caitlin and John. *The Encyclopedia of Celtic Wisdom*. New York: Barnes & Noble Books, 1996.

Mellon, Nancy. *The Art of Storytelling*. Rockport, Mass.: Element Books, Inc., 1992.

Moore, Thomas. *Moore's Poems*. New York: Thomas Y. Crowell & Co., 1895.

Psychology

Bunt, Leslie. *Music Therapy: An Art Beyond Words*. London: Routledge, 1994.

Campbell, Don. *Music and Miracles*. Wheaton, Ill.: Quest Books, 1992.

Feinstein, David, Ph.D., and Stanley Krippner, Ph.D. *Personal Mythology*. New York: Jeremy P. Tarcher, Inc., 1988.

Hall, Calvin, and Gardner Lindzey. *Theories of Personality*. New York: John Wiley & Sons, Inc., 1978.

The Journal of the Society for Psychical Research.

Jung, Carl, Ph.D. *Aion*. Princeton, N.J.: Princeton University Press, 1969.

Ortiz, John, Ph.D. *The Tao of Music*. York Beach, Maine: Samuel Weiser, Inc., 1997.

Singer, June, Ph.D. *Boundaries of the Soul*. New York: Doubleday, 1972.

Storr, Anthony. *Music and the Mind*. New York: Ballantine Books, 1992.

Tame, David. *The Secret Power of Music*. Northamptonshire, U.K.: Destiny Books, 1984.

Other Items of Interest

Ebon, Martin, ed. *The Signet Handbook of Parapsychology*. New York: NAL Penguin, Inc., 1978.

Herbert, Nick. *Quantum Reality*. New York: Doubleday, 1985.

recommended

reading

&

bibliography

Index

nut, 21, 24, 63, 139, 153, 194–195, 240,
246, 295

oak, 19–20, 23, 62, 139, 145, 151–153,
160, 164, 172, 179, 186, 194–195, 216,
265, 281, 323

occult, 39, 72, 112, 133, 137, 160, 179,
183, 203, 208–210, 260, 262

ogham divination, 177

ogham, 127, 131, 139–141, 143–147, 149,
151–157, 159–161, 163, 165, 167,
169–172, 175–184, 186, 190, 230, 280,
288, 329

ogham pole, 180–183, 185

ogham tree, 171, 175–176, 180–183, 197,
288

Old Ways, 15, 25, 50, 73, 81, 96–97,
114–115, 146, 152, 180, 187, 195, 197,
204, 228–229, 233, 238, 246, 252, 261,
264, 271, 294, 298, 303

ollamh, 184, 186, 272

omen, 24, 151, 178, 182

order, 13, 16, 35–37, 41–42, 48, 54, 59, 68,
91, 96, 104, 109, 112, 115–117, 126,
137, 139, 151, 154, 158, 167, 169–171,
174, 176–177, 183–184, 192, 204, 206,
208, 226, 228, 233, 235, 238, 245–249,
253, 280, 294, 296, 302, 307, 309–310,
315, 319–321, 323, 328

Otherworld, 14, 18–19, 24, 27, 32–33,
35–37, 39, 49–50, 53–56, 58–60, 65,
67–70, 73, 76–80, 84–85, 88, 96, 102,
105, 108, 111, 121–122, 124, 126, 128,
131, 133–134, 136, 139, 141, 146–147,
149–150, 162, 166, 170–173, 175,
177–178, 185–187, 190–194, 202–205,
207, 210–213, 215, 217, 222, 226,
228–230, 233–235, 237–239, 241, 243,
245–249, 251–261, 263–268, 272, 276,
278–279, 281–282, 284, 294–296, 299,
302, 304–305, 312–314, 320–321, 327

pantheons, 123, 168, 188, 244, 250

parable, 297

passion, 34, 38, 56–57, 78, 101–103,
105–106, 108, 110, 122, 154, 215,
227–228, 239, 302, 317–318

path, 13, 19–20, 22, 49, 58, 63–64, 68,
81–82, 96, 102, 110, 132–133,
135–137, 141–142, 149, 151, 168, 174,
178, 191, 193, 195, 203–204, 210, 218,
222, 227–229, 237, 264, 266, 268,
270–271, 273, 293, 299, 303, 305–306,
316–317, 322, 325–326, 329–330

pattern, 19, 37, 40, 57–58, 77–78, 86–88,
96, 100, 141, 155, 178, 213, 226, 277,
324–325

philosophy, 12, 14–16, 26, 29–33, 36, 49,
61, 63, 69, 131, 161, 203–204, 240,
308, 316, 319–320, 328

poet, 13, 25, 27, 42, 49, 53–55, 61, 69,
72–73, 78, 80–86, 89, 92, 100–101,
107, 121–122, 124–126, 130, 138–140,
149, 158, 160, 163, 166, 168, 170, 184,
186–188, 194–195, 202–203, 207,
209–210, 213–214, 217, 226, 234,
238–240, 251, 253, 263, 266, 271,
276–277, 279, 284, 288, 292, 306, 320

poet's wand, 140, 186

poetry, 13, 15, 18–20, 26, 36, 38, 42, 50,
53–58, 61, 63–64, 69, 72, 75–89,
91–92, 96, 100, 103, 107, 112–113,
116–118, 120–125, 127, 134, 138–141,
154, 164, 168, 170, 183, 186–188,
190–193, 195–196, 215, 227–229, 239,
244, 256, 259–260, 263, 268, 271–274,
277, 280, 294–297, 299, 302, 306–307,
322–323, 329

pole, 19, 180–183, 185, 197

polytheism, 311

pool, 20–21, 24, 40–41, 57, 68–71, 73,
116, 137, 153, 177, 195, 240, 246

portent, 127, 129, 131

potential, 35–39, 42, 46, 48, 55–56, 58,
61, 88, 120, 127, 134, 136, 141,
146–147, 166, 205, 208, 210, 213–214,
216, 225–226, 239–241, 243–244, 251,
299

practical, 14, 41, 46, 83, 150, 152, 161,
229, 265

probability, 12, 118–119, 126, 196

profane, 111–112, 115, 118, 121, 127–132,
138, 169

property, 156, 174, 178, 182, 185, 191

☾ ORDER LLEWELLYN BOOKS TODAY!

Llewellyn publishes hundreds of books on your favorite subjects! To get these exciting books, including the ones on the following pages, check your local bookstore or order them directly from Llewellyn.

Order Online:

Visit our website at www.llewellyn.com, select your books, and order them on our secure server.

Order by Phone:

- Call toll-free within the U.S. at 1-877-NEW-WRLD (1-877-639-9753). Call toll-free within Canada at 1-866-NEW-WRLD (1-866-639-9753)
- We accept VISA, MasterCard, and American Express

Order by Mail:

Send the full price of your order (MN residents add 7% sales tax) in U.S. funds, plus postage & handling to:

Llewellyn Worldwide
P.O. Box 64383, Dept. 0-7387-0285-4
St. Paul, MN 55164-0383, U.S.A.

Postage & Handling:

Standard (U.S., Mexico, & Canada). If your order is:
Up to $25.00, add $3.50
$25.01–$48.99, add $4.00
$49.00 and over, FREE STANDARD SHIPPING
(Continental U.S. orders ship UPS. AK, HI, PR, & P.O. Boxes ship USPS 1st class. Mex. & Can. ship PMB.)

International Orders:
Surface Mail: For orders of $20.00 or less, add $5 plus $1 per item ordered. For orders of $20.01 and over, add $6 plus $1 per item ordered.

Air Mail:
Books: Postage & Handling is equal to the total retail price of all books in the order.
Non-book items: Add $5 for each item.

Orders are processed within 2 business days. Please allow for normal shipping time.
Postage and handling rates subject to change.

The 21 Lessons of Merlyn
A *Study in Druid Magic & Lore*

DOUGLAS MONROE

For those with an inner drive to touch genuine Druidism—or who feel that the lore of King Arthur touches them personally—*The 21 Lessons of Merlyn* will come as an engrossing adventure and psychological journey into history and magic. This is a complete introductory course in Celtic Druidism, packaged within the framework of twenty-one authentic and expanded folk story/lessons that read like a novel. These lessons, set in late Celtic Britain circa A.D. 500, depict the training and initiation of the real King Arthur at the hands of the real Merlyn-the-Druid: one of the last great champions of Paganism within the dawning age of Christianity. As you follow the boy Arthur's apprenticeship from his first encounter with Merlyn in the woods, you can study your own program of Druid apprenticeship with the detailed practical ritual applications that follow each story. The twenty-one folk tales were collected by the author in Britain and Wales during a ten-year period; the Druidic teachings are based on the actual, never-before-published 16th-century manuscript titled *The Book of Pheryllt*.

0-87542-496-1
420 pp., 6 x 9, illus., photos $14.95

Druid Magic
The Practice of Celtic Wisdom

Maya Magee Sutton, Ph.d., and Nicholas R. Mann

Preface by Philip Carr-Gomm, Chief Druid of OBOD. Enter into the adventure of awakening the Druid within. If you want to explore the Druid mysteries, this book will help you roll up your mystical sleeves. For those who want to know who the Celts and the Druids really were, this book presents the Celtic myths, Greek and Roman writings, and archaeological evidence that allows the ancient Druid tradition to speak for itself. If you want to learn the primary tenets of Druidry, or visit the Celtic Otherworlds and lie in the "streambed of Druidic inspiration," this book will take you on that journey.

- Create Druid magical tools
- Develop yourself as a seer
- Become a Druid magus
- Live your sacred sexuality
- Hold Druid ceremonies in your back yard
- Initiate yourself as a Peregrine Druid
- Form a Druid grove
- Visit the Celtic homelands
- Learn the Druid path from nature
- Use the Celtic Tree alphabet
- Journey to the Otherworlds
- Achieve Druid inspiration through poetry, symbols, visions, and spoken word

1-56718-481-2
384 pp., 7½ x 9⅛

$14.95

To order, call 1-877-NEW-WRLD
Prices subject to change without notice

By Oak, Ash, & Thorn
Modern Celtic Shamanism

D. J. CONWAY

Many spiritual seekers are interested in shamanism because it is a spiritual path that can be followed in conjunction with any religion or other spiritual belief without conflict. Shamanism has not only been practiced by Native American and African cultures—for centuries, it was practiced by the Europeans, including the Celts.

By Oak, Ash & Thorn presents a workable, modern form of Celtic shamanism that will help anyone raise his or her spiritual awareness. Here, in simple, practical terms, you will learn to follow specific exercises and apply techniques that will develop your spiritual awareness and ties with the natural world: shape-shifting, divination by the Celtic Ogham alphabet, Celtic shamanic tools, traveling to and using magick in the three realms of the Celtic otherworlds, empowering the self, journeying through meditation, and more.

Shamanism begins as a personal revelation and inner healing, then evolves into a striving to bring balance and healing into the Earth itself. This book will ensure that Celtic shamanism will take its place among the spiritual practices that help us lead fuller lives.

1-56718-166-X
320 pp., 6 x 9, illus. $14.95

To order, call 1-877-NEW-WRLD
Prices subject to change without notice

Celtic Folklore Cooking

Joanne Asala

Celtic cooking is simple and tasty, reflecting the quality of its ingredients: fresh meat and seafood, rich milk and cream, fruit, vegetables, and wholesome bread. Much of the folklore, proverbs, songs, and legends of the Celtic nations revolve around this wonderful variety of food and drink. Now you can feast upon these delectable stories as you sample more than 200 tempting dishes with *Celtic Folklore Cooking*.

In her travels to Ireland, Wales, and Scotland, Joanne Asala found that many people still cook in the traditional manner, passing recipes from generation to generation. Now you can serve the same dishes discovered in hotels, bed and breakfasts, restaurants, and family kitchens. At the same time, you can relish the colorful proverbs, songs, and stories that are still heard at pubs and local festivals and that complement each recipe.

1-56718-044-2
264 pp., 7 x 10, illus. $17.95

Celtic Myth & Magick
Harness the Power of the Gods & Goddesses

EDAIN McCOY

Tap into the mythic power of the Celtic goddesses, gods, heroes, and heroines to aid your spiritual quests and magickal goals. *Celtic Myth & Magick* explains how to use creative ritual and pathworking to align yourself with the energy of these archetypes, whose potent images live deep within your psyche.

Celtic Myth & Magick begins with an overview of forty-nine different types of Celtic Paganism followed today, then gives specific instructions for evoking and invoking the energy of the Celtic pantheon to channel it toward magickal and spiritual goals and into esbat, sabbat, and life transition rituals. Three detailed pathworking texts will take you on an inner journey where you'll join forces with the archetypal images of Cuchulain, Queen Maeve, and Merlin the Magician to bring their energies directly into your life. The last half of the book clearly details the energies of over three hundred Celtic deities and mythic figures so you can evoke or invoke the appropriate deity to attain a specific goal.

This inspiring, well-researched book will help solitary Pagans who seek to expand the boundaries of their practice to form working partnerships with the divine.

1-56718-661-0
464 pp., 7 x 10

$19.95

To order, call 1-877-NEW-WRLD

Prices subject to change without notice

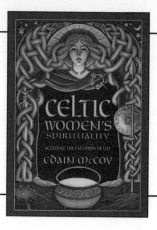

Celtic Women's Spirituality
Accessing the Cauldron of Life

EDAIN MCCOY

Every year, more and more women turn away from orthodox religions, searching for an image of the divine that is more like themselves—feminine, strong, and compelling. Likewise, each year the ranks of the Pagan religions swell, with a great many of these newcomers attracted to Celtic traditions.

The Celts provide some of the strongest, most archetypally accessible images of strong women onto which you can focus your spiritual impulses. Warriors and queens, mothers and crones, sovereigns and shapeshifters, all have important lessons to teach us about ourselves and the universe.

This book shows how you can successfully create a personalized pathway linking two important aspects of the self—the feminine and the hereditary (or adopted) Celtic—and as a result become a whole, powerful woman, awake to the new realities previously untapped by your subconscious mind.

1-56718-672-6
352 pp., 7 x 10, illus.

$16.95

Celtic Tree Mysteries
Practical Druid Magic & Divination

STEVE BLAMIRES

Trees are living, developing aspects of the Green World. So, too, is the magic associated with them. Celtic Tree Mysteries revives the ancient knowledge and lore of the trees with a practical system of magical ritual and divination.

You will learn to locate and identify each of the twenty trees and create your own set of Ogham sticks for divination. You will perform Otherworld journeys and rituals, and you will align yourself with the forces of the Green World in your area.

You will also learn to open the deeper, hidden meanings contained within the ancient Celtic legends, especially the nature poetry, which contains very precise and detailed magical instructions.

- Re-released with new cover
- Provides detailed information on the twenty trees in the Tree Ogham
- Demonstrates how to evoke spontaneous emotional experiences from your Otherworld journeys using trees in your own back yard
- Deciphers the codes in the ancient Celtic legends that reveal magical inner meanings

1-56718-070-1
304 pp., 6 x 9, illus.   **$14.95**

To order, call 1-877-NEW-WRLD

Prices subject to change without notice

Glamoury
Magic of the Celtic Green World

STEVE BLAMIRES

Glamoury refers to an Irish Celtic magical tradition that is truly holistic, satisfying the needs of the practitioner on the physical, mental, and spiritual levels. This guidebook offers practical exercises and modern versions of time-honored philosophies that will expand your potential into areas previously closed to you.

We have moved so far away from our ancestors' closeness to the Earth—the Green World—that we have nearly forgotten some very important truths about human nature that are still valid. *Glamoury* brings these truths to light so you can take your rightful place in the Green World. View and experience the world in a more balanced, meaningful way. Meet helpers and guides from the Otherworld who will become your valued friends. Live in tune with the seasons and gauge your inner growth in relation to the Green World around you.

The ancient Celts couched their wisdom in stories and legends. Today, intuitive people can learn much from these tales. *Glamoury* presents a system based on Irish Celtic mythology to guide you back to the harmony with life's cycles that our ancestors knew.

1-56718-069-8
352 pp., 6 x 9, illus.

$16.95

To order, call 1-877-NEW-WRLD
Prices subject to change without notice